PRAISE FOR JOHN KETWIG'S

... AND A HARD RAIN FELL

"...the innocents waiting offstage for service in some future Vietnam can now instruct themselves and make their task harder by adding to all those monitory texts' accounts of criminality and madness by Seymour Hersh, John Ketwig, and Michael Herr." –*The Norton Book of Modern War* 1991, W.W.Norton & Co., Paul Fussell

A magnetic, bloody, moving, worm's-eye view of soldiering in Vietnam, an account that is from the first page to last a wound that can never heal. A searing gift to his country. –*Kirkus Reviews*

...has all the immediacy and raw emotions of the best war novel, yet the reader can never escape the stark realization that this is a true story. Reading *... and a hard rain fell* drains the spirit. Mr. Ketwig's prose is beautiful, his story vivid and harsh and incredibly realistic. –*Baltimore Sun*

A searing glimpse into the heart of darkness. Essential reading, gripping, horrifying, unforgettable. –History Book Club

Ever-present in this masterpiece of war narrative is a sense of profound dread. Few books transport you in time as vividly as this. It's a reading experience you won't soon forget. A Powerful Book! –Book of the Month Club

Reading *... and a hard rain fell* is like bearing witness to the meticulous excision of a malignant tumor from a soul. It is a devastating book, shot through with horror and poetry and pain. –*Seattle Times*

Ranks among the more eloquent and powerful statements about the war. –*The Globe And Mail*, Canada

I heartily recommend this book to Americans who want to understand... –Jan C. Scruggs, President of the Vietnam Veterans Memorial Fund and the vet who made The Wall in Washington, D.C. a reality.

VIETNAM RECONSIDERED
The War, the Times, and Why They Matter

John Ketwig
Author of *...and a hard rain fell*

VIETNAM RECONSIDERED: THE WAR, THE TIMES AND WHY THEY MATTER
Copyright © 2018/2019 John Ketwig

Published by:
Trine Day LLC
PO Box 577
Walterville, OR 97489
1-800-556-2012
www.TrineDay.com
publisher@TrineDay.net

Library of Congress Control Number: 2019933152

Ketwig, John
–1st ed.
p. cm.

Epub (ISBN-13) 978-1-63424-238-7
Mobi (ISBN-13) 978-1-63424-239-4
Print (ISBN-13) 978-1-63424-237-0
1.. 2.. 3.. 4.. 5.. 6. 7.. I. Ketwig, John II. Title

FIRST EDITION
10 9 8 7 6 5 4 3 2 1

Printed in the USA
Distribution to the Trade by:
Independent Publishers Group (IPG)
814 North Franklin Street
Chicago, Illinois 60610
312.337.0747
www.ipgbook.com

DEDICATION

*This work is dedicated to the memory of Steve Mason (1940 - 2005).
I've never known a finer man.*

**An excerpt from the poem *The Children of the Sun*... from
Steve's book *Johnny's Song*:**

A billion words it seems
and then a billion more
could not explain our war to us
nor change a single lie to truth.
We fought a war in a place
one hundred billion dollars
could not buy a thing worth having
which could not be had
for five hundred piasters.
And when our nation spent it...
our money and our youth,
the monsoons came that year
as they had the past ten thousand.
When it ended there was no peace.
Only the shooting stopped.
Not one mother from either side could say,
"This that we won was worth my son."

–Steve Mason

Steve Mason was the official Poet Laureate of Vietnam Veterans of
America.

Also, this work is dedicated to the memories of Dave Cline, Dave Dellinger, Gloria Emerson, Charlie Liteky, Jack McCloskey, Wallace Terry, and Marilyn Young, wonderful people who were swallowed up by Vietnam, but helped their fellow men beyond anything that could be expected of them. Patriots all, they spoke out in defense of our country. May they all rest in peace.

ACKNOWLEDGEMENTS

Marilyn Young was a noted historian and author, but she was also a kind and gentle woman with a quick wit. Marilyn was a valued friend and colleague for years. Despite some very pressing personal obligations, she took time to read over an early version of this work and offered many valuable suggestions. I am extremely grateful, and my wife Carolynn and I are terribly saddened that Marilyn left us so soon. While she never wrote a formal blurb for the cover, her caring and influence are evident throughout this book. We are so proud to say Marilyn was a friend. My neighbor Ed Martin is a baby boomer and a (Dominican Republic) veteran, and his insights, having grown up in the same era but in the rural South, helped immensely, especially when it came to country music in the time of the Beatles. As a Pulitzer prize-winning journalist and writer, his suggestions and comments were invaluable, always offered in a supportive way, and Ed and his wife Natalie have become our dearest friends in Virginia. I must also thank author James W. "Jim" Douglass, whose book *JFK and the Unspeakable* is widely acknowledged as the finest, best researched and documented of all the studies of the assassination of John F. Kennedy. I could not have told the story of that tragic history without the wisdom and kindness of Jim Douglass. Jim's suggestion also led us to Trine Day Publishing, and I am extremely grateful. I must also say thank you to my good friends Amie Alden, Bill (W.D.) Ehrhart, Diane Fanning, Nancy Fischer, Larry Helms, "Skip" Isaacs, Ron Kovic, "Country Joe" McDonald, Bobby Muller, and Larry Shook. Each of these busy people contributed, offering insightful suggestions in ways that were always encouraging and constructive, and so very appreciated. Once in a while I read excerpts from the manuscript at meetings of the Smith Mountain Lake Writers or the Bedford, Virginia writers group, Write Now! Both of these groups, and especially their comments and suggestions, as well as their patience, are sincerely appreciated.

In moments when I was stumbling, in doubt, or in danger of losing my way, I found purpose, clarity, and inspiration in the poetry of Steve Mason.

This work has been inspired by the many high school and college students I have addressed, spoken with, or corresponded with over the years. I must especially tip my hat to acknowledge Maximilian Ottl, a student from Munich, Germany who contacted me via Vietnam Veterans Against the War (VVAW) seeking information to help him complete a term paper required for graduation from his high school. Over a number of months, Maximilian and I communicated by e-mail and his questions and observations were always organized and thoughtful. More important, his enthusiastic curiosity about the Vietnam War and the protests here in America were always inspiring to me. I was surprised to receive a copy of my young friend's final report in the mail, in the form of a slender book which includes many photographs and references. Soon after, Maximilian let me know that his paper had received the highest possible grade, and he would be graduating and was looking forward to entering university. I could mention a long list of names of students with whom I have shared ideas about the war, but Maximilian Ottl is at the top of the list and I would be remiss if I didn't mention him. I am confident he will do well in university and become very successful in life.

I have been corresponding with students from Steve Quesinberry's Vietnam class at Newnan High School in Newnan, Georgia for years, and have come to admire Steve's dedication to his work. Questions from those students have been a major inspiration for this book. To all of them, I am grateful for their thoughtful inquiries and reflections on "our" war.

I am extremely grateful to Kris Millegan at Trine Day Publishing for putting this book into print, and to Kelly Ray for editing it with understanding, enthusiasm, and patience.

Above all, I am grateful to my wife Carolynn. She has always understood, from the moment she closed her eyes and picked three names from a list of local guys in Vietnam, and, despite her reservations, she sent a letter to a Pfc. Through all the many times when this book got in the way of plans, or my help around the house, or times when it seemed I was becoming a recluse at my desk, Carolynn has always remained patient, enthusiastic and supportive. Her suggestions and contributions upon hearing my latest thoughts or reading portions of the manuscript were always on-target, insightful and vital to the completion of this work. Carolynn is the love of my life, and also my best friend. We have shared an amazing life together, and I am grateful to her in every way.

Lastly, I must mention that much of this book was researched and created with a helpful background of "smooth jazz" by Keiko Matsui and the late great Jeff Golub.

TABLE OF CONTENTS

INTRODUCTION

"The men who create power make an indispensable contribution to the nation's greatness, but the men who question power make a contribution just as indispensable … for they determine whether we use power or power uses us."

– John F. Kennedy

As this is written, it has been half a century since I was in Southeast Asia. It is January, bringing back terrifying memories of the Tet offensive, as if the memories of Vietnam ever really go away. When my year tour of duty in Vietnam was nearing an end, I was torn. I wanted to go back to my home town, Avon, New York, and the life I had known before the army, but I was scared. There were 15 months remaining of my military obligation, I had a serious romantic involvement with a young lady in Malaysia, and I thought there was a civil war happening in America. It was 1968, and the scant news reports we received in Vietnam were all about assassinations and civil strife, massive demonstrations and marches, and a bloody battle in Chicago at the Democratic National Convention. I was afraid I could be assigned to hold a bayonetted rifle against the protestors, perhaps on the steps of the Pentagon, and I knew I could not do that. I was on their side. So, instead of coming home, the goal that motivated every American in Vietnam, I volunteered to transfer to Thailand. That, too, was a one-year tour of duty, which meant I would get an "early out" of almost ninety days when I finally returned to the States. I desperately wanted and needed to get out of the army as soon as possible. It had not been "for me" from the very first day when I arrived at Fort Dix for Basic Training.

Thailand was a prime tourist location, another Southeast Asian country with scenes that would inspire a National Geographic photographer.

The American presence was all in support of the air force bases where the bombers and fighters that attacked Vietnam were serviced. There was no war going on in Thailand. Or so I thought. Still, I enjoyed Thailand. Like a scuba diver who must rise slowly from the depths or get "the bends," I needed time to get my head together after Vietnam, and to prepare to return home and walk down the street in my home town. I was anxious about that, too.

Now, fifty years later, I am still trying to understand America's war in Vietnam. Why did the army need me? At the tender age of 18, just out of high school, the draft loomed large over my future. It was a vivid, colorful time to be young. I had a nice car, long hair, and a set of drums. I was playing with a variety of rock 'n roll bands, and serving an apprenticeship that promised to lead to a fascinating career. I was skinny, certainly not the he-man type. Why did the military need me? What was the war all about? Basic training was traumatic, and then I was handed orders to go to Vietnam. Why me?

From the very start, the things I saw and experienced in basic training, then in Vietnam devastated my heart and soul. I spent the year in Thailand getting over it, which is to say I "put it in a box on the shelf" like other events from my past. Kindergarten, Cub Scouts, my first date, the junior prom, high school graduation. Vietnam was the past, and I had to look to the future. My classmates were graduating from college and getting exciting jobs. I had to play catchup. I got out of the army, came home, and before I knew it I had a job, a car payment, marriage plans, then a mortgage, and a family. I read about the protests, Vietnam veterans throwing their medals at the Capital, and I could not go. I had obligations, and I didn't want to open that frightening box on the shelf. We were living in Maryland in 1982, a young family. I had a responsible job, a wonderful wife, and two small children when that box fell and splattered its contents all over. Struggling to understand what had happened to me and what it all meant, I began to write a letter to my wife, to explain. In fact, I was reliving much of it, analyzing it, and putting Humpty Dumpty together again piece by painful piece. My letter grew to a sizable pile of paper. There were some difficult times as Carolynn became aware of all I had seen and done, but she stood by me. Then, to our great surprise, a series of totally unplanned cosmic events happened, and that pile of papers became a book! ... *and a hard rain fell: A G.I.'s True Story of the War in Vietnam* was published by Macmillan in May of 1985, and our lives would never be the same. Suddenly I was an author, asked to stand before an audience and talk about things I had never been able to discuss with anyone, even my wife. I found a Vet Center and got counseling. I learned about Agent Orange, which explained the loss of our first-born son at the age of fourteen days. It did not mitigate the hurt, but it explained.

That was forty-plus years ago, and I am still learning. That first book has stayed on bookstore shelves all these years. I have discovered "my thing," a purpose in life that was far outside my automotive career path. I have wangled invitations to speak to countless high school and college students, and the questions I have been asked formed the skeleton of this book. At first, the high schoolers had come of age with Vietnam an enormous part of their lives. Their father or brother had gone to the war, and a few were lost, but the ones who came home to be daddies all seemed to be "changed" and dangerous, mysterious, troubling influences in the maturing of their children. Many families were traumatized by the behavior of their Vietnam veterans.

I tried to explain. Their questions challenged me, and I had an insatiable need to know more, to understand what had happened to me and my country. I read books. Lots of books. Today my library shelves are overflowing with hundreds of books about Vietnam, and many more about the assassinations of JFK, RFK, Martin Luther King, and John Lennon. There are books about Nixon, FDR, the CIA, and the drug trade in Southeast Asia, the cultural upheavals of the sixties and the seventies, the Cold War. I have a lot of books about the Beatles, the Rolling Stones, Bob Dylan, and many of the other bands that impacted our world back then, and the history of rock 'n roll during that period. I have been obsessed, trying to put it all together. Trying to understand.

When our country began to interfere in Central America in the early 1980s, I got a little crazy. El Salvador, Nicaragua, Contras, Irangate, Oliver North, and Doctor Charlie Clements. We were doing it all again! I protested, carried signs, related my story and explained how it was relevant. Then came Bosnia, Serbia, Lebanon, the Sudan, 9/11, Afghanistan and Iraq. "There will be wars and rumors of wars" Revelations says, and I have brought children into the world! I have grandchildren now. The world is crazy, America bombed seven countries in 2018, and I have tried desperately to understand why. I reject the Pentagon's thinking.

This book contains many suggestions, a mosaic of historic fragments arranged to create an overall picture, colorful and heavy as chips of stone. I am confident that the events and attitudes depicted here are historically accurate. I have chosen not to include footnotes or endnotes because I think most readers ignore them, and they impede the joys of reading. I have included a bibliography with specific notes regarding which books informed which chapters, and I encourage the reader to investigate those other books and learn more from them.

Vietnam! The word carries a dark, heavy stigma. Baby boomers remember it as the seminal event of our time. Nothing seemed more important, back in the late sixties. Not the civil rights movement, not the space race, nothing. It was a time of great passions, overwhelming fears, but also a time of sincere patriotism, heroism, and stubborn optimism. Currently, there are 58,315 names of Americans killed or missing in action carved into the stone walls of the Vietnam Veterans Memorial in Washington, D.C. Approximately 153,000 Americans and about 16,000 allied soldiers were severely wounded. More than 23,000 Americans returned home 100% disabled, 5,283 lost limbs, and 1,081 suffered multiple traumatic amputations. It is estimated that somewhere between 3.5 and 5 million Vietnamese, Cambodians, and Laotians also died, mostly innocent civilians. Today it is estimated that more than 200,000 Vietnam veterans have committed suicide since returning home. The experts in the field say that number is unrealistically low. Fifty years later, in 2019, our perceptions of the Vietnam era have been impacted by countless books, movies, and the recent (autumn 2017) Ken Burns/Lynn Novick PBS TV series "The Vietnam War."

Today our government and the Pentagon have embarked upon a heavily-funded 50th anniversary "Commemoration of the Vietnam War," an ongoing series of events and publications lasting from May 28, 2012 to November 11, 2025. In announcing the Commemoration, President Barack Obama exhorted America to "pay tribute to the more than 3 million servicemen and women who left their families to serve bravely, a world away... They pushed through jungles and rice paddies, heat and monsoon, fighting heroically to protect the ideals we hold dear as Americans." Sadly, President Obama signed his name to a heavily-funded and wide-reaching Pentagon PR campaign that promises to further revise and misrepresent the truth about the war in Vietnam. I spent two years doing my country's bidding in Southeast Asia, and I did not come away feeling that the carnage and destruction I witnessed represented "the ideals we hold dear as Americans" in any way. When a G.I. was killed in Vietnam, we said he was "wasted."

There are thousands of books about Vietnam, and a few movies. Still, young people always ask me: "What was all the fuss about?" and baby boomers, especially Vietnam veterans, are finding time to re-examine the war and re-evaluate its lessons and legacies. "Vietnam" is a powerful, mysterious, even threatening word that simultaneously encompasses the far-off and mysterious Asian country, a period of overseas war and great suffering, an era of intense and passionate social turmoil here at home, and an enormous, troubling, chain of phantom historic events that impacted every aspect of our American society, culture, and government. In ways most of us cannot identify, Vietnam was a landmark event and time in American history. Today's young people sense that "Vietnam," that all-encompassing word, was important, but they don't know why. All of the books are valid, but I am not aware of one that tries to explain that all-important point. "What was all the fuss about?" This project quickly became a mosaic, requiring me to fasten a lot of random pieces together and create a multi-faceted picture of the war, the times, and why they are important today. I hope this book will help some readers, young and old, come to terms with Vietnam. As this project is about to go to print, I believe I have finally achieved that goal myself.

I am, admittedly, an angry, bitter Vietnam veteran. I have been diagnosed as having "severe" PTSD, which I define as Post-Traumatic Stress Damage. Some passages of this book will explain my thoughts and feelings in addition to the collection of historical facts. Politically, I'm not sure if I am a conservative liberal or a liberal conservative, but I am proud to describe myself as an opponent of militarism and war.

One final point must be made... It is my intention that not one word of this document reflect negatively on the common American soldiers who went to Vietnam, the neighborhood kids who were drafted or enticed to become foot soldiers. Not one word is intended to dishonor the lower-ranking Vietnam veterans, or the memory of the thousands who lost their lives. I have tried to create a tool to help people understand, and maybe even appreciate. We grew up at a colorful and exciting time. The vast majority of us weren't eager to be sent to Vietnam. Yes, some volunteered to go to the war. A few others felt so strongly that they defied the system and left the country or served time in prison instead of the rice paddies of Indochina, and I admire their courage. Looking back over the years, far too many vets have found they couldn't live with what they did in the war. I must admit, right up front, that while I do not intend any part of this book to reflect negatively upon the courage, bravery, or decency of the vast majority of Americans who served in Vietnam, I do hope it will discredit and shame the architects of the war, the greedy profiteers, and the incompetent or corrupt decision-makers who created, caused, and prolonged so much unnecessary suffering, death and destruction. And, I hope it will shame and discredit all of those who created precedents that have emboldened and misguided today's military leaders.

I wrote this book to offer a distinctly different look at Vietnam. I anticipate that some readers will say I have chosen a specific collection of facts and events because I "hate America" or words to that effect. Nothing could be further from the truth. I can assure the reader that this book is NOT anti-American. One loves the sick child but curses the disease. I believe militarism is bankrupting America both financially and morally. The facts presented within this book are genuine and true. If they have been overlooked or ignored in other works because of the author's predisposition, point of view, or agenda, well, they are presented here for the very same reasons. My experiences, the things I have seen with my own eyes, and the many things I have learned from my studies have resulted in my convictions and opinions. This book is guided by the belief that war is the most abhorrent and despicable behavior of all human endeavors, and it should not be glorified. America's war in Vietnam and Southeast Asia was a travesty and a tragedy, and the purpose of this book is to explain how and why I came to that conclusion.

Carl Sandburg wrote, "History says, 'If it pleases, Excuse me, I beg your pardon, it will never happen again if I can help it." ("Good Morning America," from *Complete Poems*, 1950). Far too many of the events chronicled in this book happened during our young adult years, when I probably should have been more attentive, more outraged, more careful, and more outspoken. There is a faint theme of apology throughout this book, and perhaps it is not so faint. If I have learned one thing, it is that no one can undo what has already been done, but anyone can look back upon the past and learn from it. Vietnam! To echo Carl Sandburg: If it pleases, Excuse me, I beg your pardon; it will never happen again if I can help it. I hope this book might cause the reader to think. I hope it will influence my grandchildren's futures, and yours, in a positive manner.

The Times They Are A-Changin'

Come gather 'round people
Wherever you roam
And admit that the waters
Around you have grown
And accept it that soon
You'll be drenched to the bone
If your time to you is worth savin'
Then you better start swimmin' or you'll sink like a stone
For the times they are a-changin'

Come writers and critics
Who prophesize with your pen
And keep your eyes wide
The chance won't come again
And don't speak too soon
For the wheel's still in spin
And there's no tellin' who that it's namin'
For the loser now will be later to win
For the times they are a-changin'

Come senators, congressmen
Please heed the call
Don't stand in the doorway
Don't block up the hall
For he that gets hurt
Will be he who has stalled
There's a battle outside and it's ragin'
It'll soon shake your windows and rattle your walls
For the times they are a-changin'

Come mothers and fathers
Throughout the land
And don't criticize
What you can't understand
Your sons and your daughters are beyond your command
Your old road is rapidly agin'
Please get out of the new one if you can't lend a hand
For the times they are a-changin'

The line it is drawn
The curse it is cast
The slow one now
Will later be fast
As the present now
Will later be past
The order is rapidly fadin'
And the first one now will later be last
For the times they are a-changin'

Chapter 1

THE TIMES THEY WERE A-CHANGIN'

To understand the Vietnam tragedy, it is important to recognize its place in the timeline of history. The generation born in the decade after America's soldiers returned from World War II came to be known as the "baby boomers," and their numbers were unprecedented in American history. They (we) grew up in the seemingly comfortable fifties, a time when the economy was strong and America tried to relax and enjoy life after the horrors of World War II. It was an exhilarating time to grow up. New technology gave us transistor radios, television, computers, commercial air travel, Corvettes, Thunderbirds, interstate highways, and the inescapable reality of nuclear weapons capable of destroying all life on our planet. Soon after the Second World War, a nasty war in Korea left 36,000 Americans dead. Peace was never achieved, but we were too young to know much about that war.

*****

The average age of an American fighting man in Vietnam was "only 19," as the historians like to point out, while in World War II the average age of an American soldier was 26. It's a curious fact, so poignant that in 1985 British jazz artist Paul Hardcastle released a single titled "19," drawing attention to the sad disparity and implying that the youthfulness of America's Vietnam army somehow made the brutality of war more heart-wrenching. While the loss of young men in war is always sad and discomforting, the author suggests that the historical significance of that statistic may be the key to understanding what went wrong in Vietnam, why it happened, and hopefully, how the United States might avoid another similar military debacle.

It's important to keep this in perspective. The largest number of Americans arrived in Vietnam soon after the Tet offensive of early 1968. The G.I. who was 19 in 1968 was born in 1949, so he probably grew up heavily influenced by all the revolutionary developments taking place. Pinned down by an enemy machine gun in Vietnam, the average G.I. felt terribly out of step with all that was happening in "The World," as he called it, and he was resentful. Suddenly, he found himself on the other side of the planet, scared to death and struggling just to survive. His life had become a terrifying, surreal nightmare, and he was hopelessly trapped by an enormous, all-powerful, uncaring and often immoral system.

Born in the aftermath of World War II, the soldiers sent to fight and die in Vietnam were raised and instructed by an adult population that had recently witnessed and indeed survived, man's inhumanity to his fellow man on an unprecedented scale. Every authority figure in our young lives had spent years reading the daily newspaper accounts of death, destruction, and suffering of Pearl Harbor, the Holocaust, the Bataan Death March, the fire bombings of Dresden and Tokyo, ad infinitum, culminating ultimately in the advent of the all-powerful atomic bombs at Hiroshima and Nagasaki.

In my Social Studies classroom in a suburban high school in western New York, we were taught that our generation must do something that no generation in the history of the world had been able to accomplish: we would have to find a way to settle our differences without resorting to war. With the shadow of a nuclear holocaust looming over the entire planet, we were taught that war had become unthinkable. We were being prepared; we would graduate and go forth to change the world, eradicate war, and bring justice to the poor and oppressed around the globe. We believed in our hearts that America was the hope of the world, that many aspects of our young lives clearly and very desperately needed to be "a' changin'," and that as Americans we were inherently privileged and empowered to challenge the *status quo* and create a genuine peace on Earth, with good will toward all men.

During the fifties, cars and super-highways put America on the road, TV sets became a common fixture in our young lives, and we gloried in the freedoms those devices bestowed. The invention of the birth control pill added another technology that would allow us to freely "make love, not war." This was our destiny as young Americans in the sixties, and we left high school determined to make a difference, and supremely confident that the new space-age technologies would help us achieve our goals. We were free to choose, free to challenge the old, worn-out dogmas in which our parents seemed to be mired, and free to help the world's poor and downtrodden. We did not believe it would be necessary to harm others. Quite the contrary. Life was to be lived and enjoyed, and the nuclear missiles would someday rust away and be retired if only we would all come together as human beings and reconcile our differences without killing each other.

As these thoughts were being implanted by our parents and teachers, young baby boomers were also receiving direction and information from outside sources as no generation before them. Throughout World War II, Americans gathered around the heavy wooden radio console in the living room to listen to big band music, dozens of dramas and comedy shows, or the news from the battlefields of Europe, Africa, and the Pacific. From 1933 to 1944, President Franklin D. Roosevelt gave a series of thirty radio addresses, or "fireside chats," designed to communicate his administration's policies in an upbeat and positive manner. As he led America out of the Great Depression, FDR seized upon the technology of the time to speak directly to every household and give cause for optimism and hope. In 1947 there were approximately 40 million radios in use across America, but their mobility was limited to the location of the nearest electrical outlet until the "transistor" portable radio was introduced in 1954. Three years later Sony came into the American marketplace with the TR-63, the first pocket-size portable radio, and by 1959 there were over six-million Japanese-made transistor radios in America.

Young Americans who would soon see action in Vietnam were coming of age with a portable radio in their pocket. The fireside chats had been replaced by powerful personal listening experiences that accompanied us everywhere we went. Popular music on the air waves began to be geared toward the affluent younger audience. About this time, a few creative musicians stretched the boundaries of musical expression by daring to combine elements of blues, jazz, gospel, and even lyrical themes from "beat" literature, and, with the evolution of amplifiers, rock 'n roll was born. We were still required to read the classic poets and writers in school, but the irresistible rhythm and the musical messages from stars like Elvis Presley, Buddy Holly, Bob Dylan, Lennon and McCartney, Jagger and Richards, James Brown, Paul Simon, Aretha Franklin and so many others spoke directly to our young hearts. They were true artists, painting the landscape in textures and colors that reflected what we were feeling, just as a landscape painter replicates scenes of mountains or seashores.

American soldiers in Vietnam were the first American fighting force to have grown up in the glow of television sets. The first public TV broadcast in America took place on May 28, 1928 at station W2XB in Schenectady, New York, although there were virtually no TV sets in American homes to receive the signals. Ten years later, the Dumont Company began selling all-electronic television sets to the public, but World War II interrupted the experiments. After the war, NBC began regular TV programming in 1945. Still, TV did not become a common accessory in most middle-class American neighborhoods until the mid-1950s. The first color TV broadcast took place in 1965, and it wasn't until 1972 that sales of color TV sets outnumbered black and white. The baby boomer generation witnessed a technological revolution, and marveled at the images of history and entertainment that appeared on a box in our living rooms.

As kids, a huge majority of the guys destined to go to Vietnam grew up in the silvery black-and-white glow of TV shows like *Rin Tin Tin, Howdy Doody, Sky King, Superman, Disney World*, the first spin-off, Disney's *Mickey Mouse Club*, and the classic morning TV show *Captain Kangaroo*, that would last 29 years. While most of us did not enjoy the idyllic family relationships in real life that we watched on *Leave It to Beaver* or *Father Knows Best*, those shows were role models every bit as much as entertainment as we moved toward adolescence. In Philadelphia, a local afternoon teen dance show called *Bandstand* began in 1952. Dick Clark took over in 1956, changed the name to *American Bandstand*, went national in August of 1957 and became an afternoon fixture for teens all over the USA. In the political arena, TV came into its own during the 1960 Presidential election, when Vice President Richard Nixon and Senator John F. Kennedy took part in a series of four televised debates. On May 5, 1961, school attendance was severely impacted as Alan Shepard became the first American space traveler, although a Russian cosmonaut, Yuri Gagarin, had become the first man in space a month earlier. By that time, televisions were widespread throughout America, and most Americans tuned in every night. TV broadcasters had developed technology and financial success that allowed them to bring news coverage from around the world into American living rooms within hours.

It was a curious time in America. Just as TV sets were becoming commonplace in our living rooms, disturbing political battles were shaking the country . In Washington, the McCarthy hearings were finding supposed Communist sympathizers in every corner, and blacklisting open-minded thinkers and creative artists in a devastating wave of intolerance. Our Social Studies teachers urged us to monitor current events, and television brought amazing images into our homes. In December of 1960 the Supreme Court had abolished racial segregation on trains, planes, and buses used for interstate transportation... and also in the terminals. This order was quietly and contemptuously ignored throughout the South, until May of 1961. The Congress of Racial Equality (CORE), an organization inspired by Mahatma Ghandi's principles of peaceful protest and passive resistance, organized a series of demonstrations aimed at asserting Black Americans' constitutional rights, and TV brought film of these actions into our living rooms. Soon after, a group of impassioned activists rode into the South on commercial buses, intent upon adding their voices to the growing chorus of Americans demanding that the Constitutional rights of American citizenship should be equally available to all, regardless of the color of their skin. These Freedom Riders, both black and white, had made their statements throughout Virginia, the Carolinas and Georgia, but in Anniston, Alabama things turned ugly. A white mob burned one bus and beat up civil rights workers. In Birmingham, the Ku Klux Klan was granted fifteen minutes of immunity by the police to beat up the Freedom Riders with baseball bats and chains. The FBI stood by without interfering. There were no arrests. It was just the beginning, and soon our televisions brought us troubling nightly news, reports of demonstrations and racial violence, killings and bombings throughout the South. We saw American citizens denied the right to vote, or even use a "whites only" drinking fountain, and we questioned. TV news brought scenes of riots, murders, children killed when churches were bombed, and we questioned it. We saw films of civil rights marchers attacked with vicious dogs and water cannons, denied entry to schools and lunch counters, and we questioned that, too. We went to school filled with those questions that our teachers were often unable or unwilling to address.

A deep and wide "generation gap" began to develop between the young and most of the adults in our lives, between our rock 'n roll sensibilities and their old-fashioned and rigid governmental and cultural institutions, which we began to call "The Establishment." Our questions were basic, and so was our sincere patriotism and belief in American Democracy. There was a desperate urgency about it all as a variety of causes gained momentum and became obsessions, and then movements. We were outraged that the travesties and abuses had been allowed to exist for so long in America, of all places, and many of us saw it as our destiny, our sacred duty, to make those things right. We would overturn The Establishment and make things fair and moral. We would make the Negro equal to the white man or woman, simply because all men are created equal, and of course that meant women, too. Who could dispute that basic truth?

Sadly, as we grew up and asked more questions, we found a huge snake-pit of intolerance and corruption that desperately needed fixing, and we took on the challenge. We were the generation inspired by the Reverend Martin Luther King, Jr., by Bob Dylan, Muhammad Ali, by John F. Kennedy, and perhaps even by Fidel Castro or Che Guevara, and there was simply no question that we would make it all right and proper, fair and honest in the spirit of America and all that was good in the world.

Americans in Vietnam were the first U.S. soldiers to enjoy easy access to automobiles prior to their military inductions. Devastated by the great depression, after World War II an affluent middle class emerged and began to enjoy the fruits of its labors. Most of the guys I knew in Vietnam had cars waiting in their driveways back home. After the war, America enjoyed a robust economy that allowed most middle-class families to own an automobile, and the face of America was changing as a result. The new phenomenon of suburbia became the most desirable and fashionable environment in which to bring up a family, and vast housing developments sprung up within commuting distance from the crowded cities. By the early 60s and the Vietnam era, changes in our culture made owning a car almost a necessity, especially for young people. You had to drive to get to your job, to school, to the shopping plaza, to this weekend's dance or the drive-in movie.

The primary avenue of communication to the masses in those days was still the printed page. The daily newspaper was a necessity, and an ever-expanding variety of magazines had become popular. In high school, the guys smuggled hot rod magazines into study halls, and discussed the latest new car models, race results, and hot rods in pinpoint detail at lunch. A guy couldn't wait to get a driver's license and a car so he could go on a date and be alone with a girl. This was the time when America's car culture became a universal obsession, and the baby boomers came of age just as space-age technology brought amazing developments to every form of transportation.

The favorite vehicle of the young during that era was the 1955, '56, or '57 Chevy two-door sedan, with hot-rod modifications that strained our wallets but made an ex-family car fast and loud. "Car guys" worked in gas stations to earn a few dollars for gas, and maybe even to afford the latest speed equipment gadget from exotic California, while the "nerds" and girls worked in ice cream shops or the neighborhood grocery. Our cars were hot-rodded to accelerate hard, just like our drag-racing heroes, but we maintained comfortable seating for a date or a trip to the drive-in movie. Of course, a cool car was necessary to attract the prettiest and most adventuresome girls, and for dates that would be imaginative and exciting. A lot of young drivers dreamed of traveling to New York City where the top bands played every night, to Indianapolis, Daytona, or Watkins Glen to see the fastest race cars, or ultimately to exotic and far-off California where we imagined the streets were crowded with outrageous hot rods, every community had a drag-strip, and the beaches were crowded with bikini-clad surfer girls. With our own cars and a few bucks for gas, there were no limits to our freedoms or our dreams. (It was not uncommon to pull into a gas station and buy fifty cents or a dollar's worth, and ride on it for a week.) To be honest, I dated driving my dad's Rambler American, or doubling with a buddy in his dad's Studebaker Hawk. But we could dream.

Technology brought drastic changes to factory-produced automobiles during the Vietnam era. The first Corvette appeared in 1953, and the first Thunderbird, a two-seat convertible, in 1955. Noting that the odd-looking rear-engine Volkswagen Beetle was gaining popularity, Ford and GM introduced the Falcon and the Corvair, small economy cars that boasted excellent fuel economy. Perhaps of more significance to the generation of young drivers who would be called upon to fight and die in Vietnam, Lee Iacocca created the sporty Ford Mustang which debuted in 1964, and then John DeLorean created the Pontiac GTO by stuffing a big V-8 engine into a lightweight Tempest sedan. Soon all the American manufacturers were building powerful V-8 engines and combining them with lightweight bodies suitable for drag racing. "Muscle cars" became hugely popular, and if we couldn't afford the latest Detroit creations, we soon learned that they were built for straight-line speed and somewhat prone to crash on rainy or curvy roads, and the power plants could often be found in junkyards just waiting to be transplanted into an older, lightweight hot rod. Drag racers like Don "Big Daddy" Garlits, Tom "Mongoose" McEwen and Don "The Snake" Prudhomme achieved cultural status equal to baseball stars, and we were enthralled by "wheelstand" exhibitions where star cars like "The Little Red Wagon" or "Hemi Under Glass" could accelerate with so much power they lifted the front of the car high in the air and dragged their rear bumpers on the ground! The guys in the lunchrooms had a hundred opinions about how they were steered.

Soon the technology that empowered satellites began to be applied to cars, and we went from 45 rpm record players hung under the dash to built-in 8-track cassette players with true stereophonic sound. It was a time of exciting innovation and unlimited optimism, and we took full advantage of all the freedoms our cars offered.

By the late 1950s, America's everyday way of life had been changed significantly by the proliferation of automobiles. In 1954, an innovative man named Ray Kroc visited San Bernardino, California and was impressed by a little hamburger joint with a long line of customers out front. The owners, two brothers named McDonald, didn't want to expand, although they sold Kroc the opportunity to open all the "McDonald's" restaurants he wanted. Of course, those drive-up restaurants were entirely dependent upon a clientele in cars. Kroc's modest investment paid off very handsomely.

In March of 1962 the S.S. Kresge chain opened the first K-Mart in Garden City, Michigan just a few months before the first Wal-Mart opened in Arkansas. By 1975 there were 125 Wal-Mart stores across the U.S. as Americans changed their shopping habits and drove to suburban shopping centers and malls instead of Main Street. Over 4,000 drive-in movie theaters were constructed. The Federal Aid Highway Act of 1956 created the Interstate Highway system, allowing (relatively) safe and efficient high-speed travel all across the country. Between 1960 and 1970, 70% of America's population growth occurred in the suburbs.

Easy access to cars gave young baby boomers mobility and the access to all manner of exciting events that no previous generation had ever known, and we were extremely reluctant to give up those freedoms when the situation in far-off Vietnam intervened.

By the early seventies, millions of young American soldiers had visited Southeast Asia and witnessed the incredible durability of Japanese cars. At the same time, Japanese companies like Toyota, Honda, Datsun, and Mazda were beginning to establish a sales presence in the U.S., especially on the west coast. In 1950, Japan produced a total of 32,000 cars and light trucks. In 1965 they built over 1.9 million. By 1974, political strife in the Middle East had brought the price of a gallon of gas to over a dollar (if you could find one)! Detroit finally saw the writing on the wall and scrambled to abandon bulky bodies with fins and to build fuel-efficient cars. While the US belatedly struggled to re-tool, European and Japanese manufacturers could not build cars fast enough to meet the demand. When I first joined Toyota at a dealership in South Carolina in 1973, we had one Corolla which was sold, but the dealer "rented" the car from its owner so we would have one solitary vehicle on the showroom floor to show to a customer. You could order a car, but no one could be sure when it might be delivered. I don't believe the Asian car manufacturers would have experienced the success they did in America had we not sent millions of impressionable young people to Southeast Asia during the Vietnam War. We saw that the Japanese cars were tough, dependable, sensible and economical at a time when American cars were not, and when we found them on sale in our home town, we had to have one.

Which came first; the chicken or the egg? At the same time the Vietnam generation was being influenced by portable radios, television, popular music, and easy access to the automobile, we became aware of a new breed of heroes and role models. Perhaps the entire world was relaxing after the horrors of World War II, or maybe people were trying to cram in all the fun they could under the threat of nuclear annihilation. Again, we were destined to right the world's wrongs, and you have to break a few eggs to make a cake. Whatever the reason, the rebel became a hero. Aided by high-tech publicity, the Vietnam generation was enthralled by a vast array of outrageously non-conformist personalities, acts, and ideas. It became fashionable to emulate the rebels, and we were proud when The Establishment referred to us as the "counter-culture."

James Dean was a symbol of teenage disillusionment, based largely upon his role in the celebrated film *Rebel Without A Cause*. Dean made only three movies before he was killed in his Porsche Spyder in 1955, but he remains an icon to this day. Other notable movie rebels were Marlon Brando, Steve McQueen, John Wayne, Clint Eastwood, Sean Connery, and Jack Nicholson on the male side, and Marilyn Monroe, Brigitte Bardot, Raquel Welch, Ann-Margret, Grace Slick and Janis Joplin among the ladies.

Elvis Presley invoked the wrath of strait-laced America primarily because he swiveled his hips keeping time with his music. Our hormones were surging! The Twist was a huge dance phenomenon, noteworthy because for the first time, couples danced without touching each other. Of course, the same older folks who objected to Elvis Presley's hip movements were also offended by the pelvic gyrations of the Twist, but by the early sixties the youth movement all around the world had gained unstoppable momentum. The immense popularity of rock 'n roll music seemed to give license to its performers, and the "rock star" replaced the crooners of our parents' generation . Rock rebels included the inimitable Jerry Lee Lewis, Little Richard, Frank Zappa, girl groups like the Ronettes and the Shangri-Las, outspoken social critics like Bob Dylan and "the Godfather of Soul" James Brown, and cutting-edge lifestyle icons like Jim Morrison and the Doors, Jimi Hendrix, Janis Joplin, The Who, and of course, the Beatles and the Rolling Stones. While discussing musical rebels of the sixties, we must also mention Liberace, whose incredibly gaudy and glamorous outfits gained more attention than his very substantial talent at the piano. All-American country or folk music rebels like Hank Williams, Woody Guthrie, Merle Haggard, and Johnny Cash portrayed Main Street America in their songs, just as painter Norman Rockwell did in his cover art for the *Saturday Evening Post* magazine. The "way it has always been done" was challenged on every front.

Even traditional sports were being challenged. Perhaps inspired by Liberace, pro wrestling featured the revolutionary, flamboyant Gorgeous George. Quarterback Joe Namath prowled New York City nightclubs in an ostentatious fur coat, often with a Hollywood starlet on his arm. Then he posed for an advertising promotion wearing panty hose! On March 2nd, 1962, Wilt "the Stilt" Chamberlain, a towering 7-foot 1-inch basketball player scored an incredible 100 points in a single NBA game. The first Super Bowl was played in January of 1967, and two years later Namath and the Jets proved that the former AFL teams were on a par with the NFL by beating the Baltimore Colts in Super Bowl III. The Brooklyn Dodgers moved to Los Angeles in 1958, to the outraged moans of millions of fans. Nothing was sacred any more.

A black kid from Kentucky became Olympic boxing champion in 1960, and then Heavyweight Champion of the World. When he became a Muslim, Cassius Clay changed his name to Muhammad Ali and refused to report for the draft in 1966 on both political and religious grounds, citing his opposition to the growing American involvement in Southeast Asia. He was found guilty of evading the draft, stripped of his title, and could not compete in the ring for four years until the U.S. Supreme Court overturned his conviction in 1971. Ali returned to boxing and took back his title twice, defeating such notable opponents as Joe Frazier, George Foreman, and Leon Spinks. Muhammad Ali was named "Sportsman of the Century" by *Sports Illustrated* magazine, and for many years was considered the "Most Admired Man in the World." Fast on his feet and a devastating puncher, Muhammad Ali's greatest weapon was his personality. He was brash, articulate, clever, entertaining, outspoken, and always inspiring.

In the 1950's, a loose-knit group of writers known as The Beats challenged many aspects of American social culture. Their alternatives focused upon the rejection of materialism, alternative sexualities, experimentation with mind-altering or hallucinogenic drugs, curiosity about Eastern religions, and explicit documentation of the plight of the American common man victimized by relentless capitalism. Above all, the Beats rejected their college professors' conservative and very formal values, preferring to eke out lifestyles of spontaneous creativity and bold non-conformity. Allen Ginsberg's epic poem *Howl* (1956), William S. Burroughs' novel *Naked Lunch* (1959), and Jack Kerouac's critically acclaimed novel *On the Road* (1957) were landmarks of Beat literature, and both *Howl* and *Naked Lunch* were subjected to widely publicized obscenity trials that ultimately contributed to more liberal publishing standards in the United States. Literary rebels like Ginsburg, Kerouac, and Burroughs inspired writers like Timothy Leary, Tom Wolfe, Ken Kesey, Betty Friedan, Hunter S. Thompson, and Helen Gurley Brown to take up their rebellious pens and expand our understanding of the world in which we lived. *Mad* magazine and its cover boy Alfred E. Neuman flippantly confronted the threat of nuclear annihilation with the classic, "What, me worry?"

The news from Cuba introduced us to the bearded Fidel Castro and his ragtag but wonderfully committed revolutionary army, and many young Americans grew beards to emulate the Cuban rebels. Fidel's lieutenant, the intense, philosophical, daring and ultra-masculine revolutionary doctor Che Guevara became a cult figure. It was only months after the rebels had tossed out Cuba's corrupt dictator Batista that Castro proclaimed his Communist leanings, igniting an uproar of cold war outrage across the neighboring United States.

In December of 1953, Hugh Hefner borrowed from his brother and mother and created *Playboy* magazine. The first issue did not include his name and was not dated, as Hefner was not confident there would be a second. The magazine soon featured America's top writers and free-thinkers, along with artful photographs of beautiful young women in the nude. The center of each monthly issue was an elaborate foldout assemblage of pictures and information featuring the Playmate of the Month, an especially beauteous young woman who would ultimately compete for the prestigious title Playmate of the Year. The magazine was hugely popular with men of all ages, some of whom bought it "just for the articles," or so they liked to say. Playboy Clubs sprang up in major cities around the world, fashionable nightclubs where top entertainers played, while nubile waitresses in abbreviated "Bunny" costumes served drinks, always hoping to attract attention and be asked to pose for the magazine.

By coincidence, the birth control pill was approved for contraceptive use in 1960. Sales reached 1.2 million in 1962, increased to 2.3 million in 1963, and 6.5 million in 1965. The same year, after vigorous court action, D.H. Lawrence's *Lady Chatterley's Lover* was published in its entirety for the first time, and in England designer Mary Quant introduced the miniskirt, which rose six inches above the knee and created controversy throughout the world. Women were actually jailed for wearing miniskirts in Greece, the Congo, and many other countries. At the same time, it wasn't considered "ladylike" for a woman to wear trousers. In post-Woodstock 1969, Judy Carne of the TV comedy show *Laugh-In* was refused entry at the trendy 21 Club in New York City, because she was wearing a tunic-topped pants suit. In true "sock it to 'em" style, she promptly took off her pants and turned them in at the coat check. She was allowed to enter, presumably in her "miniskirt." The 21 Club changed its policy the very next day. The times (and the fashions) were a-changin!

As if there was not enough political tension and confrontation across America, a new movement challenged the status quo. Influenced and inspired by Betty Friedan's 1963 book *The Feminine Mystique*, women organized and demanded equal rights, equal pay for equal work, and, as Aretha Franklin sang in the classic 1967 hit, "R-E-S-P-E-C-T." So powerful was the reaction to Friedan's book, as a concession to feminists President Kennedy appointed a blue-ribbon President's Commission on the Status of Women chaired by the iconic former First Lady Eleanor Roosevelt, which led to passage of the Equal Pay Act of 1963. The act banned gender-based pay discrimination in a number of professions, and in 1970 it was expanded to include all jobs. Betty Friedan soon founded the National Organization for Women (NOW). She left the organization in 1970 to organize the nationwide "Women's Strike for Equality," which took place on the 50th anniversary of the passage of the 19th Amendment to the Constitution, which gave women the right to vote. The Equal Rights Amendment, or ERA, had been introduced in 1921, but it wasn't until the feminist activism of the sixties that it came to a vote in Congress. The amendment was passed by a vote of 354 – 24 in the House of Representatives, and 84 – 8 in the Senate, and a nationwide debate "rattled the walls" for the next decade.

Helen Reddy had a 1975 hit record with "I Am Woman (Hear Me Roar)," which became an anthem of the movement, but ultimately the ERA failed to be ratified by the necessary majority of states within the required time. Much of the opposition to the ERA came from organized labor, fearful that the Amendment would strip away workplace protections specific to working women. Ultimately, enthusiasm for the Amendment began to fade after a campaign by conservative Republican activist Phyllis Schlafly suggested that passage would mean that women would be drafted and assigned to combat roles, alimony would be eliminated, and restrooms would no longer be segregated by sex. The women's movement gained momentum in the late 1960s and early 1970s, at the same time the United States was entangled in Vietnam. Of course, the women's movement confronted The Establishment and stirred up political emotions alongside the struggle for racial equality and civil rights that was still causing tension and strife throughout the nation. The old ways, and the staid old men who enforced them, were under siege from all sides. The Equal Rights Amendment has continued to be re-introduced in Congress as recently as 2011. At the very least, the guys who went to Vietnam had seen their masculine pre-eminence challenged, and the "little lady" that greeted them when they came home was expecting to be treated far differently.

In 1963, the 1750 novel *Fanny Hill* was published as *John Cleland's Memoirs of a Woman of Pleasure* and was immediately banned for obscenity. The publisher challenged the ruling in court, and in 1966 the United States Supreme Court ruled that the book did not meet the standards for obscenity. *Human Sexual Response* by Dr. William Masters and Dr. Virginia Johnson was published in 1966, and *Everything You Ever Wanted to Know About Sex (But Were Afraid to Ask)* by David Reuben, M.D. in 1969. By 1969 the Broadway musical *Hair* featured on-stage nudity, and those pesky hippies and rock 'n roll fans at Woodstock actually skinny-dipped in the farmer's pond! Ian Fleming's novels had come to the screen in 1962 when Ursula Andress came ashore in that amazing white bathing suit in *Dr. No*, and then in *Goldfinger* the female lead's name was, true to the book, Pussy Galore. Again, there were over 4,000 drive-in movie theaters in America in those days, and Rambler automobiles were not highly respected for their technology, but they were the first to offer reclining front seats. All of these random events, and many more, came to be known as "The Sexual Revolution." It was a glorious time to be an adolescent, male or female!

In a time of challenges to The Establishment, perhaps the ultimate challenger was John F. Kennedy. The first President born in the twentieth century, JFK came from money, but he was a war hero, a liberal, and an intellectual. Unlike the staid old politicians who ran Washington and the country during the conservative Eisenhower years, John Kennedy was a good-looking, forward-thinking young politician with a beautiful, charming wife and young children. Elected President in a very tight victory over Eisenhower's Vice President Richard Nixon, Kennedy declared a New Frontier of unprecedented challenges. The Cold War loomed over everything, but Kennedy's inaugural speech declared "The old ways will not do," and the media focused more upon his challenge, "Ask not what your country can do for you, but what you can do for your country."

John Kennedy dared to suggest that the poorest Americans should share in America's good fortune, and that the American dream was not just about the accumulation of wealth, but also the moral obligation to reach out and help the disadvantaged and needy. A dreamer, he dared America to believe in technology, and suggested that we might see a man walk on the moon within the decade! He was reluctant to involve federal forces in the civil rights movement at first, but, ultimately, he confronted the deep-South segregationists head-on, sending National Guard troops to guarantee that non-white American citizens would have access to a decent education and the right to vote. JFK negotiated with the Russians and made them take their missiles out of Cuba, he sailed, played touch football, romped with his children in the Oval Office, and his wife Jackie redecorated and restored the White House into a stately and historic mansion worthy of the most powerful man in the world.

In late 1962, Peter, Paul, and Mary's debut album was pushed out of the number one sales slot by a 33 1/3 RPM comedy album called "The First Family." The record was a good-natured spoof of the President's Massachusetts accent as it depicted a comical version of everyday life behind the scenes in the Kennedy White House. Perhaps that record helped to endear the Kennedy family to the baby boomers, or perhaps it simply mirrored the affection we were already feeling. Whatever the cause, "The First Family" was honored as the "largest and fastest selling record in the history of the record industry." One would have to stretch the imagination painfully thin to conceive of a comedy album about Eisenhower, Truman, or Nixon. John Kennedy carried out his Presidential duties with "vigor" and an engaging sense of humor. In those days, the media did not disclose that he had affairs with Marilyn Monroe, Angie Dickinson, or the former girlfriend of a top Chicago mob leader. I'm not sure it would have mattered. John Kennedy was one of us, the perfect President to help us find our way as a nation in the nuclear age, and the one person, and certainly the one politician, that young people believed might lead us into the future.

The Kennedys were special, brimming over with energy and optimism. None of us imagined that the President might be assassinated. That fateful weekend in November of 1963, we all sat in front of our black-and-white TVs dumbfounded. We saw Jack Ruby boldly shoot Lee Harvey Oswald in a crowd of police officers. We heard the muffled funeral drums as JFK's coffin was carried toward Arlington cemetery, and we saw little John-John salute his father's casket. To many of the young men who would soon find themselves viewing death close-up in Vietnam, the Kennedy assassination was our first experience with a funeral. Television made us all a part of the tragedy, and our nation has never really gotten over the shock and disappointment.

Everything seemed to undergo a subtle change with the death of President Kennedy. Suddenly the best hopes of America had been silenced, and an awful awareness crept over our generation. The truths we saw so clearly, the way forward to a new American democracy, the good and moral things, were opposed, and the opposition was utterly ruthless. Certainly, few young people could relate to Lyndon Baines Johnson. John Kennedy's successor was a typical "old style" politician, a shrewd manipulator and power broker. America's 1964 Presidential election was influenced by the fear that Barry Goldwater, the original "conservative," might actually use the atomic bomb. Goldwater's campaign slogan, "In your heart you know he's right," was offset by the opposition's wry photos of a mushroom cloud with the caption "In your heart, you know he might!"

Lyndon Johnson won the 1964 election, largely because the country couldn't stand another upheaval so soon after the assassination. By '64 the climate of the country, and most of the world, had begun to split into "the generation gap," as youth looked around at The Establishment's corruption, the plight of so many of the planet's poor and oppressed, and we dared to dream that we might make a moral, much-needed difference. The Warren Commission's report on the death of JFK seemed simplistic and unconvincing from the start. People young and old suspected that forces within the government had, in some way, been responsible for the assassination of JFK, and suddenly all government and authority was seen as morally suspect. LBJ had a prickly personality, but he played politics and passed the most wide-ranging array of social legislation since FDR's New Deal. Unfortunately, he never got his hands around the problems in Vietnam, and the disastrous war overshadowed all of his domestic accomplishments.

The late President's brother Robert F. Kennedy spoke for a generation when he said, "Some people see things the way they are and wonder why. I dream of things the way they could be, and wonder why not," and we understood because that's just the way it was. Across America and around the world, youth was energized with a revolutionary dream of peace and good will toward all men, of social justice and ethical behavior based upon a loose code of spiritual and moral values. It wasn't religious; it was just the right way to be. The point of it all was to live life to the fullest, to enjoy the new freedoms that technology had brought us, but without hurting anyone or infringing upon anyone else's freedoms. We thought we could change the world; that our generation would kick out the power brokers, the crooks and robbers, the bad guys, and we would all live in peace. It was a grand dream, perhaps a bit more idealistic than realistic, but we came by it naturally and felt it to our marrow.

So here we were, a generation brought up under the threat of imminent nuclear annihilation, and after Disney and *Captain Kangaroo*, TV began to show us the brutality of civil rights abuses in the south, along with man's first adventures in space, and the shocking tragedy of JFK's assassination. Our portable radios and televisions brought us incredible observations, fantasies, and ideas, and too many questions our teachers and other authority figures were not eager to answer. Then, as adolescents or young adults, we turned to our TV sets many evenings to watch groundbreaking, outspoken shows like *Laugh-In* or *The Smothers Brothers Comedy Hour*. The generation gap was yawning wide everywhere.

It was an exciting, colorful time. We had fast, powerful cars, exciting, meaningful music, and a boundless spirit for renewing all the social structures. We grew our hair long, wore blue jeans everywhere, turned our radios up loud to get the full effect of our music, and many of us dreamed of being an astronaut and rocketing into space, or a missionary tending to the world's poor. John Kennedy's Peace Corps was popular, allowing young people to go overseas and do good works for those less fortunate. We had high hopes, to try surfing in California, or tour Europe and stay in low-cost hostels. We hoped to gather enough money to buy a key and gain entry to a Playboy Club, or buy a ticket to a Rolling Stones or Janis Joplin concert. We dared to dream big, colorful, exciting dreams because the world was at our fingertips!

Then we were drafted or coerced to enlist. A few volunteered for all the standard patriotic reasons, but they were far from the majority. Most of us had our lives completely upended by the draft. All of the exhilarating, life-enhancing expressions of freedom mentioned in this chapter were absolutely contrary to the thought of joining the army and being wounded or killed in a place called Vietnam. We were taken against our will, yanked away from our affluent and colorful worlds, our long hair was unceremoniously sheared, and our colorful mod Carnaby Street-inspired clothes were stripped from us. From the familiar comfort and sanctuary the Beach Boys sang about in the tune "In My Room," we found ourselves in a military barracks where there was no privacy, the only mirrors were sheets of polished metal and the light bulbs were surrounded by metal cages, all to discourage suicides. Raging drill sergeants screamed at us, threatened us, and sometimes physically abused us. We were going to be shipped to Vietnam, wherever that was, to save democracy, they insisted, and fight a war against a vicious, unprincipled mob of primitive Orientals, Gooks! We didn't understand why, and the explanations offered by our superiors were clearly more propaganda than factual. It was a nightmare, but there would be no morning escape. We were caught in a machine, being processed in preparation for war. The unthinkable was inescapable.

In September of 1967, I was shipped to Vietnam. I was a young man, basically just a boy, shocked that my rock 'n roll lifestyle had been torn away and my hopes of avoiding the war dashed. I was stopped by a policeman one night, and I angrily thrust my orders for Vietnam at him. "You can write me a ticket," I growled, "but Tuesday I'm going to Vietnam. I won't be able to go to court." He let me go with a warning. The year to come would change every aspect of my head and heart and soul. By mid-summer of 1968 I was afraid to come home, and I volunteered to serve out my army obligation in Thailand. It was probably the best decision of my life, giving me time to self-medicate and contemplate, to digest all I had been asked to swallow and find the direction and courage to return to placid Avon, New York. I was no longer a boy, but I was apprehensive in a whole array of new ways and degrees. I put my Vietnam experiences "in a box on the shelf" and set out to find success.

It is pretty much universally agreed that America's failure to understand the Vietnamese was a significant factor contributing to our defeat in Vietnam. Our leaders had no knowledge of Vietnamese history, no knowledge of the language, and no regard for Vietnamese culture. Worst of all, they had absolutely no respect for the Vietnamese people, and no concern for the political dynamics behind the conflict. We were there to support a government that was corrupt, tyrannical, and despised by the vast majority of the Vietnamese. Diem and his cronies said they were opposing Communism, and that was all Washington needed to know.

Our training before we were shipped to Vietnam taught that our mission would be to help the Vietnamese resist the brutality of communism. Most of us had no understanding of what the word "brutality" meant until we got to Vietnam, and it wasn't only the communists who were brutal. We immediately learned that our military operated largely according to the MGR, or "Mere Gook Rule," which taught that a Vietnamese life was inconsequential. As young soldiers, we heard over and over again that "the only good Gook is a dead Gook," or "kill them all and let God sort them out." We had become familiar with concepts of racism and civil rights back in The World, and we were shocked, appalled and sickened by what we experienced in Vietnam. The justifications for the war, and for many of the vicious actions that happened there, just didn't square with the lessons we had learned as children, and they were not acceptable. It was obvious that the war was unwinnable, that our mission was only to kill and destroy with nothing of value to plug into the holes or craters. It wasn't about installing Democracy; it was never about making anything better for the Vietnamese people. That was a lie, a cover-up designed to placate the American public while the military tested its latest weapons and helicopters. The bloodshed and destruction rained upon the unfortunate peasants in Southeast Asia was unimaginable, but we were powerless to do anything about it. We wore the uniforms, and we found ourselves caught in a deadly trap far from home. Where conscience had become the most important trait of our generation, it was outlawed and ridiculed in the military, and we chafed at our fate as we counted the days until our "obligation" would have run its course.

We had come of age surrounded by vivid colors and an all-American atmosphere of freedoms expressed as irreverent, defiant adolescent rebellion. To be snatched away from all that, to be assigned a baggy uniform of olive drab and to find ourselves seeking cover in the Vietnamese mud while bullets shrieked overhead was not just traumatic. Far too often, our leaders in Vietnam treated us with disrespect we had never experienced before, and that included issuing orders that were clearly ridiculously hazardous or immoral. We became accustomed to suffering and death. Too many felt the impact of hot metal as it penetrated and mutilated their body. Fear became a constant companion. We saw good friends ripped and torn, bloodied and maimed.

We saw the bodies of enemy soldiers and Vietnamese civilians destroyed beyond belief. We saw lots of old men, women, children, even livestock dismembered, punctured, torn apart, burnt and bubbled, smashed and broken, their homes and fields destroyed, their lives obliterated. It was a nightmare, a "bad trip" of unbelievable proportions, and the army didn't allow any time to digest the carnage or get your head together. Human feelings were outlawed. But we were a defiant bunch: some of us committed minor acts of sabotage, while others were far more forceful in defying the carnage. In the quiet moments we remembered all that had been taken from us, and we squirreled our human feelings away in the darkest corners of our minds and simply tried to survive. We X'd off the days on our short-timer calendars and tried to imagine what it might be like if we were lucky and got to return home, to squeal the tires, dance to a rock band, or eat ice cream after dinner at the family table.

Years later, I would realize that I had feared the enemy, the Viet Cong and the North Vietnamese, but I never hated them. My army "obligation" had taught me to hate the Sergeants and Lieutenants, the Captains and Majors and all the Senators and Congressmen and Secretaries of Defense who had created and directed and profited from the war, and I have never gotten over that anger and bitterness to this day. The draft disrupted my life in 1966, and I am still bitter more than half a century later.

While it's true that the American military never understood Vietnam's culture or customs and never had a plan for success, I believe an equal reason why America lost the war in Vietnam was that the American military leadership, from the Pentagon to the platoon sergeant, did not understand or give a damn about the average American soldier's culture or customs. They did not know that the Age of Aquarius had come upon the planet. They had never floored a 450 horsepower V-8 and rocketed through a quarter mile in under eleven seconds, or danced to a Rolling Stones tune with a long-haired blonde in a mini-skirt and go-go boots. They had never heard that war had become obsolete and unthinkable, or that world peace was possible. Many had been born poor, and the military had given them their first shoes, and then their first taste of authority. They were omni-powerful, thriving in a system unchanged since the Korean War at best, backed up with a contrived, out-of-date legal system and weaponry that could obliterate the planet if need be. "We had to destroy it to save it," one "Lifer" said of a Vietnamese village that had been blown away, and we could never understand that thinking. Their war was never really our war. The Vietnamese were fighting for independence, and they were determined. We had no idea what we were fighting for, except survival. We saw oppressive cruelty and destruction that would never square with the standards of right and wrong we had been taught at home, and we saw profiteering and corruption on a scale we often could not even imagine.

After the Tet offensive, we realized that America was not going to win the war in Vietnam, but it dragged on for seven more years. We recognized that we were expendable, small cogs caught up in a very big and powerful machine, and so we concentrated upon surviving, and helping our buddies to survive too. It wasn't patriotic, and it didn't make the world a better place. A few Lifers got promoted, some guys were awarded medals or ribbons, and a lot of companies sold a lot of hardware to the Pentagon. Millions of good people died. We witnessed acts of heroism, and we saw horror, suffering and death in unimaginable quantities. If we were lucky, we survived to return home.

Morale was never good in Vietnam, and the rot soon spread throughout the American military system. By 1972, fully 25% of all Americans in military uniform *worldwide* had deserted or were openly mutinous and openly defying orders. The desertion rate was the highest for U.S. forces in any year of any war throughout our history at 73.5 per 1,000 men. "Fragging," or the assassination of commanding officers by their subordinates, began to be a factor in Vietnam about 1968, and from 1969 to 1971 the military's official statistics indicate a rate of about 240 incidents per year, eleven per cent fatal. While attempting to find the definition of fragging, I referred to my 2011 Merriam-Webster Collegiate Dictionary and was surprised to find the term is not listed. It was listed in the 1988 Random House College Dictionary. Veterans who returned from the current wars in Iraq and Afghanistan assure me that the practice still exists.

In 1971, fewer than 5,000 American soldiers in Vietnam required hospital treatment for combat wounds, while 20,529 were treated for serious drug abuse. The unsubstantiated number of "war crimes allegations" against U.S. military personnel in Vietnam had increased seven-fold to 144, at least that was the number made public by the Pentagon. The American Way of Waging War had devolved into policies and practices so cruel and horrible, many young Americans could not live with themselves due to what they had done or seen in Vietnam. Certainly, the daily experience in Vietnam, the sights of such abject poverty impacted by the vicious high-tech war, were difficult to assimilate into the minds of many American teenagers. Today, half a century later, America is losing a veteran to suicide once an hour, and about 69 percent are aged over 50, our Vietnam veterans. To paraphrase a popular sign carried by the protestors in the sixties, "War is not healthy for children and other living things." When will we accept the simple, universal truth of that sentiment?

I-Feel-Like-I'm-Fixin'-to-Die-Rag

C'mon all of you big strong men
Uncle Sam needs your help again
He's got himself in a terrible jam
'Way down yonder in Vietnam
So put down your books and pick up a gun
We're gonna have a whole lotta fun

And it's one-two-three what are we fightin' for
Don't ask me, I don't give a damn
Next stop is Vietnam
And it's five-six-seven open up the pearly gates
Why, ain't no time to wonder why
Whoopee! We're all gonna die

Well come on generals, let's move fast
Your big chance has come at last

Gotta go out and get those Reds
The only good Commie's the one that's dead
And you know that peace can only be won
When you blow them all to kingdom come

And it's one-two-three what are we fightin' for
Don't ask me, I don't give a damn
Next stop is Vietnam
And it's five-six-seven open up the pearly gates
Why, ain't no time to wonder why
Whoopee! We're all gonna die

Come on Wall Street, don't move slow
Why man, it's war-a-go-go
There's plenty of good money to be made
By supplying the army with the tools of the trade
Just hope 'n pray if they drop The Bomb
They drop it on the Viet Cong

Well come on mothers throughout the land
Pack your boys off to Vietnam
C'mon fathers don't hesitate
Send them off before it's too late
Be the first one on your block
To have your son come home in a box

And it's one-two-three what are we fightin' for
Don't ask me, I don't give a damn
Next stop is Vietnam
And it's five-six-seven open up the pearly gates
Why, ain't no time to wonder why
Whoopee! We're all gonna die

Joe McDonald (Used with permission)
© 1965/1993 lkatraz Corner Music Co, BMI

Chapter 2

THE MUSIC

As noted elsewhere in this work, the inventions of television and radio changed the cultural environment the Vietnam generation experienced as we came of age, and nowhere were the changes felt so profoundly as through music. It's not just coincidence that most of the movies, TV programs, and documentaries about Vietnam feature popular music, primarily folk songs or rock 'n roll from the era, as their background or soundtrack. Journalist Michael Herr wrote about the Vietnam soldier in his classic book *Dispatches,* fighting the war with "cassette rock and roll in one ear and door-gun fire in the other." Reviewing Herr's book, *New York Times* critic John Leonard coined the term "our first rock-and-roll war."

The historians tell us rock 'n roll evolved from Blues, Country, Jazz, and whatever. Actually, while it retained enough of those influences to still be classified as "music," it sprang from adolescent attitude, and it was entirely revolutionary, a fast-paced musical rebellion. In the mid-fifties, two guys named Clarence Leonidas "Leo" Fender and Les Paul, working separately, perfected the electric guitar and unleashed sounds that could fill auditoriums. Electric guitars required amplifiers, from the size of suitcases to huge, heavy devices that could shake the windows and rattle the walls. Rock 'n rollers loved their electric guitars.

No one talked about "high tech" in those days, but inventions and refinements brought popular music to us in amazing ways. The quality of sound reproduction became a significant marketing tool. "Hi-fi," or high fidelity, soon begat stereo, and the console stereo in the living room was a significant piece of furniture. As the Vietnam generation was growing up, record players became smaller and portable and it was not unusual for a teenager to have a record player in their bedroom. Single records were sold on 45 rpm discs with a huge hole in the center, and a successful single was usually followed by a 33 1/3 rpm album on a larger 12-inch vinyl disc with a tiny center hole. Mom and Dad's leftover records from the forties were 78 rpm, so multiple-speed record players were perfected, and with the automatic stacker-changer we were able to pile a number of discs one atop another and enjoy an assortment of tunes from a variety of artists without interruption. Disc jockeys became local celebrities, and a few like "Cousin Brucie," "Wolfman Jack" or "The Geater With the Heater" were known nationwide. Successful recording groups had always gone on bus tours, and the expansion of air travel and commercial flights in the early 60s now made it possible for big-time entertainers to abandon their buses and play coast-to-coast tours without the long travel time. It was exciting to watch a live performance of hit songs on stage in your home town, and record sales surged.

As children, the soldiers sent to Vietnam grew up with music in the background. From the large wooden radio consoles of Franklin Roosevelt's "fireside chat" era, we began to see small plastic-encased models "smaller than a bread box" that could fit on a book shelf, so Mom had radios in the kitchen, living room, and in her bedroom and was often accompanied by music, news, and weather reports while she did her housework.

For the young men destined to go to Vietnam, perhaps their first taste of popular music came in December of 1954 when *Disneyland* introduced a four-part series about the legendary frontiersman Davy Crockett. (The real Crockett hated nicknames, and insisted people address him as David.) A huge fad swept the nation, kids wore coonskin caps and carried Davy Crockett lunch boxes, and American merchants became aware of the vast buying power of the baby-boom generation for the first time. "The Ballad of Davy Crockett" theme song was sung by a group called the Wellingtons, but a number of versions became hits in 1955. Bill Hayes had the 4th largest selling record of the year with an album version of "The Ballad of Davy Crockett." The star of that first TV "mini-series," Fess Parker, recorded a version that reached #6 on the charts, Tennessee Ernie Ford's version hit #5, and a version by bluegrass singer Mac Wiseman reached #10. Other 1955 hit records were "Let Me Go Lover" by Joan Weber, "Sincerely" by the McGuire Sisters, the instrumental "Cherry Pink and Apple Blossom White," and the noteworthy first rock 'n roll hit, "Rock Around the Clock" by Bill Haley & His Comets spent eight weeks at number 1. In August of '55, newcomer Chuck Berry had the first of his many hits with "Maybellene." Elvis Presley came along in 1956, along with The Platters and Perry Como.

The importance of popular music to the history of the Vietnam War in Southeast Asia and at home is not, of course, about technology and hardware as much as it is about changing awareness and societal attitudes. Just about the time we got our first "transistor" radios and took music with us on our bicycles and to the ball game, music began to be influenced by the civil rights movement, the Cold War, television, and the contrasts between rich and poor, white and black, and the old and young. Very subtly at first, music began to explore morality and social topics. Country crossover artist Jimmie Dean had a hit with "Big Bad John," a "workin' man's" song, and Tennessee Ernie Ford sang for manual laborers everywhere with "Sixteen Tons."

Folk music was especially popular for its gentle melodies and meaningful lyrics. Tepid folk songs from The Kingston Trio, the Weavers, the New Christy Minstrels, and the Serendipity Singers began to be replaced by more topical tunes from Pete Seeger, Trini Lopez, Joan Baez, Phil Ochs, and Peter, Paul, & Mary, a very melodic all-white trio that sang from the podium just prior to Martin Luther King's "I have a dream" speech at the largest civil rights demonstration ever on the mall in Washington, D.C. Folk singers explored themes of brotherhood and justice in songs like "If I Had a Hammer," "The Merry Minuet," "Blowin' in the Wind," and "Where Have All the Flowers Gone." Most of us had been exposed to abstract forms of these ideas by our parents, church, or school, but the music coming through the radio urged us to take sides against whatever we saw as wrong or unfair as if a confrontation was imminent.

Just as the baby boomers came of age we were confronted with the threat of a cataclysmic nuclear war, TV reports of extreme poverty in Appalachia, the civil rights movement, the Berlin Wall and creeping Communism, Russian successes in space, and vast cesspools of pollution poisoning our environment. In no time, we were faced with the assassinations of a number of popular leaders, and the war in Vietnam. In September of 1965, Barry McGuire's "Eve of Destruction" was a folk song that was anything but subtle, demanding the listener acknowledge the dangers of the world situation. Some radio stations refused to play the song.

Popular music had an enormous influence on the soldiers who went to Vietnam, the folks who stayed home, and the nature of the war itself. The music of the time played a huge role in the social upheavals related to the war that shook America at home, the conduct of the war "in country" in Vietnam, and on American military bases around the globe. Growing up under the threat of nuclear obliteration, we were determined to make things better, to do the "right" things The Establishment had abandoned, and to offer a helping hand to our fellow man. As Americans, this was our inherited purpose in life. Our music was central to our feelings of freedom and individuality, our expressions of morality, and our adolescent challenges to authority. We would change the world and make it a better place! Our music supported that bold and fearless notion. Rock 'n roll gradually became the baby boomer generation's radical, even confrontational declaration of independence from our parents and authority in general. The melodic revolution of a defiant folk song or the raucous sound of screaming electric guitars and pounding drums seemed far less threatening than the risk of being vaporized by a nuclear-tipped ballistic missile, and the message of tunes like "All You Need is Love" gave us hope and confidence that we were doing the right things.

As the civil rights movement gained momentum in the early sixties, black music emerged as a hugely popular phenomenon and a separate category known as "Soul." Berry Gordy created Motown, a little recording studio in a house in Detroit, and brought us The Supremes, The Ronettes, Otis Redding, The Temptations, and Smokey Robinson & The Miracles. Black artists were nothing new; we were very familiar with conventional 50s-style music from Nat King Cole, Johnny Mathis, and Brook Benton, but the rock 'n roll beat and social commentaries of Soul music became closely associated with the civil rights movement. Artists like Sam Cooke with his beautiful "A Change Is Gonna Come," and Gil Scott Heron with "The Revolution Will Not Be Televised" pushed the boundaries, but they were so musical, honest, and valuable that radio stations, especially in the North, had to play them. Soon we heard James Brown declaring "Say It Loud, I'm Black and I'm Proud" and Aretha Franklin demanding "Respect." It wasn't really political. It was just music that spoke truth and the message was so realistic, so valid that it was enthusiastically embraced by the white audience as well as the black. Soul music made a huge contribution to breaking down racial barriers at a crucial time in the country's history.

Country, or country-western, was immensely popular, and in the early sixties a number of country records became "crossover" hits and reached the top of the pop music charts. Out and out protest songs were not plentiful in country music, but the feelings of the time were often evident if you listened closely. The Statler Brothers expressed a range of feelings about the war in Vietnam in songs like "Class of '57," "Red Clay Girl," and (years later) "More Than a Name on a Wall." Other country stars offered tunes that were rigidly supportive of the war, but as more and more of the flag-draped caskets came home to poor rural communities some of those messages became softer or more questioning. Even Johnny Cash gave voice to the skepticism of the anti-Establishment movement when he questioned the necessity of war in his 1970 song *What is Truth.*

For a time, American popular music seemed to turn its back on "real" rock 'n roll. The hit songs in early 1962 were dominated by Chubby Checker's "The Twist" and Joey Dee and The Starliters' "Peppermint Twist," but the rest of the year saw softer, more conventional hits by artists like Gene Chandler, Connie Francis, Shelley Fabares, Elvis with "Good Luck Charm," Mr. Acker Bilk, David Rose, Bobby Vinton, Neil Sedaka, and The Tornadoes with the instrumental "Telstar." Late in the year The Four Seasons had big hits with "Sherry" and "Big Girls Don't Cry," but the start of '63 saw #1 records by Steve Lawrence, The Rooftop Singers, Paul & Paula, Ruby & The Romantics, The Chiffons, and Lesley Gore. Japanese artist Kyu Sakamoto had a hit with "Sukiyaki." In July, Jan & Dean had the first #1 surfin' hit with *Surf City*, and soon after we were introduced to a new artist, Little Stevie Wonder, with "Fingertips - Part 2." (What ever happened to Part 1?) Then it was back to melody and melancholy with tunes like "So Much In Love" by the Tymes, "Blue Velvet" by Bobby Vinton, and "Deep Purple" by Nino Tempo and April Stevens. On the day JFK was shot, I'm "Leaving It All Up To You" by Dale & Grace was at the top of the charts, and following that tragic event December's #1 tune was "Dominique" by The Singing Nun, which spent four languid weeks as the most popular song in the land before it was replaced by "There! I've said It Again" by Bobby Vinton.

And then The Beatles arrived! "I Want To Hold Your Hand" brought a fresh, lively new rock sound to the top of the charts in early January of 1964, and the four Englishmen first appeared on *The Ed Sullivan Show* on February 9th, just 79 days after JFK was assassinated in Dallas. Our generation had lost its spokesman and role model, and along came the Beatles to fill the gap. They were refreshingly British, charming, fun-loving, witty, almost clean-cut, and they rocked! Their longer hair upset our parents, which wasn't necessarily a bad thing. By April 4th the top 5 records on Billboard's Top 100 were Beatles tunes, a feat that has never been equaled. The Beatles swept over popular music like a tidal wave, and a vast array of other British bands soon followed. Disk jockeys played tunes by The Dave Clark Five, The Animals, The Zombies, Manfred Mann, Peter & Gordon, Herman's Hermits, Gerry & The Pacemakers, The Searchers, and the Rolling Stones, and talked about the second British invasion. On portable radios, car radios, juke boxes, and at school dances, we waited feverishly for the next new sounds. Rock 'n roll was back, and better than ever!

For a while, the only bands able to compete with the British were the Soul artists, Frankie Valli and the Four Seasons, and the Beach Boys. Surfing was an all-American fad, especially when it was carried from California beaches to hometown theaters across the country in a series of "Beach Blanket" movies starring Frankie Avalon and America's sweetheart, Annette Funicello. We had loved her as a Mouseketeer on TV's *Mickey Mouse Club* when we were little, and she had grown up to become a beautiful, perfectly wholesome young woman. Even in a demure one-piece swimsuit, Annette made surfing popular. The British bands all wore their hair long, and the California surfers favored long, sun-bleached blonde locks, so many teenagers felt peer pressure from two sides to grow our hair as a symbol of our rebellion and defiance, or, though we would deny it, surrender to fashion.

The summer of '64 was a turning point, with classic rock hits arriving one after another. From the soulful "My Guy" by Mary Wells, our radios shifted gears to the classic hot rod tune "I Get Around" by the Beach Boys, and then "Rag Doll" by the Four Seasons lamented society's divisions by class and wealth. In August the Beatles became more insightful with "A Hard Day's Night," the theme song for their upcoming movie, and a subtle acknowledgement of the rigors of touring the world as a hugely successful rock band. Dean Martin had a week at number one with "Everybody Loves Somebody," followed immediately by the Supremes with "Where Did Our Love Go," and then The Animals with their classic rendition of "House Of The Rising Sun." Roy Orbison had a big hit with "Oh, Pretty Woman," British rockers Manfred Mann scored with Do "Wah Diddy Diddy," The Supremes brought "Baby Love," the Shangri-Las had "Leader of The Pack," The Supremes hit again with "Come See About Me," and The Beatles ended the year atop the charts with "I Feel Fine." Of course, by that time portable radios and television sets were everywhere and the vast buying power of the baby boomer generation had made rock 'n roll the most popular music in the land. The youth rebellion was under way.

A few years earlier, just as puberty exploded into the early boomers lives, the girls began to show up at the beach or the pool in daring two-piece "bikini" swim suits, and popular music reflected everyone's sexual anxieties in a 1960 tune titled "Itsy Bitsy Teenie Weenie Yellow Polka Dot Bikini." By the time we were in high school we were overflowing with hormones and discovering that adult life could be lived in the most exciting ways, and rock music gave voice to all our emotions and adolescent sexual desires. The Kingsmen's "Louie, Louie" was a party favorite, with lyrics that were supposedly obscene, but totally unintelligible. When the

Rolling Stones sang "I can't get no "Satisfaction" in 1965, or "Let's Spend the Night Together" in 1967, we were a horny and rebellious teenage audience, the guys had all studied *Playboy* magazine, and we had kissed, petted, and sometimes even more. We got our driver's licenses and then our own cars, and we took our dates to drive-in movies where we didn't always watch the action on the big white screen. We considered ourselves bold and daring, but we were still a little tentative and awkward about sex. After the Twist, dancers no longer touched during the fast tunes, and the frenzied choreographies of the Swim, the Watusi, or the Monkey served to unleash and stimulate our maturing teenage bodies. The girls wore short skirts and shook all their most exciting parts in the fast dances, the guys wore skin-tight jeans, and if you were lucky one special young lady might even snuggle close during the slow tunes. With the radio on while we were doing our homework, we were subtly introduced to musical visions of a colorful, exciting, new lifestyle that would avoid wars and replace them with the heat of sexual passion. "Make love, not war" became far more than just a slogan. It was a way of life!

The Cold War, The Bomb, and after 1965, the war in Vietnam cast an ominous dark shadow over every aspect of our young lives, and we didn't like it one bit. Clearly, the old ways embraced by grown-ups had been disastrous. The media began to speak of a "generation gap," and we took great pride and hope from the divisions that were beginning to separate our generation from everything that had come before. Rock became the moral and spiritual foundation of our bold new community. We made the transition from Davy Crockett to Bob Dylan, John Lennon, Mick Jagger, Janis Joplin and Jimi Hendrix just as naturally as we grew from diapers into varsity football uniforms or bras. Our music became our declaration of independence. Rock 'n roll music is intrinsically about youthful angst, attitude, and rebellion, but it also celebrates basic values such as love, friendship, hope, understanding, caring, and, brotherhood. From our portable "transistors" and car radios the atmosphere of young America began to be filled with songs that featured important social questions, unconventional messages, and lyrics that made us think. We had been born into a world that threatened annihilation at the push of a button, a society that in some southern states required "colored people" to drink from separate water fountains due to the color of their skin, and that often accepted poverty, illiteracy, and disease as just facts of life. As we reached adolescence, our radios began to feed us songs that recognized the hypocrisies our parents had long ignored.

We had grown up hearing about the horrors of war from the survivors of World War II, but now a new war in some far-off, primitive place called Vietnam was sucking our generation into a meat grinder, and we were not at all sure why. The questions were profound, and every step of the way, popular music was in the background to goad us, or in the foreground to challenge us. Our generation had declared a war of ideas and ideals, and when we couldn't discuss the issues with grown-ups or The Establishment, our music brought us comfort. When there were hard times, when we were tired, or our emotional energies were spent, music soothed and renewed us. We had no written creed, no formal declaration of independence or bill of rights to define our movement, but a Beatles, Rolling Stones, or James Brown tune expressed what we were all about, and the subtle harmonies of Simon and Garfunkel or Crosby, Stills, and Nash created an atmosphere where we could rest and find the energy to go on.

There had been a time, not long before, when most of us had never been to a funeral; when death seemed far removed from our loud, colorful, and exciting realities. The assassination of JFK had been a shock, and soon after it seemed the gates of Hell had been thrown open. Home towns across America hosted the funeral ceremonies for our classmates and loved ones fallen in Vietnam, and we were outraged. How could you listen to Dylan's "Blowin' In the Wind" or "Masters of War" and not be opposed to the obvious hypocrisy behind the war? Civil rights marches had become riots in our cities, with lootings and shootings and all manner of atrocities. How could you hear Sly and the Family Stones' "Everyday People" with lyrics like "There is a yellow one that won't accept the black one, that won't accept the red one that won't accept the white one and different strokes for different folks and so on and so on," and not feel that our generation with its colorful clothes and long hair could change things for the better? How could you hear Arlo Guthrie's classic "Alice's Restaurant" about the absurdities of his local draft board, listen to the Rascals' "People Got To Be Free," or hear The Fifth Dimension celebrating the dawning of the age of "Aquarius," a time when "peace will guide the planets and love will steer the stars," and not feel completely out of synch with The Establishment's world when you went to the mailbox and found a draft notice?

How could you listen to the Beach Boys' "In My Room" describing the secret place where you could lock out all your worries and fears, where you could do your dreaming, scheming, crying, sighing, and laugh at yesterday, a place where you could be alone in the dark and not be afraid, and then wake up one morning in an army barracks far from home, in a huge room filled with guys drawn from every background, warehoused on metal bunk beds with drill sergeants screaming and demeaning them as they are all being prepared to be sent to war? That transition could not, and did not, go well.

What could you believe in? Our political leaders blatantly lied to us, and our religious leaders refused to call them on it. Our schools and colleges taught the lies and misrepresentations as truth, and when students and even faculty challenged them, The Establishment hid in their corporate boardrooms and political offices and refused to change, as if the truth didn't matter. Our parents told us to cut our hair and accept that there are some things you can never change. In defiance of the established ideas, young people around the globe listened to an international chorus of recorded voices and dared to defy the old folks and believe that we could, we would change the ways of the world. There had to be a better way! We saw our heroes singing the truth on *The Ed Sullivan Show* or *The Smothers Brothers Comedy Hour* and were reinforced to learn that in some places morality still mattered.

Some people recognized that the struggle was essential to the survival of all mankind, and the rock bands and folk singers were our guerilla warriors confronting the evildoers. Hearing their harmonies and contemplating their idealistic lyrics, respect for one's fellow man seemed an achievable goal. At a moment when the concepts of morality and "peace on earth, good will toward all men" were under attack from all the halls of power, only the recording artists of the time seemed to express the loftiest ideas and simplest truths, and music, emerging from both radio and TV, played a key role in social and political discussions which were now a worldwide phenomenon. Flag-draped coffins containing classmates and friends were coming home to America from Southeast Asia, and The Establishment showed no inclination to do anything but draft replacements. It would be up to the young to make things right.

Throughout the latter half of the sixties and well into the 1970s, a wide variety of popular groups achieved music of a quality that was unprecedented and shocking, and that great outpouring of serious music will probably never be seen again. We listened, often in the sanctuary of our bedroom, or out and about with our transistor radios, and we absorbed attitudes, ideas, an undercurrent of life at the speed of a rock 'n roll rhythm, and a societal culture that seemed to develop with every new song. As our music evolved, we applauded artists as disparate as Freddie and the Dreamers, Country Joe and the Fish, Cream, Frank Zappa, Electric Flag,

Strawberry Alarm Clock, Tiny Tim, The Supremes, and Blood, Sweat and Tears. At the same time we also accepted long hair, men in flowered shirts, women in mini-skirts, surfers, hippies, the Playmate of the Month in no clothes at all, muscle cars and Volkswagen Beetles, poetry (as long as it was set to music), and the concept of free sex, although it never quite seemed to be free of significance and consequences no matter how hard we tried to embrace the concept. We gave everyone space to do their own thing. We were adolescents then, discovering the world around us, searching for our roles in the activity, and we were frightened but confident as only teenagers can be. The music of the Vietnam era was the soundtrack of our lives, and the times were vivid and exciting.

But the story of Vietnam veterans did not end with the war. Those 200,000 suicides were preceded by unimaginable struggles. This chapter would not be complete without mention of Bruce Springsteen's 1984 classic *Born in the USA*, a song that rages at the military-industrial complex and the plight of a bedeviled Vietnam veteran. The album sold 10 million copies, the song was misunderstood by some "conservative" politicians who thought it was about blind patriotism, but Springsteen gave abundantly to Vietnam veteran causes and his music and his activism are iconic to many veterans.

Throughout our lives, music has been in the background, informing, inspiring, and providing comforts. Certainly, in our time, rock 'n roll music became a legitimate art form, but its true value lies in its impact upon the common folks like those of us sent to Vietnam.

Chapter 3

VIETNAM: WHAT REALLY HAPPENED?

PART 1: THE APPROACHING STORM 1945 - 1960

You have a row of dominoes set up, and you knock over the first one and what will happen to the last one is the certainty that it will go over very quickly.
– President Dwight D. Eisenhower, April 7, 1954 regarding the pending defeat of the French at Dien Bien Phu.

All men are created equal. They are endowed by their Creator with certain inalienable rights, among these are Life, Liberty, and the pursuit of Happiness. This immortal statement was made in the Declaration of Independence of the United States of America in 1776.
– Ho Chi Minh, from the Vietnamese Proclamation of Independence, September 2, 1945.

A French Jesuit mission was established in Hanoi, in the north of Vietnam, in 1615. For many years, Europeans conducted a brisk trade with Vietnam, and established a solid Catholic presence. In 1858, the Nguyen Dynasty saw the rise of Catholicism as a political threat and began to expel French missionaries. French gunships attacked Da Nang and Saigon, and in April of 1862 the Vietnamese government was forced to cede control of three provinces to France. They continued to seize Vietnamese territory for decades. The colony known as French Indochina, roughly within the borders of the old Vietnam, was formally declared in October 1887 and Cambodia and Laos were added in 1893.

On August 15, 1945 Japan announced that it would formally surrender, effectively ending World War II. On September 2, the day the surrender documents were signed aboard the *USS Missouri*, Ho Chi Minh stood before a crowd of half a million Vietnamese in Hanoi. Vietnam had been dominated by China from 200 BC until the 10th century AD, then had enjoyed almost a millennium of independence until the French take-over. After the Japanese defeat, Ho Chi Minh declared Vietnam's independence, with the immortal words of Thomas Jefferson quoted above. Ho had lived in the United States from 1911 to 1918, and clearly modeled his Declaration of Independence after America's. The Viet Minh party formed by Ho in 1941 was a coalition of various groups with the common goal of achieving independence from French rule. During World War II, Ho Chi Minh had established a cooperative relationship with American agents from the Office of Strategic Services (OSS), the predecessor of the CIA. Although the Americans recognized Ho's affinity for Communism, the agents considered him an ally against the Japanese. Some American agents actually lived with the Viet Minh, trained their fighters, and provided arms. When Ho became ill, an OSS medic saved his life. Clearly, Ho believed that his aid in fighting the Japanese was appreciated, and after the war ended America would help the Vietnamese to resist the return of the French and establish independence.

The Japanese had ruled French Indochina during World War II, although they allowed the 'Vichy' government to administer the area after the Nazis conquered France in 1940. At the end of World War II France immediately attempted to re-establish its colonial influence over the region and, in response, Nationalist (anti-Communist) Chinese troops under Chiang Kai-shek invaded the northern area of Indochina and threatened the French with war. The Allies negotiated an agreement with Ho that the Chinese troops in the North would withdraw, and French troops would step in to help keep order. France would recognize Vietnam as "a free state" and withdraw its forces from the North in annual installments, ending in 1952. The Viet Minh would forego activity in the South. Throughout this period, Ho Chi Minh reassured his people that their American friends would help Vietnam, as the Americans understood and supported independence and self-rule. After all, President Franklin Delano Roosevelt had stated publicly that America should not help France restore its influence in Southeast Asia.

Today, most Americans think of Franklin Delano Roosevelt as one of America's greatest Presidents. He was elected to the office an unprecedented four times, which would seem to indicate that he was a popular President, but that is only partially true. When FDR was first elected President in 1933, America was suffering through the Great Depression. Unemployment was at catastrophic levels, many of America's key business-es had failed, banks had gone out of business, and the American people were discouraged, disgusted, hungry, and depressed by the unregulated pro-business policies that had precipitated the financial disaster. Voters had rejected former President Herbert Hoover, electing many Democrats who would support Roosevelt's efforts to rebuild the economy.

From the very start, FDR's "New Deal" implemented policies that would begin to put people back to work and help American workers, or Labor. Roosevelt had been born into a prestigious family of wealth and privilege, but he believed policies for the betterment of all the people would create prosperity. Many of these policies were bitterly opposed by big business. Henry Ford was especially outspoken, praising the emerging Fascist movements in Europe, and expressing virulent anti-Semitic senti-ments. His 1927 book *The International Jew,* was a model for Adolf Hit-ler's *Mein Kampf,* and the two men became mutual admirers. Hitler kept a large portrait of Henry Ford in his office throughout the second World War, and Ford sent The Fuhrer an annual birthday gift.

America's business leaders had amassed huge fortunes at the expense of their workers, and they did not welcome Roosevelt's plans to end the Depression by giving workers a bigger slice of the nation's wealth. The Russian Revolution of 1917 had brought the socialist, pro-worker theo-ries of Karl Marx to public attention. Even earlier, American labor had be-gun to organize and demonstrate for shorter hours, better pay, and bene-fits such as retirement and health care. Big business responded, often with mass killings by hired guns like the Pinkertons, and other acts of violence.

The American capitalists feared the emergence of the workers' move-ment, and derided government intervention into the workplaces on behalf of their workers as "feeding at the public trough," characterizing their em-ployees as mere animals. They formed anti-Black and anti-Semitic groups such as the Black Legion, the Wolverine Republican League of Detroit, and the blatantly pro-Nazi American Liberty League. Chemical industri-alist Irénée du Pont personally spent over a million dollars to set up a force of armed and gas-equipped storm-troops modeled on Germany's Gestapo to patrol his plants and beat up any rebellious employees. To pre-vent unionizing among auto workers, the Black Legion wore hoods and black robes with skull and crossbones. They firebombed union meetings, beat union organizers to death, and waged war upon Jews and suspected Communists in the streets and factories of America. Roosevelt's efforts to support the American worker were seen to be a threat to corporate profits and influence, and he was immediately branded a "Communist" by his big business opponents.

While researching for this book, I was shocked to come across a bit of history that has obviously been kept from most of us. Only a few months into the FDR presidency, in early 1934, the United States nearly became a Fascist state. A number of very powerful heads of industry disapproved of Roosevelt's New Deal policies, which sought to end the Great Depression by granting unprecedented benefits and financial safeguards to American workers and the disadvantaged. The group included the heads of Du Pont Chemicals, General Motors, a string of J.P. Morgan's banks, Goodyear, Bethlehem Steel, Sun Oil, Pittsburgh Plate Glass, and a wide range of other Wall Street executives and political powers, most notably FDR's political rival Alf Smith, banker J.P. Morgan, retailer J.C. Penney, and Wall Street executive and former U.S. Senator Prescott Bush, the father of future President George H. W. Bush and grandfather of George W. All of the plotters despised America's Democracy, and hoped to install a Fascist dictatorship modeled after, and cooperating closely with, Hitler's Nazi Germany and Mussolini's Italy!

The plotters put corporate profits before patriotism and enjoyed lucrative deals with the emerging fascist governments in Germany and Italy. Outraged by FDR's proposals to empower America's working class, they quietly planned a coup d'etat. The architects of the plot planned to mobilize the nation's disgruntled World War I veterans. At that time the American Legion was a very pro-Fascist right-wing organization, and the organizers were confident they could march 500,000 armed men into Washington D.C. to implement the coup by force if necessary. E.I. Dupont promised to supply weapons from his Remington Arms Company. The plot was well-funded and came near to being implemented – when they made the mistake of offering the Dictator's position to General Smedley Butler, the former head of the Marine Corps and a genuine hero to whom Congress had awarded two Medals of Honor. Butler was not a great fan of Roosevelt, but he was certainly no party to an armed overthrow of the democratic government of the United States, and he informed President Roosevelt of the plan.

The plot was investigated by the House of Representatives' McCormack-Dickstein Committee, which would later become the House Un-American Activities Committee. Remarkably, the Committee did not interview any of the plotters, none of the conspirators went to jail, and in fact none seem to have incurred any penalties at all. The Roosevelt administration desperately needed the cooperation of big business to bring the country out of the Depression, so this most alarming incident was negotiated away and played down, and it is rarely mentioned in history books. It is important to note, both as it influenced America's war in Vietnam, and because it provides interesting insight into present-day conflicts. The aborted coup revealed big business's obsession with profits and its contempt for democracy and the best interests of "We the People." From this incident, America saw John Foster Dulles and his brother Allen emerge with great influence and power that would steer America's foreign policy toward militarism and rabid anti-communism. As we shall see, those pursuits along with an all-consuming hunger for personal and corporate authority and profits were major factors in America's involvement in Southeast Asia.

Meanwhile, a wide range of American corporations enjoyed a lucrative business with the Nazis throughout World War II. GM's Chairman Alfred Sloan told stockholders his corporation was "too big" to be affected by "petty international squabbles," and throughout the war shipments of materials and information from Detroit to Nazi Germany were allowed to travel across the North Atlantic without submarine attacks or any delays. GM's Opel subsidiary supplied thousands of "Blitz" trucks from its plant at Brandenburg, and GM and Ford plants built approximately 90 percent of Germany's armored "mule" 3-ton half-tracks and more than 70 percent of the Reich's medium and heavy-duty trucks. A GM aircraft-engine plant in Russelsheim supplied conventional engines for the Nazis' JU-88 bombers, and jet engines for the ME-262, the world's first jet fighter. The Allies did not have an operational jet fighter until after World War II was over.

GM also worked with Standard Oil subsidiaries at "the urgent request of Nazi officials" to build plants to produce tetraethyl lead, which allowed raw German gasolines to supply more power. Oil baron Fred Koch, the father of today's billionaire political powers Charles and David Koch, did extensive business with the Nazis, including building a huge refinery in Hamburg, Germany to process 1,000 tons of crude oil per day and refine it into high-octane gasoline and jet fuel. GM and Exxon also created the world's first synthetic oils to supply the German war effort, without making those technologies or products available to the Allies until well after the war. In 1938, both Ford and GM's chief executives in Europe were awarded the Order of the German Eagle with Cross by Chancellor Adolf Hitler. Both American companies made elaborate plans to ensure that if Nazi Germany won the war, they would experience "business as usual."

Despite this opposition, President Roosevelt's policies proved to be good for America, and he was elected President four times. This long tenure in office allowed him three Vice Presidents. The first, John Nance "Cactus Jack" Garner, who served as Veep from 1933 until 1941, is best known for describing the office of Vice President as "not worth a pitcher of warm spit." The second, Henry Wallace, was a learned Iowa farmer, and an advocate for the common working man. Wallace, FDR's Secretary of Agriculture in his first two terms, had never run for elected office. He was Vice President from 1941 through 1945 and is best known for a 1942 speech in which he declared the Great Depression was over, and predicted the U.S. was entering a better time that would celebrate "the dignity of the individual" and "the century of the common man." Wallace was a pacifist, opposed to colonialism and the "endless deadly cycle" of economic conflict followed by military warfare and then more economic turmoil, and ultimately, more war. "With freedom," he said, "must come abundance," and the corporate power brokers hated him for planting those thoughts into the heads of the American workers.

A Gallup poll taken just before the 1944 Democratic National Convention indicated that 65% of the nation's Democrats backed retaining Wallace as FDR's running mate compared to only 2% favoring Missouri Senator Harry Truman. But big business wanted Truman, and he became FDR's new Vice President. They were inaugurated on January 20, 1945, and soon after President Roosevelt named Wallace Secretary of Commerce.

President Roosevelt died unexpectedly on April 12, 1945. Nazi Germany surrendered May 8th. Harry Truman inherited the war against Japan, and a great deal of responsibility for cleaning up the mess in Europe. President Truman authorized dropping two atomic bombs on the cities of Hiroshima and Nagasaki, and Japan surrendered on September 2nd. World War II was over, but much of Europe and Asia was in ruins. Truman appeased big business by firing most of Roosevelt's New Dealers, but he kept Henry Wallace for a time as Secretary of Commerce. Wallace ran for President in 1947 as a Progressive, but with no success. He retired to experiment with hybrid agriculture, creating a breed of chickens that became the best egg producers in the world, and he also created the honeydew melon.

The powerful business barons resented Roosevelt's New Deal policies that regulated and restricted their capitalist activities, and they were (and still are) determined to overcome them. When the war in Europe ended and the horrors of the Holocaust became known to the world, the inhuman brutality of Fascism forced the barons to drop that label, but they continued to oppose workers' rights and the basic tenets of Democracy in government.

Many of America's factories had been updated at government expense to support the war effort, and now many were re-converted to peacetime manufacturing. However, brothers John Foster and Allen Dulles had become very influential, and they were ardent opponents of Socialism in all its forms. The Dulles brothers had worked closely with bankers and industrialists on both sides throughout the war, and they were widely criticized for helping the Nazi military and business leaders dispose of vast quantities of stolen wealth, art works, and other loot during and after the war. The brothers were also effective in aiding a number of Nazis to avoid prosecution for human rights abuses, as well as helping some unsavory Nazi characters gain entry into the U.S. and find employment in prominent business or government positions. The Dulles brothers saw Communism as black and Capitalism as white, and their influence contributed greatly to the creation of the Cold War.

The American people were tired of war, but many powerful voices in government and big business feared that Communism would expand its influence in the post-war world. The Soviet Union had lost 26-million people to World War II and was struggling to rebuild its devastated cities, but the very concept of workers having a voice in government was extremely threatening to many businessmen. At the same time, the British and French insisted that America should offer military assistance to help them re-establish control over their former colonies, and their pleas often reiterated the need to "contain" Communist expansion. The great democracies on the world stage, the U.S., England, and France, turned their attention to controlling Communism and discrediting all socialist theory (although England and France adopted many socialist policies), and if those efforts led to another World War, even the nuclear obliteration of all life on Earth, (Mutually Assured Destruction, or MAD), a powerful international group of capitalists saw that as an acceptable risk.

An array of industrial and political advisors, including the Dulles brothers, rushed to convince President Truman that Communism posed a dire threat to freedom, democracy, and capitalism in Europe and throughout the world. The Soviet Union, they insisted, must be viewed as an enemy. The Dulles brothers suggested that it was critical to install an effective government in Germany, and with Hitler gone, the top leaders of the Nazi party were the most experienced and best suited for the job. They urged Truman to dismiss the genocidal killing of six million Jews as irrelevant, and to take immediate steps to establish a strong European deterrent to Communist expansion. Truman was resistant and many of the Nazis were tried for their crimes at Nuremburg, but within a few months he had fired all of FDR's cabinet members. Henry Wallace, Secretary of Commerce, was the last to go in September of 1946. He had argued valiantly for a cessation of hostilities and preparations for an ideological conflict with the Soviet Union, but ultimately Truman caved in to the rabid anti-Communist faction.

The Cold War was taking shape, and Truman was focused upon setting up NATO, the North Atlantic Treaty Organization, which was a pact of western European nations, England and the U.S. for the purpose of deterring Communist (Soviet) expansion in Europe. Truman desperately needed France to join NATO, and France agreed on one condition... that the U.S. help them regain their Southeast Asian colonial holdings. Vietnam was a particular treasure trove of natural resources for the French. French-built Michelin radial tires were the world's standard for both handling and long life at that time, and raw rubber from Vietnam was a key ingredient. The vast (31,000 acres) Michelin rubber plantation was located between the Cambodia border and Saigon and so became an important base and staging area for North Vietnamese soldiers and supplies coming down the Ho Chi Minh trail. Throughout the Vietnam War, a number of significant actions took place on the Michelin rubber plantation northwest of Saigon. It is believed that Michelin secretly paid off the Viet Cong to keep the plantation operating during the war, and the French company later demanded compensation from the U.S. for damages caused to the rubber trees during wartime operations.

World War II, the deadliest war the world had ever seen, came to an end in early September of 1945. Incredibly, American troopships were diverted from bringing G.I.s home from Europe so they could be used to transport a French invasion force (equipped with American weapons, planes, equipment and financing), to Vietnam. British troops re-armed Japanese soldiers in the South who had been disarmed by the Vietnamese, and the Japanese and British joined with the French to wage war against Ho Chi Minh's new Democratic Republic of Vietnam. The British RAF, along with remnants of the Japanese air force, bombed and strafed, while Japanese troops patrolled the important port of Saigon. When the U.S. troopships arrived in Saigon with their cargo of French soldiers, they were met by uniformed Japanese soldiers. Many American personnel were moved to write to Congress and the President in protest, to no avail.

The world focused upon rebuilding after the war, and American support for French activities in Vietnam was largely overlooked at home.

In 1950, under President Truman, America finally openly agreed to provide arms to the French in Vietnam. The first American military advisors arrived at the same time. By November of 1952, the United States provided approximately 80% of the funding for France's Indochina War. 250 U.S. pilots flew American warplanes with French markings in support of the French effort. Although the American fliers undoubtedly wrote letters home to their families in the States, the general public remained oblivious to the activity and expense.

Meanwhile, as the world tried to recover, a hard-fought civil war divided China. China's Communist party had been making gains since its inception in 1921, and after being devastated by the Japanese, Communist leader Mao Ze Dung led his forces in a long and vicious struggle against the opposing Kuomintang faction led by Chiang Kai-shek. The Communists won the struggle in late 1949, and Chiang's opposing forces were forced to flee to the island of Taiwan, where they established the Republic of China. Chiang was viewed favorably by the United States as a devout anti-Communist, but he was equally opposed to Capitalism and Democracy. His Taiwan regime imposed martial law and persecuted anyone critical of his rule. Chiang maintained strict control with a one-party political system, and he watched over an aggressive and innovative community of government-owned industries that achieved significant international business success.

On the mainland, Chairman Mao set up a very rigid and restrictive government, refusing to have any communications or business dealings with the non-Communist outside world. Opposition to Mao's policies was immediately and brutally stamped out. For decades, Communist China was viewed as a "sleeping giant," with 25% of the world's population, but only minimal participation in international politics. Anti-Communists in the U.S. and Europe tried to keep a close watch on Communist China, concerned that Mao could create an unstoppable army from China's huge population.

Korea had been part of the Japanese empire, and at the end of World War II the U.S. and the Soviet Union agreed to divide the country at the 38th parallel. North Korea would become a harsh totalitarian Communist People's Republic of Korea under dictator Kim Il Sung, while South Korea enjoyed a more democratic government under anti-Communist dictator Syngman Rhee. The two sides were aggressive rivals, and border skirmishes killed more than 10,000. In a surprise move, on June 25, 1950, 75,000 North Korean troops invaded the south. This was the first real armed conflict of the Cold War. The United Nations came to South Korea's rescue, twenty-one countries sent troops, but the United States contributed about 88% of the men and equipment. North Korea had formed close ties with both the Soviet Union and Communist China, and it was feared that the conflict might escalate to become World War III.

Initially the United Nations forces were successful, but the introduction of a large Chinese force led to North Korea regaining the offensive. The Korean War culminated in an uneasy stalemate that has endured to the present. More than 36,500 Americans died in Korea, another 92,000 were wounded, and 4,759 were missing in action (MIA). Perhaps the Korean War is best known for President Truman's firing of General Douglas MacArthur for insubordination after a series of bitter defeats and retreats. MacArthur had encouraged Truman to allow the use of nuclear weapons in Korea, and also in China and the Soviet Union if they responded by increasing their roles. After firing MacArthur, Truman's popularity plummeted to 22% approval, the lowest for any President in history. MacArthur's successor, General Matthew Ridgway, was given limited authority to use nuclear weapons under the technical supervision of the Strategic Air Command, and atomic bombs were moved into place, but never used.

The Truman administration feared Communist expansion in southeast Asia, and so it was not inclined to accommodate Ho Chi Minh's pleas to throw off the French colonial rule and install a government that might lean toward Communism. When General Dwight Eisenhower, a Republican, became President in 1953 he appointed John Foster Dulles as Secretary of State, and Allen Dulles was put in charge of the Central Intelligence Agency, or CIA, an outgrowth of the OSS with greatly expanded powers. Eisenhower agreed that Communism was a threat, and he gave his military and intelligence forces unprecedented authority and leeway.

In March of 1954, it became obvious that the French in Vietnam might face final defeat by the Communist Viet Minh at the battle of Dien Bien Phu. Washington was distraught. Chairman of the Joint Chiefs of Staff Arthur Radford proposed nuclear strikes, paratrooper drops, and the mining of northern Vietnam's key port city at Haiphong. President Eisenhower contemplated asking Congress to approve massive air strikes to save the French – but met overwhelming resistance both at home and abroad. When questioned at a press conference, the President denied contemplating air support for the French at Dien Bien Phu. Eisenhower had seen that the American public was opposed to aiding the French to take back control of Vietnam, and he abandoned all intentions of sending an overt American military force. After two months under siege, the French base fell to the Viet Minh on May 7, 1954.

On May 8th, the Far Eastern Conference of nine nations gathered in Geneva to take up the challenge of reshaping Indochina in the wake of the French defeat. By this time, Ho Chi Minh's DRV (Democratic Republic of Vietnam) had become so powerful, and the U.S.-backed regime in Saigon so corrupt and unpopular, it was clear that the Communists would win an election. After six weeks of debate, it was decided that the country would be partitioned at the 17th parallel pending reunification after future elections, scheduled for two years later in 1956. The U.S. and the Saigon government refused to sign the final agreement, but the U.S. did state that it "will refrain from the threat or use of force" to sabotage the agreements.

President Eisenhower afforded the military and the CIA great leeway, especially in Southeast Asia. The U.S. force in Vietnam at that time was 342 military men, including Air Force Colonel Edward G. Lansdale. Lansdale's official mission was to be head of the Saigon Military Mission (SMM), but he was actually a member of the CIA whose covert mission was to direct secret paramilitary operations against the Communists in both the North and the South.

The Geneva Agreements required that foreign nations could not increase the number of military personnel in-country after August 11, 1954, which meant Lansdale had to rush to establish his "cold war combat team." It should be noted that the "secret" aspect of these covert military operations was not so much to prevent the Communists from knowing that they were being attacked by South Vietnamese forces with U.S. training and equipment. It was far more important to conduct these aggressive military operations in a manner that would allow the Americans to deny involvement if discovered, and also to keep the American people at home from knowing that their tax money was being spent to participate in a clandestine guerrilla war in Vietnam. The U.S. had agreed in Geneva that it would not use force in Vietnam, so it was in effect violating the Geneva Agreements. Years later, when opposition to the war was at its peak, protestors would call the war "illegal." They were referring to these operations, among others.

Also of note in 1954, the CIA engineered its first "regime change," overthrowing President Jacobo Arbenz in Guatemala without authorization from any other branch of the U.S. government. President Eisenhower created the "President's Board of Consultants on Foreign Intelligence Activities" which found that the CIA was operating in an "autonomous and free-wheeling basis in highly critical areas," that was in conflict with established State Department policies. The Board recommended that Ike fire Allen Dulles, but he was reluctant to do so.

After World War II, the "Iron Curtain" was drawn to give the western European countries to the democratic alliance which included England, France, Spain, Italy, and the United States. Eastern Europe was dominated by Stalin's pitiless totalitarian version of Communism. So, soon after World War II, instead of peace the world was confronted with a very tense political standoff between Democracy and Communism. The dominant world powers, the U.S. and the Soviet Union, constantly squabbled. Both sides maneuvered feverishly to gain the slightest military advantage or international influence while avoiding any direct armed conflict that might escalate to a nuclear war. The tense discussions and confrontations comprised an unprecedented "Cold War" that always threatened to turn hot.

Tensions grew until, in June of 1948, the Soviets blocked all roads to the portions of Berlin, Germany's capital city, that were under Allied control. By shutting off all ground transportation in or out of the western sectors, the Soviets hoped to make it impossible for the Allies to supply Berlin, thereby allowing the Soviets to sieze control over the entire city. In response, the Allies organized the Berlin Airlift, a vast rescue mission of flights that brought food and vital supplies to the residents of Berlin for almost a year. The success of this operation embarrassed the Soviets. In May of 1949 they lifted the blockade, but Germany was divided into two separate countries, the (Democratic) Federal Republic of Germany in West Germany, and the (Communist) German Democratic Republic of East Germany. Since Berlin was located deep within East Germany, it was formally split in half, and the democratic portion, West Berlin, became a small island of democracy in a sea of Communism. West Berlin was largely supplied by air for another forty years.

In 1956, the people of Hungary revolted against their government, which had been dominated by the Soviet Union since the end of World War II. The uprising lasted only from October 23rd until November 10th, but the vicious response of the Soviet army increased tensions worldwide. Clearly, the Soviets aimed to extend their sphere of influence across the globe, and they were cruel and tyrannical once in power. America's foreign policy became focused upon containing or opposing the Communist "domino effect" that seemed to be expanding to vulnerable third-world countries around the world. This theory held that once a country fell to Communism, other countries in the area would fall like dominoes, so it was vital to prevent Communism from expanding anywhere around the planet.

President Truman had created the Central Intelligence Agency from the previous OSS in 1947. President Eisenhower's administration felt that Laos was the key "domino" in Southeast Asia, and they put considerably less emphasis on Vietnam. During the mid-1950s, however, the CIA took a very active role in the political intrigues of both Laos and Vietnam. Desperate to limit Communist influence in the region, CIA agents choreographed a vast undercurrent of political mischief and unrest that led to numerous coups in both countries. Eisenhower admired the Dulles brothers and at their urging, listened to a chorus of others who aggressively pushed for a confrontation with Communism. World War II was over, but the militarists realized that maintaining the imminent threat of another terrible war, and thereby justifying the strongest and best-equipped military, were good for the economy and also vital to maintaining their influence in American government.

Both Joseph Stalin and Nikita Khrushchev expressed surprise at America's post-war belligerence and reluctance to work with the Soviets in any way. The U.S. established a strong military presence in Europe to deter the Russians, all while our scientists were developing a new, stronger generation of nuclear weapons – hydrogen bombs. "I see no reason why they shouldn't be used just exactly as you would use a bullet or anything else," Eisenhower said, and the world took notice. Still, "Ike" loved his golf and Washington social life, and he was happy to hand off many day-to-day responsibilities to his staff.

Given an inch, Allen Dulles seized a mile and the CIA became a powerful and secretive force, almost a mini-government operating covertly alongside brother John Foster Dulles's State Department to expand America's political and military influence into all areas of the globe. During the Eisenhower years, the CIA made and implemented foreign policies and, in fact, acted covertly to overthrow leaders of other nations, sometimes by assassination, in order to ensure that American political and business interests would thrive. The American economy boomed, and the American people took comfort in our government's international struggle against any hint of Socialism or Communism. In the early 1950s the Soviet Union tested its own nuclear weapons, and the Cold War became a tense standoff. Pentagon zealots like Admiral Arthur Radford and Air Force General Curtis LeMay urged the President to consider an all-out nuclear attack upon the Soviet Union before their nuclear arsenal could be developed to equal America's. Secretary of State John Foster Dulles argued that the U.S. must overcome its reluctance to use nuclear weapons, and railed against the concept that global slaughter, even to the elimination of the human race, should present any moral dilemma to using all available weapons to conquer the world. Any delay, these forces argued, would place our nation in greater danger. Eisenhower dealt with the proponents of nuclear war as a grandfather might deal with a house full of noisy, unruly grandchildren, and he never quite allowed them to pull the trigger on a catastrophic nuclear initiative. At the same time, he did little to restrain their thunderous zealotry, and the world trembled.

In the spring of 1960, anticipating a summit meeting where he would interact with French President Charles de Gaulle, Britain's Prime Minister Harold Macmillan, and the Soviet Union's Premier Nikita Khrushchev, Eisenhower ordered the CIA to stop all U-2 spy plane flights over the Soviet Union. The head of the CIA's U-2 program was Richard Bissell. In an attempt to sabotage the President's meeting with Khrushchev, Bissell took it upon himself to order one more flight on May 1st, just two weeks before the summit meeting. Eisenhower hoped that the summit would result in a détente, or lessening of tensions, with the Russians, and looked forward to cutting America's defense budget before he left office. Piloted by one Francis Gary Powers, the U-2 departed on May 1st but developed technical problems and was shot down over Soviet territory. Powers ejected and was captured. In violation of all the rules, he carried full identification, including his Department of Defense identification card. The Soviets immediately branded him a spy and began proceedings that would end with a ballyhooed, internationally televised trial.

Eisenhower's hopes to reach some accords with Khrushchev were extinguished. Subsequently, it was found that Powers' plane had been dispatched with inadequate fuel on board, and without the usual top-secret camera so vital to its supposed mission. The plane, unlike its predecessors, wore ample U.S. identification. The path of Powers' mission was significantly different from earlier flights, putting him over known Soviet missile sites that would shoot him down if his crippled plane attempted to fly beneath the Russian radar. The U.S. tried to deny the obvious origin of the flight, but when the Soviets paraded the captured pilot and pieces of spy equipment from the crashed plane, the upcoming summit meeting was conducted under a severe chill in U.S.-Soviet relations. Francis Gary Powers was convicted of espionage and sentenced to three years in prison plus seven years of hard labor, but in 1962 he was released as part of a prisoner exchange for Soviet spymaster Rudolf Abel.

After Truman, President Eisenhower introduced a few advisors into South Vietnam, and a larger, more active CIA team into Laos. There were no significant conflicts; Ho Chi Minh's forces had very little access to arms, and the Americans succeeded in disrupting politics in Laos and Vietnam for years.

The end of World War II was greeted by the peoples of Southeast Asia as an opportunity to throw off colonial rule over the area known as French Indochina. Surely the victorious and all-powerful United States would reward the assistance of the Indo-Chinese peasants in fighting the Imperial Japanese Fascists by keeping the French away and allowing these impoverished countries to regain their independence. As demand for their natural resources was increasing, the opportunities were unmistakable. But, as we have seen, Capitalism and Communism had begun a race to dominate the various developing countries of the world, and soon their territories came to be seen as scores upon a scoreboard. Powerful forces in the American government were seeing Communists behind every tree, and the McCarthy hearings in Washington insisted that Russian agents had infiltrated to the heart of our government. The paranoia reached a crescendo when Fidel Castro led a working-class rebellion in Cuba that overcame the corrupt regime of dictator Fulgencio Batista, the puppet of strong American business interests (both legal and Mafia-owned).

America's organized crime mob had operated a chain of lucrative casinos in Cuba before Fidel Castro's revolution. Cuba was highly regarded as an unrestricted off-shore resort in the sunny Caribbean, with plenty of gambling, prostitution, and access to drugs. Batista had maintained close relations with the United States, but his regime was corrupt and brutal. He fled the country on January 1st, 1959 and Fidel Castro took over. One of his first actions was to nationalize, or seize, all American holdings on the island, including the casinos. The American mafia bosses were desperate to regain their holdings and get back to making money. Likewise, although Castro did not declare himself or his revolution to be Communist-inspired until 1961, the powerful anti-Communist community in the American government, including CIA Director Allen Dulles, viewed the Cuban revolution as a threat to the United States and all of the western hemisphere. Castro reacted to the threat of the American behemoth only ninety miles away by embracing the only world power capable of holding it at bay – the USSR.

When elements within the CIA established a secret army of Cuban refugees intent upon invading their lost homeland and wresting control from Castro, Dulles turned to organized crime in America to work with the CIA and assist the Agency in eliminating Fidel Castro by a military invasion, or by assassination. Mob bosses were no doubt pleased that the CIA had enormous (unsupervised) influence in the American government, and close ties to the rabidly anti-Communist American military commanders. Organized crime helped equip and obscure the Cuban force that had been created by the CIA during the Eisenhower years, to plan the upcoming invasion of Cuba and to develop a contingent series of assassination plots against Castro.

America was very concerned. For a very short period our nuclear weapons had provided a clear military superiority, but now the Russians also had the capability of creating a nuclear Armageddon. The devastating power of these weapons was obvious to everyone when the U.S. dropped two atomic bombs on Japan at the end of World War II. Still, government officials in Washington and Moscow were tempted to resort to a nuclear war, knowing all living things on Earth would likely be obliterated. We were the greatest country in the world militarily, economically and, the American people believed, morally. Our country stood for all that was good, just, and humane. Immigrants flocked to our shores (mostly legally in those days, through Ellis Island in New York harbor in the welcoming shadow of the Statue of Liberty.) We sent the "good ship *Hope*," a hospital ship that brought medical attention to impoverished third-world countries, and "CARE packages" of food relief and products such as blankets and school supplies to Europe, to help the people at risk of starving after the devastation of World War II. Fine American missionaries like Dr. Tom Dooley ventured all alone into the jungles of Southeast Asia to bring medical assistance to the natives. If he sometimes alerted them to the evils of Communism, all the better. America saw itself as blessed by God – we were told that the Russians were brutal and intolerant, that Communism did not allow Christianity or any recognition of God, and that the people in Communist countries were fed lies and propaganda instead of the truth. When the Russians put the first satellite into space, it was a shock to the American people, and frightening. Our innate, God-given superiority was being challenged by the forces of evil.

Meanwhile, far away in the Middle East, the U.S. and England were establishing new relationships, and sometimes even new governments, in hopes of gaining control over the region's vast supplies of oil. After World War II, automobiles had become the primary mode of transport throughout much of the world, air travel had become popular, and the internal combustion engine required petroleum-based fuels to operate. As the Americans and Europeans gained power and influence in the Middle East and Southeastern Europe, they applied moral and logistical pressures to eradicate the centuries-old heroin and opium production that had been a major business staple for the local growers for centuries.

The drug business in the Mediterranean area was also a source of enormous income and power, primarily for the Corsican Mafia that distributed the illegal substances worldwide. The other area of planet Earth where opium and heroin growing had succeeded for centuries was Southeast Asia, and the Corsicans immediately turned their attentions to the area. Like sharks swarming around the scent of blood in the sea, the international underworld converged upon the "Golden Triangle" region of Laos, Burma, and northern Thailand. Always alert to any opportunity to ply their trade, American organized crime established close "business" ties to the CIA and soon became involved in the agency's covert activities in Laos and Vietnam. Elements within the government of South Vietnam, including Nguyen Cao Ky, who would become head of South Vietnam's air force, Prime Minister from 1965 to 1967, and Vice President until 1971, allegedly helped set up worldwide drug distribution routes through Saigon's Tan Son Nhut airport in exchange for a cut of the proceeds.

Years before President Johnson announced that American combat troops would be deployed to South Vietnam, CIA operatives throughout Laos and Vietnam had been helping their underworld business associates establish a successful opium and heroin business to supply the world from Southeast Asia. The CIA's headquarters for clandestine operations in northern Laos in the village of Long Tieng contained a thriving laboratory where Burmese and Thai heroin was refined and packaged. The five dirt air strips at Long Tieng soon became the busiest airport on the planet with activity day and night. When President Johnson announced that American combat forces would be sent to Vietnam in 1965, Mafia leaders from around the world responded and had already held a summit meeting in Saigon weeks before the first Marine came ashore at Danang. It was clear that enormous riches and opportunities would soon be flowing into Vietnam, and the underworld wanted to establish territories and spheres of influence to avoid internal conflicts while they plied their trade.

Even before the Saigon summit meeting, it was estimated that the Mafia's heroin and opium exports to the U.S. alone exceeded $30 billion dollars per year. Ironically, America's organized crime community would also supply billions of dollars' worth of weapons and ammunition to the Indochinese black market, and hence the Viet Cong, throughout the war years. Under the guise of preventing Communist expansion into Southeast Asia, American "advisors" and their underworld business partners were able to lure an enormous American military effort to confront the domino theory in Vietnam, and to take full financial advantage of the situation. America's military and the strong anti-Communist faction of government were at their peak during the Eisenhower years. Fresh from a military stalemate in Korea, and with America's well-funded military backed up by the proven effectiveness of our nuclear bombs, America's leaders believed their sacred duty was to stop the spread of Communism anywhere in the world. If there were a few illicit dollars to be made in the process, of course, that was just frosting on the cake.

In the aftermath of the French defeat at Dien Bien Phu and subsequent withdrawal from the area once known as French Indo-China in 1954, President Eisenhower saw Southeast Asia as vulnerable to the "domino effect" of Communist expansion. Determined to avoid the "loss" of any countries to Communism, he turned the future of Laos over to the CIA and military. Because the people of Laos refused to support the CIA's chosen leader, Eisenhower's men could not feel confident about the situation there. Obviously, the next most vulnerable situation in Southeast Asia was Vietnam, and the Americans were determined not to let it become a dead "domino." If Laos and Vietnam fell, they feared that Communism would soon expand throughout the region, possibly even to the Philippines, New Zealand and Australia.

As Eisenhower prepared to leave the White House in January of 1961, he convinced John Kennedy of this threat, and Kennedy stated that he might even use American troops "to help South Vietnam resist Communist pressures." By 1962, the U.S. had 11,300 military advisors in South Vietnam, including Special Forces and helicopter units.

Still, America's focus of attention was certainly Laos, a desperately poor nation that had endured coups and violent governmental changes throughout its history. It must be noted that Laos was a political disaster after World War II. France set up a provisional government at the end of the war, and a coalition of Laotian groups joined together to seek an independent and free country. Prince Souvanna Phouma was the son of a

Laotian vice-king and the nephew of the King. Educated in Europe, Souvanna served as the country's Prime Minister from 1951 – 1954, again from 1956 – 1958, for a short while in 1960, and from 1962 – 1975. He recognized his tiny, impoverished country's dire predicament as the Cold War powers came calling and interfering in Laotian politics. Souvanna struggled to make Laos a neutral nation in hopes that this might avert any outbreak of actual military activities.

He was opposed by Phoumi Nosavan, an outspoken anti-Communist military man who was backed by the CIA. A series of coups kept the government in turmoil as pro- and anti-Communists gained and lost power continuously. Throughout all the turmoil, the presence of the CIA was constant, in Laos and in Vietnam. Influential forces were pressuring Washington to commit ground troops into Southeast Asia and use nuclear weapons and heavy conventional bombing to eradicate the Communist menace once and for all. Not surprisingly, most of this discussion was kept from the American public. As the Presidential election of 1960 approached, no one wanted to mention the prospect of another war. The election of Senator John F. Kennedy over Eisenhower's Vice President Richard Nixon was extremely close, and a shock to the powers in Washington. Their carefully laid plans were in jeopardy.

Shortly before turning the White House over to John Kennedy, on January 17, 1961 President Eisenhower made an impassioned farewell speech to the American people. "Ike" had been the commanding general of all allied forces in Europe during World War II and President for eight years. He was highly respected and admired as he prepared to retire to his farm near Gettysburg. Certainly, he knew exactly what he was talking about when he warned the American people, and the President-elect, of the burgeoning economic and social power of the nuclear-era defense establishment. The original text of his speech called this entity the military-industrial-government complex, but he removed the reference to the government from the final version. Was he thinking of the "free-wheeling" actions of the CIA when he spoke those words? Was he telling all he knew?

Chapter 4

VIETNAM: WHAT REALLY HAPPENED?

PART 2 ... THE KENNEDY YEARS 1960 - 1963

To those nations who would make themselves our adversary, we offer not a pledge but a request: that both sides begin anew the quest for peace, before the dark powers of destruction unleashed by science engulf all humanity in planned or accidental self-destruction.
– John F. Kennedy, from his inaugural address, January 20, 1961.

I should much prefer to have people respect us than to try to make them love us.
– Allen Dulles on "America's Role in the Ideological Struggle."

To those of us who lived through the Vietnam years, the presidency and assassination of John F. Kennedy are historical events of the greatest importance, and, after more than fifty years of unresolved debate over what really happened, the ultimate fascination. Kennedy was youthful, a genuine war hero; handsome, with a genuine smile, a glamorous wife, two playful children, a colorful and accomplished family, a genuinely heroic wartime record, and, perhaps most important, a hopeful and positive outlook about America's future. In the dark, ominous shadow of the mushroom cloud, as we came to adolescence and our teachers insisted we become familiar with current events, we responded to JFK's optimism with youthful enthusiasm. He was a new and different kind of leader, and he conveyed his visions of America's future in a manner that got most of us on board. Yes, even to land men on the moon, one of mankind's greatest adventures ever.

Looking back upon his 1,036 days in office, we see that JFK faced a variety of situations that threatened to ignite a nuclear war and destroy the planet, along with an array of domestic crises that became so confrontational we saw death, destruction, civil strife, and armed soldiers in our streets. Today, thanks to the Freedom of Information Act and the efforts of many inquisitive historians and determined investigative journalists, far more is known about the realities of those situations. At the time, the American people were largely unaware of the desperate intrigues and power struggles taking place in Washington, D.C. and the covert operations affecting events around the world. Sadly, even as many of those situations have been uncovered, they have been systematically obscured or whitewashed by a variety of forces, and most Americans remain pretty much oblivious to the sordid side of our country's history to this day.

As we re-examine the Vietnam War, an understanding and appreciation of those times and the besieged presidency of John F. Kennedy is vital. In fact, descendants of the forces that opposed JFK half a century ago are still affecting America today, in an equally threatening way. Big business wants unrestricted freedom to achieve maximum profits without regard to national interests, while the public has been led to expect democracy and support from its government, and the struggle for America's future continues to be violent and desperate. It is American history in the making, and we are all living it every day.

I suggest it is important to remember President Kennedy as a man with a young family who had taken on an immense responsibility. John and Jacqueline's first attempt at starting a family concluded with the stillborn arrival of Arabella in 1956. Caroline was born in 1957. Kennedy was elected President of the United States on November 8th, 1960, the youngest man ever to hold the office. John Jr., or "John-John," was born November 25th, so he was less than two months old when Daddy was inaugurated. One can only imagine the difficulty the Kennedys must have faced as they prepared to move their young family into the White House while planning the inaugural ceremonies, choosing a Cabinet, and contemplating the complex challenges of the national and world situations he would soon inherit.

In early 1959, a revolution in Cuba threw out the U.S.-backed and terribly corrupt Batista regime. Fidel Castro's first efforts at reforming Cuba were to nationalize U.S. companies and investments in Cuba, including closing the lucrative gambling casinos owned and operated by American organized crime groups. While Castro had earlier declared "we are not Communists," many Americans, including Vice President Richard Nixon, expressed concerns that the revolution was in fact Communist in nature. In September of 1960, Castro led a delegation to New York City to address the United Nations General Assembly. Because he had a beard and chose to wear combat fatigues on the streets of the city, he was derided as a barbarian throughout the media. However, many Americans saw Fidel Castro and his compatriot Dr. Che Guevara as dashing, brave revolutionaries who had thrown off the chains of corruption and liberated their country. Castro spoke to the General Assembly for more than four hours, passionately decrying American policies of "aggression" and "imperialism" toward Cuba and other nations around the globe. The U.S., he charged, had "decreed the destruction" of his regime and the reforms he had brought to Cuba. Most of us, as loyal American children, dismissed his rantings, but many college students and Latinos saw him as a hero.

Cuba had long been a popular Caribbean resort where the American mafia had enjoyed highly profitable gambling and other vice operations along with significant influence in every aspect of Cuban government and business. Finding themselves abruptly tossed off the island, organized crime's kingpins immediately began to pressure Washington to oppose the revolutionary Cuban government, and to support exiled Cuban groups who were plotting to take back their homeland by force. Many legal American corporations had also lost a lot of money when Castro nationalized sugar, tobacco, and other industries. In March of 1960, President Eisenhower secretly authorized the CIA to begin training and equipping these groups in preparation for an armed invasion to remove Castro from power. A few top mafia bosses were recruited to work with the CIA to overthrow or assassinate Castro. The U.S. imposed economic sanctions, limiting the importation of Cuban sugar and cigars, and Castro turned to the Soviet Union for economic and military assistance.

Suddenly, the Communist menace had a base of operations just 90 miles from America. Communism was no longer a far-off European or Asian threat – and America was told to be desperately afraid of our new neighbor. When John F. Kennedy took office in January of 1961, the CIA under Director Allen Dulles had become a major power in Washington, maintaining its own private armies, spying and conducting "covert" operations around the world, augmenting its sizable budget with proceeds from drug trafficking, and operating its own far-flung network of clandestine printing companies, banks, and airlines. From the moment of his inauguration, President Kennedy and the CIA had been adversaries. Richard Bissell politely informed the President that "the CIA was a secret state of its own." CIA asset and mercenary Gerald

Patrick Hemming later described JFK as "the last President to believe he could take power."

Under President Eisenhower, the CIA had established bases in Florida, Louisiana, and Guatemala, where they were secretly training a rag-tag army of anti-Communist rebels, former Batista supporters, and disaffected peasants. Just days before he turned the White House over to Kennedy, Eisenhower severed all diplomatic relations with Cuba. The CIA and the Joint Chiefs of Staff encouraged Kennedy to commit America's full military might to ousting the Castro regime, even suggesting nuclear attacks upon Havana. Kennedy was a dedicated Cold Warrior, but he was also a war veteran, a realist, and a daddy. His inaugural address promised to seek peaceful solutions to international problems, and to avoid a nuclear catastrophe.

In March, just a few weeks after taking office, Kennedy authorized the CIA to go ahead with its plans for an invasion by expatriate Cuban forces, but the President insisted that there was "no basis for American military intervention." The CIA and Joint Chiefs were appalled. Eisenhower had given them almost full reign to direct America's foreign policy strategies. For a few years, the U.S. had been the only nation on earth with working nuclear weapons, and there was still a strong element within the military, State Department, and intelligence community eager to use that strategic advantage to establish American dominance all around the globe. Any nations or peoples that resisted could and should be systematically eliminated, they said.

The planners of the Cuban invasion, led by Richard Bissell, the director of the CIA's Covert Operations Division, assured President Kennedy that when the invaders established a beachhead and announced that they were, in fact, a counterrevolutionary government, the Cuban people would rise up against the Castro regime and help them take back the island from the Communists. And, as soon as they landed, the invaders would declare themselves a new government of Cuba and appeal for aid from the United States. Despite the fact that Kennedy had banned any direct American military involvement, the CIA and Joint Chiefs of Staff fully believed he would succumb to public opinion and send both air support and a contingent of Marines to reinforce the invaders. The far-reaching extent of the plans included another force of covert anti-Castro guerrillas wearing Cuban army uniforms who would be brought to the island aboard a boat called the Santa Anna, and stage a fake attack upon the U.S. naval base at Guantanamo. This effort was aborted when a recon party reported strange lights and vehicle activity near the base.

The Bay of Pigs invasion took place in April of 1961. A flight of six B-26 bombers struck the Cuban Air Force in advance of the actual assault, hoping to destroy Cuba's ability to oppose the invasion from the air. The B-26s came from the fleet of retired U.S. Air Force planes that had been mothballed and stored near Tucson, Arizona. The bombers had been "sanitized" and repainted with Cuban Air Force markings. How they came to be part of the Cuban invasion force is not clear. Originally, sixteen bombers had been intended to knock out the Cuban Air Force, but at the last moment Bissell ordered only six to initiate the attack.

The raid was ineffective, as the Cubans had positioned dummy aircraft on the air field. The CIA's supposedly infallible intelligence had missed the change, and Castro's "rag-tag" fighters destroyed a number of ships carrying the invaders and their equipment toward Cuba. Within three days they suffered 40-per cent casualties and were forced to surrender. More than a thousand were captured on the beach. As it became obvious that the invasion was going badly, the planners expected the young and inexperienced President to reverse himself and order a full American effort to ensure the success of the operation. The military and CIA were shocked and deeply offended when the President flatly refused. They had miscalculated, and the Bay of Pigs was a disastrous embarrassment. The Cuban people did not rise up and revolt against the Castro regime. The CIA tried to pin responsibility for the debacle on the inexperienced President, but Kennedy was having none of it. Later, JFK would tell friends, "They had me figured all wrong."

Soon after the embarrassing failure at the Bay of Pigs, it was found that a few of the CIA planners had secretly plotted to supersede Kennedy's orders if he did not cave in and support their operation. When Robert Kennedy learned of this plot, he called it "virtually treason." JFK was outraged, and he told an administration official he wanted "to splinter the CIA in a thousand pieces and scatter it to the winds." He immediately took steps to limit the CIA's opportunity to get involved in military operations, cut back the CIA's budget significantly, and fired three of the planners of the Bay of Pigs fiasco, CIA Director Allen Dulles, Richard Bissell, and General Charles Cabell (Cabell's brother, Earle was mayor of Dallas, Texas on the day JFK was assassinated).

The significance of this operation to later events, and the planners' blatant disregard for the directions of the President, have been de-emphasized by mainstream history books. Just a few weeks after the outgoing President Eisenhower warned the American people to beware the mili-

tary-industrial complex, JFK openly defied the top anti-communist zealots and warmongers in the CIA and the Joint Chiefs of Staff, and there was
immense resentment that would resonate throughout every moment of
the Kennedy years in the White House, and beyond. The avid anti-Communists and architects of U.S. Cold War strategies did not expect their
plans or suggestions to be questioned, let alone cancelled. John F. Kennedy had been President for only ninety days. He would be challenged
again, and soon.

The President's father, Joseph Kennedy, had made a large part of the
family fortune as a bootlegger during prohibition, and he enjoyed good
working relationships with many underworld and/or mafia figures. JFK's
election victory over Richard Nixon was very close, and most observers
believe that father Joe asked Chicago mob boss Sam Giancana to influence the unions and swing Illinois to vote for Kennedy. Once in office, the
President appointed his relatively inexperienced younger brother Robert
as Attorney General, and Bobby expanded his longstanding campaign
against organized crime. JFK's reluctance to back the Bay of Pigs invasion
angered many top mafia bosses. This, and Bobby Kennedy's energetic
campaign against organized crime was viewed as an outright betrayal.

New Orleans crime boss Carlos Marcello likened the Kennedy administration to "a stone in my shoe." Bobby prosecuted Marcello for immigration violations and had him deported to Guatemala in April of 1961, but
Marcello was back in New Orleans soon after. Marcello was not reluctant
to express his hatred for the Kennedys, and after the assassination of JFK
he boasted that he had been responsible for everything but actually pulling the trigger.

Other mob leaders and their associates also hated the Kennedy brothers. Santo Trafficante Jr. had lost a number of very profitable casinos in
Cuba, and Teamsters Union leader Jimmy Hoffa, who was relentlessly investigated and hounded by RFK, was very outspoken about his hopes that
the Kennedys would be silenced soon. Chicago's Sam Giancana and Johnny Rosselli were also known to have extremely adversarial sentiments toward the Kennedys. Very significantly, in their panic-stricken zeal to erase
the Castro/Communist presence in Cuba, the CIA had partnered with
these powerful mafia bosses. Carlos Marcello was especially involved in
efforts to assassinate Castro, and he had well-documented ties to both Lee
Harvey Oswald and Jack Ruby in this regard.

While Bobby Kennedy had angered the mafia bosses by his investigations and prosecutions, the strategists recognized that if you "cut the tail

off the dog," as in eliminating Bobby, "the head can still bite. But if you cut off the head, the tail will also die." There is extensive evidence that the CIA and the mafia played key roles in the assassination of John Kennedy. Some very bizarre stories concerning the CIA and the Mafia's plots to eliminate Fidel Castro have come out, and it is extremely probable that those covert efforts continued long after John and Robert Kennedy were gone.

On November 8, 1960 Kennedy was elected president. On November 11 and 12, South Vietnam's president Diem narrowly avoided a coup. As we have seen, at that time Vietnam was not the primary Cold War concern in Asia. In meetings with Kennedy, outgoing President Eisenhower advised Kennedy that Laos, not Vietnam, was "the key to the entire area of Southeast Asia," and predicted that it might become necessary to deploy U.S. combat troops to avoid a Communist takeover in Laos. Even as a Senator, John Kennedy had been advised against committing American troops to action in Asia, from experts including World War II hero General Douglas MacArthur. When he came to the White House in early 1961, Kennedy immediately signaled his attention to the region's problems by assigning a carrier task force to the Gulf of Siam, but he was reluctant to deploy American troops to confront the region's problems. Once again, the CIA and the Pentagon were insulted and angry. The Chairman of the Joint Chiefs of Staff, General Lyman Lemnitzer, had drawn up plans for an American invasion of Laos in defiance of the President's orders, and Lemnitzer was an outspoken advocate of employing nuclear weapons in Laos, as well as Havana, Berlin, and Moscow to prevent any further Communist expansion.

Another former French Indochina colony, Laos had been granted "independence" as an associated state of the French Union in 1950. In 1954, Laos gained full independence as a constitutional monarchy, but a civil war erupted between the established government and the Communist Pathet Lao.

Perhaps the most effective political figure in Laos was Prince Souvanna Phouma. Never a favorite of the U.S. military and CIA presence in the region, Souvanna was Prime Minister on several occasions between 1951 and 1954, 1956 and 1958, for a short while in 1960, and between 1962 and 1975. The leader of the neutralist faction, he recognized that his small agricultural country could only be harmed if it became a battlefield in the struggle between Communism and the West. His main opposition, Phoumi Nosavan, was supported by the Americans despite, or perhaps because of, his extensive business interests related to gambling, drugs, and banking. Forces under his control attacked the capital, Vientiane, in 1959, but were repulsed. In early 1960, a coup d'etat under General Kong Le overthrew the government, but his own army opposed his rule and fought against him. In November of 1960, a coalition government was formed between Souvanna Phouma's neutralists, Pathet Lao communists, and the military under commander Kong Le. In December, Phoumi Nosavan relieved Kong Le, but the next day Kong Le overthrew him, and Phoumi escaped to Cambodia. On December 13, he returned and, after the Battle of Vientiane, took power back. This was the nature of Southeast Asian politics at the time, and most Americans paid little or no attention.

The CIA, meanwhile, was deeply involved in Laos. Along with the turbulent politics, there is considerable evidence that CIA operatives in Laos were looking away, or participating in the business and profiting themselves, while their old Mafia friends established a lucrative heroin and opium business in Laos, Burma, and northern Thailand with distribution routes through South Vietnam to the world.

From the earliest days of the Kennedy presidency, The Joint Chiefs of Staff, and especially Chairman General Lyman Lemnitzer, argued for a policy of "unlimited intervention" in Asia, and especially Laos. They thought the U.S. should, at the very least, deploy up to 140,000 combat troops to stamp out the Communist influence in Laos, and they urged the new president to seriously consider bombing both Hanoi and even Communist China. According to Lemnitzer, "If we are given the right to use nuclear weapons, we can guarantee victory." General Curtis LeMay was quoted as advocating that we "bomb them (North Vietnam) back to the stone age." Throughout this period, John Foster Dulles, one of the most influential men in the military and intelligence communities, believed that "we have the most powerful weapons in the world, and we should use them to eliminate our enemies."

Fresh from the embarrassment of the Bay of Pigs fiasco, Kennedy told a journalist he had "lost confidence" in the Joint Chiefs, and he directed his staff to move toward establishing a neutral government in Laos. This would, of course, include an established Communist faction with considerable input into the direction the country would take, an option the military and CIA considered unthinkable.

President Kennedy and Soviet Premier Nikita Khrushchev met at a summit conference in Vienna in June of 1961. It did not go well for the new President, but he and Khrushchev were able to agree that the best course of action in Laos would be to set up a neutral government. While this would establish a Communist presence in the Laotian government, the two leaders agreed to avoid any armed confrontation.

On July 23, 1962, fourteen nations (not including Laos) signed a "Declaration on the Neutrality of Laos" agreement. The premise of the agreement was that the Soviet Union would act as a policeman to prevent North Vietnam or Communist China from expanding their influence into Laos, but from the start the Soviets admitted that they could not effectively perform those tasks, and Hanoi soon established supply routes through eastern Laos to aid their efforts in South Vietnam. Those routes came to be known as the Ho Chi Minh Trail. In Laos, Phoumi Nosavan was ordered to merge his right-wing government into a three-way coalition under the leadership of Souvanna Phouma. When he refused, the U.S. took away its financial assistance for both the government and the army. Phoumi undertook to make up the shortfall by increasing the country's opium business, and by simply printing more money. When his troops were defeated again in May of 1962, Phoumi merged his government into a neutralist coalition headed by Souvanna Phouma, but he retained personal control of the country's Ministry of Finance and established monopolies over a far-flung empire of gambling, drugs, and even some legitimate business opportunities. Phoumi was overthrown by the military in 1964. He attempted another coup in 1965, but it failed.

Back in Washington in 1962, JFK had shocked and angered the leadership of the CIA and the military by opposing their agenda once again, and they seethed. Many of the CIA agents in Laos were making enormous profits from the opium and heroin trade, and they did not want to see America end its involvement there. The ubiquitous "Domino Theory" made it accepted that, unless we committed our full military power, Communists influenced and aided by Red China and/or North Vietnam would overwhelm the vulnerable little country, and then sweep on to Thailand, Cambodia, Malaysia, and of course, South Vietnam. Such was the hysteria of the times that it was thought even New Zealand and Australia were in grave danger.

The actual number of Americans in Southeast Asia in those early years, and their real roles, has never been clearly defined. One prominent example is Dr. Thomas A. Dooley III. Dooley was a U.S. Navy physician who was assigned to the USS Montague in 1954 to help Vietnamese refugees escape in the wake of the French defeat. Dooley spent the rest of his life working with the peasants of Vietnam and Laos; and became a popular humanitarian folk hero in America after the publication of his three books, *Deliver Us From Evil*, *The Edge of Tomorrow*, and *The Night They Burned the Mountain*. After leaving the Navy, he worked mostly in northern Laos, near the border with Communist China. While providing medical care to the Laotian peasants, he also supplied information to the CIA. Under the direction of staunch anti-Communist Allen Dulles and his supporters (even after JFK had officially removed him), the CIA was deeply involved in every facet of political intrigue throughout Southeast Asia during this period.

When he took office, John F. Kennedy was every bit a Cold War President, committed to the struggle against creeping Communist influence around the world. In July of 1961, he authorized an additional $3.25 billion for the Defense budget, as well as the addition of 200,000 recruits to the military's headcount. Kennedy, however, recognized the changing nature of military conflicts under the threat of nuclear annihilation, and he encouraged the Pentagon to emphasize new strategies such as increased reliance upon helicopter mobility and the establishment of our own guerilla war specialists, the Special Forces or Green Berets.

The numbers of Americans in Vietnam prior to the arrival of combat troops have always been difficult to determine. On January 20, 1960 there were officially 685 American MAAG (Military Assistance Advisory Group) advisers in South Vietnam. That number was doubled in April of 1960. The Department of Defense Manpower Data Center shows 760 American military personnel in Vietnam in 1959, 900 in 1960, 3,205 in 1961 under the new President, and 11,300 in 1962. When Kennedy was assassinated in late 1963, there were 16,700 American "advisers" in South Vietnam. JFK also increased economic aid to South Vietnam from $250 million to $400 million per year.

In the spring of 1962, the President considered a suggestion from John Kenneth Galbraith, the ambassador to India, to seek an accord with Hanoi that would lead to both North Vietnamese and U.S. withdrawal of all military support from South Vietnam, improving trade relations, and postponing discussion of reuniting the country. The Joint Chiefs of Staff opposed the suggestion, and during a meeting of top military decision-makers in Saigon in May, Secretary of Defense Robert McNamara asked a small group of the most influential and powerful generals how soon it would be possible to leave the war in the hands of the South Vietnamese army and withdraw U.S. forces from Vietnam. The generals were shocked when McNamara ordered them to begin planning for withdrawal. To be clear, JFK had not ordered withdrawal at that time, but he had ordered the military in Vietnam to begin planning for the day when American support might no longer be necessary. The generals had been busy planning a variety of American expansions in the country, and they felt that any consideration of withdrawal might be seen as a surrender to the Communists.

Taking full advantage of an environment of "covert" operations throughout Southeast Asia, much of the top American leadership in South Vietnam had established extracurricular sources of great wealth, and they were content to let the military's involvement continue indefinitely. Their open hostility to the suggestion of a withdrawal was common knowledge, and very little was done to respond to the Defense Secretary's request. Immediately after Kennedy's assassination, the number of American troops in Vietnam increased to 23,300 in 1964. The first American combat troops, 3500 Marines, were deployed in March of 1965, and the American presence in Vietnam totaled 184,300 at the end of that year.

Secretary of Defense Robert McNamara had been chosen for his position because he was a forward-looking, detail-oriented executive with Ford Motor Company. McNamara brought a small army of computer nerds, number-crunchers and "Whiz Kids" to the Pentagon, and he put a lot of faith in statistical data. One example was the "HES," or Hamlet Evaluation System report that generated 90,000 pages of numbers per month. At the height of the war, long before the era of personal computers, the Defense Department's computer banks in Vietnam generated 500 similar reports every month. Keeping in mind that body counts and all other signs of progress in the war were regularly overinflated, the deluge of data generated by McNamara's "Whiz Kids" was one of history's earliest and boldest examples of computerized "garbage in – garbage out."

The Bay of Pigs disaster occurred on April 17th of 1961. On April 12, 1961, Russian Cosmonaut Yuri Gagarin became the first human in space when he rode a capsule for a full orbit of Earth and returned successfully. America was shocked, and the nation's attention soon shifted to this new contest to convince the world of America's technological superiority. The U.S. launched a short sub-orbital flight by astronaut Alan Shepard on May 5th. This momentous occasion was televised in its entirety, unlike the Russian flight, and many workers and students, including the author, stayed home to watch it on TV. The outcome of the experiment was far from certain, but America breathed a collective sigh of relief when our first manned space flight was a complete success. Another sub-orbital mission, manned by Virgil "Gus" Grissom, flew successfully in, and then in February of 1962 John Glenn rode his "Friendship 7" capsule for three full orbits. Many of us missed another day of school on that occasion. In a September of 1962 speech at Rice University, JFK boldly announced "We choose to go to the moon." In the age of burgeoning missile technology and Cold War fears, the "Space Race" was seen as an indicator of America's technical expertise versus the Soviet Union's.

In May of 1961 another new phenomenon arose that had to concern the White House. Idealistic activists began to ride buses into the hot South to agitate for civil rights for blacks. These "Freedom Riders" were not welcomed by the White establishment in the South. Like so many other areas of American culture, young people were questioning and rejecting racism. The founding fathers had declared that in America "all men are created equal," and it was disturbing to learn that some American citizens were being denied their right to vote, to be served at a lunch counter, or to sit down in an available seat near the front of the bus simply because of the color of their skin. The civil rights movement was gaining momentum, and few believed that the southern segregationists' "Jim Crow" laws would be overcome without violence and bloodshed.

On August 13, 1961, backed by the Soviet Union, the government of East Germany, the Communist German Democratic Republic or GDR, closed the border around West Berlin. After World War II, the city of Berlin had been divided into four sectors, with the western sectors to be under the control of France, England, and the United States. The fourth sector, East Berlin, was to be a part of East Germany, where the city was actually located. Since World War II, West Berlin had existed as an oasis of democracy in the midst of Communist East Germany, and its success in rebuilding after the war as a center for business, commerce, and the arts stood in stark contrast to the bleak atmosphere of its Communist neighbors. East Germans had enjoyed visiting West Berlin; many worked there, and over two million of East Germany's best and brightest had emigrated through Berlin to escape Communism. Now, suddenly the border was ringed with East German guards who were ordered to shoot anyone attempting to cross into West Berlin. Within a few days a wall was constructed, along with an elaborate obstacle course of barbed wire and guard towers. President Kennedy would not be intimidated, and he sent Vice President Johnson to Berlin to greet a large convoy of American troops who were driving through East Germany to West Berlin.

It must be acknowledged that President Kennedy was a World War II veteran and hero, and also a prolific womanizer. The author suspects that some of the president's bold sexual adventures might have been fueled by a taste for adrenalin, perhaps related to PTSD. At any rate, JFK's favorite companion was a sophisticated blonde named Mary Pinchot Meyers. Deeply opposed to war, there is reason to believe that she had a profound effect upon the president's thinking. As his presidency progressed, he became more and more determined to seek peaceful solutions to the frightening international conflicts erupting all around the world. This despite the outspoken advice from many powerful military and diplomatic advisors to solve foreign policy dilemmas by simply blowing the enemy away regardless of the consequences.

We now know that President Kennedy and Soviet Premier Nikita Khrushchev, also the father of a small child, carried on a secret personal correspondence of letters smuggled back and forth between the White House and the Kremlin. Beginning in September of 1961, the two leaders shared their thoughts on life, expressed the immense pressures they were both feeling from their hawkish militaries, and agreed to communicate privately to avoid any conflict that might unleash a nuclear holocaust. "Whatever our differences," Kennedy wrote to Khrushchev on October 16, 1961, "our collaboration to keep the peace is as urgent – if not more urgent – than our collaboration to win the last world war." These exchanges did not become known to historians until 1993.

The Berlin Wall effectively cut off East Germany and East Berlin from contact with the West, dividing families and creating another tense international crisis. Along with the debate over Laos, the President was now forced to defend his policies toward Berlin to the military. Generals Lemnitzer and Curtis LeMay insisted they be given authorization to use nuclear weapons to settle the disputes in both Laos and Berlin. President Kennedy walked out of those meetings, saying, "These people are crazy." He appointed retired General Lucius Clay to be his personal representative in West Berlin, and in October Clay, acting on his own initiative and without informing Washington of his intentions, attempted to escalate the crisis by preparing to knock down the wall with American tanks. Soviet spies watched the tanks being prepared and moving into position, and advised Premier Khrushchev of the situation. By this time the two leaders had begun their secret correspondence, and Khrushchev realized that Kennedy was being undermined by the American military. The President was in New York City to give his first speech to the United Nations when he received a conciliatory note from Khrushchev, and he told the U.N.,

Today every inhabitant of this planet must contemplate the day when this planet may no longer be habitable. Every man, woman, and child lives under a nuclear sword of Damocles, hanging by the slenderest of threads, capable of being cut at any moment by accident or miscalculation or by madness. The weapons of war must be abolished before they abolish us... It is therefore our intention to challenge the Soviet Union, not to an arms race, but to a peace race—to advance together step by step, stage by stage, until general and complete disarmament has been achieved.

American military leaders and businessmen were appalled.

Undeterred, on October 27th Lucius Clay ordered ten American tanks, some with bulldozer blades, to approach the Berlin Wall at Checkpoint Charlie, the most visible point in the center of the city. Ten Soviet tanks arrived almost immediately to meet them, and then twenty more. Another twenty American tanks rolled up, and the Americans and Russians aimed their guns at each other. The confrontation lasted for sixteen very tense hours. Kennedy contacted Khrushchev via their secret channel of communication, assuring him that if the Russian tanks backed off the Americans would follow suit within thirty minutes. Finally, the Russians moved away, and the American tanks withdrew.

On January 5 of 1962, *Time* magazine named John F. Kennedy its Man of the Year for 1961.

In 1959, a steel-workers strike had hurt the American economy. Soon after taking office, the fledgling Kennedy administration got involved in negotiations between ten of America's biggest steel companies and the United Steelworkers Union. An agreement was reached on March 31st of 1961, and it implied that the steel companies would not raise prices to cover the cost of a moderate increase in fringe benefits for their union members. On April 10th, the CEO of U.S. Steel, the largest of the steel companies, announced that U.S. Steel and five other companies would be raising their prices by 3.5%.

The President saw this as a corporate double-cross that would lead to inflation and damage the nation's economy, and in a press conference he described the price hikes as "a wholly unjustifiable and irresponsible defiance of the public interest." He criticized the "tiny handful of steel executives whose pursuit of power and profit exceeds their sense of public responsibility." Two big steel firms announced that they would not increase prices, and the Defense Department, run by former auto executive Robert McNamara, a bean counter who recognized the impact the price increase would have on manufacturing, let it be known that a lucrative submarine construction project would be awarded to one of the steel companies that had not raised prices. By April 13 all of the firms had abandoned the price increase, but their management's anger toward the President was a bitter political reality. Now the Kennedy administration had angered the CIA, the military, and big business. Tensions throughout Washington, D.C. were at a critical stage.

In the autumn of 1962, American spy planes saw Soviet missile installations being built in Cuba. President Kennedy began blockading ships and demanded that all Russian missiles be removed from proximity to American soil. Premier Khrushchev had been concerned by American missiles in Turkey aimed at key Soviet targets, and he had intentions of setting up a similar line of defense just ninety miles from Florida. The result was a crisis that brought the world to the very brink of all-out nuclear war, and the Joint Chiefs of Staff urged Kennedy to attack the missile sites in Cuba with nuclear weapons to ensure success. When an American U-2 spy plane was shot down over Cuba, the American military demanded an immediate attack with so much enthusiasm that the President sent his brother Robert Kennedy to meet with Soviet ambassador Anatoly Dobrynin. The Attorney General told Dobrynin with urgent emphasis, "If the situation continues much longer, the President is not sure that the military will not overthrow him and seize power." Kennedy asked the Soviet leader to turn the ships around, promised to remove the missiles from Turkey and Italy, and pledged not to invade Cuba.

Khrushchev immediately responded to Kennedy's letter by announcing that the Soviet Union would remove all missiles from Cuba in exchange for Kennedy's promise not to invade Cuba in the future. It must be noted that a number of top American Generals, especially Lemnitzer and LeMay, strongly urged the President to consider direct military intervention and nuclear attacks wherever crisis flared. They had urged him to use The Bomb to support insurgents at the Bay of Pigs, in Laos, and again during the missile crisis. The Joint Chiefs were outraged by Kennedy's refusal to attack the missile sites, and by his pledge to take no further military action against Castro. This effectively crippled the resource-starved Cuban resistance, and the President was accused of being "soft" on Communism. The political atmosphere in Washington was so tense that President Kennedy confided to close friends that he was concerned his opponents within the American military and intelligence establishment might actually attempt a violent *coup d'etat* by the military and intelligence communities.

Khrushchev was also keenly aware of the pressures being brought to bear upon the President. The two had formed avenues of communication that had defused international situations and may well have avoided an all-out nuclear war, and Khrushchev valued Kennedy's willingness to compromise. The Soviet Premier knew that no other American who might succeed Kennedy would so boldly work to achieve peace. Khrushchev ordered the Soviet missiles be removed from Cuba, and the world narrowly avoided nuclear annihilation.

It should be noted that, in October of 1962, this situation of the warmongering military and intelligence communities openly defying the President came less than two years after Eisenhower's famous "military-industrial complex" speech as he was leaving the White House in January of 1961. Three days after Eisenhower's grave warning, Kennedy's Inaugural Address had voiced his intention that "Both sides begin anew the quest for peace, before the dark powers of destruction unleashed by science engulf all humanity in planned or accidental self-destruction." As he was saying those words, John Kennedy the Cold Warrior was fully committed to containing the threat of creeping Communism. But he was also feeling the great responsibility inherent in commanding America's ability to destroy all life on planet Earth at the push of a button. The nuclear button was on his desk while Caroline and John-John played at his feet.

JFK did not intend to defy America's militant Cold Warriors, but he recognized that nuclear war must be avoided, as well as his obligation to work toward a peaceful alternative to all-consuming war. It was not a welcome message in all of the nation's halls of power. The President fully recognized the possible consequences of his actions to steer the nation toward peace instead of war, but he felt the potential benefits to America and the world community made his personal risks necessary.

Americans who had come of age during the depression and survived World War II have been tagged, primarily by former NBC News anchor and author Tom Brokaw, "The Greatest Generation." While their childhood years were marked by poverty and uncertainty, they did not have to rationalize nuclear attack drills in school, the sight of a neighbor preparing an underground bomb shelter for his family, or the very real fear that the entire population of the planet might be obliterated any day in a nuclear holocaust. That fear still exists today, of course, but we have survived a number of years, and have seen a few realistic, reasonable men negotiate and avoid the all-out nuclear war that only The Bomb could promise. The Baby Boomer generation has had to face a more terrible and immediate threat than our parents, and one wonders if Mr. Brokaw's opinion is not somehow related to the fact that our generation was the first to lose an American war... in Vietnam?

In June of 1963, President Kennedy defied the nation's banking establishment by issuing Executive Order 11110. This order essentially revoked the privately-owned and intensely secretive Federal Reserve Bank's authority to loan money to the U.S. government, or to charge interest upon its loans. When most people hear the term "Federal Reserve Bank" they think it is an agency of the U.S. government. But the Federal Reserve is a very profitable corporation, largely owned and operated by the Rothschilds and their banking associates, that prints money for the government and charges interest for every dollar it produces. In effect, Kennedy's order put the Federal Reserve Banks out of business and returned to the federal government, and specifically, the Treasury Department, the Constitutional authority to issue currency. The order established the guideline that the Treasury could create money by issuing silver certificates only as backed by "any silver bullion, silver, or standard silver dollars in the Treasury." More than $4 billion worth of $2 and $5 United States Notes were issued, and a supply of $10 and $20 United States Notes were being prepared when the President was assassinated.

After his death, United States Notes were immediately removed from circulation. Federal Reserve Notes (with no actual backing) have continued to be the accepted U.S. currency ever since. While Kennedy's order has never been rescinded, repealed, or amended, it has been universally ignored by Congress, Wall Street, and the nation's bankers and moneyed interests. As this is written, America's national debt is approximately $21.8 trillion, and virtually all of that debt has been incurred since 1963. It seems the "liberal" President Kennedy had attempted to return the United States to a financial system dictated by the Constitution, a most "conservative" goal, while wiping out the profits and authority of the Federal Reserve (company), and in doing so he created many bitter enemies among the country's money moguls. It is curious to note that *every* American president to actively oppose the Federal Reserve system has been assassinated!

In October of 1962, President Kennedy moved to eliminate a unique and very costly tax break called the Oil Depletion Allowance. Texas oil men were aghast. Under the Oil Depletion Allowance, they could offset 5 per cent of their initial drilling costs against taxes, yearly, into the endless future. It was estimated at the time that Kennedy's action would cost the industry $300 million per year, the equivalent of more than $3 billion at 21st century prices. The 8F Group, named for the hotel suite where they usually met in Houston, included a powerful array of wealthy oil men, Texas Governor John Connally and Attorney General Waggoner Carr, and many prominent Texas businessmen and bankers. They were all personal friends of Vice President Lyndon Johnson. The 8F Group financed J. Edgar Hoover's annual vacation at a Mafia-owned and run California resort, and they were confident their donations had bought favor throughout the halls of power in Washington, D.C. The Oil Depletion Allowance was considered sacred in Texas, and the oil community agreed that President Kennedy had gone too far.

Early in his presidency, JFK had issued Executive Order 10925, which required federal contractors to "take affirmative action to ensure that applicants are employed and that employees are treated during employment without regard to their race, creed, color, or national origin." His election over Richard Nixon had been a close victory, and he was very apprehensive about taking any bold civil rights stand that might alienate conservative southern democrats. Civil rights leaders, including Reverend Martin Luther King, Jr., pressured the President to issue a broad-reaching executive order that they saw as a kind of second Emancipation Proclamation, but he resisted.

In September of 1962, James Meredith announced his intention to become the first black enrolled at the University of Mississippi. In hopes of avoiding any worsening of the situation by sending military troops, Attorney General Robert F. Kennedy sent 400 federal marshals, a force he had successfully called upon to deal with previous threats to the Freedom Riders. The situation on campus turned into a violent riot, and the President had to send 3,000 troops to restore order. Two students died and dozens were injured, but James Meredith was finally able to enroll and begin classes.

Meanwhile, President Kennedy was encountering foreign policy challenges from a number of regions. His father, Joe, had been a notorious anti-Semite, and the powerful Jewish community in America was leery of the new president. JFK tried to gain Israel's allegiance by creating a close working relationship with Israel's Foreign Minister Golda Meir, but he also instructed the State Department to contact Israel's Arab enemies and explore the possibilities for a peaceful settlement of their conflicts. Tensions grew when U.S. intelligence learned that Israel had begun to develop nuclear weapons. Prime Minister David Ben-Gurion, one of the founding fathers of the State of Israel in the wake of World War II, believed an arsenal of nuclear weapons was necessary for Israel's survival. Kennedy and Ben-Gurion met briefly in 1961, and immediately detested each other.

There were suspicions that an American company, NUMEC, owned by Jewish-American Zalman Shapiro, was supplying enriched uranium to Israel's secret nuclear plant at Dimona. Aided by the Communist Chinese, the Dimona plant, supposedly an "agricultural research establishment," had begun to produce weapons-grade nuclear material. Kennedy demanded that Israel allow American inspectors to visit and examine the Dimona facility. Ben-Gurion refused and the pro-Israel lobby in America assailed the president. Tensions ran high. At Ben-Gurion's order, a bogus facility was hurriedly constructed near Dimona, and inspectors were invited in to tour a plant obviously dedicated to producing electric power. The CIA immediately recognized the ruse, and President Kennedy threatened that if Israel did not comply with his demands, "the U.S. commitment to Israel would be seriously jeopardized." Ben-Gurion, feeling immense pressure from a scandal at home, promptly resigned. Kennedy immediately wrote his successor, Levi Eshkol, demanding that American experts be allowed to examine the real Dimona site, or America's ties to Israel would be, as indicated previously, "seriously jeopardized."

In the summer of 1963, Israel's secret service, the Mossad, learned that powerful elements within America's Mafia had begun to discuss eliminating the brash young president. If that should happen, Israel knew that Vice President Johnson was, and would be, a staunch ally.

In Vietnam, the Strategic Hamlet Program was initiated early in 1962, authorizing the ARVN (Army of the Republic of Vietnam) to designate certain villages as communist strongholds within their assigned areas. In theory, these communities would benefit from increased military security and closer ties to the Saigon government, while particularly vulnerable residents would be relocated into the secure areas to protect them from the Viet Cong. In reality, many thousands of Vietnamese were relocated, taken away from their rice paddies and livestock, and also from the graves of their ancestors. The Strategic Hamlet Program was terribly unpopular with the peasants of Vietnam, but it allowed local level politicians to send their opponents away, and to seize land, crops, and livestock. The Strategic Hamlets were basically concentration camps, and they converted a great many peasants to the Viet Cong. Unrest was growing throughout South Vietnam.

John Kennedy understood the turmoil his policies were stirring in Washington, but he did not hesitate to push his agenda ahead. On June

10th, JFK signed the Equal Pay Act of 1963, a major step toward equal pay for both sexes. Later in the day he delivered one of his most important speeches at American University. As we have seen, in the wake of the Bay of Pigs disaster and the Cuban Missile Crisis, the President had secretly exchanged a series of personal letters with Soviet Premier Nikita Khrushchev. Both of these men had children, both recognized the imminent threat of nuclear annihilation, and both were under considerable pressure from their militaries to accelerate the Cold War or, if provoked, to initiate a nuclear exchange before the other country could become any better prepared. In America, a grassroots movement had gained momentum, demanding an end to nuclear development and testing, and favoring a disarmament treaty with the Soviet Union. The "arms race" had become desperate and costly, and now the "space race" was threatening to introduce nuclear warheads into the heavens. Tensions were running high around the globe.

The text of the President's speech was kept confidential in hopes it would not "set off alarm bells in the more bellicose quarters in Washington" before he made his bold suggestions public. Kennedy was becoming increasingly concerned that a *coup d' etat* might be imminent. However, Khrushchev had offered some opportunities to pursue peace between the two nations, and Kennedy was driven to respond in kind. He stood bravely and declared that America wanted to pursue peace with the Soviet Union:

> What kind of peace do I mean," he asked, "and what kind of a peace do we seek? Not a Pax Americana enforced on the world by American weapons of war. Not the peace of the slave. I am talking about genuine peace, the kind of peace that makes life on earth worth living, and the kind that enables men and nations to grow, and to hope, and build a better life for their children – not merely peace for Americans but peace for all men and women, not merely peace in our time, but peace for all time." Unafraid, he challenged his audience: And is not peace, in the last analysis, basically a matter of human rights – the right to live out our lives without fear of devastation – the right to breathe air as nature provided it – the right of future generations to a healthy existence?"

In his speech at American University, Kennedy announced that the U.S, Britain, and the Soviet Union were beginning discussions about a comprehensive nuclear test ban treaty, and, as a gesture of good faith, he promised that the U.S. would no longer conduct nuclear tests in the atmosphere so long as other countries also refrained. "We must labor on …," he said, "not towards a strategy of annihilation but towards a strategy of peace." John Kennedy realized that he had few allies among the powerful military and intelligence communities, and that his declarations would be seen as defiance of their eager propensity for war as well as a personal affront to their honor and patriotism. He had been pushed to the very edge of a nuclear nightmare, and this was his response. In what he regarded as the best interests of mankind and all life on planet Earth, he had bet everything on peace.

The speech at American University indicated that John F. Kennedy had taken a bold new stand. The former Cold Warrior had realized that only one inevitable conclusion could come from the Cold War and the arms race, and it was too awful to imagine. Kennedy knew full well that his words would be unacceptable to those powerful forces who saw war, even a nuclear holocaust, to be not just a viable path to America's future, but the most promising one. The resistance to his peacemaking was building, and he was heard to quote Abraham Lincoln on a number of occasions: "I know there is a God – and I see a storm coming. If he has a place for me, I believe that I am ready."

Civil rights clashes were erupting throughout the South. On June 11, 1963, the day after the American University speech, Kennedy intervened when Alabama Governor George Wallace stood in the way of two black students attempting to attend the University of Alabama. That evening, Kennedy addressed the nation on television and radio, proposing widespread civil rights legislation and promising federal protection of voting rights and equal access to schools regardless of the color of the student's skin. That evening, prominent NAACP activist Medgar Evers was assassinated in the driveway of his home. The next day, the President's legislation to combat poverty in Appalachia was defeated in Congress, with the majority of negative votes coming from southerners. Many black leaders criticized the President for waiting too long to embrace the civil rights movement. Tensions were increasing, both at home and overseas.

On August 7th, 1963, the President's second son, Patrick Bouvier Kennedy, was born prematurely. He died two days later, a severe blow to the First Family.

On August 28th, 1963 the Reverend Martin Luther King Jr. stood before an unprecedented crowd numbering over a quarter of a million on the National Mall, and from the steps of the Lincoln Memorial delivered his famous "I have a dream" speech. This peaceful gathering in clear view of the Capitol and the White House could not be ignored.

In the summer of 1963, tensions were also coming to a boil in South Vietnam. President Ngo Dinh Diem had held power since Vietnam was divided into North and South in 1956, but his regime was becoming more and more unpopular. A staunch anti-Communist and an unmarried Catholic, Diem was a hard-line dictator. His brother, Ngo Dinh Thuc, was the Roman Catholic Archbishop of Hue. He resided in the Presidential Palace, and was a major influence upon Diem's decisions. Ngo Dinh Nhu, Diem's younger brother, and his wife Madame Nhu also lived in the palace, and were major players on the Vietnamese political stage. Although he held no official title, Nhu directed the Can Lao political party and chose its members, all of whom swore allegiance to the Ngo family. Nhu ran the secret police, controlled the Army's Special Forces, ruled the southern portion of the country, and commanded a number of private militias. He competed with his brother Ngo Dinh Can, who managed the northern half of the country, for U.S contracts and black-market goods. Ruthless and utterly corrupt, Nhu is thought to have been responsible for 50,000 deaths and 75,000 imprisonments of "Communist suspects," or political adversaries, in the years leading up to 1963.

Since President Diem never married, his sister-in-law Madame Nhu presented herself as Vietnam's First Lady although she had been raised in a family that collaborated with the French, and she was unable to write Vietnamese. Madame Nhu pushed Diem to favor Catholics over the far more populous Buddhists, and to ban abortions, contraceptives, and divorce; to criminalize adultery, and to close many Saigon opium dens, gambling halls, nightclubs and dance halls. Extremely outspoken, she openly suggested that the United States was trying to topple the Diem government by creating unrest among the Buddhists. In June, an elderly Buddhist monk sat cross-legged in a busy Saigon intersection where he doused himself with gasoline and set himself afire. Other monks soon duplicated the act. Photographs of these incredible protests caused outrage against the Diem regime around the world. Madame Nhu did not help the situation by laughingly referring to the self-immolations as "barbecues." "Let them burn," she told a reporter, "and we shall clap our hands."

Diem and Nhu had begun a countrywide purge of Buddhists, sending the Special Forces dressed as regular army to turn the Buddhists' anger toward the army, to round up thousands, even children. While the Americans were trying to choreograph a war against the Communists, Saigon was more intent upon creating a religious war against the country's huge Buddhist population. As their atrocities became more outrageous and their victims numbered in the thousands, Diem and Nhu were becoming aware that the generals were gathering support for a coup. Nhu called upon a Polish diplomat to carry a message to Ho Chi Minh in Hanoi, suggesting the two countries begin exchanging economic and cultural gestures and perhaps reunite Vietnam as a neutralist nation like Laos. Ho had come to see America's "imperialism" as the true enemy and sent word that they would be willing to work with the South if the Americans were not involved. Before that word could be delivered, Nhu and Diem were dead.

Some historians have pointed to a number of incidents of this sort and speculated that perhaps the divisions between North and South Vietnam were not really so defining, and that the war was largely a sham that brought billions of American dollars and goods into the impoverished land. If that was the true situation, the conspirators failed to recognize the American military's eagerness to confront Communism, to test themselves and their strategic theories in a "real" combat situation, and to enjoy the opportunities for career advancement that a war would offer. All of Vietnam would soon be devastated and drenched in blood.

On October 11, 1963 President Kennedy quietly issued National Security Action Memorandum (NSAM) 263, which called for the withdrawal of 1,000 military personnel from Vietnam by the end of the year, and the "the bulk of U.S. personnel" by the end of 1965, if the war was going well. Robert McNamara described discussions between the President and members of the National Security Council as "heated debate," and said "we battled over the recommendations." Kennedy was leery of the withdrawal of 1,000 troops by the end of 1963, but McNamara countered that the declaration would quiet opponents such as Senator J. William Fulbright of Arkansas who felt that America was "bogged down forever" in Vietnam. "It reveals we have a withdrawal plan," McNamara said.

Also in October of 1963, the President announced that he would sell a large quantity of America's wheat surplus to Russia, where food shortages were having a terrible effect upon the common people. Vice-President Johnson called it "the worst political mistake he ever made," and most of the members of his Cabinet were opposed to any deal with "the enemy." To the surprise of many, the sale was greeted with optimism by a large majority of the American public. The Nuclear Test Ban Treaty was seen as a significant step toward peace, and Americans considered the wheat sale another move in the right direction. There was opposition, of course, but it was far more prevalent in Washington than in Hometown U.S.A. In spite of the opposition, the President saw hungry people and an abundance of food, and he chose to do the humane thing even if it would further anger his opponents. It was a gesture of peace, and one more entry on a long list of anti-war concessions to the Communists.

It is also noteworthy that President Kennedy repeatedly extended invitations to Premier Khrushchev that the Russian space program join with ours to work toward a joint mission to the moon. Kennedy hoped that a mutual effort of that sort might end the race between the two countries to develop ever more powerful missiles, and that it might even render the Cold War obsolete. Khrushchev told his son Sergei, about a week before Kennedy's death, that he had decided to accept the President's invitation. Kennedy never knew that, but in anticipation of a collaboration with the Soviets he issued NSAM 271 on November 12, 1963 instructing NASA to implement "my September 20 proposal for broader cooperation between the United States and the USSR in outer space, including cooperation in lunar landing programs." Not only did Kennedy envision peace with the Russians, he undertook dramatic actions to bring it about.

As mentioned above, in the autumn of 1963 President Diem's brother Nhu sent his Special Forces to attack Buddhist temples and gatherings, leaving hundreds dead, wounded, or imprisoned and tortured. He tried to blame the military and the Viet Cong Communists, but the military leaders turned against the entire Diem family regime. The generals planned a coup, and asked the U.S. for assurance that America would back a new government and continue to supply economic and military assistance to maintain their struggle against the communists. The military, the State Department, and the CIA were all fully and enthusiastically committed to a regime change in Vietnam. America's ambassador, Henry Cabot Lodge, favored the coup, and had actually defied the President when Kennedy had urged him to seek some softening by Diem that might avoid or delay the generals from taking over the country. Kennedy was very reluctant to support the generals, but finally agreed after receiving assurances that Diem and Nhu would not be harmed. On November 2nd of 1963 Vietnamese generals seized control of the country and assassinated President Diem and his brother. When President Kennedy heard this news, others in the room described his reaction as "a look of shock and dismay," "somber and shaken" and "depressed."

Less than three weeks later, on the morning of November 21st, President Kennedy told Assistant Press Secretary Martin Kilduff:

"I've just been given a list of the most recent casualties in Vietnam. We're losing too damned many people over there. It's time for us to get out. The Vietnamese aren't fighting for themselves. We're the ones who are doing the fighting. After I come back from Texas, that's going to change. There's no reason for us to lose another man over there. Vietnam is not worth another American life."

The next day, at Parkland Hospital in Dallas, Martin Kilduff officially announced that President Kennedy had died.

When he heard the news, Nikita Khrushchev wept openly. An emissary from the President was actually meeting with Fidel Castro when the news of Kennedy's assassination came. Shortly before his death, President Kennedy had also initiated a secret avenue of communications with Castro, and there was reason to be optimistic that relations between the U.S. and Cuba might be restored. Obviously distraught at the news of the assassination, Castro exclaimed, "This changes everything." It would be half a century before the U.S. resumed diplomatic relations with Cuba in 2015.

It has never been determined who pulled the trigger (or triggers) that eliminated President Kennedy, or precisely who planned and coordinated the murder. About three hours after Lee Harvey Oswald was arrested, FBI Director J. Edgar Hoover ordered his agents to stop investigating the assassination and to prepare a report stating that Oswald had been the lone assassin. Legally it was not a federal offense for an individual to murder the President, but if two or more people were involved the case would no longer be a local Dallas matter. No one has been tried for the crime, although New Orleans Prosecutor Jim Garrison did bring Clay Shaw to trial for his role in the assassination, but Shaw was acquitted.

Ironically, Allen Dulles, fired by JFK after the Bay of Pigs fiasco, was named to the Warren Commission by President Johnson and played a key role in steering the investigation of the assassination away from the CIA and other powerful Washington intelligence and military entities. The original Warren Commission report was obviously severely flawed and is considered to be part of a cover-up, as it is inconceivable that, unless purposely subverted, a group of highly respected lawmakers and responsible government officials could fail to investigate so many pieces of readily-available information, or neglect to interview so many witnesses to the crime of the century. To this day, a great many Americans believe that John F. Kennedy was murdered by a conspiracy, and so too were his brother Bobby, Reverend Martin Luther King, Jr., and possibly Malcolm

X. Over the years some questionable "conspiracy theories" have been put forth, but a great wealth of additional information has become available through dogged investigations and the painfully slow release of official government records and documents.

Today the body of knowledge concerning the assassination of President Kennedy clearly points to the likelihood that some combination of high level government officials, including recently fired officials from the CIA, along with influential individuals from the military-industrial complex, working in complicity with the FBI, the Secret Service, the Dallas police force, organized crime, and the Cuban refugee movement, murdered President Kennedy because he still maintained that war is a bad thing, and that life is sacred. In short, it seems JFK was eliminated primarily because he was a peacemaker. To the anti-Communist zealots and warmongers, and the big business interests who supplied the Pentagon, those kinds of thoughts were dangerous and must not be allowed to affect or infect government policy or the public's thinking. In her book *A Farewell To Justice*, author Joan Mellen quotes a CIA asset describing John Kennedy as "the last President to believe he could take power." Sadly, it has become clear that President Kennedy recognized the enormous threat posed by modern war machines and tactics, and had decided to use his position to work for disarmament and world peace despite the obvious personal risks.

Half a century later, our government still holds some of its records in classified vaults, and the unanswered questions about the assassination remain. Clearly America's destiny was drastically altered by the assassination of JFK. The baby boomer generation who witnessed that terrible TV weekend in November of 1963 will never see our government offer a full and honest explanation of the murder of the President. It is extremely unlikely that anyone will ever be held accountable. If the assassination was orchestrated within the government and the military, it was simply a coup d'etat. That concept was unthinkable in 1963 America, it is rarely discussed in history books or classes even today, but there is no reason America should be seen as immune to an armed overthrow of our government. As we have seen, a closely-related group of rabid anti-Communist businessmen had plotted to overthrow Franklin Roosevelt's New Deal in 1934, and to install a Fascist regime that would have sided with Hitler and Mussolini in the build-up to World War II. From those beginnings a deadly movement grew.

John Foster Dulles had been a financial friend to the Nazis, and as Secretary of State under Eisenhower he was an avid proponent of launching nuclear missiles to eliminate Communism. Dulles was the spokesman for a powerful force within the Eisenhower administration until he died in 1959. His brother Allen, who had close ties to many Nazi officials and was the staunch anti-Communist architect of the CIA's forays into regime-change via assassinations in Guatemala, the Congo, and Iran, remained an influential and powerful force long after being fired by the President over the Bay of Pigs disaster. John Kennedy recognized the powerful forces he was opposing, and he was not deterred.

Suddenly, late in 1963, Lyndon Baines Johnson had become President of the United States, inheriting all the domestic and international problems. Johnson had been chafing in his role as JFK's Vice President. He openly hated both the Kennedy brothers. Still, LBJ was a crafty politician, and he realized the nation was traumatized. Lyndon Johnson had long enjoyed powerful alliances with many of the men who had opposed Kennedy, and he hurried to change the nation's course.

Four days after the assassination, President Johnson issued NSAM-273, effectively reversing the United States' position on the war in Vietnam from Kennedy's NSAM- 263. From that moment forward the U.S. would be fully committed to help the South Vietnamese "win their contest against the externally directed and supported Communist conspiracy." Kennedy's withdrawal schedule was scrapped. LBJ's challenge was how to sell the war to the American people, especially since he would have to seek re-election in 1964. He chose to appease the generals and intelligence chiefs, and to appear to be standing strong against creeping worldwide Communism. But everyone remembered World War II and Korea and feared The Bomb, and the majority would not support anything that threatened another world war. To those in charge in Washington and Southeast Asia, the truth was not an option. They agonized over how to "spin" the escalation of the war to gain the support of the American people.

It must be noted that on December 22, 1963, just one month after the assassination of JFK, former President Truman wrote a scathing op-ed article in the *Washington Post* charging that when he had created the CIA, its only mission had been to aid the President by monitoring and consolidating intelligence from the many sources already operating, and in effect boil it down so that the President could understand and respond to it as easily as possible. He "never had any thought" when he established the CIA "that it would be injected into peace-time cloak and dagger operations." Truman observed that "this quiet intelligence arm of the President has been so removed from its intended role that it is being interpreted as a symbol of sinister and mysterious foreign intrigue." He stated that he "would like to see the CIA be restored to its original assignment," and "its operational duties be terminated." Ultimately, Truman declared, "There is something about the way the CIA has been functioning that is casting a shadow over our historic position and I feel that we need to correct it."

Would the Vietnam War have escalated into a killing ground for thousands of Americans and millions of Southeast Asians if John Kennedy had lived? By signing NSAM 263, he had clearly started the process of leaving Vietnam's future to its own people. "Vietnam is not worth another American life," he said, the day before he died. Certainly, if John Kennedy had been allowed to pursue his vision for world peace, American history since 1963 would be far different. The number of Americans in Vietnam was approximately 9,000 in June of 1962, and within a year that number had grown to almost 15,500. At the same time, government memos and reports recognized the increased influence of the Viet Cong, and also the growing political opposition to the Saigon regime. Clearly, without increased American assistance South Vietnam would soon fall to Hanoi and the Viet Cong.

In September of 1963, President Kennedy told Walter Cronkite, "In the final analysis, it is their war. They are the ones who have to win it or lose it." A week later, in an interview with NBC TV, he was asked about the possibility of withdrawal from Vietnam and replied, "I think we should stay. We should use our influence in as effective a way as we can, but we should not withdraw." Did this mean the President favored keeping military advisors in Vietnam, along with the vast array of diplomats, CIA "spooks," and political advisors who were trying to "influence" the Saigon regime? It is important to remember that the U.S. did not have combat troops in Vietnam at the time of that interview, or when he was assassinated. The President was probably aware that some of the Green Beret advisors were taking part in combat operations alongside their South Vietnamese students, but his determination to get U.S. personnel out of Vietnam, despite political opposition, was obvious.

The assassination dramatically changed the course of American policy and history, and the conduct of our government since that fateful event has been stubbornly militaristic. The sounds of gunfire at Dealey Plaza in Dallas heralded the advent of increased militarism throughout America's foreign policy, and an intense, war-like campaign against anyone who opposed the military-industrial machine. America's foreign and domestic policies have been guided by an almost religious reliance upon fear, death, and destruction ever since. Whatever JFK might have done about Vietnam and a myriad other issues had he lived, the simple fact is that he was denied the chance. The American people were deprived of their elected leader, an enormous and terrifying cover-up conspiracy was unleashed, and as a result millions of the world's people have died horribly under a barrage of American weaponry throughout all the years since. None of the Communist countries have enjoyed the affluence of the United States, and most of them have adopted an aggressive capitalist business community while maintaining strict totalitarian controls over human rights.

Chapter 5

VIETNAM: WHAT REALLY HAPPENED?

PART 3 ... 1964 – 1967

I would like to see American students develop as much fanaticism about the U.S. political system as young Nazis did about their political system during the war.

— President Lyndon Johnson, 1965.

A few hours after President Kennedy was pronounced dead in Dallas, Vice President Lyndon Baines Johnson was sworn in as President of the United States. Only four days after Kennedy was murdered, President Johnson signed National Security Action Memorandum (NSAM) - 273, a curious document that asserted America's total commitment to assisting Saigon to achieve victory over the Communists in Vietnam. This statement seems to be in direct contradiction to President Kennedy's NSAM- 263, which had ordered the withdrawal of 1,000 troops by year's end and the planning for a complete withdrawal of American forces by the end of 1965. An ominous aspect of NSAM- 273 is that it was written November 21st by McGeorge Bundy, the day *before* the murder, while most of Kennedy's cabinet met in Honolulu between November 20th and the 22nd. (The out-of-town meeting was unprecedented, but no one noticed until the events of November 22nd in Dallas.) Did Bundy know that the President would soon be eliminated? How many other top government personalities knew?

In June of 1964, General William Westmoreland was assigned to command Military Assistance Command Vietnam (MACV), replacing General Paul Harkins. Westmoreland would remain at the helm until 1968, and his management of the war is highly controversial at best. "Westy" implemented a strategy that would become known as the War of Attrition, relying upon American firepower, mobility, and air support to inflict extreme misery and pain upon the enemy until the Vietnamese people would no longer support the Viet Cong or North Vietnamese. It must be noted that this strategy would aim the most powerful military in the history of the world far more at America's ally, South Vietnam, than at the enemy Communist regime in North Vietnam.

In Vietnam, after the coup in early November of 1963, the new government was supposedly headed by former Vice-President Nguyen Ngoc Tho, but the real leader was General Duong Van Minh, known as "Big Minh." The next few months were chaotic. A number of setbacks in early 1964 were blamed upon General Minh's fledgling government, and he was overthrown by General Nguyen Khanh, who was himself overthrown a week later. Khanh regained power within days, but seven more coups in the next twelve months created chaos and allowed the American CIA and military to control the war. Of course, this political turmoil was not in the best interests of the Vietnamese people, but the expanding American presence is indicative of the immense importance the Cold War planners in Washington placed upon Vietnam. It was considered imperative that we stop the spread of Communism, and our military was assigned the task, despite South Vietnam's political turmoil.

Within a few weeks of the Kennedy assassination, the military and intelligence communities in Washington were preparing for increased activities in Vietnam. In March of 1964, Secretary of Defense Robert McNamara, a carryover from the Kennedy administration, toured South Vietnam on a fact-finding mission that was also a public relations campaign to show U.S. support for the new Khanh regime. Undersecretary of Defense William P. Bundy, a bureaucrat highly regarded by top CIA and military powers, drafted a set of recommendations for the strategic bombing, blockading, and punishing of North Vietnam, and delivered it to President Johnson. Normally, he noted, to carry out operations of this scale would require a declaration of war, but it was generally agreed that the American public would not support another formal war. What was needed was a congressional resolution that would give the President the authority to conduct military actions without declaring war. Although at that time there was no situation available that would excite such a response from Congress, a document was prepared that would, when presented, presumably win approval for the Pentagon's wish list.

Since the Geneva Conference of 1954, the CIA had orchestrated a top-secret program to destabilize and harass the Communists in both North and South Vietnam. Small groups of South Vietnamese guerrillas were trained and sent to organize dissidents in the North's hamlets and villages, to disrupt government and military operations, conduct raids, abduct or assassinate officials, gather intelligence, and distribute propaganda. The guerrilla volunteers were primarily refugees from the North who had joined the South Vietnamese army, so they were expected to be able to blend into northern communities. However, these operations proved far less than successful in the North, and nearly all of the guerrilla insurgents were either killed or captured soon after arriving.

While covert operations in Vietnam had been carried out very judiciously under President Kennedy, the Joint Chiefs of Staff recognized a fresh new opportunity under President Johnson. Within days of LBJ taking office they launched OPLAN 34-A, a more aggressive program that included greatly expanded covert sabotage and propaganda missions into North Vietnam, intensified surveillance and interception of Communist ships bringing goods into North Vietnamese harbors, increased espionage and intelligence-gathering activity, and planning for strategic air and naval attacks and even an amphibious invasion of the North by American and South Vietnamese combat troops.

The increases in activity along North Vietnam's coastline alerted Hanoi, and the Soviet Union began to install sophisticated radar and antiaircraft missiles around the key cities, and along the coast. South Vietnamese commandoes were deployed to harass the coastal radar installations so that American ships in the Tonkin Gulf, equipped with the latest intelligence equipment, could detect, monitor, and measure the North's electronic message and surveillance capabilities.

One OPLAN 34-A mission on July 30, 1964 saw four "swift boats" full of South Vietnamese commandoes leave Danang and head north along the coast. Early on the morning of the 31st, two of the boats attacked the tiny island of Hon Me, seven miles off the coast of North Vietnam. Intending to blow up a radar installation with satchel charges, they encountered stiff resistance and instead resorted to firing at the island with machine guns and cannons. At the same moment, the other two boats opened fire on the island of Hon Ngu, near the busy North Vietnamese port of Vinh. Of course, these attacks resulted in a flurry of radio signals and concentrated radar surveillance, all of which was monitored by the USS *Maddox*, cruising off shore in international waters.

In the early morning hours of August 2nd, the *Maddox* found itself surrounded by an armada of North Vietnamese junks. An intercepted message indicated that the North Vietnamese were preparing for "military operations," but the *Maddox* was ordered to remain in place. Late in the morning, in broad daylight, three Communist patrol boats approached the *Maddox*, and its Captain ordered his men to fire at them. Undeterred, the patrol boats came closer and began firing deck guns and torpedoes. Fighter jets from the nearby aircraft carrier *Ticonderoga* riddled two of the boats, and the *Maddox* damaged one. Only one North Vietnamese bullet had struck the *Maddox*, while two of the patrol boats were incapacitated and the third was sunk.

Back in Washington, President Johnson was engaged in a presidential election campaign against Arizona Senator Barry Goldwater, an Air Force Reserve fighter pilot who had advocated dropping nuclear bombs on Hanoi, Beijing, and Moscow. Johnson did not want to appear to be taking the nation to war, but he also did not want to be seen as weak or ineffective when provoked. He forbade reprisal for the North Vietnamese attack, informed Soviet Prime Minister Khrushchev of the incident, and LBJ ordered the *Maddox* and another destroyer, the *Turner Joy*, to continue the mission in the Tonkin Gulf, with instructions to fight back against any force that might attack them. He also warned Hanoi that "grave consequences would inevitably result from any further unprovoked offensive military action" against American vessels "on the high seas" off the North Vietnamese coast.

While Johnson returned to his Sunday afternoon activities, the State Department and the Joint Chiefs of Staff seized upon the opportunity to magnify the incident. A fleet of fighter-bombers was ordered to South Vietnam and Thailand, while the generals poured over maps of the installations along North Vietnam's coast, and the aircraft carrier *Constellation* was sent to the South China Sea to reinforce the *Ticonderoga*. The *Maddox* and the *Turner Joy* were ordered to venture closer to North Vietnam's coast, noting that the North Vietnamese had "thrown down the gauntlet" and should be "treated as belligerents." Meanwhile, the OP 34-A swift boats were dispatched again, to attack mainland targets. The Captain of the *Maddox* was, of course, monitoring the North Vietnamese radio traffic, and aware that the Communists were expecting the swift boat attacks. He requested permission to move away – but was ordered to stay in place in hopes the American destroyers might divert attention from the commando raids.

The night of August 4th saw the two destroyers inundated by thunder storms. Blinded, they relied upon instruments to track North Vietnamese movements. Atmospheric conditions disrupted both sonar and radar. The *Maddox* intercepted North Vietnamese communications that seemed to indicate an attack was imminent. The Captain called for air support from the *Ticonderoga*, and eight fighter jets responded. Their pilots were unable to find anything threatening, but about nine o'clock the *Maddox* and the *Turner Joy* perceived that they were being attacked with torpedoes. They began a series of evasive maneuvers, and both began firing wildly. Sonar seemed to indicate that twenty-two torpedoes had been aimed toward the two vessels, but none scored hits. The American ships continued firing until after midnight and reported sinking two or perhaps three Communist vessels. When the action was over, the Captain of the *Maddox* reported that "the entire action leaves many doubts." Not a single sailor on either American vessel, nor the pilots in the jet fighters, had actually seen or heard anything! That same evening, (for the second consecutive night in a row) two flights of Laotian fighter-bombers, commanded by the CIA and piloted by Thai mercenaries, attacked border posts in southwestern North Vietnam.

Even as those raids were taking place, President Johnson was leery of initiating any type of attack upon North Vietnam without the authority from Congress. On August 6th, he sent Defense Secretary McNamara, Secretary of State Dean Rusk, and the Chairman of the Joint Chiefs of Staff to testify before a variety of congressional committees. The record shows that McNamara blatantly lied to the Senate Foreign Relations Committee. The President's men assured Congress that the resolution they proposed, prepared weeks earlier, would prevent any increase of hostilities as the Communists would recognize America's resolve and our great military might, and they would surely avoid any further actions that might ignite hostilities.

On August 7th, the Gulf of Tonkin Resolution passed the House of Representatives by a unanimous vote, giving President Johnson authority to unleash America's military power as he saw fit to support the anti-Communist government of South Vietnam. Only two Senators dissented, Wayne Morse of Oregon and Ernest Gruening of Alaska. President Johnson immediately ordered air strikes against four North Vietnamese naval bases and a fuel storage site. Two American planes were shot down, one pilot was killed, and Lt. j.g. Everett Alvarez, Jr. became the first prisoner of war held by the North Vietnamese. In South Vietnam, General Khanh took advantage of the situation to declare a state of emergency, re-impose strict censorship measures, and clamp down on dissenters. Throughout the long years of war to come, the Gulf of Tonkin Resolution was seen to give both Presidents Johnson and Nixon the authority to wage undeclared war in Vietnam.

It must be noted that the President's attention was also torn by developments in Mississippi where, on the evening of August 4th, three civil rights workers disappeared in the vicinity of Meridian, Mississippi, after a black church had been burned. On August 6th, a rally in New York City recalled the anniversary of the atomic bombing of Hiroshima; and decried the bombing of North Vietnam and American military actions in Vietnam while nothing was being done to protect blacks and civil rights activists against hostile actions by white segregationists in the American south.

On August 29, 1964 the Defense Department issued an official casualty list, revealing that 274 Americans had died in Vietnam since December of 1961. LBJ said his administration had "tried very carefully to restrain ourselves and not to enlarge the war," and "it is better to lose 200 than to lose 200,000." On November 1, just two days before the American election, the Viet Cong infiltrated the U.S. air base at Bien Hoa, just outside Saigon, and simultaneously launched a heavy mortar attack. Five American military personnel were killed, along with two Vietnamese, and six American bombers were destroyed. The Viet Cong escaped unscathed. The Johnson administration suggested that attacks of this nature must be expected when we commit to help other nations militarily. The next day, candidate Goldwater challenged LBJ to tell the American people the truth and admit that the U.S. was involved in an undeclared war in Vietnam.

In the weeks leading up to the Presidential election, LBJ had told the American public that he was the peace candidate, the one who would prevent a wider conflict in Southeast Asia. In contrast, Republican Barry Goldwater, who declared himself a "conservative" (the first time that word was introduced into a major American political contest), charged that the President was weak and soft on Communism, and recommended using nuclear weapons and bombing to discourage the "Commies," perhaps even initiating a concentrated campaign of bombing raids upon Communist China and North Vietnam. Goldwater told American voters that "extremism in the defense of liberty is no vice," and his campaign slogan was "In your heart you know he's right." The Johnson campaign countered with images of a nuclear mushroom cloud, and the message "In your heart, you know he might." Johnson won the election by the largest margin in history, but at the edges of the campaign a new phenomenon had begun to assert itself into the national debate. Peace and anti-war rallies had cropped up in a number of American cities.

As the calendar changed to 1965, South Vietnamese troops were generally ineffective against Viet Cong (supposedly Communist) guerrilla activities, and American military advisers began to speak openly of their frustration, and even disgust, with the lack of aggression by South Vietnamese troops. However, at the end of 1964 the American military reported that the "kill ratio" of Viet Cong guerrillas compared to South Vietnamese forces was at its most favorable level since 1961. At the new year, South Vietnamese forces were soundly defeated in a battle near the hamlet of Binh Gia, despite their American-supplied tanks, artillery, and helicopters. Repeated coups and political upheavals in Saigon began to affect the mood in Congress and among U.S. military leaders in Vietnam. President Johnson ordered a campaign of sustained bombing in North Vietnam called "Operation Rolling Thunder," and the White House informed officials in a number of allied nations "in strictest confidence" via secret cables. The Soviet Union responded by building anti-aircraft installations around the North Vietnamese capitol of Hanoi.

Sunday, March 7, 1965 became an important date in U.S. history when 600 peaceful demonstrators attempted to march from Selma, Alabama to the state capital in Montgomery to protest voting rights restrictions that kept up to 98% of Alabama's blacks from registering to vote. When the march reached the Edmund Pettis Bridge they were met by a force of Alabama state police armed with billy-clubs and tear gas. The police rushed the crowd and brutally beat a number of the marchers. The attack was filmed and shown on national TV news, enraging many Americans and increasing the resolve of many civil rights and religious leaders. On March 8, 1965 the first American combat troops landed near Danang in South Vietnam.

By July, there were over 71,000 American troops in Vietnam, and General Westmoreland had requested an additional 125,000. U.S. bombers conducted 3,600 missions over North Vietnam in April, and 4,800 in June. In Washington, Undersecretary of State George Ball submitted a report to President Johnson that stated "The South Vietnamese are losing the war to the Viet Cong. No one can assure you that we can beat the Viet Cong, or even force them to the conference table on our terms, no matter how many thousand white, foreign troops we deploy." The President felt he could not turn back.

As the first American combat troops were being introduced into the war in Vietnam, it must be noted that the long-term South Vietnamese strategies would be to influence the politics of every small village and hamlet, convincing the population that the government in Saigon was, in fact, benevolent and fair, and a much better alternative than anything the local Viet Cong or distant Hanoi Communists might offer. Communities suspected of being friendly to the Viet Cong were forcefully relocated under the "Strategic Hamlet" program, the inhabitants moved to camps where their thoughts and activities might be monitored and influenced to embrace the Saigon regime. These strategies were generally called "pacification," and the concept would be a significant influence on the allies' overall strategy throughout the war. As the first Marines landed in Vietnam, their leadership agreed with the concept of pacification and began to operate in this manner. This was in direct opposition to General Westmoreland's concept of a war of attrition, and his program of "search and destroy" interventions designed to find and eliminate the enemy. The Marines sought to reinforce each pro-Saigon hamlet's sense of community by civic actions to improve the villagers' quality of life, bringing medical assistance and agricultural advice along with tactics and weaponry that would increase the community's ability to fight off Viet Cong activities.

The Marines soon found that the ARVN military and other South Vietnamese government agencies were inconsistent, corrupt, and undependable, but they believed the war could be won by working closely with the Vietnamese citizenry and improving their living conditions. General Westmoreland insisted upon a more offensive or confrontational military approach to "winning the hearts and minds" of the Vietnamese citizenry, and if some individuals were reluctant to embrace the Saigon government, they would be imprisoned or killed.

These two policies were at odds with each other throughout America's involvement in Vietnam, both in actual practice in the field and in the "image" projected to the media for distribution to the public at home and around the world. To a great degree, this was the basic dichotomy that defined and obscured America's mission in Vietnam. Were we really there to make things better for the Vietnamese people, or was our goal simply to demonstrate the awesome military response that could be expected wherever Communism might try to expand its borders? And of course, as the might of the American military came to the defense of the people of Vietnam, the American military-industrial complex enjoyed unprecedented benefits. It seemed to be a win-win situation – but not for the common people of Vietnam – who suddenly found an all-out war raging in their homeland. The "Strategic Hamlet" program's forced relocations removed thousands of peasants from their ancestral homes and the gravesites of their ancestors, actions which deeply offended their centuries-old traditions and loyalties. Herded to compounds that resembled concentration camps, many escaped to join the Viet Cong and help with efforts to drive out the American invaders and the power-hungry, disrespectful Saigon government.

General Westmoreland was busy positioning his forces to implement his war of attrition, bringing in a massive helicopter presence and surrounding the war zone with air support from aircraft carriers and fighter bases in-country, and heavy bomber bases in Thailand and the Philippines. The 4-star General planned to set up a network of hilltop firebases with artillery in remote areas, to be supplied by helicopters. These bases would send out "search and destroy" patrols looking for signs of enemy influence in the hamlets and villages. Upon finding any indication of Viet Cong activity, the "destroy" aspect of the program encouraged G.I.s to burn village homes, destroy food supplies and crops, poison the wells, and kill any local who protested. To some extent, the patrols would also serve as bait, enticing the enemy to show himself so that he could be clobbered by artillery and air support, then quickly finished off by helicopter-borne infantry. Because the enemy had no air support, the helicopters gave American forces a decided advantage. When a fight broke out, U.S. or South Vietnamese forces could immediately call in reinforcements, which the enemy could not.

Westmoreland believed American hardware, mobility, and technology would overwhelm the enemy. Of course, the famous "Huey" helicopters were the workhorses of the American strategy, but there were also Chinooks, the odd-looking, banana-shaped craft with huge rotors front and rear, and the ability to carry heavy loads of cargo. G.I.s called them "shithooks," but they proved indispensable to the mobile war.

Although the Air Force's B-52 strategic bombers were the signature weapons of the American air war, they actually dropped less than 25% of all the tons of bombs that fell on Vietnam during the war. A single B-52 carried as much as 30 tons of bombs, and its lethal payload would utterly destroy every living thing in an area .6 of a mile wide and 1.2 miles long. The U.S. conducted 126,652 B-52 missions during the Vietnam War, approximately 80% of them against targets in South Vietnam, our ally and an impoverished agricultural society approximately the size of New

Mexico. Bombers dropped both high explosives to destroy enemy infrastructure such as bridges, buildings and roads, and also "anti-personnel" bombs designed to inflict maximum damage to human flesh and bone. "Cluster bombs" contained as many as 600 small bomblets inside the main container, and those smaller anti-personnel weapons were thrown out as much as thirty feet in every direction upon impact. Each bomblet contained a cargo of ragged metal ball bearings or other shrapnel scientifically designed to impose the maximum damage to the human body. Many of America's bombs contained shrapnel made of razor-sharp plastic slivers, as plastic would not show in an X-ray. Massive 500 or 700-pound bombs left craters 300 feet in diameter and 15 to 20 feet deep, unleashing a deadly cloud of shrapnel to cut down any living thing unfortunate enough to be in the impact zone. White phosphorous bombs spewed a chemical that ignited at 86 degrees Fahrenheit and burned at 10,000 degrees until consumed. "Willie Peter" could not be extinguished, even inside human bodies, causing unimaginable damage and agonies. The sight of a human body burned by white phosphorous is not easily consigned to memory. The smoke is extremely toxic to the mouth and throat and causes the disintegration of the jawbone. White phosphorous weapons were widely used in Vietnam, in bombs and in grenades that were effective in Viet Cong tunnels because they consumed so much oxygen that VC hiding in the tunnels would be asphyxiated. White Phosphorous weapons used for anti-personnel purposes were later prohibited as chemical warfare by Protocol III of the 1980 Convention on Conventional Weapons signed by 80 nations, but the U.S. refused to sign that agreement. American forces used white phosphorous weapons in Fallujah, Iraq in 2004, and Israel has used them in Palestinian communities in Gaza as recently as 2014.

The U.S. also dropped 400,000 tons of napalm, mostly upon South Vietnam. Napalm is chemically enhanced gasoline jelly that cannot be wiped away when it lands upon skin. As the bombs land they unleash a huge fireball. This consumes all the available oxygen so anyone below who might be protected from the firestorm is asphyxiated. The main purposes of the hellish napalm in Vietnam were to burn people alive, destroy villages and crops, and also to terrorize anyone who witnessed the effects of the weapon. Napalm is also chemically configured in such a way that it causes human flesh to melt, so survivors often were grotesquely and terrifyingly deformed. Again, more than seventy percent of the most intense bombing in the history of warfare, fell upon South Vietnam, the population we were supposedly trying to save from Communist "brutality. Today, over forty years after the end of the war, thousands of Vietnamese continue to be wounded, maimed, or killed by unexploded ordnance. The Vietnamese government has estimated that it will take another fifty years to completely eliminate the leftover bombs and land mines.

From the air, converted C-123 cargo planes affectionately called "Puff the Magic Dragon" were equipped with mini-guns that fired 6,000 rounds per minute, and could supposedly put a bullet into every square inch of a football field within one minute. I never did the math to verify that legend. To watch "Puff" operate at night was just awesome, as the squiggly line of tracers formed a red trail slashing down from the sky not unlike a protracted lightning strike, while the sound was an ongoing roar like a (hypothetical) dragon's growl. Watching "Puff," you couldn't imagine that the Viet Cong would continue the fight for long. There must have been huge numbers of enemy soldiers killed under such an onslaught, and any enemy activity was bombed or strafed, so it is not likely that many of the dead were ever returned home for funerals. The North Vietnamese list over 300,000 troops missing in action during the war.

Other American weapons were equally vicious. The firebases were equipped with "beehive" *flechette* artillery rounds consisting of thousands of tiny metal arrows. Intended for use against a human wave attack, supposedly these arrows could pin a man to a tree and leave his body less than an inch thick, a deterrent sign to any other enemy in the area. The bullet from an M-16 rifle was scientifically designed to tumble so that, upon contact with any part of a human body, it would cause maximum damage. It must be noted that the assault rifles in wide use by civilians in America today utilize the same technology. They are anti-personnel weapons, not suited for hunting animals.

The American war of attrition was based upon activities that would separate the Viet Cong guerrilla warrior or sympathizer from the rest of the people in his community, a very difficult determination because guerrillas do not wear uniforms or march to battle in orderly formations. It bears repeating that the American "search and destroy" strategy required the G.I.s to sweep into hamlets and villages, rout all of the inhabitants from their huts, and then search the people and the community for any signs of enemy affiliation. Villagers judged to be friendly to the government in Saigon, and to the American presence, were usually relocated to "Strategic Hamlets," or refugee camps. Their homes and crops were destroyed so that they could not be used by enemy forces. Those peasants judged to be Viet Cong or enemy sympathizers were imprisoned, tortured or killed. Civilians were encouraged to report their neighbors for any enemy activity, and it was not unusual for someone to report a rival neighbor to the authorities. The American "search and destroy" patrols were especially prone to ambush, which caused as much as eleven percent of G.I. deaths during this period of the war.

From the first, the South Vietnamese army, or ARVN, troops were unreliable and ineffective. Low-ranking soldiers were paid little, if their commanders paid them at all. Corruption among the Vietnamese cadre was almost universal, and actual fighting was viewed by most officers as an interruption to their profiteering. Throughout the American experience in Vietnam, desertions by ARVN troops were consistently over twenty percent.

American leaders came to Vietnam intending to win the fight against global Communism, but also to establish themselves as genuine heroes wherever possible. There were thousands of offices and desks in the Pentagon, and a successful war record could earn promotion and a cherished career opportunity. Americans in Vietnam were not taught the Vietnamese language, and they were not encouraged to include Vietnamese forces in planning or operations. Eager to record successes, American leaders soon found that things worked better if the South Vietnamese were not involved. As a result, the South Vietnamese military felt marginalized and excluded from their own war, and many became resentful of the American efforts.

As an example of the changes the U.S. was bringing to the war, Operation Masher/White Wing in the heavily populated coastal region of Binh Dinh was supposed to convince the enemy that America had come to town like a gunslinger entering a Wild West saloon. Years before the term "shock and awe" was adopted to describe America's air attacks, B-52 bombers and smaller fighter-bombers combined to drop 750 tons of explosives upon the area, along with 292,000 pounds of napalm, while American gunships provided artillery support. The damage to this South Vietnamese agricultural area cannot be calculated. The Viet Cong had never experienced this level of firepower before, and the American brass fully expected them to give up the fight. Despite heavy losses, the enemy did not quit. Thoughtful U.S. soldiers began to suspect that, no matter what the cost, they never would.

In late October of 1965, the Viet Cong attacked a U.S. Special Forces camp at Pleime in the central highlands. A few days later, a force of South Vietnamese and U.S. troops stumbled upon a major North Vietnamese staging area and base of operations in the IaDrang Valley west of Pleiku.

The most significant and bloody battle of the war became famous years later via the 1992 book, *We Were Soldiers Once… And Young,* and the 2002 film, *We Were Soldiers,* starring Mel Gibson.

While the battle in the IaDrang Valley was raging, in Washington a young man walked to a position in full view of Robert McNamara's Pentagon office. On the afternoon of November 2, 1965 he put his fifteen-month-old daughter Emily safely out of harm's way, then doused himself with gasoline and struck a match. Norman Morrison had chosen to make a statement against the war in Vietnam in the same manner as had Buddhist monks in Saigon. His widow said, "He was protesting the government's deep military involvement in this war. He felt that all citizens must speak their true convictions about our country's actions." A friend said Morrison believed "that his self-sacrifice was a giving, not a taking of life." A week later, a member of the Catholic Worker movement, Roger Allen LaPorte, repeated the act outside the United Nations headquarters in New York City. In all, eight American protestors would mimic the Buddhist monks in Vietnam and die by self-immolation to protest the war.

In a 1965 memo to President Johnson, Defense Secretary McNamara warned that a military success was not imminent, and "U.S. killed-in-action can be expected to reach 1000 a month." After the war, a Defense Intelligence Agency analysis reported that "the idea that destroying, or threatening to destroy, North Vietnam's industry would pressure Hanoi into calling it quits seems, in retrospect, a colossal misjudgment." At the end of 1965 there were more than 180,000 American troops in Vietnam, and General Westmoreland was assured that he would get another 250,000 in 1966. The Pentagon requested a staggering $12.7 billion to conduct the war in 1966. American combat losses in 1965 were 808, compared to 561 killed in the previous years of activity in Vietnam since January of 1961.

1966 saw a significant increase in the bombing of North Vietnam, including attacks upon the capital city of Hanoi, and the key shipping port of Haiphong for the first time. While there were few big battles on the ground in Vietnam, in early November an operation in Tay Ninh province sought to destroy a Viet Cong command center. More than 20,000 allied troops met intense resistance by a force of the best-equipped and best-trained Viet Cong and North Vietnamese troops in South Vietnam. An estimated 1,100 enemy soldiers died during the engagement.

Terror attacks by both sides increased, especially in the Saigon area, and mines in roads and rivers took a toll on civilians as well as combatants.

A fire aboard the American aircraft carrier Oriskany killed 43 sailors and wounded 16, and another fire on board the carrier *Franklin D. Roosevelt* killed eight. At home, organized protests against the war were increasing. Campus speeches by Defense Secretary McNamara and Chairman of the Joint Chiefs of Staff Earle Wheeler were interrupted by student protests. In November, McNamara forwarded a report to President Johnson advising that additional troops deployed to Vietnam had not resulted in any significant victories, suggesting that General Westmoreland's strategy of attrition was not proving effective. The White House rejected the report.

The *New York Times* office in Saigon reported that approximately 40 percent of American economic and military assistance and goods sent to Vietnam were failing to reach their intended destinations due to widespread theft, black-marketing, bribery, and currency manipulations. The military investigated and Navy Captain Archie C. Kuntze was ultimately court martialed for his activities in setting up and operating the American port and interactions with the business community in Saigon. (Kuntze was found innocent of corruption charges; but was convicted of "Conduct Unbecoming an Officer" due to his affair with a beautiful local woman. See chapter 12.)

In early December, Viet Cong sappers entered Saigon's Tan Son Nhut Airport, a major Vietnamese and U.S. air base, and blew up a reconnaissance jet and numerous supplies and equipment. The attack was thwarted and 18 V.C. saboteurs were reported killed, but the guerrillas attacked again later the same evening, losing eleven more of their number but thoroughly disrupting the airport's operations. This type of bold attack became the nature of the ground war in Vietnam. Later in December, a massive barrage of hundreds of tons of napalm and other bombs from U.S. planes was followed up with a ground assault by 6,000 South Vietnamese troops in the Mekong Delta southwest of Saigon. 104 Viet Cong were reported killed and 18 captured, ending the year with a noteworthy success for allied forces.

In response to American bombing raids in North Vietnam, which averaged 25,000 missions per month, the Soviet Union supplied additional MiG fighters and North Korean pilots began to train North Vietnamese pilots. TASS, the Soviet Union's official news agency, and a number of other European newspapers reported that American bombs were falling upon civilian areas of Hanoi. U.S. officials issued carefully worded statements denying that civilians were being targeted. The *New York Times'* Harrison Salisbury actually went to North Vietnam to determine the truth, and his report described the effects of U.S. bombing of civilian neighborhoods in a number of North Vietnamese cities. Finally, the Defense Department acknowledged that "It is sometimes impossible to avoid all damage to civilian areas."

At the end of 1966 there were approximately 1,138,000 allied soldiers in Vietnam, including 380,000 Americans in-country and another 60,000 on ships operating off the coast. South Vietnamese forces numbered about 750,000, South Koreans 46,000, and additional troops from Australia, Thailand, New Zealand, and the Philippines made up the balance. It is noteworthy, however, that 116,858 South Vietnamese troops were reported to have deserted in 1966, as usual about 20 percent of the ARVN army.

In December, Secretary of Defense McNamara testified before a Senate committee that Communist forces in South Vietnam numbered approximately 275,000, including about 45,000 North Vietnamese regulars. The Saigon government's *Chieu Hoi* ("Open Arms") program reportedly attracted 20,242 Viet Cong to lay down their arms. Despite massive bombing of the Ho Chi Minh Trail, McNamara remarked that disease was causing more casualties along the Trail than American bombing. The total number of Operation Rolling Thunder bombing missions in 1966 was 148,000, approximately 128,000 tons of bombs were dropped, and 318 American planes were lost. The total cost of the war in 1966 was estimated at $1,200,000,000. The CIA estimated that 24,000 North Vietnamese had died as a result of the bombing, and American bombing was costing U.S. taxpayers ten dollars for every one dollar's worth of damage done to North Vietnam. The Department of Defense reported 5,008 American deaths in the war in 1966, and 30,093 wounded. The report also noted that blacks accounted for about 10 percent of the American force in Vietnam, but they were suffering approximately 16 percent of the loss of life. In his New Year's Day message, French President deGaulle urged the U.S. to end its "detestable intervention in Vietnam."

At the beginning of 1967, Great Britain proposed an international conference to seek an end to the war. North Vietnam rejected the suggestion because the NLF, or National Liberation Front, the political arm of the Viet Cong in South Vietnam, would not be invited. In his State of the Union address to Congress, President Johnson asked for a 6 percent surcharge on personal and corporate income taxes to fund the war in Vietnam for the next two years, or "for as long as the unusual expenditures associated with our efforts continue."

In New York, a U.S. Court of Appeals ruled unanimously that young men who were eligible for the draft could not be reclassified to 1-A (immediately draft-eligible) status as punishment when they were found to be protesting the war.

In Vietnam, 1967 began with a massive attack by about 16,000 U.S. and 14,000 South Vietnamese troops on an area northwest of Saigon believed to contain key enemy base camps and supply sites. Operation "Cedar Falls" was successful, with over 700 enemy reported killed and 488 captured. A massive tunnel complex was discovered and destroyed, and tens of thousands of suspected Viet Cong sympathizers were relocated to camps south of Saigon. American planes flew 1,229 bombing missions. In March, during an even larger operation designed to disrupt Viet Cong operations near the Cambodian border, America's First Infantry Division and 173rd Airborne Brigade each suffered heavy casualties. Later that month, the First Division overwhelmed a North Vietnamese force, killing 210, and then another Operation "Junction City" push resulted in 606 Viet Cong killed, and yet another at the end of March killed an additional 591. On the ground in Vietnam, the conflict had become a full-scale war.

In January, American helicopters fired upon a group of civilians in the Mekong River Delta, killing 31 and wounding 38. On February 1, American artillery and air strikes hit a hamlet near the U.S. base at Danang, killing 8 and wounding 18. On February 13, an errant U.S. artillery shell landed on a First Cavalry Division position, killing 7 G.I.s and wounding four. In March, the village of Languei was accidentally bombed by two U.S. Phantom jets, killing 83 and wounding 176. Also in March, the Defense Department announced that it intended to triple the chemical destruction of crops and defoliation of jungles "in Viet Cong areas" of South Vietnam using Agent Orange and other chemicals.

Noting that the North Vietnamese were sending large quantities of men and supplies into the South through the demilitarized zone (DMZ) between the countries, the U.S. and South Vietnam initiated a major offensive to build a fortified defensive zone along the southern boundary of the DMZ. This offensive met strong resistance, and American forces suffered heavy casualties. In April, the enemy destroyed two key bridges between Danang and Quang Tri, disrupting American supply shipments to the DMZ area.

Throughout 1967, bombing missions over North Vietnam were regularly increased, and the target areas were adjusted closer and closer to the capital city of Hanoi and the key port city of Haiphong. In February, Secretary of Defense McNamara reported that the bombing was disrupting operations in the North and slowing the movement of goods to the South.

Over 300,000 North Vietnamese civilians, according to McNamara, had been diverted to repair damage to supply lines. In March, U.S. bombers hit a key iron and steel manufacturing complex near Hanoi, the first bombing of a major industrial site in North Vietnam, and in April 86 fighter-bombers attacked two Haiphong power plants. American planes began to drop mines into North Vietnamese harbors, as American leaders were becoming amazed and concerned at the enemy's ability to continue the fight while sustaining such severe damage to their infrastructure.

At home, Senator Robert F. Kennedy proposed a plan to help end the war, suggesting that the U.S. stop bombing in the North, and both America and Hanoi gradually withdraw their troops from South Vietnam, to be replaced by an international peace-keeping force. The plan was rejected by Secretary of State Dean Rusk. In March, Chairman of the Joint Chiefs of Staff General Earle Wheeler was quoted as saying that the North Vietnamese "don't expect to win a military victory in South Vietnam" but "expect to win a victory in the war right here in Washington, D.C."

President Johnson replaced the American Ambassador to South Vietnam, Henry Cabot Lodge, with Ellsworth Bunker. In Chicago, the Reverend Martin Luther King, Jr. led an anti-war march and declared that the war in Vietnam was "a blasphemy against all that America stands for." He would become more outspoken against the war, tying it to the civil rights movement as another example of American injustice. With the coming of spring, massive protests took place in a number of American cities. A new expression of rebellion, the burning of draft cards, became widespread. The Justice Department found that 570,000 men had violated the draft laws during the war years. Of those, 206,775 names were forwarded to federal attorneys for prosecution, 25,000 were actually indicted, and more than 9,000 were found guilty. Approximately 3,250 American men went to prison for non-compliance or resistance to the draft.

In Saigon, an agreement was signed that would increase American aid to the government of South Vietnam to $700 million per year. General Westmoreland flew to Washington to request an additional 200,000 troops. The State Department began a review of policies, weighing giving Westmoreland the additional troops with the intent of "possible intensification of military actions outside of South Vietnam, including invasion of North Vietnam, Laos, and Cambodia." The other alternatives were to approve a far smaller increase in forces, which would prevent having to call up the reserves, and limiting bombing in North Vietnam to targets south of the 20th parallel. It was hoped that this might prevent any aggravation of neighboring Communist China after Beijing had reported shooting down two American Phantom jets in Chinese air space.

But Arkansas Senator William Fulbright was quoted as saying he no longer believed reports of the situation in Vietnam from President Johnson, Secretary of State Rusk, or Defense Secretary McNamara. Fulbright also suggested that some pro-war members of Congress were motivated in their enthusiasms by the vast amount of defense contracts flowing to their home industries. Questions about the conduct of the war were becoming common in Washington, and even some in his administration began to send the President suggestions that he curtail the bombing and troop increases. A significant number of Americans were becoming opposed to the war, and public protests were becoming commonplace. In August, Abbie Hoffman, Jerry Rubin, and Stewart Albert infiltrated the sacred halls of capitalism, the New York Stock Exchange. From the balcony they scattered thousands of real and play-money dollar bills onto the trading floor, completely disrupting business as the stock traders on the floor abandoned trading to scurry and scuffle after the money falling from above.

In Vietnam, activity increased throughout the northernmost areas of South Vietnam, near the DMZ, in the second half of 1967. Initially, U.S. Marines defeated a force of North Vietnamese regulars in the mountainous area near a small airbase near Khe Sanh. North Vietnamese artillery pounded the American Marine base at Con Thien. Frustrated, a force of 5,500 U.S. and South Vietnamese troops invaded an area of the DMZ to destroy enemy equipment and supply routes leading to the South. American losses from the activity near the DMZ were considerable. On Hill 174 near Con Thien, for example, 164 Marines were killed and 999 wounded. Bombing in North Vietnam began to target air bases where MiG fighters were stationed, and railroad yards and electrical power stations within the city of Hanoi. Bombing missions in the harbor at Haiphong resulted in damage to British and Russian ships. The U.S. apologized. By late summer, ground actions near Con Thien intensified, with heavy losses to both sides. Enemy activity was also increasing in the Central Highlands, causing heavy casualties to U.S. forces.

In July, Secretary McNamara flew to Saigon to discuss the actual number of additional troops needed with General Westmoreland. McNamara was a numbers cruncher, and he observed that the American forces in Vietnam were not being utilized effectively, noting that of the 464,000 Americans currently in-country only 50,000 were actually available for combat. McNamara informed Westmoreland that his request for 200,000 additional troops had been denied, but he had approved a maximum of 543,000, a sizable increase from the 431,000 Americans currently in-country. Back in Washington, prominent Senator Mike Mansfield suggested cutbacks to America's commitment to Vietnam, and Republican Senator George Aiken of Vermont suggested that the administration should pay more attention to Senators than "certain military leaders."

President Johnson personally gave approval to bomb a number of additional targets in or near civilian populations in Hanoi and Haiphong. In a further blow to America's enthusiasm for the war, a fire aboard the aircraft carrier *Forrestal* off the coast of North Vietnam killed 134 U.S. sailors and injured 62, damaging or destroying 63 of the 80 airplanes on board. Still, there was considerable public support for the war and efforts to stop the spread of Communism. "Hard-hats," construction workers wearing plastic helmets, harassed and even got physical in opposition to anti-war protest demonstrations in New York and other cities. The war was dividing the American public, and passions were extreme.

In July, a Gallup poll found that over half of the American people thought the U.S. was either losing the war in Vietnam or making no progress. 52 percent disapproved of LBJ's strategies for conducting the war. Opposition to the war was growing at home and around the world. In Sweden, an "International Tribunal on War Crimes" accused the U.S. of aggression in Vietnam and "widespread, deliberate and systematic bombing of civilian objectives." Even Defense Secretary McNamara was becoming discouraged about the lack of real progress in the war. He had gathered data and information from a broad range of Washington and Saigon authorities, a report later known as the Pentagon Papers. Clearly, the prospects for a military success in Vietnam had become grim. McNamara suggested to President Johnson that the U.S. cut back its bombing to the 20th parallel, limit troop deployments to only 30,000, and consider a more limited objective in Vietnam. The Joint Chiefs responded by suggesting serious increases in troop strengths and bombing, suggesting that the cutbacks might "no longer provide a complete rationale for our presence in South Vietnam." A national "Teach-in" at 80 colleges and universities discussed and exposed the history of American involvement in Vietnam, and current policies and military tactics and their effects upon the country. United Nations Secretary General U Thant expressed concern that China might enter the conflict, leading to World War III.

In September, a widely anticipated election in South Vietnam returned Nguyen Van Thieu to the Presidency, with flamboyant Air Force Commander Nguyen Cao Ky as Vice President. The election was surprisingly peaceful, although after results were announced the Buddhists held demonstrations. Bombing in the North intensified, with attacks upon railroads, bridges, and air bases where the enemy's MiG fighters were based. Air Force officials suggested that many MiGs were flying out of air fields in Communist China, but President Johnson refused to allow bombing raids into China. American bombing raids had expanded to destroy MiG bases and areas of Hanoi and Haiphong that had not been attacked previously, but the cost was dear as a number of American planes were shot down. North Vietnam appealed to "all governments" to help stop the U.S. bombing, citing civilian casualties and destruction of homes and schools.

This was a most difficult period for President Johnson. Various interest groups, not the least of which was the Pentagon, demanded a variety of bold and expensive actions to create some semblance of progress in Vietnam, which would hopefully calm the storm of public division and dissent in the streets of America. The war was not going well. After the bold move of introducing American combat troops into the situation, there were a lot of flag-draped coffins coming home, but virtually no prospect of a military victory in the foreseeable future. LBJ had carefully sidestepped the real cost of the war for a time, but in his 1967 State of the Union address he had to ask the American public for another tax increase to fund the war, with no offsetting real progress to report.

For years, the infiltration of troops and supplies from North Vietnam across the DMZ and down the Ho Chi Minh Trail had frustrated the generals. Massive bombing of the industrial centers in the North, and rail and shipping targets, had proven largely ineffective, but costly. In fact, an in-depth study of Operation Rolling Thunder had concluded that American bombing in the north had "no measurable effect" on the enemy's ability to supply its army in the South and admitted there was evidence that the massive bombings had resulted in increased resolve in North Vietnam. Pressed by their Commander-in-Chief, the Pentagon came up with two suggestions. With a significant increase in men and materials, they could invade North Vietnam and crush the war effort at its source. However, the risk that China might intervene, as it had done in Korea when American forces had invaded the North, was a major concern. Communism as a worldwide movement was stronger now, and tensions were high. It wouldn't take much to ignite World War III.

Without resorting to all-out and unlimited war, LBJ's key advisers suggested that a real victory in Vietnam would not happen soon, if at all.

Westmoreland's war of attrition had seemed a solid strategy a year and a half before. Certainly, America's state-of-the-art military, with its unparalleled firepower, mobility, tradition and commitment would make short work of the primitive enemy, especially if we were partnered with the South Vietnamese ARVN forces. America's war machine would inflict damages upon the Communists that they could not afford, and they would soon collapse. It was terribly difficult for Washington to accept that we were simply unable to kill and destroy enough to defeat the enemy. We simply but certainly could not break their will to kick us out.

In September, a delegation of American activist leaders met with North Vietnamese leaders in Czechoslovakia to discuss possible ways peace might be accomplished. Seven of the Americans were invited to visit North Vietnam and view the damage to civilian areas, and they reported what they had seen upon returning home. Predictably, they were viewed as traitors by The Establishment, and their eyewitness reports had no effect upon the conduct of the war. However, throughout the summer of '67, most of the prominent groups in the anti-war movement had come together to plan a massive protest for October. Always entertaining, Abbie Hoffman announced that a huge throng of people were coming to Washington for the purpose of focusing the power of their love and "levitating" the Pentagon and changing its color to orange. The "Old Left" counterculture had struggled to maintain a "respectable" image, discouraging anti-social behaviors like ragged or dirty dress, pot smoking at demonstrations, and any overt demonstrations by pro-Communist groups. But the movement had become frustrated, and Abbie Hoffman and others proclaimed a "New Left" that welcomed everyone to the resistance movement and hoped to tear down most of America's institutions and allow the people to create a new, free-fall society. Anything would be better than The Establishment.

The government, of course, heard these pronouncements and took precautions, including infiltrating a large number of informers and saboteurs into the movement. As the October date approached, the CIA and FBI set up elaborate electronic surveillance equipment around the Mall in Washington and the Pentagon across the Potomac River in Virginia. Radio and telephone communications between the protest leaders would be monitored, jammed, or even "hacked" with false messages designed to confuse and disrupt the demonstration. The defense of the capital city was planned to operate as a military-style campaign. Hundreds of police officers from all around the region were teamed with the National Guard and about 10,000 soldiers to defend the Pentagon and keep it firmly on the ground. Mysteriously, all across the country, buses that might have been used to transport protestors to Washington were unavailable, but a wall of buses was set up to circle the White House and keep the protestors away.

The crowd for the October protest was estimated at somewhere between fifty and a hundred thousand. Daniel Ellsberg, a trusted Rand Corporation analyst, watched the protest alongside Robert McNamara from the Defense Secretary's office windows. The protest, perhaps inspired by Abbie Hoffman's off-the-wall nature, took on a number of bizarre aspects. The famous photograph of a female demonstrator putting a flower into the barrel of a soldier's rifle became symbolic of the deployment of armed soldiers against the civilian protestors, and indeed, the protestors were surprised to find that many of the soldiers were not adversarial to their cause.

At midnight the protestors were informed that their permit had expired and they had to clear the area. When they didn't hurry to comply, the authorities released tear gas and resorted to some force. Just under 700 of the demonstrators were arrested, including Abbie Hoffman, and a few hundred more were detained but released. Writer Norman Mailer was among those arrested and jailed, and his book *Armies of the Night*, describing his experience, later won a Pulitzer Prize. The Pentagon remained firmly attached to the ground and did not change color.

President Johnson became incensed, and authorized various government agencies to use unprecedented measures against the opposition, which he described as a group of Communists. LBJ ordered the CIA to look into the trips to Czechoslovakia and North Vietnam as indications that the opposition to the war was under the influence of foreign powers, but they were unable to find any evidence. The President would not be deterred, and committed a massive force of government, military, and intelligence forces against the unruly crowd of American citizens attempting to exercise their constitutional right of Freedom of Speech. On the other side of the globe, Johnson ordered yet another increase in the bombing of Hanoi and Haiphong.

Way back in 1964, General Westmoreland had suggested building a barrier across the southern border of the DMZ and the eastern portion of Laos where the Ho Chi Minh Trail shipments were staged. Westy thought this barrier could be manned by an international force protected, of course, by American Marines. The idea had generated no enthusiasm, but perhaps it deserved a second look, with some high-tech enhance-ments. This was the second alternative, and LBJ personally approved it with NSAM-358, the only hands-on directive related to the war that John-son issued after being elected President. In September, Defense Secretary McNamara announced plans to construct an electronic barrier across the southern edge of the DMZ, to monitor and deter enemy movements. Once the "McNamara Line" was in place, any enemy activity could be dealt with by artillery and air strikes. The barrier would consist of remote acoustic and chemical sensors and anti-personnel mines. The latest high-tech mines were not detectable by mine detectors, and they fired plastic pellets which would not be detectable by X-rays. The initial estimate was that 240 million of these new mines would be required in the first year. The proposed budget also called for over $2 billion to implement the bar-rier, and something over $1 billion per year to maintain the system and modify it as the enemy learned ways to defeat it.

The Pentagon was not enthusiastic about the plan, preferring to in-crease the number of conventional troops on the ground in Vietnam, and continue all the requisite air, naval, and covert activities that had not proved effective to this point. Construction of the McNamara line was actually begun before the Defense Secretary's public announcement, and the barrier was expected to be completed in July of 1968. Marines as-signed to plow the broad strip immediately came under intense fire. Gen-eral Westmoreland expressed his disappointment with the performance of the Marines – and ordered them to do a better job.

In October, the Marine base at Con Thien came under siege from North Vietnamese artillery followed by a ground attack that was only re-pelled after fierce hand-to-hand combat. A month later, the largest-scale and bloodiest battle of the war to date occurred in the Central Highlands around the American base at Dak To. The battle began when Americans from the 4th Infantry and the 173rd Airborne found large numbers of North Vietnamese troops moving into positions surrounding the base. Intense fighting went on for almost three weeks and climaxed with a hard-fought struggle for Hill 875, which was won by the Americans. Casualties on both sides were heavy.

Opposition to the war was growing across America, including with-in the government and Lyndon Johnson's Democratic party. There were massive demonstrations in Washington, including the October march upon the Pentagon. Similar protests were occurring throughout America, Europe, in Japan, and in many other corners of the world. The President was becoming tired and concerned. He gathered a number of America's most distinguished leaders and statesmen to a secret meeting and simply asked them, "How do we unite the country?" The response was that the White House should find "ways of guiding the press" to offer reports from the war zone that would convey the perpetual optimism of the Generals and the Pentagon. It never dawned on them that the reporters on the scene might be telling the truth. Reports from the war, they said, needed to be more optimistic.

Later that month, LBJ summoned General Westmoreland home to explain and defend the war to Congress and the press. The General built no bridges by declaring that "the protests and unpatriotic acts at home" were giving the enemy hope that they might "win politically that which he cannot win militarily." Anti-war congressmen objected, and the General appeared before a joint session of Congress in hopes of gathering support for the war. In an interview with the press, Westmoreland was quoted as saying, "We have reached an important point, when the end begins to come into view," and in a televised news conference he stated emphatically that he could see "light at the end of the tunnel." It was actually an approaching train.

Chapter 6

Vietnam: What Really Happened?

Part 4 ... 1968

*Our brave young men are dying in the swamps of Southeast Asia.
Which of them might have written a poem? Which of them might have
cured cancer? Which of them might have played in a World Series or
given us the gift of laughter from the stage or helped build a bridge or a
university? Which of them would have taught a child to read? It is our
responsibility to let these men live... It is indecent if they die because of
the empty vanity of their country.*

– Robert F. Kennedy, 1968

Lyndon Baines Johnson was an experienced and skillful politician, one who could twist an arm or pour a drink to cajole an adversary into seeing things his way. He wanted to be known for his domestic policies, the Civil Rights Act, the War on Poverty, the various social programs that would leave America a "Great Society." Unfortunately, he never quite got his hands around the war in Vietnam, and it ultimately proved his undoing. Johnson was walking a slender tightrope. On one side, he found himself leading a head-on confrontation against Communism in which he could not fail and "lose" Vietnam. However, he was of course aware of the Chinese invasion of Korea a few years previous, and he could not risk bringing Communist China into a war in Southeast Asia that might easily become World War III. In October of 1964, China had detonated its first nuclear weapon and become the fifth nation with The Bomb. President Johnson needed to stop Communist expansion in Vietnam, but avoid expanding the conflict to an all-out war. A veteran political figure, he also had to think about winning re-election, and maintaining the Democratic Party's dominance in an election year.

At the end of 1967, protest, dissent, and resistance to the war were widespread in America, taking a great toll on Johnson's domestic agenda. There were few signs of progress in Vietnam, and the generals expected the war to go on for some time. LBJ wanted it over by Christmas of 1968, and General Westmoreland repeatedly asked for more troops and equipment, but he would not predict when the war might be won. Since February of 1965, the American and South Vietnamese air forces had dropped more than 1,500,000 tons of bombs on Vietnam, including a substantial portion on South Vietnam, our supposed ally and an impoverished, agricultural country. In 1967 alone, the U.S. had lost 779 airplanes in southeast Asia. In South Vietnam, we had lost 500 helicopters in combat and 1,000 helicopters and planes due to accidents. The war had cost $21 billion in '67, plus 9,353 American lives, and just under 100,000 wounded. The ARVN had reported 11,135 killed, and our other allies had lost 189. The American military's "body count," the only measure of progress in this guerrilla war, claimed to have killed 90,400 enemy in 1967, but no one really believed that statistic.

In November of 1967, Defense Secretary Robert McNamara gave President Johnson a personal report in which he argued against any further escalation of bombing or adding American troops to the struggle in Vietnam. McNamara encouraged the President to shift the responsibilities of the war to the South Vietnamese. He had studied the history of the war in great detail, compiling inputs from a variety of involved sources into the document that would come to be known as the Pentagon Papers, and he had concluded that the government of South Vietnam was "political quicksand," and that "military force ... especially when wielded by an outside power ... just cannot bring order in a country that cannot govern itself." A number of LBJ's closest advisors were echoing those sentiments, but the President could not have a Secretary of Defense steering the war while doubting both the strategy and the ability of the Saigon regime. President Johnson announced that Robert McNamara had been appointed to be the President of the World Bank. Clark Clifford, an old friend and ally of LBJ, would be the new Defense Secretary.

The President was also hearing optimistic reports from a number of sources, most notably national security advisor Walt Rostow, who viewed the American involvement in Vietnam to be necessary and heroic. LBJ felt the public needed to hear more positive news about the war, so he set up a subcommittee group within the National Security Council to be headed by Rostow. The Vietnam Information Group (VIG) was created with the specific intention of influencing public opinion about the war. Today we would say the purpose was to "spin" the news from Vietnam to give the impression of progress and offset the influence of the growing anti-war movement. One issue immediately identified by the VIG was the controversy between the CIA and the military leadership in Vietnam over the "order of battle," or the number of enemy troops facing the American forces. In March of '67, Chairman of the Joint Chiefs Wheeler had instructed General Westmoreland that data reflecting enemy troop strengths, especially those showing increases in the enemy's strength, would undermine support for the war at home. After that, Westmoreland kept a rigid control over reports of the enemy numbers by excluding whole categories of Viet Cong. This controversy came to a head at a conference in Saigon in September of 1967, and the military's lower numbers became official. The CIA believed there were as many as 600,000 enemy troops opposing the U.S. effort in Vietnam, but the agreement reflected only 208,000 total, and 118,000 North Vietnamese regulars. After the war, documents released by the North Vietnamese showed that they had 278,000 combat troops in South Vietnam in preparation for the Tet offensive. The VIG debated ways to feed the lowered numbers to the public in a manner that would show increased "body counts" as an indication of real military successes in Vietnam, but not raise questions about how so many enemy combatants had come to be in the South in the first place.

North Vietnamese troops and supplies continued to flow into the South across the DMZ in large quantities. In 1966, as part of the effort to construct the McNamara Line, General Westmoreland had ordered a small Special Forces camp and an old French airstrip be converted into a significant Marine base camp. Located about 14 miles south of the DMZ and 6 miles from the Laotian border, the base at Khe Sahn was in a remote area and surrounded by heavily forested mountains. In January of 1968, large numbers of North Vietnamese regulars began massing around the base. The new audio sensors had picked up the signs, and the Marines felt something big was coming.

On January 21, North Vietnamese artillery in the hills surrounding Khe Sanh began a bombardment, hitting the base ammunition dump and killing 18 Marines, wounding another 40. The heavy guns had been hand-carried into place through the mountains and forests, and they were very effective. The 3500 Marines and 2100 South Vietnamese were pinned down day and night by constant, heavy siege as enemy troops dug trenches to within a few yards of the base perimeter. Estimates of the enemy force surrounding the camp at Khe Sanh varied from 15,000 to 80,000, but it was the artillery that did the most damage. "The eyes of the nation, the eyes of the entire world, are on that little brave band of defenders who hold the pass at Khe Sanh," President Johnson said, and he had a scale model of the Khe Sanh area built in the White House basement. The President prowled the basement in his bath robe at all hours of the night, eager for any word from Westmoreland, who was sleeping on a cot at MACV headquarters and under orders to personally report on the battle every day. LBJ told General Wheeler, the Chairman of the Joint Chiefs, "I don't want any damned 'Dinbinphoo'." The terrain and the situation reminded everyone of the French defeat at Dien Bien Phu. General Westmoreland was extremely concerned, especially as other events took place in the days to come, and asked permission to use tactical nuclear weapons if "necessary," reminding the President that the two atomic bombs dropped on Japan at the end of World War II "had spoken convincingly." That permission was denied, and we can only wonder about how the general intended to drop a nuclear weapon on Khe Sanh without making matters a whole lot worse for the thousands of Americans trapped there by the siege.

The North Vietnamese had carefully positioned their artillery in caves in the mountains overlooking the Marine base, so that the guns could be rolled out, fired, and then rolled back into the caves to escape the American bombing and artillery response. North Vietnamese regulars were not so fortunate, and after the war ended it was disclosed that some units lost as much as 90 percent of their men. The siege would ultimately last 77 days, until April 6th. Throughout that period, American planes dropped an average of 5,000 high explosive and napalm bombs daily, or the equivalent of five times the explosive power of the two atomic bombs dropped on Hiroshima and Nagasaki. It was the heaviest bombardment of any target in the history of war. The Marine artillery returned fire with as many as 2600 rounds per day. All of the ammunition and food had to be brought in by air, and two U.S. cargo planes were hit on the runway, with considerable loss of life and obstruction to future flights, but the Marines fought on valiantly.

The siege of Khe Sanh began on January 21, 1968. On the evening of the 22nd, the TV show *Laugh-In* appeared (in America) for the first time with its cutting-edge humor and clever social commentary. The very next day, to add to the anxiety at the White House and the Pentagon, an American spy ship operating off the coast of North Korea was captured. The *USS Pueblo's* crew would be held for eleven months, starved and tortured by the North Koreans. They were finally freed in December, but the ship remains on display as a Korean museum to this day.

One week later, on the evening of January 30, Vietnam appeared calm. A cease fire was in effect in honor of Tet, the Vietnamese New Year and the most important of all Viet holidays. Suddenly, in the dead of night, every major city and town came under attack simultaneously. A squad of Viet Cong sappers even penetrated the U.S. Embassy in Saigon, and another got into Tan Son Nhut air base and penetrated within a few hundred yards of Vice President Ky's home. So many calls for help were coming across the American radio net that it broke down. Destruction was heavy. In every population center, the Communists had lists of civilians who worked for or with the Americans, and they went door to door and tortured, and killed as they worked their way down the list. The entire country was in chaos.

Historically, most of the cities were re-taken within a week, and the Communists suffered severe losses. They had expected the citizens to come out of their homes and join the fight, and that never happened. In the ancient Imperial city of Hue, it took almost a month of grueling house-by-house fighting to regain control, and mass graves were unmistakable evidence of the enemy's brutality. Militarily, the Tet Offensive was a defeat for the Viet Cong and North Vietnamese, but psychologically the logistics of the attacks cast an unmistakable spotlight upon the American leadership's lack of any meaningful intelligence capability or military strategy. The "light at the end of the tunnel" had been exposed as wishful thinking or political grandstanding, and the realities came home to America in an unprecedented and shocking cargo of flag-draped coffins.

Clearly, the American command in Vietnam was stunned by the Tet Offensive. There had been unmistakable signs, most notably sightings of large forces of North Vietnamese and increased supply shipments down the Ho Chi Minh trail. Stanley Karnow, in his landmark book *Vietnam* relates that "a West Point textbook on the war, published years later, attributed the 'complete surprise' achieved by the Communists to a U.S. "intelligence failure ranking with Pearl Harbor." Westmoreland predicted an enemy offensive, but when in-country intelligence reports indicated the current enemy force at over 600,000 men the good General ordered that any and all reports back to Washington be capped at 350,000. In 1982, this situation was presented in a CBS-TV documentary titled *The Uncounted Enemy: A Vietnam Deception*. Westmoreland sued CBS for "besmirching his honor," and the case went to trial late in 1984. The first of

Westmoreland's former staff to testify was Colonel Gains Hawkins. Reportedly, twenty-seven additional field grade officers were waiting in line to say that yes, those were the orders they had received from "Westy," and the artificially low numbers had made the Tet Offensive much more effective for the enemy. Immediately after Col. Hawkins' testimony Westmoreland dropped his suit and CBS agreed not to "further question the General's honor." Not surprisingly, no one was ever held accountable for the oversights, errors, or mistakes that resulted in the unnecessary death and destruction of the Tet offensive. Today, video of that CBS program is virtually unobtainable.

The Tet offensive was widespread and initially extremely successful, and the American media reported it as it happened. In Saigon, at the height of the battle, National Police Chief General Nguyen Ngoc Loan walked up to a captured Viet Cong, put his pistol to the man's temple and blew him away. The encounter was filmed by an American news photographer, and widely broadcast throughout the U.S. on February 2. It became one of the most iconic images of the war. On February 27, CBS-TV news anchor Walter Cronkite, "the most trusted man in America" reported, "To say that we are closer to victory today is to believe, in the face of the evidence, the optimists who have been wrong in the past." President Johnson remarked that if he had lost Walter Cronkite, he had lost the country.

In all the history books I've seen, the emphasis has been on the impact the Tet Offensive had upon "the best and the brightest" in Washington, and upon Walter Cronkite and the American public. There has been scant recognition of the impact of that enemy action upon us, the American troops in foxholes in Vietnam. We felt we were experiencing another Pearl Harbor, another devastating sneak attack that killed unprecedented numbers and destroyed equipment, supplies, morale, and our leadership's strategies. Our best hope of getting home in one piece was the skill and understanding of our officers, and we suddenly had to face the sobering fact that they had "no freaking idea" what was going on, or they didn't care. Ol' General Westy smiled and recited his unrealistic and irresponsible litany about imminent victory, and we heard the news reports of V.C. sappers in the embassy in Saigon and watched and heard the sounds of battles raging in every city and town throughout the country, and we were scared more than ever before. Frightened, bewildered, and feeling betrayed, we smoked C-ration cigarettes and laughed at somebody's suggestion that Westy was just a cheerleader, that he should take off his four tarnished stars and put on one of those overstuffed Vietnamese padded bras and a short skirt before he took his pom-poms back to Washington to report to Congress the next time.

The war was lost. We had felt it from the first day in-country, and it was blatantly obvious now. And no one wanted to be among the last few to die for a lost, and utterly absurd, cause. No one wanted to see any more killing, any more destruction. All of the blood and napalm and explosives were accomplishing nothing. Certainly, our presence in-country was not bene-fitting the common people of Vietnam in the slightest. Quite the contrary. Politicians and Generals in Saigon, Washington, and, we suspected, even Hanoi, a few civilian contractor firms, and a number of corporations with lucrative Defense contracts were profiting while Americans and Vietnam-ese peasants were dying horribly and in ever-increasing numbers. We wanted to go home. And, because the brass would not admit that the war was lost, because they recited Westmoreland's ridiculous lies, we resented them and called them F***ing lifers. The morale of the American troops in Vietnam was the greatest casualty of the Tet offensive, and as hostages, as slave labor, many of us expressed our anger in small acts of sabotage and defiance, kept our heads down as we crossed off the days until we could catch that flight to home. There was no enthusiasm for the war; there were only three realities and they were survival, death, or dismemberment. We trusted our buddies and looked out for them, as they looked out for us. The World was far, far away.

On February 5, a massive force of North Vietnamese followed nine Russian-built tanks and overran a camp at Lang Vei, about seven miles west of the besieged Marine base at Khe Sanh. Over 300 allied soldiers died, including eight Americans. The terrain was so hilly that the tanks were unable to travel to Khe Sanh. Instead, the North Vietnamese began to dig trenches closer and closer to the besieged Marines. At one point there was hand-to-hand fighting, but the Americans held. The trenches were devastated with napalm every day, but they were dug closer every night. Westmoreland called in the heaviest concentration of bombing in the history of warfare, with the colorful name Operation Niagara. The hills around Khe Sanh were littered with electronic sensors from the Mc-Namara Line initiative, and they proved very effective for monitoring the movements of enemy ground troops and calling in effective artillery and air strikes. Still, the siege dragged on and on, and the press reports showed Americans caught in a desperate situation.

On February 8, officers of the South Carolina Highway Patrol con-fronted a group of about 150 student protestors at South Carolina State

University in Orangeburg. The students had been protesting segregation in the city, and especially at a nearby bowling alley, for two nights. Things got out of hand, a policeman was struck by a thrown object, and the police opened fire at close range. Two college students and one high school student were killed, and twenty-eight were wounded. Most of the wounded were shot in the back as they tried to escape. Once again, racial tensions were heightened across the country. This was the first time the authorities had actually fired upon a protest, and the incident seemed to signal to both sides that the stakes of speaking out had been raised.

Of course, after the Tet Offensive there was a flurry of activity throughout Vietnam. On March 16 an American platoon entered the hamlet of My Lai-4. The Americans had suffered numerous casualties since Tet, and the area around My Lai-4 was thought to be a Viet Cong stronghold. Charley Company had lost twenty percent of its members to snipers and booby traps in the past few weeks without ever sighting an enemy soldier. The night before Captain Earnest Medina had ordered them to "kill everything" in the village, or "kill everything that breathes." When asked, "Are we supposed to kill women and children?" Medina responded, "Kill everything that moves." The next morning, Charlie Company encountered no enemy fire as they approached the village. They found only civilians peacefully fixing breakfast. While the army has steadfastly refused to reveal precise numbers of Vietnamese killed that morning, a 1970 study concluded that 347 Vietnamese men, women, and children died. Most were simply herded to three drainage ditches and gunned down, but some were killed when grenades were tossed into their huts without bothering to look inside. One woman was hauled out of a hut by her hair and shot in the head, while another emerged from a hut with her baby in her arms. The mother was shot, and when the baby hit the ground it was hit with a burst of M-16 fire. Numerous women and young girls were raped, dead bodies were mutilated, throats cut, ears and tongues cut off for souvenirs, homes were burned, and the community's drinking water was fouled.

Experienced helicopter pilot Hugh Thompson was covering the operation at My Lai that morning, hovering low to try to draw enemy fire. There wasn't any. As he watched the action below, Thompson realized he was watching a massacre. He landed his chopper between a group of G.I.s and some terrified villagers. Thompson ordered the Americans to back off, and loaded four Vietnamese adults and six children, including one severely wounded boy, into the chopper and flew them away to safety. On the ground, at least four G.I.s took unorthodox actions to save approximately 80 civilians. They were never honored by the military. Although there was not a single shot fired in opposition, the U.S. army reported a victory over a "significant enemy force" with 128 Viet Cong killed without the loss of any American lives.

There were actually 4 My Lai villages in the hamlet of Song My, called "Pinkville" by the Americans. At the same time as the massacre was happening at My Lai-4, a similar action was taking place at nearby My Khe-4, killing approximately 100 more Vietnamese civilians. The army very systematically tried to cover up these atrocities, but they were (later) revealed by Pulitzer Prize-winning author Seymour Hersh. Although numerous American military officers were charged, only Lieutenant William Calley was tried. Found guilty, Calley was sentenced to life in prison but President Nixon released him and allowed him to remain under house arrest in his quarters until he was paroled after serving just forty months.

There is no official record of the term "Mere Gook Rule" being used during the investigation or trial, although Hersh mentions it in his book *Cover Up*. The "Mere Gook Rule" or MGR was an unofficial directive by Americans in Vietnam that Vietnamese citizens were "mere Gooks" and less than human. Therefore, any abuse, rape, pillage, murder or other atrocity against them could and would be condoned. The massacre at My Lai would have been recorded as just another victory over the V.C. were it not for a soldier named Ron Ridenhour who was not at My Lai, but heard his comrades describing what had happened. When he returned to the *World* he bucked the tide and reported the massacre. Ridenhour's campaign attracted the attention of Seymour Hersh, who investigated and published articles about the massacre. Finally, an article in *Life* magazine, including pictures taken at My Lai by army photographer Ron Haeberle, attracted sufficient public outcry that the military was forced to account for its actions. Unfortunately, My Lai was far from the only action of its type in Vietnam, but very few atrocities were investigated. The American public did not want to know, and the American military certainly did not want these situations to be revealed. The American Way of Waging War had come to fruition.

In the aftermath of the Tet offensive U.S. advisors realized that Saigon's pacification program was not working. Clearly the enemy had developed a vast infrastructure of sympathizers, "enemy civilians," and guerilla fighters throughout South Vietnam. While the military continued to view the war as a traditional confrontation between standing armies, the CIA and intelligence community increased their influence, urging the South Vietnamese local militia and police forces to accept more responsibility by monitoring and controlling enemy activities in the hamlets, villages, and neighborhoods throughout the country. The Phoenix Program created local Vietnamese committees to monitor grass-roots activities and pinpoint key enemy agents and Viet Cong cadres. Anyone identified as being V.C., or suspected of having knowledge or information about enemy activity would be "neutralized" either by capture and imprisonment, torture, or assassination. The local units were originally called "Counter Terrorism Teams," but the CIA quickly realized that any use of the word "terror" in describing America's new strategy would not play well in the newspapers back home. The teams became "Provincial Reconnaissance Units" or PRUs. The CIA turned its attention to creating a network of PRUs and regional interrogation centers, or torture facilities, across South Vietnam. By 1970, over 700 U.S. advisers were overseeing the Phoenix Program throughout South Vietnam. Records-keeping for this type of activity was understandably suspect, but it is generally accepted that between 1968 and 1972 the Phoenix Program "neutralized" 81,740 suspected enemy agents and supporters, with approximately 26,000 to 41,000 killed.

It was during this period that the term "winning hearts and minds" came into use to describe America's efforts in South Vietnam. While the strategy of rooting out enemy activities at the hamlet level seemed promising, the Saigon government immediately turned its focus to aiding the CIA in setting up PRUs and interrogation centers, and it severely cut back programs to build schools and provide health care to its citizens. Neighbors and family members were encouraged and rewarded to report enemy activities, and it was not unusual for local authorities to turn in their political opponents as enemies, or to solicit and accept bribes from neighbors to keep their names off the reports. Torture was widely used at the interrogation centers. Of course, the enemy soon recognized the new pacification strategy, and the Viet Cong began to issue quotas for the "neutralization" of Phoenix officials. Aspects of the Phoenix Program continued until Saigon fell in 1975, but by 1973 widespread corruption had once again sabotaged the Americans' plans and the CIA abandoned the effort. While the American military's questionable body counts became symbolic of the Vietnam War, no statistics regarding the hearts and minds won, or lost, by the Phoenix Program were ever reported.

After the Tet offensive, every aspect of America's involvement in Vietnam came under intense scrutiny. President Johnson nominated his old friend and colleague Clark Clifford to be Secretary of Defense, and appointed General Westmoreland to become Army Chief of Staff, promoting General Creighton Abrams to command of U.S. forces in Vietnam. Clifford was known as a hawk and a staunch supporter of the military. After assessing the situation, he surprised the President by describing the war as a "real loser." In late March, Johnson called together a nine-man panel of trusted experts, his "Wise Men," to discuss the outlook of the war. After two days, they advised the President against any further additions to U.S. troop strengths, and suggested that he renew efforts to negotiate a peace with Hanoi.

On March 31, President Johnson spoke to the nation and announced that he had ordered a cessation of air and naval bombardments of North Vietnam, except in areas just north of the DMZ where the enemy was continuing to stage attacks into the South. The President committed an additional 13,500 troops to Vietnam, and announced that he would request additional defense expenditures totaling more than $5 billion. At the end of the broadcast, looking tired and drawn, the President shocked the nation and the world by announcing "I shall not seek, and I will not accept, the nomination of my party for another term as your President." Unlike our Commander in Chief, those of us in the military were not allowed to quit and go home.

On April 3, North Vietnam finally announced that they would be willing to talk about peace, but only after the U.S. stopped all bombing of the North. President Johnson immediately announced "We will establish contact with representatives of North Vietnam." A 34-day discussion ensued regarding the location for the talks before it was agreed to meet in Paris. However, only the U.S. and North Vietnam would be talking; the government of South Vietnam and the NLF or Viet Cong would not be invited to take part. The talks began in secret with days of negotiations over the shape of the meeting table. The U.S. resumed and intensified its bombing of North Vietnam.

After Tet, the American military in Vietnam became obsessed with preventing another enemy offensive. On May 5, 1968, a second major Communist offensive began with heavy shelling of 119 key targets and a furious ground assault upon the Saigon region. This assault was finally overcome after seven days. Then in late May another offensive erupted around Saigon and took over a week to be put down.

The *New York Times* reported that the siege of Khe Sanh ended April 7th. It is estimated that more than 10,000 enemy had been killed, compared to about 500 Marines and their South Vietnamese allies. America, hit by tragedy at home, hardly noticed. In Memphis, Martin Luther King, Jr. was assassinated on April 4th. Throughout America, angry blacks rioted and portions of 100 cities were burned.

Readers should be aware that in 1999 the King family brought a civil action suit for $100 charging a Memphis bar owner, Loyd Jowers, and "other unknown conspirators" with wrongful death in the assassination. Reverend King's friend, attorney William F. Pepper, had investigated the case and represented the family. Both the King family and Jowers alleged that the U.S. Government had been complicit in the assassination, and a great deal of evidence was presented. Seventy witnesses described an elaborate conspiracy that involved the FBI, the CIA, personalities within the U.S. military, Memphis city police, and organized crime. Because they were not named as defendants in the suit, government officials were not allowed to contest the charges. The jury took one hour to find for the King family.

On June 5, 1968 Senator Robert F. Kennedy was assassinated after winning the Democratic presidential primary in California. RFK had become a very outspoken critic of the Johnson administration's policies in Vietnam, and with the California victory he had taken the lead in the race for the presidential nomination. Anti-war sentiments were then focused upon Senators Eugene McCarthy (D-MN) and George McGovern (D-SD). America was wounded and divided, wondering what would happen next.

Everything changed after Tet. Blacks coming over to Vietnam from The World were angry that the civil rights movement had been stalled by the war, and now they were on the wrong side of the planet, wearing the uniform of the oppressive Establishment, and in grave danger of being killed or maimed for no real reason whatsoever. "No Vietnamese ever called me nigger," Muhammad Ali had said before he was screwed over by The Establishment, and every poor black kid knew he was right. They came angry, with a chip on their shoulders, and in April when Martin Luther King was assassinated, it got worse. Racial tensions began to flare up in Vietnam, just as at home. "Black Power" had become a rallying cry and a new and very real force in the turbulence and divisions of the American political scene.

In colleges and universities across America and around the world, students took over administrative offices or classrooms to stage sit-ins, simply sitting down on any available flat surface to disrupt the day-to-day operations and demand that the schools modify their curricula to better reflect reality and morality as well as to introduce meaningful discussions of current social issues, especially the war in Vietnam. At other schools, students conducted strikes, staying away from classes en masse to protest the war. Here again, The Establishment was being questioned as students demanded their tuition dollars' worth of appropriate courses that would prepare them to be successful in a most challenging post-graduation environment. College students were exempted from the draft as long as they maintained good grades, but they were usually subject to being drafted immediately after graduating.

In late June, MACV announced that American troops had begun to evacuate the base at Khe Sanh.

In early August, the Republican National Convention nominated Eisenhower's former Vice President Richard Nixon as its candidate, to run on a platform aimed at achieving an honorable peace in Vietnam by shifting more of the responsibilities for fighting to the Vietnamese. Nixon pledged to improve negotiations with Hanoi while maintaining America's strength. Later in the month, Viet Cong forces launched the most intense series of attacks since the Tet offensive, rocketing Saigon and the U.S. air field at Da Nang, and key cities from Hue to Quang Tri. A Special Forces camp at Du Clap was overrun by North Vietnamese regulars, but finally retaken just as the Democratic National Convention began in Chicago.

If the Vietnam War was ostensibly about defending freedom from the threat of creeping Communism, the Soviet Union chose a particularly conspicuous moment to invade Czechoslovakia. For the past nine months, a youthful revolution in that country had challenged conventional Stalinist Communism, softening the message as it sought to improve the lot of the Czech people. Just a few days before the start of the Democratic convention, the Soviets invaded and very forcefully ended the experiment. The youth movement around the world was shocked and depressed. In America, presidential candidate Eugene McCarthy shot himself in the foot by commenting that "it's not as if Hitler were marching in" and "I do not see this as a major world crisis." The Cold War was still threatening a nuclear holocaust, and the American public recognized that the Senator had little understanding of the grave situations at home or in Europe. At the very last minute, Senator George McGovern announced that he would be an anti-war candidate at the upcoming convention. McCarthy's thoughts on the war in Vietnam would certainly be challenged from every side in Chicago.

The nation's focus turned to the Democratic National Convention. The delegates were asked to consider two very different positions on the war, either advocating a halt to the bombing and negotiations that would lead to a withdrawal of American and North Vietnamese troops along with increased pressure on the Saigon regime to create a coalition government with the Viet Cong. The other alternative fully supported the LBJ administration's conduct of the war and asked Hanoi to "respond affirmatively" to America's initiatives to scale down the war. By now, the two candidates were Senator Eugene McCarthy representing the anti-war contingent, and Vice President Hubert Humphrey, representing President Johnson and the status quo. Humphrey had attempted to bridge the gap, noting that more than 75% of all voters in the Democratic primaries had voted for anti-war candidates Bobby Kennedy or McCarthy, but the President insisted that his policies and positions were not subject to discussion.

Outside the convention hall, a huge throng of youthful anti-war demonstrators had gathered, wishfully hoping that the American system might actually work. They had seen their movement shake The Establishment nationwide, but here at the national gathering of the nation's political powers, they fully expected their champion Eugene McCarthy would stand up to the big machines and the people would have their way. The nation was distraught over the war, still reeling from the assassinations, and the youth movement was especially desperate to see the voice of the people triumph over The Establishment and its corrupt "good ol' boy" alliances. Unbeknownst to the faithful throngs in the streets, the assassination of Robert Kennedy had destroyed McCarthy's resolve, and he had become despondent, quiet and ineffective at the most crucial moment of his life.

At the kickoff of the convention, McCarthy announced his potential choices for his cabinet, and Democrats everywhere were shocked to hear that he proposed to appoint millionaires and Republicans, but no experienced Democratic politicians. Then he told the press that Vice President Hubert Humphrey had the nomination locked up. The delegates and the crowds in the streets had all come to Chicago expecting the convention to be confrontational, and suddenly it seemed that Eugene McCarthy had folded, tossed in his cards and slunk away from the table a defeated man. The news did not sit well. Americans, not to mention Vietnamese peasants, were dying in Vietnam while this conclave enjoyed a big party.

In the weeks leading up to the convention, the enthusiasm and moral outrage of the young anti-war community across America had morphed into a loosely structured and utterly irreverent "Yippie" or Youth International Party, not quite so pacific as the so-called "hippies," but equally colorful and revolutionary. The brainchild of satirical spokesmen Abbie

Hoffman, Jerry Rubin, and Paul Krassner, the Yippies were as entertaining as they were committed to the revolution, and they were making plans to come to Chicago for the joint purposes of partying in a rock-concert atmosphere and speaking out to force America to change. Darlings of the press, the Yippies talked of dumping vast quantities of LSD into the Chicago water supply during the Democratic convention, conducting a demonstration of 10,000 nude bodies floating on Lake Michigan, and organizing mass seductions of convention delegates to change the nation's course by seizing the leaders' genitals. Other, less extreme activists planned a wide range of more conventional political activities to convince the convention that the time had come to end the war and change America's priorities. When the pro-Johnson platform won, their hopes began to crumble.

From the start, Chicago Mayor Richard Daley had made it clear the protestors were unwelcome in his city, refusing to grant permits for any visitors to camp in the city's parks. So sophisticated had the government's counter-activities become, the FBI had sent out a bogus list of homes that would welcome demonstrators to stay for the convention, so upon arriving in Chicago a huge number were shocked to find themselves homeless and living on the streets. Meanwhile, the CIA had infiltrated the movement, and would anticipate and disrupt many of the activities and demonstrations. (The CIA was forbidden by law from operations within the United States, but the challenge posed by the movement had become so threatening that all available resources had been called in to fight the scourge.) Years later, the army estimated that one out of every six demonstrators in Chicago had been some variety of government agent. In a series of minor skirmishes throughout the week, the protestors called the police "Pigs!" while the cops responded with "Kill the Commies!"

On Wednesday the pro-LBJ platform was adopted and a large number of convention delegates interrupted proceedings as they sang "We Shall Overcome" or chanted "Stop the war!" A priest knelt to pray for peace, and delegates throughout the hall contributed their "Amens." The demonstrators outside the convention had become bitter and disenchanted. They came together in Grant Park, just across the street from the hotel where Humphrey and McCarthy were staying. When a group, including at least one undercover police instigator, surrounded a flag pole and removed the American flag, the police attacked with clubs, tear gas, and mace. It was totally unexpected, vicious and bloody – the war had come home to America, and television crews recorded the scene as onlookers chanted "The whole world is watching."

Inside the convention hall, attempting to nominate George McGovern for President, Senator Abraham Ribicoff told the convention, "With George McGovern as President, we would not have to have such Gestapo tactics in the streets of Chicago." Mayor Daley responded, although there were no microphones nearby, with what appeared to be an obscenity, and Ribicoff shook his head. "How hard it is to accept the truth," he said to the world. "How hard." The convention had deteriorated to bedlam. On the convention floor, CBS-TV journalist Mike Wallace was slugged on the jaw as he attempted to cover the convention for a new show to be called *60 Minutes*. To regain order, a filmed tribute to Bobby Kennedy was shown eliciting a long and very emotional spontaneous singing of *The Battle Hymn of the Republic*. When the week was over, Hubert Humphrey said, "We ought to quit pretending that Mayor Daley did something that was wrong. He didn't condone a thing that was wrong. He tried to protect lives." With its wavering resolve on the important issues, the Democratic Party had lost the support of both the anti-war community and mainstream, middle-class Americans – Humphrey didn't stand a chance.

In Vietnam, fighting continued with no significant victories for either side. American officials declared emphatically that the use of chemical defoliants such as Agent Orange had not had any negative effects upon humans or animals, despite testimony by the U.S. Department of Agriculture that the chemicals had caused "undeniable ecological change," and would continue to impact the country far into the future. In early October, U.S. Marines returned to the abandoned base at Khe Sanh to set up artillery fire-bases. Back home in San Francisco, for the first time, an anti-war demonstration was organized and led by Vietnam veterans and active-duty soldiers and reservists. Also for the first time, the Department of Defense announced that it would be necessary to send 24,000 soldiers back to Vietnam involuntarily due to a shortage of available personnel. In London, 50,000 English citizens marched to protest the Vietnam War. On October 31, LBJ announced that he had, due to encouraging developments at the peace talks in Paris, ordered a cessation of all bombing over North Vietnam. Air raids on the Ho Chi Minh Trail and infiltration routes were consequently increased three-fold. South Vietnamese President Thieu responded that his Saigon regime would no longer participate in the Paris talks because the Viet Cong would be taking part, and Vice President Ky announced that, due to the bombing pause in the North, South Vietnam could "trust the Americans no longer."

The evening of October 6, the "promotional film" for the Beatles' massive hit song *Hey Jude* was debuted on *The Smothers Brothers Comedy Hour* on CBS TV. The film is viewed as a predecessor to music videos. The flip side of the 45 RPM (vinyl) single record was the song *Revolution*, which stated the band's support for social activism, but also their physical limitations *"We're all doing what we can,"* and John Lennon's moral declaration, *"but when you talk about destruction, don't you know that you can count me out."*

On November 6, Richard Nixon was elected President by a resounding majority over Hubert Humphrey. Most Americans hoped that Nixon had a "secret" plan for ending the war, or that his actions would acknowledge that the vast majority of Americans wanted the war to end soon.

In December, Vice President Ky disrupted the peace talks in Paris by complaining about seating arrangements at the table, and U.S. Secretary of Defense Clark Clifford warned that the U.S. was prepared to negotiate without the Saigon government. Clifford made it clear that the U.S. felt no obligation to maintain the current number of American troops in-country until a final political settlement could be reached, and suggested that the U.S. and Hanoi should pursue discussions without Saigon's participation.

1968 was one of the most important years in American history. 14,314 Americans died in Vietnam, doubling U.S. losses since January of 1961 to more than 30,000, with more than 200,000 wounded. During 1968, 20,482 South Vietnamese military personnel were killed, along with 978 soldiers from other allied countries. Since 1961, over 439,000 Communists were reported killed, and estimates of the number of innocent civilians killed or wounded were in the hundreds of thousands to over a million. The U.S had spent nearly $30 billion in Vietnam in 1968, with little progress to show for it.

Chapter 7

VIETNAM: WHAT REALLY HAPPENED?

PART 5: 1969 – 1973

They wrote in the old days that it is sweet and fitting to die for one's country. But in modern war, there is nothing sweet nor fitting in your dying. You will die like a dog for no good reason.

– Ernest Hemingway

I don't want him [General Abrams] to short-change our efforts to destroy North Vietnam in order for a half-assed effort to do something in South Vietnam.

– Richard Nixon, May 6, 1972

Before leaving office, President Johnson sent his final budget to Congress, with $25,733,000,000 for the war in Vietnam for fiscal year 1970.

Richard Nixon took office on January 20, 1969. After the traumas of 1968, America was desperate for a change. Nixon promised to end the war and bring the divided nation together. Just days before the inauguration, an agreement was reached in Paris that would seat all four parties, the U.S., North and South Vietnam, and the NLF or Viet Cong, at a round table without flags or identification by political alignment. With 539,000 troops in Vietnam, plus untold thousands of diplomats, intelligence "spooks," contractors, journalists, and visiting politicians, America's commitment had grown far beyond that of the French at the height of their struggle, but the U.S. had little to show for its huge expenditures. Nixon's strategy was focused upon "Vietnamization" – turning over more of the actual war-fighting responsibility to the South Vietnamese army and air force.

The Communists were not in control of the government in Saigon, but they had established a powerful presence in provinces and villages throughout the country. In late February, they staged another offensive that hit Saigon and all the significant cities in the South. American forces had feared another major offensive for a year, since the Tet offensive, and they brought great force to bear in an effort to squash the uprising quickly and decisively. President Nixon announced that there would be no reduction in the number of American troops in-country until he could see a decrease in ground activity in the South and progress at the talks in Paris. Clearly, Nixon's peace plan was to meet aggression with force, and a negotiated settlement would not happen soon. On March 15 the President and National Security Council approved bombing of supply lines and support bases in Cambodia for the first time, but this escalation of hostilities was kept secret from Congress and the American people. Nixon's new Secretary of Defense, Melvin Laird, went before Congress to request an additional $156 million to train South Vietnamese troops. (This after how many years of "advisors" and training for the ARVN?)

In Chicago, eight prominent anti-war activists were indicted on charges of conspiracy to incite a riot for their activities prior to and during the Democratic National Convention. At the same time, seven Chicago policemen were indicted on charges of assaulting demonstrators. The anti-war organizers became known as "The Chicago Eight," and their ensuing trial became a circus and a travesty of justice.

In early March, it was revealed that American ground troops had entered Laos in an effort to slow the flow of troops and equipment to the South along the Ho Chi Minh trail. This was the first time the U.S. had acknowledged any actions in Laos other than bombing. At about the same time, Cambodia formally complained about American reconnaissance flights over its territory. President Nixon reaffirmed that the U.S. respected Cambodian sovereignty and its borders, and Prince Sihanouk accepted the apologies for flights that had strayed over Cambodia. But in Vietnam, heavy bombing was concentrated on enemy supply routes near the Cambodian border. There was intense ground action in areas near the border, and when North Vietnamese artillery bases within Cambodia shelled allied troops in Vietnam, U.S. bombers attacked them.

On an episode of the popular and controversial TV show, *The Smothers Brothers Comedy Hour,* guest folksinger Joan Baez attempted to bring attention to her husband, David Harris, who was going to federal prison for his refusal to report when drafted. Her remarks were censored by CBS to simply say that Harris was going away. April 4th saw the final Smothers Brothers episode, as they refused to submit tapes to CBS censors ten days prior to airing and the network abruptly cancelled the show.

President Nixon was allowed a short period to evaluate the war and develop a strategy, but in May Republican Senator George Aiken of Vermont spoke out, advising the administration to begin withdrawing American troops from Vietnam. The *New York Times* disclosed secret B-52 bombing raids over Cambodia, and the FBI was assigned to discover who had leaked information about the bombing. The FBI began a widespread but secret program of wiretapping government officials and reporters. Responding to a 10-point plan from the Communists in Paris, the President outlined a suggestion for withdrawal of U.S. and North Vietnamese troops from the South, and supervised elections in South Vietnam. The North Vietnamese rejected the proposals, insisting that the U.S get out of South Vietnam before there could be any realistic hopes for peace. Legislation was introduced in the House of Representatives that would require the unconditional withdrawal of 100,000 American troops and a cease-fire, but there was limited support for the measure.

Also in May, in an effort to halt enemy troop and supply movements from Laos into South Vietnam, a major American and ARVN offensive in the Ashau Valley met stiff opposition. After ten days and ten agonizing and bloody attempts to take hill 937, the allied forces finally succeeded on the 11th try. G.I.s called the place "Hamburger Hill." 46 Americans were dead, and more than 400 wounded. They were immediately ordered to abandon the hill, and then were ordered to retake it eight weeks later. A wave of protests erupted at home. A poll found that 52% of the American people felt the war was "not worth the cost." After intensive air and artillery strikes, fighting in the Ashau Valley was vicious and bloody.

In early June, President Nixon and South Vietnamese President Thieu met at Midway Island in the Pacific, and Nixon announced that 25,000 American troops would be withdrawn before September. Thieu described the strategy as "a replacement, not a withdrawal," as South Vietnamese troops would take the place of the departed Americans. In Vietnam, the NLF or Viet Cong announced a Provisional Revolutionary Government (PRG) to rule South Vietnam, a direct challenge to the Thieu regime. The PRG was immediately recognized by Communist governments around the globe.

The U.S. government admitted that it had wiretapped the "Chicago Eight" prior to the Democratic National Convention, claiming that it had the "right" to eavesdrop without court approval on individuals or groups it perceived as acting to subvert or undermine the government.

In Boston, an appeals court reversed the conviction of famed baby doctor and author Dr. Benjamin Spock on charges that he had conspired to counsel young men about how to avoid the draft. Dr. Spock's book, *Baby and Child Care*, first published in 1946, was considered a textbook for raising children throughout the baby boomer era. Spock encouraged parents to be gentle and understanding with their children. When he became an outspoken critic of the war in Vietnam, pro-war advocates charged that Spock's book had advocated permissiveness and an expectation of instant gratification that ultimately resulted in a generation that was "soft" and unable or unwilling to fight effectively in Vietnam. Later in the year, Spock would lead a "March Against Death" from Arlington National Cemetery to the White House. Headed by relatives of servicemen killed in Vietnam, the march was followed two days later by the largest anti-war demonstration in American history. Groups of protestors attempted to march to the South Vietnamese embassy and the Justice Department but were dissuaded by heavy tear gas. Rocks and bottles were thrown, resulting in several policemen injured and well over 100 demonstrators arrested.

In July of '69, President Nixon visited South Vietnam and met with President Thieu. A few days later, in a meeting with India's Prime Minister Indira Ghandi, Nixon described Thieu as one of the four or five best leaders in the world. The remark was not widely reported in South Vietnam, as Thieu's government had shut down most of South Vietnam's newspapers a few months earlier. Nixon would also meet with South Korea's President and thank him for sending 50,000 troops to aid the efforts in Vietnam, while promising 250 million American dollars to cover the costs.

In late August, a major battle broke out south of Danang. When a U.S. helicopter was shot down, American forces met extremely stiff resistance while trying to reach the downed chopper. Finally, after suffering heavy casualties, one American infantry company refused to continue the mission. The battalion commander sent his executive officer and a sergeant to "give them a pep talk." Subsequently, the company's leader, a Lieutenant, was relieved of his post and reassigned, but neither he nor his men were disciplined. G.I. resistance to the American Way of Waging War had become a factor.

North Vietnam's President Ho Chi Minh died on September 3rd, 1969 at the age of 79. He was replaced by a four-man team led by Ho's principal deputy, Le Duan, who had long pressed for more military activity in the South, and General Vo Nguyen Giap, who had led the Viet Minh resistance to the Japanese occupation in World War II and was considered the mastermind of the North Vietnamese victory over the French at Dien Bien Phu, as well as the Tet offensive and the siege of Khe Sanh. When he died at the age of 102 in 2013, General Giap was recognized as one of the 20th century's most brilliant and effective military leaders.

Late in September, Secretary of the Army Stanley Resor announced that murder charges against eight U.S. Special Forces soldiers would be dropped, stating that the army was "helpless" to enlist the aid of the CIA in investigating the incident that killed a Vietnamese civilian.

In meetings and negotiations with the North Vietnamese and especially the Russians, national security adviser Henry Kissinger had dropped numerous hints that President Nixon was irrational, mentally unstable, perhaps crazy, and sometimes sufficiently volatile that he might initiate an all-out nuclear war. This impression had been carefully disseminated to the Soviet Union, Cuba, and Hanoi as a major Kissinger strategy.

On October 27, 1969 President Nixon played the role suggested by Kissinger and deployed 18 B-52 Stratofortress bombers heavily laden with the most lethal nuclear weapons in the American arsenal. The B-52s gave every appearance that they were bringing a nuclear holocaust to the Soviet Union. The "Operation Grand Lance" B-52s roared across the Pacific Ocean toward the eastern coast of the Soviet Union, apparently in attack mode. For three days they flew to the very edge of Soviet air space, patrolling as if awaiting orders to deliver their nuclear payloads to Moscow. Each airplane carried hundreds of times more explosive capability than the bombs that had destroyed Hiroshima and Nagasaki. Clearly, President Nixon wanted the Communists to believe he was crazy enough to start World War III in response to frustrations over the war in Vietnam. Information regarding this incident was kept classified for 35 years before a few documents were uncovered via the Freedom of Information Act. Nixon, and especially Kissinger, expected the Russians to panic and insist that the North Vietnamese break the negotiation logjam in Paris and make some meaningful concessions to the "crazy" Americans. There was, of course, a very real chance that the Soviets would launch their own nuclear fleet in retaliation for the perceived American attack. Wiser heads prevailed, but clearly Nixon and Kissinger had gambled with the future of the planet.

I had just returned from Southeast Asia and processed out of the army in September, and, like the rest of the world, had no idea how close we had all come to a nuclear holocaust. I was busy absorbing the Beatles' *Ab-*

bey Road album and joyfully prowling the ice cream aisles of all the area supermarkets.

Meanwhile, journalist Seymour Hersh, who had revealed the massacre at My Lai, reported that he had interviewed soldiers who had taken part in the action, and the *Cleveland Plain Dealer* published a number of photos taken at the scene. In Vietnam, reporters interviewed survivors of the massacre, and the various stories and photos of the atrocity brought a swift and very negative reaction from the American public. An investigation ordered by the Secretary of the Army and the Army Chief of Staff (General Westmoreland) immediately reported that the massacre had never happened and recommended that no further action be undertaken. The army announced plans to court martial a sergeant and eleven other low-ranking participants in addition to Lt. Calley. In March of 1970, the army charged Captain Ernest Medina, Lt. Calley's company commander, and four others, with a variety of atrocities at Song My (both the hamlets of My Lai and My Khe were in the "village" of Song My.) in March of 1968 Medina was held responsible for 175 murders of civilians. The charges also included rape, and maiming a suspect while interrogating him. A few days later, 14 other officers were charged with suppression of information, dereliction of duty, failure to obey regulations, and false swearing, or perjury, for a variety of actions intended to whitewash or obscure reports of murder, rape, and abuses at Song My, where the military acknowledged that approximately 28 civilians were killed.

In Paris, America's chief negotiator, Ambassador Henry Cabot Lodge and his deputy resigned. 1969 had been another hard year in Vietnam. The U.S., Australia, and the Philippines had begun to withdraw a small but significant portion of their troops, and intelligence reported that there were also fewer enemy troops in-country, but 9,414 Americans died in Vietnam in 1969. Total deaths in the war had now topped 40,000, with over 260,000 wounded and 1400 missing or captured. After nearly four years of intense air and ground war, American troops were finding the poor and primitive "mere Gooks" to be a formidable enemy. Morale was deteriorating among the G.I.s, drug use had become widespread (allegedly supplied in large part by CIA flights from Laos), "fragging" incidents had increased, and the army had convicted 117 soldiers of "mutiny and other acts involving willful refusal to follow orders," up significantly from 82 the prior year. At home, opposition to the war was now a predominant concern as unprecedented numbers of American citizens were traveling to Washington, D.C. and other major cities to protest and call for an end to the war. In Chicago, the National Guard had to be called out to contain a series of demonstrations against the trial of the Chicago Eight. A coordinated chain of demonstrations across the U.S. called for an immediate end to the war, the first action of its kind in the history of America. A Gallup Poll found that 57 percent of Americans supported the total withdrawal of American forces in Vietnam by the end of 1969. In Washington, D.C., protestors were tear-gassed as they peacefully attempted to march to the South Vietnamese embassy.

The Communists began the year 1970 with a flurry of bold actions throughout South Vietnam. A Viet Cong team invaded a refugee camp and threw explosives into houses, killing civilians. Another team planted mines at an Officers' Training School near Saigon, killing 16 South Vietnamese cadets and their instructor. North Vietnamese and Viet Cong forces attacked a South Vietnamese Marine command post in the Mekong Delta, while others attacked a fire base north of Saigon, killing 13 Americans and wounding 3 when they blew up the ammo dump. An American F-105 jet fighter was shot down by anti-aircraft missiles over North Vietnam, and the American military was forced to admit that air actions against the North continued to be met with resistance – but had not been made public because they were "insignificant."

It must be noted that in 1970 there were no personal computers and no internet where the American public could easily seek information. Many government personnel were feeling besieged by requests for information, and even Freedom of Information Act requests were often met with reluctance and extensive use of redactors' black pens. Still, information about the conduct of the war was seeping out. An article in the *Ladies' Home Journal* in January of 1967 had made the country aware of napalm, and the terrible damages done to a human body by this chemically altered gasoline jelly dropped in bombs to create a vast inferno. The article described children with their flesh melted, pooling and growing in masses so thick the victims were unable to move their heads or limbs. When gangrene set in, there was no alternative to amputation. However, the article pointed out, "the only thing they cannot cut off is their head." A number of American doctors had formed a group and offered to treat Vietnamese children burned by napalm at no cost, but the State Department callously refused to allow those children to enter the United States. Only after considerable political wrangling were a few allowed to be treated in the U.S.

Campus protests were happening across the country, and protestors began to harass or disrupt the recruiting activities of Dow Chemical, the sole manufacturer of napalm. Campus protests were focused upon military recruiters and ROTC programs, CIA recruiters, draft policies, and the very lucrative research activities for military and defense industries. The national conscience had become inflamed, and many college and university personnel warned their students about the sinister activities "secretly" happening on campus. Of course, many others in college administrations were reporting student activists to the FBI or police.

Student actions were becoming increasingly bold. Dow Chemical's recruiters on many American campuses were blockaded by sit-ins, organized primarily by the Students for a Democratic Society (SDS), making it impossible for job applicants to meet with them. A number of schools reacted to these disruptions by summoning police, and soon the confrontations became bloody. A few institutions, however, actually banned Dow and other companies with close ties to the war from their campuses.

In February of 1970 it was announced that U.S. B-52 bombers were striking northern Laos for the first time, but those raids were being shown in military records as routine missions against enemy supply routes in South Vietnam or southern Laos.

On April 30, 1970, President Nixon spoke to the American people via television and announced that he had authorized U.S. troops to enter areas of Cambodia to destroy Communist supply depots and command bases. "This is not an invasion," the President said, since the American troops would not set up any permanent bases, and the areas were under North Vietnamese domination. A flurry of protests erupted across America, including the burning of an ROTC building on the campus of Kent State University in Ohio where, two days later on May 4th, National Guard troops fired into a throng of student protestors, killing four and wounding eleven. On May 15, city and state police at Jackson State College in Jackson, Mississippi fired into a crowd of students protesting the invasion of Cambodia, leaving two dead (one was a visiting high school student) and a dozen wounded. The "unthinkable" had happened once again in the USA.

Over 500 colleges and universities shut down (51 did not reopen that year!) as students at 1350 schools went on strike in protest, and the presidents of 37 universities and colleges drafted a letter to President Nixon urging him to clearly show his determination to end the war. ROTC facilities at 30 colleges were burned or bombed. Protests were widespread throughout America. On the weekend of May 9th, four million Americans protested in the streets, including 130,000 in Washington, D.C.

President Nixon got out of town, spending the weekend at Camp David despite major renovations under way there. More than 250 State Department employees signed a letter to the Secretary of State protesting the expansion of the war into Cambodia. An anti-war demonstration on Wall Street in New York City was attacked by construction workers, injuring more than seventy. A few days later, over 100,000 construction workers, office workers, and stevedores marched in New York in support of President Nixon's policies.

The Nixon White House was shocked by the size and passion of the anti-war protests. The invasion into Cambodia had been a limited success, with large numbers of weapons seized, but no major or significant battles. The shootings at Kent State had divided the nation even further, with the government, military, and police arrayed against the citizens. America was on the verge of civil war. In June, the President announced that the incursion into Cambodia was "the most successful operation of this long and difficult war"; he had ordered an end to air support for South Vietnamese troops remaining in Cambodia, and resumption of American troop withdrawals from Vietnam.

On April 10th of 1970, Paul McCartney made a public announcement that he was leaving the Beatles. Also in April, NASA's Apollo 13 moon mission encountered mechanical difficulties, abandoned a moon landing, and barely made it back to Earth. Jimi Hendrix died of a drug overdose on September 18th, and Janis Joplin on October 4th.

On June 7, 1971 the *Armed Forces Journal* ran a long and rambling article by Colonel Robert D. Heinl, Jr. entitled "The Collapse of the Armed Forces." The Colonel stated:

The morale, discipline and battle-worthiness of the U.S. Armed Forces are, with a few salient exceptions, lower and worse than at any time in this century and possibly in the history of the United States. By every conceivable indicator, our army that now remains in Vietnam is in a state approaching collapse, with individual units avoiding or having refused combat, murdering their officers and non-commissioned officers, drug-ridden, and dispirited where not near mutinous. Elsewhere than Vietnam, the situation is nearly as serious. Intolerably clobbered and buffeted from without and within by social turbulence, pandemic drug addiction, race war, sedition, civilian scapegoatise, draftee recalcitrance and malevolence, barracks theft and common crime, unsupported in their travail by the federal government, in Congress as well as the executive branch, distrusted, disliked, and often reviled by the public, the uniformed services today are places of agony for the loyal, silent professionals who doggedly hang on and try to keep the ship afloat.

The Colonel went on for about 15 pages, lamenting the fact that there was no discipline in the Vietnam-era military, but he offered no suggestions or alternatives. It was as if he thought the Colonel's eagle insignia on his collar made him an authority, but he could only whine and complain. He was blissfully unaware that he was the problem! Active duty soldiers were certainly *not* "disliked and often reviled" by the public in hometown America, but statements like this one began to create the great myth. This type of career soldier was known as a "lifer," and yes, their orders were often ignored because they were clueless, and they could and did get good men hurt or killed.

In an unprecedented move, the U.S. Senate voted to cut off funding for American operations in Cambodia after July 1st. The act would also bar any military advisors or air support in Cambodia without congressional approval. This was the first time in American history that a Congress limited a President's powers as Commander-in-Chief during a time of war. The House of Representatives did not pass the amendment. FBI wiretaps of congressmen helped the Nixon people target the votes they needed, and sometimes provided personal information they could use to influence the congressman's vote. In the public realm this practice would have been extortion, but when practiced by the highest offices of government against legislators in 1970, it was just business as usual. The White House had adopted a defensive posture that considered anyone who disagreed with policy a "subversive," and the FBI was ordered to target all subversive individuals and groups.

FBI Director J. Edgar Hoover recognized the legal implications of such activities and referred these directives to legal counsel, quietly ignoring those which were patently illegal. Still, much of America's government and military had taken on an adversarial role against the forces opposing the war. President Nixon called the protestors "bums," and Vice President Agnew referred to them as "psychotic and criminal elements" and "traitors and thieves and perverts." When it was reported that U.S. planes were providing support for South Vietnamese operations in Cambodia, MACV issued a confidential directive that all air activity in Cambodia be described as interdicting shipments of troops or supplies from North Vietnam to protect U.S. troops in South Vietnam. The truth was obscured and manipulated at every level of the government. President Nixon railed against the protestors, then ordered a car to take him to the Lincoln Memorial where he talked football with a group of striking Syracuse University students. The students said they thought he appeared "tired." The President announced that all American troops would be out of Cambodia by June 30th.

The invasion of Cambodia did not yield much in the way of military success, either for American or South Vietnamese forces. The invasion did not allow Saigon much time to prepare, and they were not attracting large numbers of recruits. Their draft was relatively ineffective, as draftees could buy their way out. Approximately 150,500 South Vietnamese ARVN soldiers deserted in 1970, up from 123,000 in 1969, and 140,000 in 1968. Desertions peaked during the planting and harvesting seasons, and some of the deserters eventually returned to duty. It was estimated that about 24,000 returned in 1970.

On August 29, 1970 a Los Angeles rally by the Chicano Moratorium, a southwest U.S.-based organization of Chicano activists opposed to the war, attracted an estimated crowd of 30,000 participants. Police claimed they had received reports that a nearby liquor store had been robbed, and they chased the "suspects" into the midst of the protest. The march was immediately declared an illegal assembly, tear gas was employed, and police confronted the protestors. A struggle ensued, stores were looted and burned, 150 were arrested, and four protestors were killed, including Ruben Salazar, an award-winning journalist, news director for a local Spanish language TV station, and a columnist for the *Los Angeles Times*. Salazar was reportedly killed when a tear gas canister was fired into a café, and an inquest ruled that his death was a homicide but no one was prosecuted.

In October, a pro-war rally in Washington drew approximately 20,000. South Vietnamese Vice-President Ky had intended to speak at the rally, but was dissuaded by Henry Kissinger. The experts were convinced that the long years of bombing in the North and ground war in the South must have worn the Communists in Hanoi down, so President Nixon returned to TV with a speech requesting a ceasefire and renewed negotiations to end the fighting. The Communists promptly denounced Nixon's initiative and repeated their demand for the withdrawal of all U.S. troops. President Thieu reassured his National Assembly that he would never accept a coalition government with the Communists, stated that the allies now controlled 99.1 percent of the people of South Vietnam, and borrowed a phrase from General Westmoreland to insist that "we are seeing the light at the end of the tunnel." On October 19, 1970 the *New York Times* reported that the CIA estimated there were upwards of 30,000 people in the Saigon government who were more or less cooperating with the Viet Cong, and that their numbers were expected to reach 50,000 "soon."

At the end of 1970, American combat troops in South Vietnam numbered 334,600, including about 274,000 actual combatants. U.S. forces lost 6,081 killed in 1970, and 24,835 wounded. Another withdrawal of 60,000 was planned for spring.

In the very first days of 1971, the U.S. Congress passed a law forbidding the use of U.S. ground troops in Laos or Cambodia. However, U.S. bombers pounded areas of South Vietnam, Laos, and Cambodia, especially supply routes along the Ho Chi Minh Trail and missile sites north of the DMZ. President Nixon and National Security Advisor Henry Kissinger spoke publicly of troop withdrawals and "Vietnamization" of the war, but privately they were concerned that lower troop levels would benefit the enemy. Despite the failure of the Cambodian invasion a few months earlier, they began to plan for a second, simultaneous with an invasion of southern Laos to interrupt the flow of men and supplies down the Ho Chi Minh Trail. (This strategy was originally suggested by Admiral John McCain, Commander-in-Chief of the Pacific Command and father of prisoner of war, future U.S. Senator, and 2008 Republican candidate for President, John McCain III).

Because Congress had forbidden American troops to take part in any more ground incursions into Cambodia or Laos, the strategy called for Americans to mount a major offensive right up to the DMZ, and set up long-range artillery bases and supply routes to support an ARVN invasion of Laos, which would also be sustained by U.S. Air Force fighters and bombers.

Over 9,000 Americans and their heavy artillery were moved into position just south of the DMZ, and 20,000 South Vietnamese troops crossed into Laos on February 8th. Almost from the start, a key ARVN tank unit failed to carry out its agreed-upon mission. North Vietnamese artillery pounded U.S. positions with both range and accuracy that were superior to the American big guns. Rain made the supply routes mostly impassable, enemy ambushes delayed supply convoys, and sapper squads disrupted a number of American bases. President Nixon had decreed that journalists not be allowed to cover the offensive on-site, but the American press passed on reports from their European and Asian counterparts, and as the operation floundered, the President's poll numbers dropped by fourteen points. President Thieu ordered that his troops abandon the offensive when they incurred 3,000 casualties, and the ARVN armored unit stopped again as if to wait for that eventuality. American generals conferred with the South Vietnamese, but nothing happened. By the end of February, the invasion had become another disaster. ARVN troops took heavy losses, and abandoned the fight in droves. One famous photograph showed a number of panicked troops clinging to the skids of a departing helicopter. On March 9th, President Thieu ordered all South Vietnamese troops to withdraw from Laos. At the same moment, the second ARVN offensive into Cambodia also failed badly.

President Nixon had gambled, sending a large force of American troops to the very edge of the Laotian border seemingly in defiance of Congress, and it was obvious that the concept of an invasion of Laos by Vietnamese forces had originated from the American command. On the ground just south of the DMZ, American troops attempting to withdraw were being cut to ribbons by North Vietnamese artillery. The only road out of the area, Route 9, became known as "Ambush Alley" and was virtually impassable. Ordered to recover some damaged equipment, one American unit flatly refused. Another, ordered to travel "Ambush Alley" as a convoy, defied orders and slipped through in individual dashes with minimal losses. Another artillery battery lost two-thirds of its big guns attempting to flee through Route 9. The White House and Saigon tried to picture the Laos invasion as a success, and blamed the journalists for "negativity," despite severely inhibiting their access to the action.

As things went badly, President Nixon became frustrated and, always a spiteful man, blamed American commander General Creighton Abrams for the failed offensives, then ordered another 100,000 troops withdrawn over the next twelve months. Nixon hoped the troop withdrawals would pacify the American public while a renewed emphasis on American air power would bomb the enemy into submission. "We're going to level that goddamn country!" he told Kissinger. The enemy responded by striking hard throughout the northern half of South Vietnam, and increased truck traffic on the Ho Chi Minh Trail to 2,500 vehicles per month.

Meanwhile, the White House had learned that the peace movement was planning a major demonstration in Washington for the May 1st weekend with the intent of disrupting traffic and shutting down the government. On March 1st a bomb exploded in the Capitol building, injuring no one but doing considerable damage. A new anti-war group, the Weather Underground, claimed responsibility and said the bombing was to protest the invasion of Laos. At the same time, Congress was conducting hearings into the widespread corruption of the PX and clubs serving American G.I.s in Vietnam, (See Chapter 12, "Corruption and Profiteering"), and the news media were reporting on the trial of Lieutenant Calley for the massacre at My Lai. The cover of the January 11, 1971 issue of *Newsweek* featured a photo of a G.I. in Vietnam with crisscrossed ammo bandoliers over his shoulders, and a gleaming peace sign pendant clearly visible suspended from a chain around his neck. "The Troubled Army in Vietnam," shouted the headline; and the feature article reported poor morale, refusal to obey orders, and rampant drug abuse among the G.I.s in Vietnam.

Late January and early February are not ideal times to visit Michigan unless you enjoy winter sports, but for three days in early 1971 a number of Vietnam veterans came together at a Howard Johnson's motor lodge in Detroit. Vietnam Veterans Against the War (VVAW) had evolved from a chance meeting of six veterans at a 1967 anti-war demonstration in New York City. The group grew quickly. Never before had U.S. veterans gathered together to speak out against their government's policies while an active war was going on. Now a nationwide organization, the vets had worked for months to plan, fund and publicize a public outpouring, a forum where they might tell the American public what they had seen and experienced in Vietnam, and how they felt about it. They had chosen Detroit in an effort to connect with America's blue-collar working class, the segment of society most endangered by the war. The White House, the Pentagon, and the FBI knew about the planned event, and presented many logistical obstacles for the veterans to overcome. The Howard Johnson's Inn was the third location for the meeting in Detroit, after the first two mysteriously fell through. The telephone company refused to make service available, and a number of participants, both Americans and Canadians, were stopped at the border and not allowed to enter from Canada.

During the American Revolution, the colonial army had endured desperate conditions at Valley Forge during the winter of 1776. Many soldiers simply went home. Patriot Thomas Paine wrote of those that stayed, "These are the times that try men's souls. The summer soldier and the sunshine patriot will in this crisis shrink from the service of his country; but he that stands it now, deserves the love and thanks of man and woman."

VVAW called their hearing in Detroit "The Winter Soldier Investigation," stating that America was once again, "...in grave danger. What threatens our country is not Redcoats or even Reds; it is our crimes that are destroying our national unity by separating those of our countrymen who deplore these acts from those of our countrymen who refuse to examine what is being done in America's name." The Winter Soldier Investigation offered over one hundred veterans an opportunity to testify publicly about the American Way of Waging War, the nature of the war in Vietnam, and acts they had witnessed or participated in which they believed fit the agreed international definition of war crimes. The massacre at My Lai was "no unusual occurrence," they declared, and "…we intend to tell more. We intend to tell who it was that gave us these orders; that created that policy; that set that standard of war bordering on full and final genocide."

The organizers had vetted the participants with great care, ensuring that every vet's role in the war was thoroughly documented, and the testimonies were selected to present a wide variety of atrocities, units, locations, and dates. The Winter Soldier revelations were not widely reported by the media. The testimonies were published in a paperback book, but it was not a best-seller. The entire testimony was read into the Congressional Record by Senator Mark Hatfield on April 6 and 7 of 1971, but no change in America's national policies resulted. VVAW's strategy of locating the event in Detroit had probably been a mistake, but news of the Laos invasion came and they began to plan another attention-getting event for the center of Washington, D.C. In February of 1969, elements of the Third Marine Division had invaded Laos for a few days. The operation was called "Dewey Canyon." American efforts to support the South Vietnamese incursion into Laos were called Operation Dewey Canyon II, so VVAW called its action Dewey Canyon III.

VVAW and supporters such as a number of "Gold Star Mothers" (who had lost sons in Vietnam) began to arrive on Sunday, April 18th. On Monday, about 1,100 protestors, mostly veterans, moved across the Potomac to the gates of Arlington National Cemetery where they were denied entrance. They left two wreathes and marched to the Capitol where four Congress-people made speeches, and VVAW formally presented sixteen demands to Congress. From there, the vets moved onto the Mall and established a campsite, which the Justice Department attempted to block, but a Court of Appeals lifted the injunction. On Tuesday about 200 vets attended hearings by the Senate Foreign Relations Committee on proposals to end the war, and then another contingent returned to Arlington Cemetery, where the Superintendent attempted to bar them entrance but finally backed down. After another group of vets staged a guerilla-theater performance on the steps of the Capitol, Senators Claiborne Pell and Gary Hart hosted a fund-raising party for the vets.

The party atmosphere was disrupted when it was announced that the Supreme Court, in the speediest decision in all American history, had ruled that the vets must break camp the next day. In a remarkable instance of poor timing, the Pentagon announced that "fragging" (attacks upon officers by their own soldiers) had more than doubled in 1970 compared to '69. Wednesday, amidst a variety of activities, the vets learned that the Supreme Court had ruled that the veterans could stay on the Mall, but, absurdly, anyone who fell asleep would be arrested. The vets voted to sleep. The cast of the musical *Hair* arrived to entertain them, and Senator Ted Kennedy visited and sang with the vets. History does not record the quality of the Senator's singing, but the vets were allowed to sleep. On Thursday, a group of vets on the steps of the Supreme Court inquired as to why the constitutionality of the war had not been challenged. They began to sing *God Bless America* and 110 were arrested for disturbing the peace, which may have been an indicator of the quality of their singing, but more likely for other reasons.

Also on that Thursday, veteran John Kerry testified before a special session of the Senate Foreign Relations Committee. "How do you ask a man to be the last man to die for a mistake?" Kerry asked; and he declared,

> We saw Vietnam ravaged equally by American bombs and search-and-destroy missions, as well as by Viet Cong terrorism, and yet we listened while this country tried to blame all of the havoc on the Viet Cong. We rationalized destroying villages in order to save them. We saw America lose her sense of morality as she accepted very coolly a My Lai and refused to give up the image of American soldiers who hand out chocolate bars and chewing gum. We learned the meaning of free-fire zones, shooting anything that moves, and we watched while America placed a cheapness on the lives of Orientals. We watched the United States' falsification of body counts, in fact the glorification of body counts. And now, we are told that the men who fought there must watch quietly while American lives are lost so that we can exercise the incredible arrogance of Vietnamizing the Vietnamese.

Other VVAW members testified before an assortment of congressional venues, and their accounts brought a number of the Pentagon's misrepresentations into the light of day.

On Friday, April 23, 1971, VVAW finally got the media coverage they wanted when more than 1,000 veterans, in a very orderly but passionate manner, briefly explained their reasons and then defiantly threw back their medals onto the steps of the Capitol. Scenes of that protest became some of the most iconic of the war, and America was finally forced to confront the desperation felt by many of the kids-next-door who had seen what was really happening in Vietnam. Inside the Capitol building, hearings continued. The vets broke camp, planted a symbolic tree on the Mall to honor life and the environment, and then went away. Not one act of violence had been committed over the five very emotional days in America's Capital city.

On April 24, over 200,000 protestors demonstrated on the Mall in Washington, while another 156,000 marched in San Francisco. Demonstrations in Washington were never able to "shut down" the government, but the week had certainly given lawmakers some new information to consider. Demonstrations continued through May 5, and almost 13,000 protestors were arrested, a new record. When those arrested came to court, the U.S. Government was found to have violated the civil and constitutional rights of most of the demonstrators, and they were released.

On June 13, the first portion of the report ordered by Secretary of Defense Robert McNamara in 1967, commonly known as the Pentagon Papers, was published by the *New York Times*. The Pentagon Papers contained 47 volumes of material, and only a small amount was ever printed in the daily newspapers. One can only pity the poor newsmen tasked with reading all of the material and separating out the most important bits for publication. Still, the implications of the material were very clear. The architects of U.S. involvement in the affairs of South Vietnam in the Kennedy and Johnson years had consistently lied and misled the American people, Congress, the press, and even their fellow bureaucrats up the hall. Within a couple of days, the Justice Department had sued both the *Times* and the *Washington Post*, but the Supreme Court ruled in a 6-3 vote that publication could continue.

The FBI had identified Daniel Ellsberg as the leaker, and President Nixon soon made every effort to destroy him. White House counsel Charles Colson, often recognized as the President's "hatchet man," recruited a covert special operations team that the President had created to stop information leaks, to search for any information that might discredit or embarrass Ellsberg. The "Plumbers," led by former CIA officer E. Howard Hunt, were unable to find anything in the records of Ellsberg's long career with the Defense Department, so they sought to satisfy the President by burglarizing the office of Ellsberg's psychiatrist. (Colson was the first of the Nixon insiders to be tried and sentenced to prison for his role in the break-in, which came to light as part of the Watergate scandal in 1974.) Nothing that would embarrass Daniel Ellsberg was ever found.

The Pentagon Papers, by their very volume, convinced the American public that a huge government conspiracy had involved us in Vietnam, and that we the American people had been systematically misinformed and manipulated. The Nixon administration could not ignore the growing numbers of Americans who were sick and tired of the war. They created elaborate contingency plans to deal with future demonstrations in the nation's Capital, with the ability to mobilize a force of Army and National Guard troops equal to one-fifth the size of the U.S. Army presence in Vietnam. In addition, the President called upon all levels of the intelligence community to escalate surveillance of the anti-war movement, including a large number of infiltrators, who were not only ordered to listen to what was going on in planning missions; they were trained and instructed to instigate illegal activities by anti-war groups, and to gather documents and other information that would lead to arrests of protestors wherever possible. Phones were tapped, meetings disrupted, and computer files compiled on 18,000 American "enemies," including members of Congress and civic leaders. President Nixon confided to friends that the White House felt like the Alamo.

On December 26, 1971, VVAW undertook a coordinated nationwide flurry of protests which included occupying the South Vietnamese consulate in San Francisco, the Lincoln Memorial, the Betsy Ross House in Philadelphia, barricading themselves in the Statue of Liberty and displaying the U.S. flag upside down from her crown – an international distress signal. It was a passionate time, and despite its success VVAW was reluctant to accept that a majority of Vietnam veterans were content to come home from the war and try to resume their old, familiar lives. Many thought VVAW's over-the-top theatrical demonstrations were silly or embarrassing, and a significant number of veterans were convinced that the peace movement was too supportive of the enemy they had recently faced, and their buddies were still facing in Vietnam.

By the end of 1971, a total of 45,627 Americans had died in Vietnam; fewer than 5,000 Americans in Vietnam had required hospitalization for combat wounds, but more than 20,500 were hospitalized due to serious drug abuse. A Congressional review described heroin addiction among the in-country troops as an "epidemic." G.I.s using heroin had increased from two percent in 1969 to twenty-two percent in '71, and it was estimated that 14% of the fighting force was using hallucinogenic drugs regularly. Investigators found that Vietnamese customs inspectors earned several dozen times the amount of their legitimate salaries by overlooking the heroin coming into the country. The Vietnamese said, accurately, that the heroin trafficking was an American problem and refused to do anything to stop it. Amidst the devastation of the war, the drug trade was bringing great wealth to Vietnam, and many saw the heroin addiction of American soldiers to be a subtle but effective front in the war against the American invaders.

While fragging incidents had not been a factor until 1969, in 1971, the military recorded 240 attacks upon officers, 11% fatal. 8,100 expensive American war planes had been shot out of the sky in 1971, and the scent of tear gas had become commonplace on the Washington Mall. In Paris, the peace talks had achieved nothing. South Vietnam flatly refused to accept any Communist or Viet Cong involvement in its affairs, and North Vietnam was confident that it would soon achieve a total military victory.

In December of 1971, American intelligence predicted that there would be a series of offensive actions at the beginning of the dry season, as happened every year, but this time the attacks would be intended to show that the Communist infrastructure had not been seriously damaged by the invasion of Laos. Despite elaborate electronic surveillance, MACV was confident that the reports of increased shipments along the Ho Chi Minh Trail were mistaken. Their own inflated reports of damages a few months earlier indicated that Hanoi should have nothing left to ship, and the trail should be impassable due to bombing. Buildups along the DMZ were thought to be defensive, perhaps a signal that the prior year's invasion of Laos had made the North Vietnamese more respectful of the ARVN's capabilities. Another interpretation of the increased numbers of trucks moving south along the Ho Chi Minh Trail construed them as a temporary compensation after the interruptions to traffic caused by the invasion. By the time they realized that a major offensive was imminent, American leaders in Saigon found President Thieu to be noncommittal and unconcerned. American troop strength was down to 156,000 and the president had committed to withdraw another 47,000 by July. MACV prepared to counter the upcoming offensive with air power.

President Nixon ordered the Air Force to emphasize bombing North Vietnam's anti-aircraft emplacements and air force installations, and the President ordered Air Force General John Lavelle and all the top layers of American leadership in Vietnam to describe all attacks as "protective reaction." According to the international rules of military engagement, these actions could only be reactive, and could only target the specific guns that had fired upon American aircraft. The President called for an all-out attack, especially targeting enemy radar installations and air defenses. An American airman realized that his colleagues were defying international rules and notified his congressman, and Congress began an investigation. The President expressed regrets to Henry Kissinger within the confines of the Oval Office, but when Nixon had every opportunity to tell the truth and save General Lavelle from humiliation and the destruction of his career, he told the media, "It was proper for him to be relieved and retired." Lavelle was demoted and forced to retire in disgrace. No other official was held responsible. Until his death, Lavelle maintained that he had acted under orders from the Joint Chiefs of Staff, Defense Secretary Melvin Laird, and General Abrams. In 2010, researchers examining the transcripts of tapes from Nixon's Oval Office discovered that the President had indeed, in full accord with Henry Kissinger, ordered the bombing. In 2010, the Senate restored John Lavelle to his full four-star rank, posthumously.

President Nixon, responding to criticisms that his administration had not made sincere efforts to end the war, revealed that Kissinger had held a dozen secret negotiations in Paris with Hanoi's highest-ranking officials. Thailand withdrew its forces from Vietnam in February of 1972, at the same time South Korea began withdrawals of its troops. The U.S. was now conducting the heaviest bombing of the war, with a decided emphasis upon targets in the Central Highlands of South Vietnam. By late February, the Communists were staging significant attacks in the Mekong Delta and near Da Nang on the coast. The U.S. began a "limited duration" bombing offensive against North Vietnamese artillery positions, and a surprising number of American planes were shot down by surface-to-air missiles (SAM).

President Nixon journeyed to Beijing and met with Prime Minister Chou En Lai to re-establish relations with Communist China after 25 years of diplomatic silence. Nixon promised to reduce America's military presence on the island of Taiwan, or "Nationalist China," and North Vietnam feared that the American effort signaled a new era of cooperation between the U.S. and its old rival China. In fact, Nixon's visit to China changed the entire character of the Cold War, ultimately aligning Communist China with the U.S. against the Soviet Union. Nixon described the visit as "the week that changed the world," perhaps because his old employer, Pepsico, would now be allowed to sell its products to the vast population of China. The "Pepsi Generation" had just acquired a billion new thirsty customers.

The North Vietnamese contingent walked out of the next meeting of the peace talks in Paris after only seventeen minutes. By March 7, the number of U.S. bombing raids over the North eclipsed the total number in 1971. Unlike the Tet offensive of 1968, Communist forces in the South hit intermittently, but effectively. American bombing had become a major factor. By late March, a large force of North Vietnamese swept southward across the DMZ and routed the ARVN, pushing on into the provincial capital city of Quang Tri, where the entire South Vietnamese 56th Regiment promptly deserted. In the Central Highlands, the Communist forces seized the critical highway between Pleiku and Kontum, while another force attacked the American air base at Cam Ranh Bay. B-52s increased bombing in North Vietnam, and two additional American aircraft carriers were deployed to the South China Sea to reinforce the four already there. Two squadrons of B-52s were added, and the number and scope of bombing missions increased to the greatest intensity of the war. The B-52s were now ordered to hit supply and storage facilities in Hanoi and Haiphong, but the vast majority of bombing missions continued to pound targets in South Vietnam.

In response to news of the increased bombing, a new wave of protests and demonstrations swept America. The National Guard was ordered onto the University of Maryland campus, where hundreds of students were arrested. Thousands of protestors marched in all the major cities as the presidents of all eight Ivy League colleges and MIT issued a joint statement opposing the bombing and encouraging orderly anti-war protests. Protestors closed Columbia University and occupied Lewisohn Hall for 17 days. In May, the presidents of sixty Midwest colleges issued a statement calling for the immediate withdrawal of all U.S. forces from Southeast Asia. 1972 was a Presidential election year, and the statement was delivered to President Nixon and all the anticipated candidates.

On May 1, Communists troops finally captured Quang Tri city as the ARVN 3rd Division disintegrated and deserted. Hundreds of thousands of refugees from Quang Tri and Hue fled on foot, moving south toward Da Nang. The government of South Vietnam announced the evacuation of all civilians from Kontum and Pleiku.

President Nixon announced that he had ordered the mining of all North Vietnamese ports, and his intention to seize any foreign ships suspected of bringing weapons and military hardware from Communist China or Russia. U.S. planes would bomb rail shipments from China and do whatever might be necessary to slow the flow of supplies to the North. Announcement of the mining of North Vietnam's harbors ignited a bitter season of protests across America, and condemnation from many foreign governments. The Defense Department promptly requested additional funding to carry out the mining operations. With the addition of the *Ticonderoga*, the U.S. now had seven aircraft carriers in the waters off Vietnam, along with six destroyers. In late May, a major North Vietnamese force swept into the Mekong Delta, south of Saigon.

In early June, journalist Seymour Hersh released a secret report which showed clearly that the entire commanding officer staff of the Army's American Division had suppressed information pertinent to the investigation of the My Lai massacre. Hersh also revealed that the nearby hamlet of My Khe was the site of a gruesomely similar massacre of approximately 94 civilians on the same morning as the atrocity at My Lai.

On June 17, 1972, five men were arrested for breaking into the offices of the Democratic National Committee located in the Watergate complex in Washington, D.C.

Journalist Kevin Buckley of *Newsweek*, with Alexander Shimkin, published an article titled "Pacification's Deadly Price" that brought to light a 1968 "Operation Speedy Express" in which U.S. soldiers working in the Mekong Delta province of Kien Hoa may have killed as many as 5,000 civilians as part of the pacification program. The official army records show 10,899 enemy combatants killed but only 748 weapons captured. Interviews with survivors indicated that most of the "enemy" killed were actually unarmed farmers working in their fields. The story received little attention in the U.S., and General Westmoreland declined to investigate the matter. Later the story was corroborated in a number of books, including *Steel my Soldiers' Hearts* by Col. David Hackworth, and *Kill Anything That Moves* by Nick Turse. A number of accounts by soldiers assigned to the army's 9th Division and investigative journalists indicate that the 9th Division operated under a policy requiring G.I.s to create an outstanding "body count" by whatever means necessary. This policy was implemented and strictly enforced by 9th Division Commander General Julian Ewell. It is estimated that as many as 9,000 innocent civilians were killed during Operation Speedy Express. No one was ever held responsible for the mass killings. Indeed, when he promoted General Ewell to command the II Field Force, the U.S. commander in Vietnam, General Abrams, described Ewell as a "brilliant and sensitive commander... And he plays hard," and noted that "the performance of this division has been magnificent."

In July, U.N. Secretary General Kurt Waldheim announced that he had confirmed reports that the U.S. was intentionally bombing North Vietnamese dikes that were necessary to prevent flooding during the rainy season. President Nixon and his top cabinet officials insisted that any damage to the dikes was accidental, and Nixon said Waldheim was "well-intentioned and naïve." Within a few days, a CIA report claimed that the dikes had been damaged in 12 places and those damages could be catastrophic for North Vietnamese civilians. Hanoi reported the dikes had been damaged in 149 places. Bombing of the dikes was advocated by a number of U.S. military strategists throughout the American effort in Vietnam but had been rejected by previous Presidents because it would cause disastrous results for thousands of Vietnamese peasants.

In late July, former U.S. Attorney General Ramsey Clark visited North Vietnam as part of an International Commission of Inquiry into U.S. War Crimes in Indochina. He was primarily interested in alleged bombing of non-military targets in North Vietnam. Clark reported via Hanoi radio that he had seen bombing damage to the dikes, hospitals, schools, and civilian residential areas. Some Americans were critical of his visit and his reports, while others had become resigned to the American Way of Waging War.

By August, Communist forces controlled all major supply routes into Saigon. Despite heavy fighting, South Vietnamese forces were unable to maintain control of those key highways. On August 11, the last U.S. ground combat unit in Vietnam was withdrawn, bringing the total number of troops actually in-country to less than 45,000. A report smuggled from Saigon indicated that over 10,000 South Vietnamese had been arrested, and many were being transported to Con Son jail by the CIA's Air America airline for the purpose of torture. U.S. advisors did not deny the reports.

In Paris, Henry Kissinger resumed private talks with the North Vietnamese negotiators as the end of the rainy season allowed the U.S. to resume bombing. Thousands of anti-war demonstrators attempted to disrupt the Republican National Convention in Miami. Some of this activity was pictured in the 1989 movie *Born on The 4th of July* starring Tom Cruise, and taken from the book of the same name by paralyzed Marine veteran and anti-war activist Ron Kovic. In October, a racial disturbance injured 46 crewmen aboard the aircraft carrier *Kitty Hawk* off the coast of Vietnam. In San Diego, 123 black sailors were reassigned when they refused to return to the aircraft carrier *Constellation* after onboard racial incidents left them fearing for their lives. Other racial incidents happened at a naval installation at Midway Island in the Pacific, and also at a Navy correctional facility in Norfolk, Virginia. Throughout the U.S. military worldwide, fully 25% of all Americans in uniform were either deserted, AWOL(absent without leave), refusing orders, or openly mutinous. The desertion rate was 73.5 per 1000, the highest for any year of any American war in history. Fully 176 of every 1000 American servicemen were simply absent – not available for duty. Among those that remained, morale was terrible. Many historians feel that America did not end the Vietnam War due to the efforts of the peace movement back home, but because morale had so deteriorated throughout the American military that it could no longer function.

During the years of the Vietnam War, more than 500,000 American soldiers, including about 170,000 Vietnam veterans, received an "other than honorable" discharge from the military, making them ineligible for G.I. Bill benefits or medical attention at VA medical facilities for the rest of their lives.

In October of 1972, a bomb hit the French Embassy in Hanoi as the U.S. intensified bombing across the North and the South. The peace talks in Paris finally yielded the first signs of a cease-fire agreement. Henry Kissinger flew to Saigon to get President Thieu's acceptance, but Thieu rejected the plan. Because North Vietnam's Premier Pham Van Dong announced the cease-fire to the press, military units throughout Vietnam, Laos, and Cambodia attempted to establish their control as much as possible before peace would be established. In a show of respect for the North Vietnamese concessions at the peace talks, President Nixon ordered a halt to all bombing north of the 20th parallel in North Vietnam.

But the war was far from over. Almost immediately, the talks in Paris broke off again due to South Vietnam's insistence that all North Vietnamese troops be withdrawn. Richard Nixon was re-elected President by a wide margin over Democrat George McGovern, who was very enthusiastically supported by the young and anti-war communities, but not by many mainstream Democrats. This was the first Presidential election, after passage of the 26th Amendment, in which 18-year-olds could vote. Nixon certainly benefitted from his rapprochement with China, and the general feeling that he was very near to ending the war.

By late November, the North Vietnamese were focusing their attacks upon the northern provinces. It was revealed that the U.S. was bringing a large number of Defense Department contractor personnel to Vietnam to replace the military advisors being withdrawn. Plans called for as many as 10,000 of these civilian mercenaries to remain in South Vietnam after the final American military forces would be withdrawn, as "independent businessmen" would not be affected by a ceasefire treaty. There were now less than 27,000 American troops in Vietnam. However, U.S forces in Thailand, Guam, the Philippines, or on ships off the coast were not being depleted. In fact, areas near Hanoi and the port facility at Haiphong, along the Ho Chi Minh Trail in Laos and Cambodia, and conflict areas throughout South Vietnam actually underwent increased bombardment. By mid-December, President Nixon and Henry Kissinger were becoming frustrated at North Vietnam's reluctance to negotiate the South's future. The President ordered the Air Force to prepare to deliver the heaviest bombing of the war, and to target areas of Hanoi and Haiphong that had never been bombed previously. Kissinger charged Hanoi with delaying a peace agreement and Nixon announced a full resumption of bombing and mining operations, to end only when all U.S. prisoners of war were released and a peace agreement in effect. Australia withdrew the last of its personnel from Vietnam.

The "Christmas bombing" of 1972 was the most devastating of the war, targeting heavily populated areas of Hanoi and Haiphong that had not been hit previously. American ships also conducted a heavy bombardment of North Vietnamese targets, as more than 100 B-52 bombers delivered thousands of tons of bombs day and night. Hanoi announced that the suffering of civilians was at its worst in ten years, while the White House reported significant damage only to military targets. The U.S. was condemned around the world for its attacks upon non-military targets. American bombs hit the Cuban, Indian, East German, and Egyptian embassies and Hanoi's largest hospital. Eleven B-52s were shot down. The bombing of North Vietnam between December 18th and 24th was the equivalent of twenty of the atomic bombs dropped on Hiroshima, Japan at the end of World War II. After a short pause for the Christmas holiday, on December 26th American bombers pounded Hanoi continuously for more than forty minutes. Five more B-52s were shot down. In Australia, the Seaman's Union announced that it would refuse to unload American ships to protest the bombing. Italy, Sweden, the Netherlands, Austria, and Belgium officially protested the bombing. Marches in the streets of England and France demanded their governments take action against the slaughter, but the governments took no official actions. The intense bombing ended on December 31.

Despite the withdrawals, 4,300 flag-covered caskets were shipped home to a dispirited American public in 1972. Apollo 17, the sixth NASA mission to land men on the moon, came home on December 19. It was the final manned flight to the moon, and the culmination of mankind's greatest technological accomplishment – but America's pride was severely overshadowed by concerns about the disintegrating war.

Chapter 8

VIETNAM: WHAT REALLY HAPPENED?

PART 6 ... 1973 – 1975

Having failed to eliminate the "Viet Cong" with 500,000 American troops and 15 million tons of bombs and shells, it was absurd for the Americans to hope for their disappearance through negotiations.
– Activist Tom Hayden, *Boston Globe*, 1973.

Power always has to be kept in check; power exercised in secret, especially under the cloak of national security, is doubly dangerous.
– Senator William Proxmire.

The peace negotiations in Paris resumed in early January of 1973. On January 15, President Nixon suspended all bombing, shelling, mining, and all other military actions against North Vietnam, and on the 18th, the negotiators announced that they had reached a peace agreement. On January 23, 1973, President Nixon announced that the agreement had been signed in Paris, and a cease-fire would go into effect on the 28th. Henry Kissinger also announced that he expected peace treaties soon in Laos and Cambodia.

In anticipation of a peace accord, the U.S. had poured weapons and equipment into South Vietnam for months, making the South Vietnamese Air Force the fourth largest in the world. South Vietnam was still unwilling to recognize the Viet Cong or their Provisional Revolutionary Government, so two separate versions of the peace agreement were prepared, one for the U.S. and both Vietnams, and another just between North Vietnam and the United States. The agreement stipulated a cease-fire throughout all of North and South Vietnam; the withdrawal of all

American combat troops and advisors and dismantling of all American bases within 60 days; release of all Prisoners of War within 60 days; withdrawal of all foreign troops from Cambodia and Laos; continuation of the 17th Parallel as the border between North and South until the country could be reunited "through peaceful means"; and establishment of an international commission to oversee the agreement. North Vietnam would respect the right of the people of the South to "self-determination" of their government; President Thieu would remain in power pending elections; there were to be no military movements across the DMZ; and no use of force to reunify the two Vietnams.

From the start, the two Vietnams accused each other of aggression. Hanoi released the first of 587 American POWs on February 12, and the last in late March. The last U.S. military personnel left Vietnam on March 29, 1973, with the exception of a small contingent of Marine guards at the U.S. Embassy in Saigon. Approximately 8,500 American civilians remained in-country, including reporters, businessmen, and Defense Department contractors. The U.S. continued to bomb Communist operations in Cambodia. Opposition to any further military operations in Southeast Asia was very apparent in Washington, although Nixon and Kissinger proposed continuation of air attacks until August 15. Congress finally agreed, but after that date Congressional approval would be required for any military operation in Indochina.

Recalling that Laos was supposed to be a neutral country, the Senate Armed Service Committee investigated reports that the Air Force conducted thousands of B-52 raids into Laos and Cambodia in 1969 and 1970. The Pentagon admitted that the raids had taken place, and claimed they were authorized by President Nixon and Defense Secretary Melvin Laird. The State Department claimed Laotian ruler Prince Sihanouk had requested the raids, but he denied that assertion. Laird and Henry Kissinger denied they had known or authorized the falsification of records. Again, no one was held accountable. Laos had been subjected to the most intense bombardment in history. It is unknown how many civilians died.

U.S. bombing of Cambodia ceased at midnight, August 14, 1973. This was the definitive end of U.S. military activity in Southeast Asia. Nixon appointed Henry Kissinger as Secretary of State a few days later, when William Rogers resigned.

Vice President Spiro Agnew resigned on October 10, 1973 after the U.S. Justice Department uncovered widespread evidence of corruption, including allegations that he had regularly accepted bribes. In a familiar case of hypocrisy, Agnew had been an outspoken proponent of the rule of law when running for office. He was succeeded by Gerald Ford, a longtime political ally and friend of President Nixon.

In October, Kissinger and North Vietnam's chief negotiator Le Duc Tho were awarded the Nobel Peace Prize for ending the Vietnam War. Le Duc Tho declined to accept the award until a real peace would finally be established in his country.

Congress passed the War Powers Resolution, which required congressional approval before any deployment of combat troops to any future overseas conflict. President Nixon vetoed the bill, stating it would impose "dangerous restrictions" on presidential authority. Congress overrode the veto a few days later and this law remains in effect today, although it is usually ignored and the majority of Americans don't even know it exists.

Early in January of 1974, President Thieu announced that the war had restarted.

In February, the National Academy of Sciences reported that the use of herbicides such as Agent Orange in Vietnam had done damage to the country's ecology that might last as long as 100 years.

By the summer of 1974, South Vietnam reported that the North was preparing a major offensive, and the White House requested increased military aid to the Saigon government. Congress rejected the request. Soon after, Congress set limits on aid to South Vietnam of $700 million in 1974 and $300 million in 1975. In 1973, military aid to the Saigon regime had been $2.8 billion.

In early May of 1974, the House of Representatives Judiciary Committee began impeachment hearings against President Nixon over the Watergate break-in and subsequent cover-up. On July 30, they voted to impeach the President on three counts. America was adhered to its TV sets as the hearings presented a stunning scenario of lawbreaking, arrogance, and covert illegal actions against supposed "enemies" of the White House. Finally, on August 9, 1974, Richard Nixon acknowledged his untenable position and resigned. Vice-President Gerald Ford became President and soon after he pardoned Nixon from all criminal prosecution.

On January 6, 1975, North Vietnamese forces overran Phuoc Binh, the capital of Phuoc Long Province. Hanoi had expected America to come to the aid of South Vietnamese forces, and they prepared for a major offensive. President Ford requested emergency funds for the Saigon regime, but Congress declined any further assistance. By March, the North Vietnamese captured Ban Me Thuot in the central highlands. A huge number of refugees moved south to escape the advancing army, and a large number of South Vietnamese troops deserted to help their families escape. President Thieu ordered all ARVN forces to withdraw from the central highlands and to defend the coastal city of Hue. Once again, many of the ARVN troops retreated and deserted. Within two weeks, Thieu ordered his army to abandon Hue. Over a million refugees were streaming south on foot, expecting the military to stop the Communists at Da Nang, the site of a huge American air and combat base. President Ford announced that he had ordered American Navy ships to assist in the evacuation of refugees. Da Nang fell to the North Vietnamese on March 29th, seemingly without resistance. ARVN troops actually shed their uniforms and joined the flood of refugees moving south ahead of the advancing Communist forces. No one, including the North Vietnamese, had expected the ARVN to offer so little resistance. The Communist offensive rolled on, and all of South Vietnam was in a state of panic.

On April 3, as the situation worsened, President Ford announced "Operation Babylift." Perhaps to put a caring, decent gesture on record at the end of the struggle, or perhaps as a grandstand last-minute humanitarian appeal for emergency funding, the Air Force began evacuating Vietnamese orphans from Saigon. Tragically, on April 4, a C-5A jet crashed shortly after takeoff, killing over 150 children and the crew. The evacuation was ultimately able to remove about 2,000 children before Saigon fell, and most of them were brought to the States. Although many of the orphans had been fathered by U.S. servicemen, they were not generally welcomed to America.

The situation in Saigon had become so dire that American authorities began planning a final evacuation. The Pentagon wanted to evacuate all American personnel as quickly as possible to ensure their safety, but U.S. Ambassador Graham Martin wanted a very low-key process, for fear the South Vietnamese would turn against the remaining Americans when they realized an evacuation was in process. Henry Kissinger opposed any evacuation, fearing that it would show a lack of faith in President Thieu and weaken him at a critical time. President Ford approved an interim plan to remove all but the most essential 1,250 Americans, a number that could be evacuated by helicopters in a day, and as many refugees as possible. The President was still hoping Congress would approve an additional $722 million in emergency funds for the Saigon government. There were also legal concerns about whether the President could deploy military personnel to evacuate Americans or refugees without requesting congressional approval under the War Powers Act. Meanwhile, in Saigon the situation was desperate and getting worse by the day. Americans had to get to Tan Son Nhut airport through huge crowds of panicked Vietnamese. Government offices in Saigon were besieged with throngs of desperate people offering handfuls and briefcases of money for a passport and exit visa. The price of escape by air or sea was going through the roof. Citizens with relatives or friends in America reached out requesting sponsorship so they could escape to the U.S., but there was little time to make arrangements through official channels.

Many Americans refused to leave without their Vietnamese friends and dependents. A number had not been able to negotiate the complex paperwork to become legally married in the eyes of the U.S. government, and technically it was illegal to move these people to American soil. In the atmosphere of utter panic, sometimes with the sound of North Vietnamese rockets landing near the city, eventually the American authorities began illegally flying some undocumented Vietnamese to Clark Air Force Base in the Philippines, where their paperwork could be completed.

In early April, a force of South Vietnam's most capable soldiers was overrun at Phan Rang. Over two-thirds of South Vietnam was now controlled by the Communists. A final line of defense was formed at Xuan Loc, just north of Saigon, and both sides brought in reinforcements for the final battle. The South Vietnamese held on for almost two weeks before they ran out of ammunition and supplies. Their air bases had fallen to the North Vietnamese, and on April 21 the last remaining defenders finally abandoned their posts and retreated into the city. Rockets began to fall on downtown Saigon. There was utter chaos in the streets.

On April 12, all American Embassy staff evacuated Phnom Penh, the capital of Cambodia. On April 16, the government of Cambodia surrendered to the Khmer Rouge and the People's Assembly under leader Pol Pot. Over the next three years, the Pol Pot regime murdered approximately two million Cambodians.

South Vietnam's President Thieu deftly handed off the leadership of South Vietnam to his Vice-President Tran Van Huong and escaped to Taiwan on April 25. On April 28, Huong handed over all authority to General Duong Van Minh. "Big Minh" had been active in South Vietnamese politics for many years, and the North Vietnamese had indicated they would be willing to negotiate with him.

On April 29, the largest helicopter evacuation in history began removing the last Americans from Saigon. Over 1,000 Americans were evacuated along with 6,000 Vietnamese. Those who had worked closely with the Americans were especially fearful of the Communist takeover – and desperate throngs attempted to escape by all means possible. Two fliers became the last Americans to die in Vietnam when their evacuation helicopter crashed.

On April 30, 1975, North Vietnamese troops moved into Saigon, and soon their tanks crashed through the gates of the Presidential Palace. "Big Minh" announced an unconditional surrender and by nightfall, after thirty years, Vietnam was finally reunited. Saigon was re-named Ho Chi Minh City. The war was over.

* * *

In a world of injustice, peace cannot be expected for long. But peace itself is a value we should cherish, a value threatening to a system geared for war. We should cherish the thought that the skies of Vietnam are clearing, that the long-suffering guerrillas may embrace their families by day, that our machinery of death is being repelled and restrained. If we feel the happy possibilities of just this moment, we will fight all the harder to keep it this way forever.
– Activist Tom Hayden, 1973.

Only recently has the whole and fully documented truth come out about President Nixon's "negotiations" to end the war behind the scenes. In his amazing 2015 book *Fatal Politics: The Nixon Tapes, The Vietnam War, and the Casualties of Reelection*, author Ken Hughes reveals that Nixon and his National Security Advisor / Secretary of State Henry Kissinger conspired to abandon the war in Vietnam in a manner that would not jeopardize the President's chances of being re-elected in November of 1972. There is a common impression that Congress betrayed the new President, the military, and South Vietnam by refusing Ford's desperate last-minute request for $722 million dollars in emergency aid for the Saigon regime as the North Vietnamese were marching almost unopposed toward the capital in early 1975.

Author Hughes has spent many hours listening to Nixon's secret tape recordings from microphones hidden under the President's desk in the Oval Office. Briefly: in December of 1970 Nixon and his staff had realized that the war in Vietnam was unwinnable. The President planned to announce that he would withdraw all American troops from Vietnam by December 31 of 1971, but Kissinger reminded him that he would have a hard time getting re-elected in late 1972 if he would be the President who had finally lost Vietnam to the Communists. Ultimately, in those many secret meetings with Le Duc Tho in Paris, Kissinger worked out a deal whereby the U.S. would continue to withdraw troops in increments until early 1973 – a "decent interval" after the election to be held in November of 1972, and then we would *not* re-enter the fray and oppose the North's takeover of South Vietnam.

Official numbers show that the U.S. had lost 45,267 soldiers in Vietnam as of December 31, 1971. Ultimately, the total number lost presently stands at 58,315. This means that more than 13,000 American soldiers lost their lives needlessly so Nixon could win re-election in 1972. In the best-selling book *The Final Days* by Bob Woodward and Carl Bernstein, (Simon & Schuster, 1976), Henry Kissinger is quoted as describing American military personnel as "dumb, stupid animals to be used." Richard Nixon is long dead, but Henry Kissinger is still alive, and sometimes interviewed on TV as if his opinions are valuable. Of course, Mr. Kissinger need not worry that he will ever be held accountable for participating in actions which killed 13,000 American "dumb, stupid animals" and countless thousands of Vietnamese, Laotian, and Cambodian peasants. The great tragedy of the Vietnam War is that none of those responsible were ever held accountable. That precedent is proving to be very threatening to America's position in the world, and our future.

* * *

As this is written, the total number of names on the Vietnam Veterans Memorial is 58,315. Three were added in 2010, so names are occasionally added if the Defense Department rules the death as attributable to the war, even four decades after it ended. All of the numbers regarding the war are approximate. One wonders how the computer "whiz kids" under Secretary of Defense Robert McNamara could fail to accurately record the number of Americans deployed to Vietnam, the number of women, the numbers of killed and wounded, the financial costs of the war to the American taxpayer, or any other statistics that would inform the American people about the true costs of the wars in Southeast Asia. Approximately 350,000 G.I.s were wounded, of which approximately 160,000 were classified as serious.

The percentage of Americans who actually faced Viet Cong or North Vietnamese troops in battle is relatively small, but it is estimated that approximately 75% of all Americans who went to Vietnam experienced incoming mortars or rockets during their deployment. Approximately 55% saw a fellow soldier wounded or killed. (Am I the only one confused by those last two sentences?) The concept of Shock Trauma emergency medical care originated in Vietnam, and helicopters brought the wounded to the medics in record time. As a result, over 80% of seriously wounded G.I.s survived, compared to 71 % in World War II and 75% in Korea. Approximately 10,000 Americans lost at least one limb, which was more than the total from World War II and Korea combined.

The United States did not resume diplomatic relations with Vietnam until 1994, and in fact maintained a very strict economic embargo that drastically inhibited Vietnam's ability to rebuild. The U.S. offered no medical or health-related aid to our former "ally" or its people, despite having subjected them to the most intense bombardment in human history. A few American religious workers have managed to gain admittance to Vietnam over the years and aid the Vietnamese people. Unexploded ordnance, or UXO, continues to kill and maim civilians, and Vietnamese officials have predicted that the country will not be free of this threat until approximately, or hopefully, another fifty years. In 2015, the U.S. finally allocated $12 million to help with the cleanup. Birth defects presumed to be related to Agent Orange and other defoliants have continue to occur forty years after the war ended.

The Communist takeover of South Vietnam was brutal and merciless, as anticipated. Many thousands of Vietnamese sought to escape, usually by sea. The "boat people" refugees overwhelmed many neighboring countries such as Thailand and Malaysia, and many were turned away. It is estimated that 300,000 were allowed to enter the United States.

Chapter 9

THE AFTERMATH

Americans cannot perceive – even the most decent among us – the suffering caused by the United States air war in Indochina, and how huge are the graveyards we have created there.
    – Gloria Emerson, *New York Times* correspondent in Vietnam.

Vietnam:

In the aftermath of the war, it is estimated that between 1 and 2.5 million Vietnamese were sent to re-education camps after the Communists conquered South Vietnam, and as many as 165,000 are estimated to have died there. Somewhere between 50,000 and 250,000 were executed. The United Nations High Commission for Refugees estimates that as many as 200,000 to 400,000 boat people died at sea, while other estimates are much higher. The government of Vietnam claims unexploded bombs, land mines, and artillery shells have killed 42,000 since the war ended. While that number cannot be independently verified, several American groups are active in Vietnam, aiding the cleanup effort. Their reports, along with government data, indicate that 500 civilians were wounded or killed by unexploded ordnance in Laos, Cambodia, and Vietnam in 2012 alone. Since 1998, the U.S. has contributed more than $65 million to aid the cleanup campaign in Vietnam, but it is estimated it will take another fifty years to finally make all areas of the country safe.

Chemical defoliants, especially Agent Orange, have caused illnesses and birth defects in both U.S. servicemen and the population of Vietnam. The principle dangerous ingredient of Agent Orange, Dioxin, is considered by scientists to be the most toxic substance in the world. Between 1961 and 1971, 18.2 million gallons of Agent Orange were sprayed over South Vietnam. While the U.S. has basically confirmed that Agent Orange was toxic, the government has shielded chemical companies from prosecution, and has allowed only minimal funds for research or health benefits to G.I.s affected by the chemicals, or their offspring. The Vietnamese government claims that 4 million of its citizens were exposed to Agent Orange, and 3 million have experienced health problems as a result. American civilians working with the Vietnamese, some of them veterans, report that birth defects are still showing up in the grandchildren of Vietnamese exposed to Agent Orange, and illnesses such as cancer are much more prevalent in areas where the heaviest spraying occurred. The Red Cross of Vietnam estimates that up to one million Vietnamese are experiencing health problems related to exposure to chemical defoliants used by the Americans during the war, which ended more than forty years ago. In August of 2012, the U.S. committed to helping Vietnam clean up toxic chemical sites at DaNang Airport. This marks the first time the U.S. has officially been involved in any cleanup of toxic chemicals left over from the war. This initial project is budgeted at $41 million, and other infected sites are being considered.

The U.S. began to normalize diplomatic relations with Vietnam in 1991. In 1994, President Bill Clinton ended the trade embargo that had been in place since the end of the war, and a year later relations between the two nations were normalized. Vietnam has enthusiastically endorsed capitalism and free enterprise, but the authoritarian government continues to maintain tight controls over individuals and newspapers that attempt to speak out or criticize those in power. While foreign companies have built factories in the urban centers, people outside the cities still live in abject poverty.

Cambodia:

Cambodia's position along the western border of the two Vietnams made it an extremely important factor in the Vietnam War. With wars developing in neighboring Laos and Vietnam its leader, Prince Norodom Sihanouk, attempted to keep his country neutral in order to avoid the damages that involvement would bring. In the early 1960s he gave permission to North Vietnam to establish resupply points and base camps near the border with Vietnam, in return for North Vietnam's guarantees that it would not attempt to influence Cambodian politics. North Vietnam created the famous Ho Chi Minh Trail through southeastern Laos and then on through Cambodia to infiltrate South Vietnam at various locations. Because Cambodia was officially "neutral," bombing of these sanctuaries was limited under President Johnson, consisting of raids upon specific targets, with no carpet bombing by B-52s. Targets were determined by approximately 2,000 secret spy missions by CIA, Special Forces and reconnaissance teams operating within Cambodia.

In January of 1969 as President Nixon took office, a rocket attack on Saigon was launched from the NVA's main base in Cambodia. Nixon was encouraged by American General Creighton Abrams, the Joint Chiefs of Staff, and Security Advisor Henry Kissinger to increase the bombing of Cambodia significantly, and Prince Sihanouk secretly gave his approval, though he later condemned the bombing in public speeches.

In March of 1969, the Communists launched an offensive in South Vietnam, and President Nixon, who had stopped the bombing of the North in an effort to encourage the peace talks, felt betrayed. Nixon authorized an intense series of carpet bombing raids on North Vietnamese bases and supply routes in Cambodia. Over 3,800 B-52 missions dropped approximately 110,000 tons of bombs on "neutral" Cambodia. As we have seen previously, each B-52 bomb run would effectively devastate an area approximately .6 miles wide and 1.2 miles long, leaving nothing living in its wake. In Washington, Nixon and Kissinger kept these missions secret, knowing that the public would disapprove of escalating the Vietnam War by bombarding a nearby neutral country.

In March of 1970, Prince Sihanouk was deposed and Cambodia came under the rule of General Lon Nol, a friend and ally of the U.S. Within days, North Vietnamese forces attacked Lon Nol's weak army and seized most of eastern Cambodia. In response to this development, the allies invaded. South Vietnamese troops were the first to enter Cambodia on April 29, 1970. American forces invaded Cambodia on May 1, and conducted a series of missions until the end of June. They discovered large caches of enemy supplies, including weapons, ammunition, rockets, communications equipment, and a number of U.S.-built trucks. Most of the weapons and ammunition were delivered to Lon Nol's army for use in the struggle against the Khmer Rouge. Although the Allied forces never found the North Vietnamese headquarters they were seeking, the invasion was considered a success due to the amount of supplies and ammunition taken out of the enemy's hands.

The invasion of Cambodia resulted in a wave of protests in America, including the shooting of students at Kent State University. In Cambodia, the Communists supplied weapons and advisors to the Khmer Rouge forces, and a bitter civil war ensued. Lon Nol recognized a large community of Vietnamese refugees in his country, and he ordered his army to round up all Vietnamese men. Approximately 800 of those captives were executed and their bodies dumped into the Mekong River, to be carried into South Vietnam and serve as a warning. President Nixon complained to Kissinger that the American Air Force was being "unimaginative," and demanded an increase in the intensity and target areas of the bombing. Years later, Nixon was heard on tape exhorting Kissinger to "crack the hell out of them. There is no limit on mileage and there is no limit on budget. Is that clear?" Kissinger knew that this order ignored Nixon's promise to Congress that bombing missions into Cambodia would not go beyond thirty kilometers of the Vietnamese border. Over two million tons of bombs were rained upon Cambodia, resulting in total destruction of vast amounts of territory, and incalculable loss of life. Survivors gravitated to the Khmer Rouge in large numbers, increasing the Communist army's manpower from 5,000 to more than 200,000. The carpet bombing continued until 1973 when Congress cut all funding for the wars in Southeast Asia.

In 1973, the Senate Armed Services Committee uncovered the truth regarding the bombing of Cambodia, and the Nixon administration's extensive program to expand the Vietnam War without informing Congress. By that time, Nixon was facing impeachment in relation to the Watergate break-in, and the full story of his deceptive bombing campaign in Cambodia became known. Washington was in turmoil, the American people were sick and tired of war, and so Congress turned off the finances. Although the covert bombing of Cambodia was never added to the list of "high crimes and misdemeanors" for which Nixon was to be impeached, both Congress and the top-level officers of the military were deeply offended that the President and his men had lied to them in defiance of the Constitution, further undermining Nixon during the Watergate investigation and impeachment hearings.

Cambodia fell to the Khmer Rouge on April 17, 1975 and the government of South Vietnam fell on April 30. Despite twenty years of American involvement, the expenditure of about 377 billion American dollars, the deaths of more than three million people, the majority of whom were innocent civilians, and the devastation of three agricultural countries without war ever having been declared, Communists now controlled Vietnam, Cambodia, and Laos. More than two million Cambodians had been left homeless, in utter poverty. Many thousands were wounded and unable to work. The Khmer Rouge under Pol Pot proved to be one of the most brutal regimes in world history. In four years of rule, they murdered somewhere between 1.4 and 2.2 million of their countrymen in the most horrible and inhuman campaign of genocide since Nazi Germany. In 1979 they were removed from power in an invasion by the Socialist Republic of Vietnam. The new government was moderate, and Cambodia has slowly recovered from the holocaust. Factions of the Khmer Rouge survived for many years as a resistance movement based in western Cambodia and areas of northern Thailand. Pol Pot formally dissolved the Khmer Rouge party in 1996, and he died without ever standing trial in 1998.

Cambodia has set up a number of organizations to deal with unexploded land mines and bombs, with considerable success. The number of Cambodians injured or killed by leftover explosives has declined from a high of 4,320 in 1996 to 286 in 2010, 45 in 2012, and only 23 in 2013. In 1997, a Mine Ban Treaty signed in Ottawa, Canada by a number of nations resulted in a promising effort to ban the use, production, or shipment of land mines. The late Princess Diana of England was a strong supporter and spokesman for the movement to ban land mines. At latest count, 157 countries have signed on to the treaty, but 39 countries have refused, including the United States, China, North Korea, and Russia. The U.S. has not used anti-personnel land mines since 1991, and has not exported them since 1992. Officially, no land mines have been produced in the U.S. since 1997, but it appears that America has a stockpile of up to ten million anti-personnel mines ready to be used at any moment.

Despite its refusal to sign onto the treaty banning land mines, the U.S. has done more than any other country in recent years to support efforts to remove them around the globe. Cambodia has received more than $80 million from the U.S. for this purpose since 1983. Approximately twenty to thirty square miles are cleared per year in Cambodia, and a total of about 270 square miles have been made safe, but as of 2017 about 250 square miles are still waiting to be cleared. The U.S. established full diplomatic relations with Cambodia in 1993, but broke off relations following political turmoil in 1997 that resulted in human rights abuses and mass murders. As a result, humanitarian assistance such as clearing unexploded ordnance is done by non-government organizations.

Laos:

The U.S. dropped more than two million tons of bombs on Laos from 1964 to 1975. At that time Laos had a population of slightly less than two million, so the bombing amounted to about one ton for every man, woman, and child in this impoverished agricultural country. In 1969, it was reported that 85% of the population of Laos was living underground in bomb shelters or tunnels to escape the American bombing. Many areas of Laos remain uninhabitable due to unexploded bombs. In 2012, explosions from live ordnance killed 12 and injured 41 Laotian people. It is estimated that up to 80 million "bombies," or small bomblets from American cluster bombs, are still live and waiting throughout Laos, along with an unknown quantity of high explosive and other anti-personnel bombs. In 2014 the U.S. finally appropriated $12 million to help clear the unexploded ordnance. Laos has had a Communist government since 1975, but in the 1990s the leadership began to encourage tourism and some private enterprise.

Laos has been criticized by groups such as Amnesty International and Human Rights Watch for its policies and human rights violations against political opposition and religious groups. Because the Hmong tribe worked closely with Americans in the 1960s and 1970s, they have been subjected to severe persecution and abuses. Many Hmong have sought refuge in Thailand, but the Thai government has closed its refugee camps and actually deported some refugees back to Laos. In 2003, the U.S. allowed 15,000 Hmong to resettle in America, but many thousands are still in Thailand living a very unsettled existence. In 2006, despite opposition from human rights organizations, the U.S. resumed normal trade relations with Laos. America has worked closely with the Laotian government to control the cultivation of opium, which has been the country's primary cash crop.

Certainly, the American war did tragic damage to all three of these countries. The United States will never be held responsible for those damages, there will be no "50-year commemoration" or celebration of the wars in Southeast Asia, and the true nature and history of the war cannot be allowed to be misrepresented.

Chapter 10

THE DRAFT

"The real enemy of my people is here. I will not disgrace my religion, my people or myself by becoming a tool to enslave those who are fighting for their own justice, freedom and equality. If I thought the war was going to bring freedom and equality to 22 million of my people they wouldn't have to draft me, I'd join tomorrow. I have nothing to lose by standing up for my beliefs."

– Muhammad Ali

The time not to become a father is eighteen years before a war.

– E.B. White

While those who are most opposed to the war have been silenced, the system that provides the personnel for war crimes continues to function smoothly... We do not seek jail, but we do this because as individuals we know of no justifiable alternative.

– David Harris, former head of the student body at Stanford University, who refused to be drafted and served 15 months in federal prison for draft evasion.

I correspond with a lot of high school and college students in relation to their studies in a variety of courses focused upon the Vietnam War. Recently, a high school senior from Newnan, Georgia inquired about my memories of the draft, and I replied that being pursued by the draft board and ultimately forced to enter military service against my will was one of the most traumatic periods of my life.

His response was thoughtful and to the point. "I totally understand not wanting to be drafted into the war fresh out of high school. I have my whole life ahead of me and would not want to have a huge risk of dying before I even got to live."

I graduated from high school in June of 1965, and in early July my buddy got me a job at a large and very successful Chevy dealership in Rochester, NY. I had a few scholarship offers, but my father was ill and I couldn't afford to go on to college, and in fact I wanted to get under the hood of a car far more than I wanted to sit in another classroom. At first, I was a car-jockey, moving cars in and out for the mechanics, but soon the company sent me to GM training school and enrolled me as an official apprentice auto-body and fender repairman. I was privileged to work with a very talented group of guys, and I was enthusiastic. I saw terrible wrecks reassembled and put back on the road, with care and attention to detail that convinced me the cars were probably better built than they had been when they left the factory. I got to work with, and around, some really exciting vehicles. It was the age of muscle cars, and the western New York winters caused extensive salt damage so we also did restoration work. I recall repairing a rusted fender on an antique Bentley using lead, a very expensive but lasting repair procedure. Years later, I would become a factory representative for the Rolls-Royce and Bentley Motor Company and come to appreciate that, for a teenage apprentice in 1966, to be around and work on those incredible classic cars every day was an honor. At the time, the fact that my apprenticeship earned me a draft deferment was nice, but not a major consideration.

I was also playing drums in a band as much as possible, and in the style of the times, I had long hair. If I wasn't playing music, I traveled far and wide to see the top bands, or to date a pretty girl if the opportunity came along. It was a very exciting time, and I looked forward to a successful future as a craftsman and artist.

One afternoon I was directed to move a Corvette from the paint shop to a nearby glass shop. This had been a severe wreck, but it was all back together and painted, and it was time to replace the broken windshield before the final polishing of the fresh paintwork. The car had been off the road for months, and the atmosphere in the shops was extremely dusty. I had a hard time getting the engine started, and it was barely able to move outside into the street. I played with the accelerator and gradually it cleared, but it was a big 400-cubic inch monster and noisy, and it emitted an awesome cloud of thick, dark smoke. Before I knew it, I was in the boss's office. I thought I had done something extraordinarily skillful in bringing the recalcitrant engine back to life. There had been a lot of noise and smoke from the beast, but I had cleared it out and made it drivable, and I took great satisfaction in that. The boss was not so enthusiastic. He thought I was hot-rodding a customer's car, and insisted that other customers had seen my actions and complained. Then, as if the two situations were related, he complained about my appearance, and began to insist that I get my hair cut.

In 1966, the British Invasion was on, young guys grew their hair, and older folks often disapproved. It was the beginning of a new era, and they weren't ready for it. We loved to point out that Jesus had long hair, and that it wasn't the length of an employee's hair that should be considered, but the quality of his work. My boss was an older man, the type who wore a suit to run an automotive service department, and his opposition to long hair was deeply ingrained.

My work situation, which I had enjoyed so much, began to be uncomfortable, and I started to look around for other opportunities. I found one, as a second body-fender repairman and painter in a smaller, more suburban Pontiac and Cadillac dealership. I gave my notice and started in the new position, and thankfully my new co-worker was very talented and willing to show me his techniques. There were just the two of us, and I enjoyed the increased responsibilities. On Labor Day weekend I took some vacation days and traveled with my friends to the "National Drags," the biggest drag race event of them all, in Indianapolis. We ran two cars, didn't do particularly well, but I got to see all the stars from the magazines, and to hear the sound of nitro-methanol fueled dragsters! It was a fabulous event, and I was on top of the world. Within a few weeks, I got an official letter demanding my attendance in Buffalo for a pre-induction physical. In my new job, I was no longer deferred.

As I have tried to describe throughout this book, the sixties were a time of unprecedented freedom. The music, the cars, and the attitudes, especially of the opposite sex, were all emancipated to the extreme – colorful and loud. We were surrounded by sensory overload, and a thousand varieties of incredible fun were popping up everywhere if only we could find the time, money, and endurance to experience them. You could drink at 18 years of age in New York in those days, and we all had "fake proof" in the form of altered or contraband draft cards. I had turned 18 in January of '66, so now I had a legitimate draft card and I could go to any bar, buy a beer and enjoy live music, and I did. I worked every day. I wasn't making a lot of money but I could afford my car payment, gas, an occasional beer, a date, and a pack of condoms. I wore flowered shirts and a wide leather belt in my weathered jeans, and Beatle boots with Cuban heels. When I played with the band, we wore snow-white jeans and madras shirts, and a couple of the guys wore riding boots, but I couldn't work my foot pedals wearing knee-high boots. Besides, I was the drummer, hidden back behind everyone. I was playing with a couple of city bands, just waiting for someone to hear us and discover America's answer to the Beatles. I drove a Thunderbird, with the most luxurious and sporty interior you could invite a young lady into, and I was "pit crew" on two magazine-quality drag cars. Life was extremely fast-paced and fun. And then I opened that letter.

My sweet life turned sour overnight. I couldn't conceive of the possibility that I would be torn away from my beautiful life and turned into a soldier. I was skinny, not at all the he-man type. I was a musician, a hip cat, into Beatle-influenced concepts of peace and love. I was learning a trade, creating a career for myself, and beginning to pick up some odd jobs doing custom body or paint work. I knew nothing about war. I began to hear the word "Vietnam"; I could hardly imagine such a place, but I knew I wanted nothing to do with it. The draft physical was terrifying. There were hundreds of guys, most of them just like me. You could smell the fear as we were herded like animals and probed in every humiliating manner, and soon after I got another letter and a new draft card; I was classified 1-A, a prime candidate for military service.

I was in shock. It was a nightmare, and it was closing in on me fast. I looked desperately for alternatives. The National Guard and Reserves had waiting lists a mile long, and I really did not want to be a soldier, not even once in a while on weekends. I couldn't afford to go to college. My employer did not want to take on the paperwork involved in a formal apprenticeship program. He thought I was a skilled worker, and seemed to bristle at my efforts to avoid military service. It started to be hard to get dates. I wasn't good at keeping secrets, and girls seemed to disappear when they learned the draft was after me. The band got word of my predicament and suddenly they didn't need me anymore. They had to look to the future. Hey, I hadn't been drafted yet! Everywhere I turned, the message was the same. "It's just a matter of time. If you're walking and breathing, you're going." It was a nightmare, but there was no waking up to escape it. I heard it from every direction: "It's inevitable. You're 1-A? You're gone; you just haven't opened the letter yet." I found a club in the city with an acoustic folk-rock band and a lot of college-educated beatnik types, candles on the tables, and deep, passionate discussions of issues like civil rights, nuclear proliferation, and the war in Vietnam. It all sounded sordid, so contrary to what America was all about. I listened, but I still couldn't imagine that I would be drafted and sent to the other side of the planet to fight in a war. To kill, or be killed.

I heard all the arguments against the war. I didn't always accept everything I heard, but it was overwhelmingly negative information. I cannot claim that I was unaware. In those days there were very few Americans escaping to Canada to avoid the war, but I was aware that the possibility existed. I was from a small town, and if I ran away to a foreign country to escape my "obligation" or my "duty" as an American, what might my family have to undergo as a result? If I ran away and tried to start a new life in some other part of the U.S., I would be caught and put in jail. Of course, I could simply refuse to be drafted and go to prison, but my reservations about the war were not strong enough to justify that. My friends were being drafted too, including one with a very serious heart condition. There was just no way to avoid it. In the end, I caved. I enlisted to get "my choice" of schooling, which added a year to my commitment. The recruiter assured me I had done the best thing; that I would "probably" be sent to Germany where I would live in a barracks that would be nicer than most college dorms. And, of course, I would have a wonderful benefits package when I got out. I reported on December 30, 1966. I was 18 years old, and I thought I was scared to death. Soon I would learn the real meaning of the term.

If we consider the Vietnam War period to be from late 1964, when LBJ approved assigning combat troops, to 1973 when the last combat troops were withdrawn, approximately 1,850,000 Americans were drafted. Many of them had the luck to draw other duty stations around the world, but the Vietnam meatgrinder was the primary reason the draft increased its numbers during that time.

In the late 60s, the draft was aimed precisely at America's underprivileged young men. No matter what the recruiters said, it wasn't about opportunity; the draft supplied the cannon fodder, the raw meat to be butchered in the jungles of Southeast Asia. They needed strong, healthy guys who might be able to withstand the heat and exhaustion, and they wanted them young and impressionable so they wouldn't ask questions or tell a sergeant to stick it where the sun don't shine. In 1966, Secretary of Defense Robert McNamara and company lowered the standards for draftees, obscuring their plans behind the façade of "Project 100,000" that they billed as a program to assist and benefit America's underprivileged youth. This program *required* the military to fill 20% of all openings from the guys who scored lowest on pre-induction general aptitude tests. Another 10% would be taken from men who would have been rejected as "unfit for service" before Project 100,000, most often because they had been convicted of felonies. Officers and especially sergeants did not want to deal with "McNamara's Morons," but units were encouraged to maintain maximum headcount, so they were rarely allowed to send the substandard, disabled, or convicted criminals home. The recruiter had been honest when he told me that draftees were most likely to be assigned to the infantry and Vietnam. In the emotion-charged atmosphere of protests in the sixties, those draft policies were largely viewed as discrimination "against low-education, low-income, underprivileged members of society" by the kids most likely to be taken, their families, loved ones, and communities. Like so many uncomfortable situations in American life, it was all about supply and demand.

To their credit, the Selective Service system of the sixties did not record a person's race. In '65 and '66 the percentage of black combat troops in Vietnam was about 20% compared to blacks composing about 11% of the American population, but that statistic became more representative as the war dragged on. The deciding factor was wealth. Money equates to opportunity in capitalist America, and it was especially so in the Vietnam-era draft. After high school, those who went on to college were deferred throughout their first four years as long as they maintained passing grades. Deferments for graduate school were not uncommon. Reserve and National Guard members were deferred, along with R.O.T.C. and students taking military training, and aviation cadets. There were deferments for a few specific occupations, especially agriculture. At President Kennedy's order, fathers were deferred, and most local draft boards were reluctant to draft married men. It was not unusual in those days to get married to avoid the draft. There were deferments for severe financial hardship, for sole surviving sons, and for members of the U.S. armed forces, the Coast and Geodetic Survey, and the Public Health Service. Conscientious objectors could be drafted for noncombatant service, usually as medics, but a CO could be deferred if he was deemed by the draft board to be performing civilian work that contributed to the national health, safety, or interest, or had completed work in those endeavors. Aliens were exempt from military service, as were clergy and divinity students.

After World War II, Americans had felt secure that our nation's superior technology would guarantee the U.S. would remain the world's pre-eminent power. Then, on October 4, 1957, the Soviet Union launched Sputnik, the first man-made object in space. American families stood in the yard on clear nights and watched the satellite pass over like a blinking star, and many became fearful. Perhaps American know-how was not better than everyone else's! Industry criticized the American education system for not teaching the latest technologies. In truth, if those classes had been offered in the early '60s, they probably would not have been well-attended. Although we had always maintained good schools, many Americans placed more value on less-educated workers who displayed common sense, the ability to tinker with mechanical devices, or the ability to produce things, than they did on the college-educated candidate with no mechanical skills. Common folk could not understand Einstein's accomplishments, but mechanical men like the Wright brothers, Henry Ford, Thomas Edison, Lee Iacocca, "Big Daddy" Don Garlits, and John DeLorean were hugely admired.

Sputnik, Walt Disney and John Kennedy changed all that. For years, Disney's *Tomorrowland* TV programs and amusement attractions had predicted a day when space travel would actually happen, and Kennedy reacted to the Russian success by challenging America to go farther and faster into space. In order to accomplish that, our schools would have to supply space-age intellectuals. Suddenly, colleges and universities took on unprecedented importance. President Kennedy pointed to education as the key that would unlock America's future, and as the Russians put a man into space and brought him safely back to earth, the intellectual JFK stressed the importance of educational excellence over all other national priorities. President Kennedy challenged us to enter the "New Frontier," and many young people took that to mean exploring space and other areas of computerized, transistorized high technology. It was a most exciting era, and America soon scored a number of its own successes until, in 1969, we put American footprints on the surface of the moon and brought our brave space pioneers home again safely. Throughout this period of great national endeavor and accomplishment it was almost as if the Vietnam War was pulling the country in the opposite direction. Rocket scientists were not drafted.

In the wake of JFK's assassination, Lyndon Johnson enthusiastically agreed that excellence in education was necessary to beat the Russians in the Space Race, the Arms Race, and in every measure that counted. College students were excused from the draft, and they began to see themselves as special, perhaps even the most important segment of American society. If the baby boomer generation was destined to right the world's wrongs and make war obsolete, the college students would be at the vanguard of the new civilization. Some students complained and protested the draft because they were only deferred while actually attending school, and they had critically important work to do after graduation. It was simply unthinkable and disrespectful to face the threat of graduating and, instead of joining the emerging space-age high-tech industry, being drafted and sent to Vietnam to wallow in the mud and possibly be "wasted" by an enemy bullet or booby trap!

"I thought what I was doing at Texas A&M was important," Texas Senator Phil Gramm intoned years later when his pro-war sentiments seemed at odds with his history of student deferments to avoid the draft. College campuses were the scenes of many protests and demonstrations during the late sixties, and it is noteworthy that among the policies being challenged, many old-fashioned or traditional schools were actually taken over by their students who demanded that courses and curricula be modernized and updated to be more appropriate to the expanding high-tech workplace. Burning draft cards was not unusual, but it was a crime that could send you to prison. Draft counseling and lessons in how to avoid being drafted were available on most campuses and in many poor urban neighborhoods. Sadly, most rural communities had no such alternative training available.

The draft peaked in 1966, when it inducted 340,000 men. Still, throughout the war years the draft was always a focus of resistance, and the protests and demonstrations had more severe social and economic consequences as the war dragged on and on. By 1968, resistance to military service was widespread throughout America and resisters, evaders, or "draft dodgers" were becoming somewhat respected by the public if they weren't too "anti-American" in their outbursts. Increasing numbers were defiantly burning their draft cards in public, while others chose to confront the system by openly refusing military service. The record shows that 3,250 young Americans chose to go to prison rather than be drafted.

In the later years of the war, about a quarter of a million young Americans were reported to authorities because they simply neglected to present themselves when summoned to physicals and pre-induction testing or broke the draft laws in other ways. Only about 25,000 were actually indicted, and it is thought that another 360,000 broke the laws but were never reported. A significant number left the country, around 125,000 moving to Canada and others to Sweden. Many came home when President Carter announced amnesty, but Canadian Immigration records say more than 30,000 became citizens and left the United States behind. Got that, America? About 58,300 died in Vietnam (not all by enemy actions) and 30,000 or more actually left the country and renounced their citizenship, rather than take part in something so wrong! Over 3,000 brave souls chose to go to prison for their convictions, though some people called them cowards. It was a very emotional time.

The number of young men who received deferments during the Vietnam era is estimated at 15 million. Historian Arthur Schlesinger, Jr. wrote, "The war in Vietnam was being fought in the main by the sons of poor whites and blacks whose parents did not have much influence in the community. The sons of the influential were all protected because they were in college."

As the 60s faded into the 70s, President Nixon formed a commission to study the draft and perhaps suggest alternatives. After a great flurry of debate, it was decided to end the draft and implement an all-volunteer military. This solution would take away the draft as a focus of protests which were now large-scale events that seriously disrupted Washington, D.C. and other prominent cities. Draftees were proving to be angry and alienated within the military, and morale in all the armed services was disintegrating. An all-volunteer force would be far less likely to complain, and hopefully morale would improve over time. (Draftees were only obligated to two-year service, so they would cease to be a factor and positive results could be anticipated in a fairly short term.) If the military could be composed entirely of three-year enlistees, the result would be a more experienced army with less turnover.

A few personal notes on the draft are in order.

- I have thought long and hard about this and I feel that at least 90% of the lower-ranking G.I.s that I met and/or served with were there only because they were drafted, and they deeply resented that. Morale suffered.

- I enlisted in the U.S. army against my will (to get my choice of training) ONLY because it was inevitable that I would be drafted. During that era, it was a popular joke that guys like me had "enlisted to beat the draft."

- One acronym that is rarely used by the military is the one for Draft-Induced Enlistee (DIE).

- My draft notice arrived when I was already in Vietnam. My father mailed it to me, and I took it to the Company Commander. "Sir, it says here I have to be in Batavia, New York next Wednesday." He responded, "Nice try," and grinned.

- By enlisting, I added a year to my obligation. I spent that year in Thailand. I disliked the military immensely, but I am grateful for the opportunity to visit Thailand, which was friendly to the U.S., and gave me the opportunity to explore their culture, language, religion, food, music, and customs in depth, and to learn that my government's position that "The only good Gook is a dead Gook" was genocidal propaganda designed to brainwash me into becoming a soldier who would kill Oriental people for no reason. Despite their poverty, I believe the Thai people are the happiest people I have ever known. If I had been drafted for a two-year "obligation," I would not have the perspective to know these truths.

• In the Spring of 2014 I took part in a Cognitive Processing Therapy (CPT) course to deal with PTSD at the VA Medical Center in Salem, Virginia. A total of five veterans took part: one Iraq War vet, myself, and three other Vietnam vets. I was surprised to find that all four of us Vietnam veterans were still experiencing "stuck points" of anger and bitterness at being taken away from our lives by the draft some forty years previous – and some were even more bitter and negative than I.

• In Vietnam, we took up a collection to buy our Vietnamese barber's way out of the draft. A few weeks later he was shot dead, creeping through the barbed wire in the dark of night with explosive satchel charges, a Viet Cong sapper.

The inequities of America's draft system during the Vietnam War led to so much public outcry and rancor that finally the draft had to end. Ironically, the universally despised General Lewis Hershey, the national director of the Selective Service System, issued an order in October of 1967 directing the nation's local draft boards to immediately reclassify anyone caught, or even just observed or rumored to be participating in any form of demonstration against the draft to make them immediately eligible to be drafted. "The Hershey Directive" was predictably very unpopular with college students, and resulted in increases in both the number and intensity of protests. The order was challenged and finally deemed unconstitutional by the U.S. Supreme Court and voided on January 2nd, 1970. General Hershey was removed from his post by President Nixon a few days later. Sadly, he was not reassigned to Vietnam.

President Nixon had campaigned on the promise that he would do away with the draft. The Joint Chiefs of Staff and other powerful forces within the military opposed the idea, as did many members of Congress. Nixon appointed a commission to explore the feasibility of an all-volunteer military, and in February of 1970 the Gates Commission's report suggested that the idea would be beneficial to both the military and the country. The Defense Department and the White House requested that the current system be maintained for about two years while the details of the all-volunteer force could be worked out. The measure was passed after considerable debate. In preparing for the end of the draft, Congress increased military pay rates and the army began to advertise for recruits on television.

The draft lottery began with the first drawing of birthdates in December of 1969, to determine the order in which eligible candidates would be called for examinations and subsequently inducted in 1970. Similar lotteries were held in 1970, '71, and '72, and the draft was finally abolished in 1973. The last men to be drafted entered the service in June of 1973, after the last American combat troops had been withdrawn from Vietnam.

The all-volunteer military has been fairly successful overall, but it does not usually attract college graduates. During times of economic recession such as the years from 2008 to 2014, enlistments were buoyed by the limited availability of good jobs in the civilian marketplace.

It must be noted that the Selective Service System is still in place and young men ages 18-25 are required to register in case it ever becomes necessary to reinstate the draft. As of 2018, it has become likely that young women might also be required to register, as females are now being admitted to most combat assignments.

In 1986, as the U.S. was on the verge of invading Nicaragua to oust the Contras, a bill was quietly introduced into Congress. Because the military's health care facilities were seriously understaffed, bill H.R. 3646 would have required all health care professionals in the U.S. between the ages of 18 and 46 to register with Selective Service, including proof of their training and qualifications in the medical professions. Had the bill become law, failure to comply within 60 days would result in a fine not to exceed $250,000 and imprisonment for five years. At that time, our children were six and nine years old, and my job required a great deal of travel. I could not imagine that my wife, who is a registered nurse, would be drafted! We obtained a copy of the bill, added a passionate plea, and distributed it to every health-care professional we knew. They were shocked, and presumably contacted their congressman to voice opposition to this bill. It was never passed, and the invasion of Central America never happened due to widespread opposition across the country. It was a time of great anxiety, and I developed ulcers.

Today, we still hear a few voices calling for a return to the draft. Some people think drafting from every segment of American society, including women, would help to galvanize public opposition to militarism. Others believe every American young person has some sort of obligation to "serve" the country by enlisting for a few years. "Freedom is not free," they say, but where is the freedom in enforced servitude? What would be the options if, or when, the U.S. embarks upon another ill-advised, unnecessary, or unwinnable war? 9/11 proved that Americans will join up to fight if our country is invaded or attacked, but America's history post-9/11 clearly shines a spotlight on the threatening nature of America's modern Way of Waging War, basically unchanged since the Vietnam era. One of these days we have to admit that the Pentagon's basic strategy simply doesn't work, and it is unnecessarily cruel, expensive, and wasteful. As this is written, the war in Afghanistan has gone on for 17 years, under the leadership of 17 Generals. When will we question what they are teaching in West Point? Despite the economic pressures on the poor, military recruiters are struggling to meet their quotas for good reasons. To paraphrase the old John Kerry statement, no one wants to be the last person to die for a mistake in Iraq or Afghanistan.

The Vietnam era draft was a focal point for resistance to the war. The baby boomers were gloriously alive in an environment that gave us an exaggerated sense of freedom, and also a burning desire to focus our energies on doing something constructive. To be taken away against our will and be required to wear combat fatigues, heads shaved, and be sent to an illegitimate war on the other side of the planet was simply unthinkable. To be drafted was like being sentenced to prison, except that experiencing the horrors of war made it far worse.

Chapter 11

THE MEDIA

Vietnam was the first war ever fought without any censorship. Without censorship, things can get terribly confused in the public's mind.
– General William C. Westmoreland.

If we let people see that kind of thing, there would never again be any war.
– A Pentagon Official (unnamed) ...
explaining why the U.S. military censored
graphic footage from the Gulf War.

It is not the journalist's job to be patriotic. How can patriotism be determined anyway? Is patriotism simply agreeing unquestioningly with every action of one's government? Or might we define patriotism as having the courage to speak and act on those principles one thinks are best for the country, whether they are in accordance with the wishes of the government or not?
– Walter Cronkite, from his autobiography, *A Reporter's Life*, 1996.

I am constantly asked about the role of the media in the outcome of the war in Vietnam, and the ways the war is remembered. There is a perception that the media, especially those journalists actually reporting from Vietnam, were somehow intent upon discrediting the overall mission, the conduct of the war, and the American soldiers on the ground. Did that actually happen? Did the reporters and correspondents poison the opinions of their readers back home by showing all the ugliest scenes and ignoring the successes or the good that was occurring? Others contend that the media were too soft on the politicians and generals who completely mishandled the situation, resulting in widespread death and destruction without anyone held to account. Looking back after forty to fifty years, is the more prevalent first view simply denial by a segment of veterans or history aficionados who stubbornly refuse to accept that America lost the war because (A) We had no business being there in the first place; and (B) Our military leaders were incompetent, obstinate, and too busy profiting from corruption to pay attention to the war itself? Or, do books like Michael Herr's *Dispatches* overstate the bravery of the journalists while they underplay the courage and commitment of our American troops? The debates and discussions have not subsided over the years.

In high school we were taught that Alexander the Great conquered most of the known world, and Julius Caesar conquered Gaul. Baloney! If either of those great leaders had climbed on a horse, drawn his sword and charged off into enemy territory he would have been killed immediately. The truth is, both of them gathered large armies, mostly of everyday citizens, equipped them and led them away to far-off lands where many would die and the injured would suffer terribly. Unfortunately, most of us remember little about the struggles of those foot soldiers, or the families left behind. The Greek poet Homer contributed legendary accounts of ancient war and its aftermath in *The Iliad* and *The Odyssey*, apparently 150 to 200 years after the Trojan War. While his books are fictional, he was one of the first to ponder the deeper emotions of the low-ranking foot soldiers in war, and to suggest that there are emotional after-effects of combat upon the warrior.

As recently as the American Civil War, it is generally acknowledged that the horrific photos of Gettysburg after the battle by Alexander Gardner, Timothy O'Sullivan and James F. Gibson were rearranged, with bodies and weapons repositioned to make their pictures more effective. At the time, the technology did not exist to allow widespread distribution of those images in newspapers and many of the photographs were considered too graphic to be made widely available. Everyone knew that deaths occurred in war, but photographic evidence of the carnage was considered indecent and disrespectful in polite society. Author Stephen Crane, who was born years after the end of the Civil War, felt that the literature from the war failed to tell how it *felt* to experience combat, and he created *The Red Badge of Courage* after interviewing numerous veterans. The story first appeared as a series in a number of newspapers, and was released as a novel in 1895. *The Red Badge of Courage* is a classic book, as are *All Quiet On The Western Front* by World War I veteran Erich Maria Remarque, and *Johnny Got His Gun* by Dalton Trumbo. Still, it is one thing to read a carefully crafted novel about the horrors of war, and quite another to watch actual combat on a color TV while eating dinner. To be a participant in a war on the other side of the planet, with combat, war machines, and the threat of maiming or death always close seems indescribable, but many brave journalists have involved themselves and tried to describe the horror to folks relaxing at home in their favorite easy chairs.

America's war in Vietnam was the first significant conflict to be reported on television. At the start, this was viewed as a good thing. Modern film cameras made it possible to record operations and battles in the jungle on the other side of the planet, and to transport those films back to the network broadcast centers for broadcast within a day or so. The American TV audience gradually became familiar with viewing far-off and exotic Vietnam, which might have helped reinforce the perceived necessity of the war. However, the journalists in Vietnam also reported the realities of combat, and TV delivered the horrors of war to America's living rooms as never before. Meanwhile, TV crews in the States interviewed politicians, generals, and even the families waiting anxiously for their sons to return. In his book *A Reporter's Life* retired CBS TV news anchor Walter Cronkite quotes an article by an un-named Marine major from *Military Review*, the official journal of the U.S. Army. "More than any other factor, it was the television camera that brought home the reality of war that shocked the nation and broke its will. What we need, contrary to the wide-open and unrestricted policies of Vietnam, is not freedom of the press, but freedom from the press, more specifically, freedom from the television camera and its interference. *In the next war, the television cameras must stay home.*" (Italics and underlining from the original.) Note that the major, despite his contempt for the 1st amendment, did not accuse the television media of altering the facts in any way. Their offense was bringing home "the reality of war" to the American public, and so that reality caused the American public to turn against the war. Isn't it possible that the real villain is the concept of America's exceptionalism, the belief that we are entitled to cause unlimited horrors, death, and destruction, all in the name of spreading our capitalist system regardless of the costs, or despite human standards of morality and decency? Someday, and soon, America must confront this question before all the peoples of the world turn against us.

The Nixon administration considered the press an opponent. A variety of top administration spokesmen repeated the White House position that, by showing actual film of the war and conditions in Vietnam, and also film of the demonstrations against the war, the media were not simply reporting the news, but influencing their audience. They accused the press of being less than patriotic by reporting opposition to the government's activities. Speaking in Des Moines, Iowa in November of 1969, Vice President Spiro Agnew claimed that the impact of network TV coverage "represents a concentration of power over American public opinion unknown in history." A few sentences later, he suggested, "The views of this fraternity do not represent the views of America." Agnew, like most of the Nixon administration and the Establishment in Washington, chose to ignore the massive protest marches that actually represented the views of America. The Vice President also complained that the news anchors all lived and worked in "the geographical and intellectual confines of Washington, D.C. or New York City … communities that bask in their own provincialism, their own parochialism. We can deduce that these men thus read the same newspapers, and draw their political and social views from the same sources. Worse, they talk constantly to one another, thereby providing artificial reinforcement to their shared viewpoints."

Walter Cronkite, the CBS news anchor known as "the most trusted man in America," begged to differ. "…while it is true that a handful of people decided what would be on the three network news broadcasts each evening, there wasn't the slightest… not the slightest… consultation among them. Indeed, their intense rivalry prescribed just the opposite."

Agnew was investigated on charges of extortion, tax fraud, bribery and conspiracy; and in the autumn of 1973 he was allowed to plead no contest to one charge of tax evasion, with the condition that he resign as Vice President. Soon after, President Nixon resigned in disgrace to avoid impeachment for the assortment of crimes and cover-ups related to the Watergate burglary. Those crimes were uncovered by a Bob Woodward and Carl Bernstein, *Washington Post* reporters who became influential heroes as a result.

Serious studies have been done, reviewing countless hours of TV coverage and pouring over endless reams of printed reporting from the Vietnam era. Critics have written scathing reviews, only to be criticized in turn as lacking specific examples of slanted reporting. No article or study known to the author has undertaken to group the myriad reports and articles about the war into columns of pro-versus-con so they can be "scored" by words, sentences, paragraphs, or whatever method. It is doubtful anyone would take the time to read such a collection anyway, and it is almost certain that the critics would disagree with the findings. This is a controversy that will never be resolved. The reporting from and about the war in Vietnam, whether via newspapers, magazines, books, radio, or television, constitutes a huge body of information, and the zealot of any persuasion can probably find some evidence to back his individual theory. Ultimately, it is useful to recognize that reporters are trained to be objective, to report only the facts, but they are always human and prone to human failings. They can be influenced, especially when reporting an event as dynamic as a war. That's why their work is usually reviewed by editors before being printed or broadcast. As evidenced by the Pentagon Papers, the most powerful men in the land were very consciously misleading and lying to the news media. As their plans and strategies failed time after time and year after year, the failure of the war was never the fault of the press, who regularly reported what they were seeing or experiencing. Or, as in the case of the Pentagon Papers, discovering facts hidden from public view in the nooks and crannies of government.

"Reporting Vietnam," a special 2015 display at the Newseum in Washington, D.C., gave the viewer numerous examples of correspondents' reports from Vietnam being extensively censored before they were allowed to be published or aired. Clearly, TV producers and newspaper editors were under considerable pressure from the White House and the Pentagon to avoid negative reporting about the war, no matter how truthful that reporting might be. Of course, the correspondents on the ground in Vietnam were exposed to considerable risk. Sixty-three journalists were killed reporting from Vietnam, and their hard-won observations deserved to be delivered to the public intact.

In the extreme environment of a war zone, the reporter is exposed to the most vivid of images. In the introduction of his wonderful book, *War is a Force That Gives Us Meaning*, war correspondent Chris Hedges writes: "The enduring attraction of war is this: Even with its destruction and carnage it can give us what we long for in life. It can give us purpose, meaning, a reason for living. Only when we are in the midst of conflict does the shallowness and vapidness of much of our lives become apparent."

At the very end of his soul-wrenching book, Hedges tells us "My translator in Kosovo, Shukrije Gashi, a poet, vanished. (I returned to Kosovo that summer to find her family was searching for her in mass graves.)" Adrenaline and emotion, Hedges is saying, will inevitably color the reporter's observations, and the elemental humanity residing in his heart might, hopefully, affect the words that come to mind as he attempts to describe what he has seen or experienced. Hedges, with a background in theology, ultimately left the *New York Times* to free himself from the paper's censorship.

The television cameraman may target one scene over another without ever moving his feet, and his editor miles away will choose which images will be broadcast. How might anyone recording the realities of modern warfare convey such scenes of human desecration without any influence from their personal feelings? And, should they try? Should we really encourage them to sugar-coat the truth? Isn't that more the role of the politician than the journalist? Since Vietnam, the Pentagon has severely limited the Media's access to combat situations. Reporters in Vietnam were not "embedded," and they went "where the action was." Their testimony was true and realistic overall, and sometimes more so than the Pentagon or the White House could accept.

How does a reporter tell the truth about war? War is not about statistics, the number of buildings destroyed, or "body counts" tabulating the number of combatants, or innocents, killed. War is too often presented as data, and there are those who accept that perspective as valid. Secretary of Defense Robert McNamara thought his "whiz kids" could steer the course of the Vietnam War by statistics and data, and the war was a debacle. I suggest that those poor statisticians live apart from the mainstream of human activity, perhaps in fortified castles like the Pentagon or the Kremlin. The average human being finding himself surrounded by a war will recoil and despair at the damage done to tissues and bone, to dreams and achievements represented by buildings and schools and cultivated fields, and the destruction done to our universal notions of civilization. I acknowledge that there may be awe at witnessing the technology of death, the mechanics that allow one human being to eradicate numbers of his fellow men, women, and children efficiently and well. Today's weaponry boasts potency and efficiency light years removed from what we saw in Vietnam.

Is the reporter obliged to resist human emotions when viewing the devastating results of war? Regardless of whether his side has won or lost the battle? As the audience, do we not hope to view the TV news or read the morning paper and get a vicarious exposure to those scenes? How much realism is appropriate? Will we be disappointed if the correspondent doesn't deliver the proper amount of horror, of patriotic heroism, or nationalistic empathy? Is the journalist's job to produce popular reporting that attracts high ratings, or is he more obligated to show or tell us the whole truth, even if it is upsetting? And what if his observations harm the mission in some way? If the reader or viewer were standing in the reporter's shoes, wouldn't they be equally affected, or even more? In general, we must have faith that journalists strive to report in a mostly objective, impartial manner, at least until they make their biases obvious. I believe the journalists who reported on the Vietnam War did so in a fair and impartial manner. Some were better at their jobs than others. Some were more daring as they went into the fray to get the stories. Some questioned more, and some less. And, at about 6:30 this evening, I believe the TV network news anchors will report today's news in a similar, generally impartial manner. For whatever reasons, I am free to choose NBC, CBS, ABC, Fox, HLN, CNN, MSNBC, or the Comedy Channel to learn about the day's events. Most of those shows will have on-site footage from around the planet, via technology that is now also far advanced from the days of Vietnam. Still, I like having the "talking heads" reporting what they have experienced, in all its humanity. I'm very grateful when I see them on the scene, sometimes even taking risks to show me what's happening.

The alternative to reporting by humans is no reporting at all, which the U.S. military began to implement during the invasions of Grenada in 1983 and Panama in 1989. Newsmen were excluded from the Grenada invasion for the first two days, and clearly, they missed a number of great acts of heroism. Approximately 5,000 G.I.s took part, and almost 9,000 medals were awarded. But the truth is, more Americans died as a result of accidents and "friendly fire" than enemy action.

In Panama, Secretary of Defense "Dick" Cheney delayed notifying the press of the invasion "with full knowledge," in his words, keeping the media away until the action was nearly over. The official Pentagon report put civilian casualties at less than 200, but the Panamanian people pointed to mass graves where they said thousands were buried by bulldozers. The bombing of the hamlet of El Chorrillo was so intense the survivors called it "little Hiroshima." The whole truth will likely never be known. After the invasion, the Defense Department's official review, known as the Hoffman Report, criticized Secretary Cheney and others for "an excessive concern for secrecy." There was little outcry from the American public, and Cheney and the Pentagon planned even tougher controls upon the media, restrictions that would be seen in the Middle East in early 1991.

Vietnam was reported by a large cast of characters, including a fair number of journalists who became the most respected in their profession. Walter Cronkite was described as "the most trusted man in America" at the time. Other prominent reporters included David Halberstam, Stanley Karnow, Michael Herr, Mal Browne, Peter Arnett, Morley Safer, Frances Fitzgerald, Bernard Fall, Seymour Hersh, and Gloria Emerson. I would also suggest writers like W.D. Ehrhart, Jan Barry, James Hamilton-Paterson, Arnold "Skip" Isaacs, Wallace Terry, Gerald Nicosia, Marilyn Young, Tim O'Brien, David Harris, Myra MacPherson, John Prados, Robert Jay Lifton, Nick Turse, Elizabeth Becker, Philip Caputo, Lynda Van Devanter, Dr. John Parrish, Larry Heineman, Neil Sheehan, and the poet to whom this work is dedicated, Steve Mason, have all contributed to our understanding of what took place. This is supposedly the Age of Information, and input from writers, reporters, and commentators has continued to come at us abundantly in all flavors and colors. Freedom of the press as guaranteed by the first amendment lives on regardless of those who would keep the truth from us! The first amendment is a bedrock of American democracy.

I graduated from high school in 1965. Today's students studying Vietnam are looking back at a war that ended in 1975! After so much time has passed and so many analyses have been published, it must be difficult for today's student to ferret out the truth about Vietnam. The war and the times, so important in our lives, has become ancient history to our children. I am amazed and pleased that so many of them are intensely curious about "our" war.

Vietnam was very different from World War II. Somewhere between the two conflicts, someone had dreamed up a perfected version of the concepts of marketing and merchandising. "The medium is the message" declared Marshall McLuhan in 1964 as he attempted to explain that the new medium of television was impacting how messages are perceived. John Kennedy had become President in large part because he had more charisma and delivered his message better during the first televised presidential debates than had Richard Nixon. Suddenly the White House, Congress, the Pentagon, and the army on the ground in Vietnam all had to deliver their viewpoints to the American people via newsprint, radio waves, and television ... and, they had to compete with the messages coming from Bob Dylan, the Beatles, the Reverend Martin Luther King, Jr., the John Birch Society, the Smothers Brothers, Barry Goldwater, and Peter, Paul and Mary through the same media.

As we have already seen, the government's policy toward the war changed drastically within a few days of JFK's assassination. To the average American consumer, the policy seemed to change depending upon which newspaper or magazine one read, what radio station or TV channel one chose. Indeed, the conduct of the war evolved as time went on. President Johnson brought General Westmoreland to Congress in late '67, and the good general announced that he saw the light at the end of the tunnel. Soon after, the Tet offensive changed everything. Viet Cong guerrillas entered the Embassy in Saigon! Americans at home experienced, "up-close-and-personal," the shock and horror of seeing a boy's brains blown out by a South Vietnamese general with a pistol. More Americans died that week, and that month, than at any other time in the ten-year history of the war. The light had gone out, and it was terribly hard to report that to the audience back home. Still, reporters did report, and General Westmoreland became very defensive about his personal "honor."

To a kid "humping the boonies," trying to survive, the news media was his only link to the nation's policy, the reason why he was in this predicament. When the news reports were not 100% supportive of his mission, he felt betrayed. He needed his country's support to make sense of it all. It was a matter of life and death, on a horrendous scale. All too often Washington could not provide that, MACV could not provide that, his immediate officers or NCOs could not shed any light, and the media reported the truth and that seemed adversarial. It was just reality. And it sucked!

The war dragged on for seven more years after Tet. Pentagon spokesmen proudly announced changes of policy from the war of attrition to pacification and strategic hamlets to the Phoenix Program's assassinations to Vietnamization. There was widespread recrimination, and amidst all the turmoil some folks perceived the intrepid journalist steadfastly doing his job as the most stable target in the gallery, and they took their shots. Most of us did not blame the journalists. It was plain to see that they didn't make the policies. But the passions of the time were intense, and the reports from the war were rarely optimistic. The messengers were easy targets.

The press did not lose the war in Vietnam. It was a new kind of war, and when the new tactics didn't work the Generals and Secretaries and Joint Chiefs had no alternative plans. Unfortunately, some of them were more intent upon getting rich or powerful than they were concerned about success in the contest, or the preservation of human lives. The reporters tried to be objective, to report both sides, to reflect all the contrasting opinions, positions, and policies, to allow the readers and viewers to make up their own minds. There came a point where they could no longer report that the moon was made of green cheese simply because the White House, the Pentagon, MACV, or a recent West Point graduate declared it to be true. They began to call the difference between the truth they saw with their own two eyes and the official pronouncements from MACV, the Pentagon, or the White House "the credibility gap" and in fact CBS reporter Morley Safer was often seen off-camera in Saigon wearing a tongue-in-cheek button that said "I was ambushed at the credibility gap."

By 1968, the vast majority of G.I.s knew the war would never be won. It went on until '73, and for the Vietnamese until 1975, and it was awful. The most disgusting aspect was that it was all so unnecessary. Yes, we tested our latest state-of-the-art weapons and tactics. The profiteers made millions, while communities around the globe had to make room for more than three million graves... if there was enough left to be buried. Some people thought the press shouldn't call it awful, afraid that those pronouncements might get in the way of their next atrocities or tragedies, medals, career advancements, or profits. Parents and spouses did not want to hear that their loved ones were being sacrificed for lies, misrepresentations, or for nothing. Added to the screams of the wounded and the widowed, the unfeeling and unrealistic statements from the politicians and generals just added to the cacophony of the tragedy. The hard truth was usually available, but it was not always popular.

Chapter 12

CORRUPTION AND PROFITEERING

Never think that war, no matter how necessary, nor how justified, is not a crime.

– Ernest Hemingway

When the President does it, that means it is not illegal.
– President Richard M. Nixon

Corruption and profiteering from the misery of others were integral to America's wars in Southeast Asia. The average G.I. who might stumble upon an unusual situation was prone to think of it as an aberration, a one-of-a-kind oddity. While the infantry units and other combat troops were "humping the boonies" and fighting for their lives, a large community made up mostly of American "advisors," contractors, military officers and NCOs (sergeants) in support positions were busy stealing, cheating, and conspiring to take away incredible profits from the war. The average G.I. had no idea these activities were going on, the scale of the operations, nor how common they were. It is interesting to note that many of these schemes involved stealing large sums of money from the clubs and PXs that were intended to offer some minimal pleasures and comforts to the American troops in a war zone. That those thefts should be perpetrated by higher-ranking military professionals, some of whom were honored for their exemplary contributions to the welfare of their subordinates, just serves to underscore the degree to which they sold out their personal integrity. It is shocking to discover the scope of these schemes, the involvement of the world's top Mafia leaders, and to discover that some of these schemes had been going on for years at U.S. bases in Germany, Korea, and at home in America before they converged upon the easy pickings in Vietnam.

The currency manipulations involved billions of dollars, money that was in fact stolen from America's taxpayers. A coalition of Americans, Vietnamese, Asian Indians, and Chinese was able to cooperate, effectively manipulate, and transfer enormous sums of money around the globe during a time of great international and societal strife. It seems corruption and theft were better motivators than peace on Earth, good will toward all men. If there is a good side to this story, perhaps we should note that it is possible for people from disparate cultures to work together if there exists enough opportunity for personal gains. The negative side would be that these syndicates are probably still involved in today's wars, and that the uncontrolled spending to facilitate modern warfare always attracts world-class crooks and profiteers.

If the American military operations in Southeast Asia were "low hanging fruit" to crooks, we can only wonder what new schemes are sucking the blood out of current American efforts in the long wars in the Middle East. We do know that in May of 2004 something in the neighborhood of, well, $6.6 to over $18 billion dollars in American $100 bills were unloaded in Iraq, and a very large portion of that money disappeared! (I have long been an opponent of increased "defense" spending, but this situation convinces me that the Pentagon needs to invest in calculators.) Loaded onto pallets, this was so much American cash that it required 21 flights by C-130 cargo planes to deliver it to Baghdad. It just disappeared! Ahhh, but that's another story. Until the disappearance is investigated and the perpetrators punished, there is no end to the story. As an American taxpayer, if you wonder how we could accumulate a national debt of more than $21 trillion, the government's indifference to this theft is a glaring clue. (See chapter 21)

But back to the war in Vietnam. In January of 1967, in response to reports of widespread and systematic corruption and mis-appropriation of incoming goods to the black market, the Agency for International Development (AID) reported to President Johnson that "no more than 5 – 6 percent of all economic assistance commodities delivered to Vietnam were stolen or otherwise diverted." In retrospect, this was probably a carefully worded response designed to placate Washington while the coalition of thieves were reaping enormous profits from a very well-organized and country-wide thieving binge. What exactly were "economic assistance commodities"? A very large proportion of the military supplies coming into Vietnam were stolen or diverted to the black market, or sold by unscrupulous military officials to equally unscrupulous South Vietnamese,

Thai, Cambodian, or Laotian businessmen. Many U.S. personnel availed themselves of the opportunities to steal from the huge cargoes of goods coming into the country, and throughout all of Southeast Asia.

When I arrived in Thailand in early September of 1968, I was surprised to find that my platoon had no sergeant. He had been decapitated by piano wire stretched across the road in the path of his motorcycle. I soon learned that the entire base at Korat had recently been shaken by a black-marketing operation that involved some of the highest-ranking army officers. For many years, I thought this was an anomaly, a unique incident upon which I had stumbled. I was just a low-ranking enlisted man reassigned to the unit, and I only heard the whispers and saw the frantic maneuvering from a distance as those responsible rushed to save their heads, their prestige, and, everyone assumed, their ill-gotten profits.

The transportation battalion where I had been assigned was in turmoil over a corruption scandal. Korat, Thailand was the site of a major U.S. Air Force base. Trucks and jeeps in brand-new condition were shipped there, and upon arrival classified as "damaged, only fit for salvage." They were rugged military vehicles, unlike anything available in the Thai civilian marketplace, and they were sold to Thai businessmen. The quantities and dollars involved were never reported, but it seems our ex-platoon sergeant had become aware, or possibly been a part of, the operation. Supposedly, the officers involved didn't want to split their profits with a mere sergeant. They double-crossed the poor sarge, and he threatened to blow the whistle, so they paid some Thais to kill him. But the Thais were stupid, they killed the sergeant on the army post, and when they were questioned at the gate they got scared and admitted the whole thing. Within a couple of hours, the colonel and the major were on a plane headed home to the States. At the height of the frenzy, one young enlisted clerk who worked in battalion headquarters was suspected of knowing what was going on. He was given some mail to take to the Post Office, and asked to stop by the mess hall and bring back some coffee. When he arrived back at HQ, he was arrested and charged with losing classified information. "Digger" was court martialed, found guilty, and sentenced to fifteen years in Leavenworth prison. Amazingly, his mother and her lawyer mailed him legal books, and he represented himself and won his appeal. He was sent home a few days after I met him. There is no indication that there was ever any investigation, or that the corrupt battalion commander and his colleagues ever faced any disciplinary action. We can only assume that they were able to transfer their ill-gotten wealth home safely.

Walking into the new assignment and hearing all this, I thought I was seeing an anomaly, a bizarre and unique situation. It was only years later that I began to read about the underbelly of the war in Vietnam and realized that corruption and profiting of this sort were very commonplace throughout the American involvements in Southeast Asia. In fact, so great were the opportunities to make money from the American war effort, international Mafia leaders held "summit meetings" in Saigon to discuss whose organization would get what part of the pie, and to prevent anyone stepping on a colleague's toes.

A friend heard my story about the salvage truck operations in Korat and recommended I read a book titled *The Greedy War*, by James Hamilton-Paterson. In fact, because the book was so hard to find he let me borrow his personal copy. As I read *The Greedy War*, I immediately realized that the events I had witnessed in Thailand were anything but unusual, and I began to understand why the war in Vietnam dragged on so long after it was essentially lost in 1968. *The Greedy War* was also published in England under the title *A Very Personal War*. It is the story of Cornelius Hawkridge.

Cornelius Hawkridge was born into a British family that was immersed in police work in Hungary, and raised in a rigid 19th century family environment, surrounded with fine literature and music, and an appreciation for all things cultured and beautiful. When he was a teenager, World War II brought the Russians into Hungary to evict the Germans, and as is always the case, the war destroyed all that was serene, artistic, beautiful or civilized. The Russian invaders were ruthless, and they soon established an environment of danger, fear, and brutality. By the time he was seventeen years of age, Hawkridge had become active in the underground resistance. On a number of occasions, he was captured, imprisoned, physically abused, and released.

Others might have quit the fight, but Hawkridge valued principle above all else. His father had been killed, and his mother's business seized by the state. From a life of comfort and affluence, they had been relegated to poverty and hardship. Hungary had become a totalitarian police state, and Hawkridge became an underground warrior, a guerrilla saboteur. In early 1948 he was arrested, tortured for fifty-one days, and then mysteriously released. In 1949 he was arrested again, attempted to escape, but was captured. After two and a half agonizing years in solitary confinement he was tried, convicted and sentenced to life in maximum-security within Stalin's gulag system. In 1953, after Stalin died, Hawkridge was transferred to work in the coal mines. He tried to escape and was sent back to solitary for six months, with chains locked upon his legs.

In 1956, Cornelius Hawkridge was unexpectedly released. He made his way back to Budapest, found a job shoveling coal into a boiler, and rejoined the resistance. In October, the Hungarian revolution broke out and he immediately joined the fight. After a few days the Russian tanks arrived. Hawkridge and a few friends slipped away and walked through occupied Hungary for eight days until they reached the border with Austria. Eventually, he met some American agents who valued his information about the Russian camps, and they brought him to the U.S. To his great surprise, once he had told the State Department all he knew, he was tossed out to fend for himself.

After a series of demeaning jobs and setbacks he was enlisted by a company working with USAID to go to the Dominican Republic where American troops were supposedly guarding the safety of American students from a popular uprising billed as Communist-inspired. Lured by the possibility that he would be fighting Communism, Hawkridge was very troubled by the realities he found in the Dominican Republic. While the capitol city of Santo Domingo was an ornate, beautiful and genteel enclave, immediately outside the moneyed walls the poverty was desperate, and universal. Vast shipments of money and materials from the United States, sent with the best of intentions, were directed or diverted to the affluent and powerful in Santa Domingo. As the rich got richer, the peasants became more angry. Hawkridge saw that the Dominican poor were not revolutionaries, and they were not espousing Communism or any other political ideology. They were hungry, barely able to clothe their children, and they were desperate. All the wealth that was being donated to ease their plight was being seized by the ruling military regime, and the American troops were charged with maintaining that regime in place. Hawkridge heard the locals shout "Yanqui go home!" and understood their despair. President Lyndon Johnson had seen Fidel Castro come to power in Cuba six years earlier, and he was determined that no other Caribbean country would turn Communist while he was President.

Cornelius Hawkridge was concerned by the careless ways the Americans maintained their equipment. He had seen the Russian army's extremely rigid and efficient methods, and he saw the Americans as inefficient and chaotic. Most troubling, however, was the observation that the Americans had absolutely no regard for the welfare of the Dominican people. Hawkridge had matured, and he kept his feelings to himself. When the American presence in the Dominican Republic began to be drawn down in 1966, he was asked if he would like to transfer to Vietnam and help in the refugee camps. The pay would be better, and the opportunity to challenge Communism would certainly be available in the war zone.

From the very first, Hawkridge was shocked by what he found in Vietnam. The refugee camps were abysmal, overcrowded, filthy, and utterly degrading. There were no sanitation facilities. When he asked about the lack of supplies, he was told that they were stolen before they could be delivered. As he was being prepared for the assignment he had learned that huge sums of money had been allocated by the American government to care for the innocent victims of the war, but very little of the desperately needed material ever made it to the refugee camps. He visited a number of camps, and the deplorable conditions were universal. Then Hawkridge ventured into a Vietnamese market and, to his great dismay, found it stacked to overflowing with all manner of American goods – weapons and hardware, uniforms, food, beer and liquors, and even American refrigerators and TV sets. This was the "black market," and the vast display of attractive American goods had obviously all been stolen.

When the American combat forces came to Vietnam, agreements were signed with the Vietnamese government regarding the handling of incoming freight. Americans were forbidden from unloading their own planes or ships, or delivering the goods to their destinations. Those chores were handled by the Vietnamese, or by Korean stevedores and port operators hired for the purpose. Trucks were loaded at the ports and driven, in broad daylight, directly to warehouses or shops in the cities where the goods were sold for cash, or to Viet Cong camps northwest of Saigon, or in Cambodia. The Americans were helpless to do anything; it was a police matter, and the Vietnamese police were profiting handsomely from the arrangement.

Archie Kuntze had set up a very profitable system for everyone involved. Cornelius Hawkridge saw every type of American weapon and ammunition displayed at the markets, and when he inquired, he was offered jeeps, trucks, helicopters and armored personnel carriers for purchase. A tank would take "a few days" he was told, because it would have to be delivered from Saigon. Vietnamese military vehicles, helicopters, and planes arrived at the docks and loading zones constantly, to be filled with American goods. They departed without the slightest security inquiry, to peddle their contraband goods across the country and throughout Southeast Asia. Hawkridge quickly observed that the South Vietnamese military could transport these goods with relative ease, as they had the benefit of detailed American intelligence about Viet Cong activities to help them avoid any troublesome delays to their deliveries. He became convinced that the American troops were fighting the war while their Vietnamese comrades were profiting from it by every corrupt means imaginable.

Hawkridge also discovered that foreign banks, primarily Indian and Chinese, were running money-exchanging scams throughout Vietnam. The Americans paid their troops in Military Payment Certificates (MPCs) instead of real American dollars. The official exchange rate was 118 Vietnamese piasters to an American dollar, but the black market paid as much as 240 piasters to the dollar.

A number of Americans, especially Defense Department contractors, took advantage of these rates. Americans would transfer funds from their hometown banks back in The World to accounts operated by the black marketeers, and be paid in piasters at the higher rate. These could easily be converted to American MPCs, which were soon deposited in the checking accounts to start the process again. The black-market accounts were available in a number of prestigious American banks, including Manufacturers Hanover Trust in New York City where the "Prysumeen" account handled more than $1.5 million a month. Overall, the currency transactions were stealing as much as a billion dollars a year, and no one was doing anything to interrupt the practice.

Intensely outraged, Hawkridge began photographing the evidence and writing letters to the various levels of the American effort, up to and including General Westmoreland. His letters were not answered. When he was able to arrange a face-to-face meeting with a lower-ranking American commander, he was advised to stop being a trouble-maker; to get on board and make few thousand dollars and he would feel much better. He wrote to many government agencies in Washington and again received no replies. In 1968 he was newly married and working near Seattle when he was contacted by the Senate Subcommittee on Investigations, asking him to testify about the corruption he had seen in Vietnam. Unfortunately, before he could testify, Hawkridge was involved in a very suspicious auto accident. His wife was killed, and he was seriously injured.

Hawkridge was still in a wheelchair in March of 1969 when he went to Washington, D.C. to tell the Senators about the corruption and mismanagement that were wasting enormous amounts of the taxpayers' money in Vietnam, only to find that he would only be allowed to talk about one very limited facet of the money-laundering operation. Hawkridge challenged the Committee, especially Senator Abraham Ribicoff, naming names and Chinese-run banks, and asking why he had been able to see all of this but the more than 5,000 CIA agents working in Vietnam had not. There was a feature article in *Life* magazine, but it was extensively censored.

In the end, no one in a position of authority wanted to hear what Cornelius Hawkridge was saying. The war dragged on, American G.I.s continued to die, and the corrupt profiteers stole billions of America's tax dollars. Many young Americans saw corruption like the salvage trucks scheme in Thailand, and, like the author, thought they were viewing a unique occurrence. Cornelius Hawkridge attempted to make us aware that these scams and conspiracies were the norm. The author believes Cornelius Hawkridge was one of the real heroes of the Vietnam War. In the spirit of full disclosure, the author admits that Cornelius Hawkridge became a highly valued personal friend.

The history of corruption in Vietnam is very colorful. At the end of World War II, many of Europe's sources for heroin, especially Afghanistan, had been lost. The principal traffickers, the Corsican Mafia, or "French Connection," quickly established sources in Southeast Asia, especially Saigon. They also created a "kind of truce" with influential Americans such as Lt. Col. Lucien Conein, a CIA agent deeply involved in the 1963 coup that overthrew President Diem, and General Edward G. Lansdale, who had come to Vietnam in 1953, ostensibly as a military advisor; but his real work was as a chief operative of the CIA.

In October of 1964, soon after President Johnson announced that he would deploy American combat troops to Vietnam in early 1965, organized-crime bosses from around the world met at Saigon's Continental Palace Hotel to organize the international traffic of narcotics, and to coordinate the various Mafia activities in Vietnam. Clearly, there was more than enough available for all. One notable attendee was Florida mob boss Santo Trafficante, Jr., who visited Saigon throughout the war years for meetings with his peers. Trafficante had been a major figure in the Mafia's gambling operations in Cuba, and he had lost millions when Fidel Castro closed the casinos, resorts and bordellos. Trafficante wanted his businesses back, and is widely thought to have played a significant role in the assassination of President Kennedy.

Perhaps by coincidence, General Lansdale returned to Saigon in 1965 as a special assistant to Ambassador Henry Cabot Lodge, and was a strong supporter of South Vietnam's Premier Nguyen Kao Ky. The flamboyant Ky allowed the Corsicans to fly large shipments of drugs into and out of Saigon, supposedly in exchange for a percentage of the profits. The CIA's heroin processing facility at Long Thien in Laos was the source of many of those flights, and the five dirt airstrips at Long Thien soon became the busiest airport in the world.

One of the key figures involved in official corruption in Vietnam was Navy Captain Archie Kuntze, commonly known as "The Mayor of Saigon." Kuntze graduated from the Naval Academy in 1942, had an exemplary career throughout World War II and Korea and was awarded 22 medals, including a Purple Heart and the very prestigious Legion of Merit medal with a Combat "V."

In 1965, Captain Kuntze was placed in charge of HSAS, the Navy's Headquarters Support Activity in Saigon. Essentially, his duties were to convert Saigon's city port facility into a major military port, and to set up operations throughout Vietnam in preparation for the arrival of American combat troops. Kuntze was in charge of disbursing pay for all American military personnel in South Vietnam, and he was responsible for obtaining and running all bachelor officers and enlisted men's quarters in the city. Kuntze controlled a field hospital and dental clinic for American troops, and he was responsible for food and entertainment in mess halls and clubs throughout Vietnam. He set up and ran all the commissaries and PXs, and his office supplied food, drink, and professional entertainment to every officers', NCOs', and enlisted men's club in Vietnam.

Whatever you wanted in Vietnam, Archie Kuntze could get it for you, for a price. HSAS operated independently of MACV and Kuntze never got along with General Westmoreland. He was in charge of the American vehicle fleet, so he was chauffeured around the city in a Buick sedan, the only vehicle in all of Vietnam with whitewall tires, while Westmoreland was assigned a drab Chevy. When Westmoreland's wife visited and requested that more ladies' toiletries be made available in the PX's, Kuntze officially declined the request just to show Westmoreland his power.

In contrast to Westmoreland's straight-laced and formal old-school military style, Archie Kuntze was flamboyant, but he was also very efficient. He worked sixteen-hour days, attended every important event, and developed a reputation as a "get-things-done type of guy." He could cut through American or Vietnamese bureaucratic red tape and find the people in authority to approve anything he needed. Under his direction, facilities throughout Vietnam were ready when the first Marines landed, and Archie Kuntze was in line to be promoted to Rear Admiral.

Soon after he arrived in Saigon, Kuntze met a bright, attractive young Taiwanese woman at an embassy party. By every account, Jannie Suen was a sleek and ravishing beauty, and Archie Kuntze fell head-over-heels for her. He had recently divorced his wife back in California and, two weeks after they met, Kuntze moved into a grand, luxurious villa in Saigon with Jannie. Accompanied by his Chinese lady, Archie began to host Saigon's most luxurious and elegant parties, and the villa soon became known as "The White House." Archie's lavish get-togethers attracted the highest-ranking political, military, and diplomatic personalities in the city, visiting celebrities, and an endless queue of men who were doing business with Archie Kuntze, or seeking to do so.

By all accounts, Jannie enjoyed the good life. She was often seen riding alone through Saigon's crowded streets in Archie's enormous Buick sedan. She was well-known at all of Saigon's upscale stores, where her chauffeur would hurry to open her door, and to stow her latest purchases in the trunk. Before long, both the car and the lady were known in Saigon as "offensively loud and insistent as well as shameless." Despite those reports, Jannie knew how to be polished and elegant, and she presided over the lavish affairs at "The White House" as First Lady to Kuntze's "Mayor of Saigon" persona. Their swanky parties were the finest affairs in all of Vietnam, and Archie's influence was felt throughout the country. He could be counted on to show up at every news event, good or bad, prancing in his pure white Navy uniform, brandishing a pistol as he kept an eye out for the press photographers.

Like the watered-down *Life* magazine article about Cornelius Hawkridge, stories about corruption in Vietnam began to appear in American publications. The American public was tired of the war, and feeling the pain of the new taxes President Johnson had implemented to pay for it. The cost in American lives had become unbearable, and reports that billions of taxpayer dollars were being diverted to a few fat cats caught the public's attention. From Saigon, General Westmoreland complained about Archie Kuntze to Secretary of Defense McNamara. The abundance of U.S. goods available in neighborhood markets throughout Vietnam was unmistakable. American bombing had made it arduous and dangerous to bring weapons and ammunition down the Ho Chi Minh trail, but the Viet Cong had found it safe and easy to steal from the American ports and shipments. No one could miss the scope of the black market in Vietnam, and Archie Kuntze was responsible for running every aspect of America's port operations.

Like all men with great power and authority, Archie Kuntze was both admired and resented by powerful American and Vietnamese businessmen, and as his antics became more bold and blatant, an investigation was begun. In January of 1966, several bolts of fine silk from Thailand were delivered to Jannie Suen's father's tailor shop in Saigon. The Vietnamese government seized the material, and when neither Jannie nor her father could show any receipt for payment of customs on the shipment, Jannie was arrested and put in jail. The "Mayor of Saigon" was desperate to use his influence to get her out, but at precisely that moment a special Naval Board of Inquiry arrived in Saigon to investigate matters regarding Kuntze's relationship with Jannie Suen, and the disappearance of materials unloaded from ships in the port of Saigon. Kuntze was questioned in great detail, and the investigators went through his personal bank statements where they found large sums of cash had been deposited. Clearly those amounts could not be justified by his salary. The investigators recommended Kuntze be officially reprimanded, but no action was taken at that time. A second board of inquiry was sent to Saigon to further investigate many of the same transactions.

Investigators found that Kuntze kept a stash of $23 million in cash in a freezer adjacent to his office, and his personal bank accounts were again examined in detail. Kuntze explained that the large quantities of cash being deposited and withdrawn were all just a part of doing business. He had won some money gambling, he said, and though he was unable to supply any proof, the investigators found no specific evidence of criminal activity. However, they did find some very unusual transactions. Kuntze had ordered 150,000 cans of hair spray to stock the shelves of PXs in Vietnam, but there were only 750 American women in-country who were authorized to shop at the PXs. Huge quantities of PX supplies were missing, similar goods were seen in abundance on the black market, and the investigators found evidence of his involvement in currency manipulations.

Kuntze was ordered back to San Francisco where he was charged with twelve violations, including importing the Thai silk "in excess of his personal needs," illegally converting $12,000 of MPCs and Piasters into American dollars, giving false testimony, violating an order, making official statements intended to deceive, and conduct unbecoming an officer. He was found guilty of only two counts of conduct unbecoming an officer for allowing Jannie to live in his quarters and to be chauffeured in his official car, and for importing the silk from Thailand. Kuntze received an official reprimand and he was moved down 100 points on the list of officers eligible for promotion. He retired from the Navy shortly after. Although Jannie Suen came to San Francisco at the time of the court martial, Kuntze was never seen in her company again. He returned to Wisconsin, married an American woman, and died in 1980.

The "Mayor of Saigon" had not only offended General Westmoreland and MACV, which represented the Pentagon in Vietnam, he had also stifled the business aims of one William Crum. Crum had made a lot of money supplying the American army in Korea during and after the Korean War, gaining access to the PX, mess halls and clubs supply systems via a sophisticated campaign of bribes and kickbacks. He had started supplying liquor to American PX's in Korea and used his status as an army contractor to import goods duty-free, which he then sold to the black market. His operations attracted attention from army investigators in 1955, 1957, and a 1959 probe was interrupted by high-ranking Pentagon officials. Crum fled Korea in 1959, a multi-millionaire, and the investigation was halted by American military command influence.

William Crum turned up in Saigon in 1962. By 1965, as American combat troops arrived in Vietnam, William Crum was already well established in Southeast Asia. Crum knew the American presence offered the opportunity to make huge sums of money, and he quickly renewed old friendships and created a vast underground empire, a "consortium of criminals" one reporter called it, with influence from MACV headquarters to the black-market stalls throughout Vietnam. He had established himself with several top civilian officials in the PX system, paying each of them a monthly retainer of $1600 (about ten times the monthly pay of a Private First Class in those days) to look out for his interests, along with providing them a very comfortable Saigon villa, a chef, a maid, and plenty of booze and women.

Soon Crum had set up the same operations that had been so successful in Korea, and began selling equipment to Archie Kuntze's fledgling American clubs and PX systems. In fact, Crum supplied the luxury villa and other personal luxuries for his competitor, Kuntze. Crum soon established his companies as primary suppliers to the HSAS and clubs throughout Vietnam, importing, duty-free, restaurant equipment and materials such as beer and liquor into Vietnam and on to Saigon's bustling black market. Kuntze was leery of Crum, but Crum had many contacts and he took good care of his friends.

Crum was also competing with Frank Carmen Furci, a young American entrepreneur who had come to Saigon as soon as it was announced that combat troops would be deployed to Vietnam. Furci, the son of one of Tampa, Florida Mafia boss Santo Trafficante, Jr.'s lieutenants, had been dispatched to Vietnam in search of lucrative construction and service contracts, and he was also interested in supplying equipment and supplies to the clubs and PXs. The clubs sprang up as soon as the G.I.s established their bases, and they were run by a brotherhood of senior army NCOs, mostly Sergeant Majors. During the early 60's, a group of sergeants had been investigated for a lucrative scheme involving the clubs at the Twenty-Fourth Infantry Division in Germany.

In partnership with Frank Furci, an influential American sergeant major named William Wooldridge set up a company called Maradem, Ltd. and when the American army went to Vietnam, Maradem obtained a large portion of the club supply business. Later, investigators learned that many of the clubs were run by the same sergeants who had been busted in Germany. Of course, that was not just coincidence. In the meantime, Wooldridge had been promoted to Command Sergeant Major of the Army by Chief of Staff General Harold Johnson. In this role, Wooldridge was the highest-ranking NCO in the history of the U.S. military.

A subsequent investigation indicated that Wooldridge, along with a core group of seven other sergeants, had capitalized upon their positions controlling a huge chain of American PX's and clubs in Germany. The sergeants controlled all operations of the network, and they had set up an elaborate and very profitable scheme that included bribes and kickbacks from vendors offering equipment, beer and liquors, snack foods, and bands. Investigators found the sergeants had skimmed money from their slot machine operations and demanded large cash kickbacks from anyone who wanted to do business with the clubs. Maradem regularly charged clubs a transportation fee of $600 per delivery, even though the materials were shipped across the Pacific along with all other military goods. It was later disclosed that each of the sergeants had Swiss bank accounts containing hundreds of thousands of dollars.

When Wooldridge came to his powerful Pentagon position, he arranged for his sergeant friends to be transferred to Vietnam, where they would manage the new chain of clubs being installed there. Of course, both William Crum and Frank Furci also wanted to sell equipment to the clubs, and they were willing to offer competitive kickbacks to get the orders. Crum did not appreciate the competition and suggested to officials that Furci had been getting rich on currency transactions, and an investigation was started by a general to whom Crum paid $1,000 a month. Vietnamese customs raided Furci's offices and he was fined $45,000. Furci left Saigon soon after, to open a restaurant in Hong Kong. He was, of course, still part of Maradem, which did over $1.2 million a year in sales to the clubs in Vietnam. William Crum reportedly died in a mysterious fire in Hong Kong in the early 1970s.

After Santo Trafficante, Jr. visited Furci in Hong Kong in 1968, a Filipino courier ring began to transport Southeast Asian heroin to the Mafia in the U.S. Soon they were supplying up to 20% of America's heroin traffic, worth billions of dollars.

However, things were not going well for Sergeant Major Wooldridge. Wooldridge and several of his accomplices, now known as the "Khaki Mafia," were summoned to discuss corruption in the army's PX and club systems with the Senate in 1969, and they repeatedly took the 5th amendment. They were finally indicted in federal court on a variety of charges including conspiracy to defraud the U.S., and a widespread system of bribery, kickbacks, currency manipulations, skimming from slot machines, and altering club records to disguise the money they were taking illegally. In 1973 Wooldridge and the Department of Justice reached an agreement whereby Wooldridge pleaded guilty to accepting stock equity from a corporation engaged in providing merchandise to the non-commissioned officers' clubs in Vietnam. Although Wooldridge admitted to having a Swiss bank account containing hundreds of thousands of dollars, the court found no wrongdoing on his part while serving as the Sergeant Major of the Army. Rank has its privileges.

Wooldridge had been protected by Major General Carl C. Turner, who was the Provost Marshall, or "top cop" of the army. Turner knew that Wooldridge had been involved in questionable operations regarding the clubs in Germany, and he later admitted that he had hindered the investigation by the army's Criminal Investigation Division (CID). When the Senate Subcommittee under Senator Abraham Ribicoff attempted to locate the records of the CID investigation, they were "missing" from the army files. Wooldridge had been caught trying to smuggle liquor from Vietnam to Hawaii aboard General Creighton Abrams' plane, and General Turner had covered up the report. He also covered up the records of Wooldridge's court martial for petty theft in 1943, and two AWOL infractions, which would have made the sergeant ineligible for his position as the highest-ranking NCO in the history of the U.S. military. Turner explained that Wooldridge was "just a good old country boy."

General Turner was also found guilty of accepting 700 confiscated handguns from the police departments of Chicago and Kansas City, ostensibly for the army's use, then keeping some for himself and selling many of them without paying taxes on his income. Both Turner and Wooldridge were stripped of their prestigious Legion of Merit medals. Turner was convicted in federal court and went to prison for three years. Wooldridge was able to plea bargain and stay out of jail, but his career was ruined. He retired from the military, under conditions "to be determined" instead of a normal honorable discharge.

The corruption went further. Brigadier General Earl Cole had been the ultimate authority over the PX system, and when it was uncovered that he had helped William Crum avoid paying duties to Vietnamese Customs, and had interfered with CID investigations of Crum, he was demoted to Colonel and allowed to retire. Colonel David Hackworth was an acknowledged hero, having won a total of 91 medals, including two Distinguished Service Crosses, 10 Silver Stars, 8 Bronze Stars and 8 Purple Hearts. Hackworth spoke out against the Vietnam War during a TV interview in 1971, saying the war could not be won. Soon after he was charged with currency manipulation in Vietnam, but his military record was so exemplary the Secretary of the Army allowed him to retire. Hackworth went on to become an author, a correspondent for *Newsweek*, a critic of the American military, and a spokesman for the peace movement in America.

At this point, the author finds it necessary to mention his personal experiences in Vietnam and Thailand because something unusual happened on pay-days in Thailand, and I've never seen any mention in all the books about the war. Are my memories somehow related to the problem of currency manipulation in Vietnam? I don't know. I am certain that we were paid in MPCs in Vietnam, and it was easy to convert some of your MPCs to Piasters for transactions involving the Vietnamese. For instance, we paid the house-girls and the barber in Piasters. The Vietnamese did not like MPCs, because every so often the American military would issue new MPCs with artwork drastically changed, making the previous generation worthless.

When I arrived in Thailand, I was surprised to find that we were paid in American greenbacks. Pay-days were the first day of each month, and it was a very formal occasion. Somewhere around the beginning of 1969, a new wrinkle appeared on paydays. After you received your pay, you went to an officer at the end of the table, usually a lieutenant, and showed him the twenty-dollar bills in your pay. We were told the North Vietnamese government was introducing large quantities of counterfeit U.S. $20 bills into the Thai economy. In earlier times, prior to 1954 if I remember correctly, the oval framed portrait of Andrew Jackson was "zoomed out," so that all four fingers of his left hand could be seen gripping his robe. After 1954, the portrait was "zoomed in" just a little, and only two fingers were visible. The supposed Communist counterfeits were dated after 1954, usually in the early 1960s, but they had the portrait with all fingers showing. The friendly lieutenant looked at all our bills, and when he found a counterfeit he very happily exchanged it for real money. It seems odd that I have never seen any reference to this situation, especially in light of the billions of dollars stolen by the currency manipulators in Vietnam. I can't imagine that the Thailand counterfeit $20 bill exchange was anything but legit, but it was just odd enough to make me wonder.

* * *

Anna Chennault was the widow of General Claire Chennault, a highly regarded Air Force personality who was twice forced to retire from the U.S. military due to disagreements with his superiors over tactics. The general is best known for his work in support of Chiang Kai-shek, the leader of Nationalist China, in the early days of World War II. Chennault formed the famous "Flying Tigers" squadron, a mercenary group of American fighter pilots and aircraft maintenance personnel allowed to "retire" from their U.S. positions and join the Chinese Air Force squadron to fight the Japanese. After the war, Chennault created a company called Civil Air Transport (CAT) and aided the Nationalist Chinese in a struggle against Communist forces under Mao Ze Dung until the Nationalists were forced to retreat to the island of Taiwan. Chennault sold CAT to the OSS, which soon became the CIA, and the company's name was changed to Air America. The general died in 1958 at the Ochsner Foundation Hospital in New Orleans, an institution founded by Dr. Alton Ochsner, who had close ties to the CIA efforts to assassinate Fidel Castro, and for a time had an employee named Lee Harvey Oswald.

Anna, an accomplished Asian journalist, moved to Washington, D.C. and became a popular socialite and hostess. Known in Washington circles as "The Dragon Lady," Anna was active as a broadcaster for Voice of America, and as a national committeewoman for the Republican Party. Ms. Chennault was known to have close personal relationships with many prominent Asian political personalities, and she expressed her strong anti-Communist convictions by fund-raising for the Republicans.

In October of 1968, at the height of the presidential election campaign between Richard Nixon and Democrat Hubert Humphrey, Chennault visited the South Vietnamese ambassador, Bui Diem. The election would be very close, she told Diem, and the President had announced a halt to the bombing of North Vietnam and urged all parties to convene in Paris and find a solution to end the war. Candidate Richard Nixon felt President Johnson had timed the action to influence the election and improve Humphrey's chances. Nixon had campaigned upon the idea that he had a "secret" plan to end the war in Vietnam, although he never announced what that plan might entail. Anna Chennault had previously met with candidate Nixon and his campaign manager John Mitchell, and Nixon had confidentially designated her to be his "sole representative" to the Vietnamese government in Saigon. When she was seen visiting the ambassador, President Johnson ordered the FBI to keep her under surveillance, and to wiretap the Vietnamese embassy's phone.

Three days before the election, the wiretap revealed that Chennault contacted the ambassador to tell him she had received a message from "the boss," who she did not name, asking her to reassure the ambassador that he should "hold on, we are gonna win." She had previously assured the Saigon regime that the staunchly anti-communist Nixon would be far better for South Vietnam than either LBJ or Humphrey. Within hours, President Thieu announced that the Saigon government would not be sending a delegation to the Paris peace talks. This meant the war would not be ended before the election, and Nixon narrowly defeated Humphrey a few days later.

President Johnson was incensed, and described Nixon's actions as "treason." Americans were dying in Vietnam, and to delay or interfere with the possibility of an end to the war was simply unconscionable, and blatantly illegal. The Logan Act of 1799 prohibits private citizens (Nixon held no elected office at that time) from interfering in negotiations between the U.S. government and foreign nations. Johnson informed Humphrey of what had happened, and the candidate declined to make the information public so near to the election. There were concerns that President Thieu might learn that the CIA had bugged his office. When Johnson confronted Nixon by phone, the president-elect insisted he would "never do anything" to delay the peace process.

Immediately after the election, FBI Director J. Edgar Hoover met with president-elect Nixon in a New York City hotel room and suggested that the FBI had tapped both Chennault's home phone and Nixon's campaign plane. It wasn't true, but president-elect Nixon eagerly reassured the 73-year-old Hoover that he would be kept on in his position at the FBI. Mrs. Chennault had discussed the election almost every day with

Nixon himself or John Mitchell and the president-elect was frightened. He soon learned that LBJ had transferred his records to the site where the Johnson Presidential Library was being constructed in Austin, Texas. However, recognizing its importance, Johnson had given the files on the Chennault-Nixon affair to his aide Walt Rostow, designating them the "X-File." Rostow kept the envelope sealed, and ultimately donated it to the Johnson Library with the provision that it be kept sealed for fifty years – but it was opened in 1994.

For some reason, Nixon thought the files concerning this incident were stored at the offices of the Brookings Institute, a liberal think-tank in Washington. On June 13, 1971 the *New York Times* began to publish the Pentagon Papers, which created a nationwide outburst of anti-war fury. Clearly, if the public became aware that candidate Nixon had impeded peace talks and possibly prolonged the war in Vietnam, the consequences would be immediate and disastrous for the President. Four days later, Nixon ordered his closest associates to enlist the aid of loyal friends from the intelligence community and break into the Brookings Institute's offices, "blow the safe and get it."

Plans began to be made, and CIA officer E. Howard Hunt was enlisted to put together a team. On June 30, an impatient President Nixon told his White House Chief of Staff H.R. Haldeman, "I want the break-in. Hell, they do that. You're to break into the place, rifle the files, and bring them in. ...Just go in and take it. ...I mean, clean it up." Hunt's group never actually broke into the Brookings Institute, although an attempted break-in was reported, but Hunt's Special Investigations Unit, known as "the Plumbers," was arrested a year later, on June 17, 1972, breaking into Democratic National Headquarters at the upscale Washington office and apartment complex known as the Watergate. The President was desperate to cover up the incident, probably because a full investigation would have exposed the group's original objective of burglarizing the Brookings files, and the evidence of the Chennault affair.

It is also possible that the Watergate burglars were trying to install wiretaps and hidden cameras, and to steal embarrassing information related to the favorite call-girl operation utilized by the Democrat National Committee to entertain important guests and clients. There is considerable speculation that Nixon's White House Counsel, John Dean, had sent the Plumbers to extract any and all information related to Erica "Heidi" Rikan, aka Cathy Deter, who was a girlfriend of D.C. crime boss Joe "Possum" Nesline, and also the roommate of Dean's girlfriend and future wife,

Maureen "Mo" Biner. The ladies provided entertainment for a very distinguished clientele, particularly foreign diplomats and visiting politicians referred by both the Democratic National Committee and the White House. This aspect of the Watergate scandal has been documented in a number of books, but was not widely publicized as the Nixon administration was being exposed on national TV by the House of Representatives Judiciary Committee.

It is not difficult to conclude that thousands of brave young Americans were being wounded and killed in Vietnam while a shocking number of their superiors, up to and including the candidate who would become their Commander-In-Chief, resorted to every imaginable avenue of corruption and disdain for the law in order to rake in profits or enhance their personal circumstances, using the war as an unprecedented opportunity. Perhaps the saddest legacy of the Vietnam War is that the cheaters, crooks, and scoundrels who profited from the suffering were never brought to account for their actions.

The precedents set by the Vietnam example have certainly been exploited in more recent times, and at even greater cost to the United States of America. While we don't know the specifics of the official curricula at West Point, Officer Candidate Schools, or ROTC, the lack of any formal consequences for this type of misbehavior sets a very dangerous precedent. The techniques and rewards of all the scams and corruption are sure to be discussed if only during off-duty get-togethers of the good ol' boys' fraternities. How many Americans died because their superiors were planning to get rich instead of focusing on the business of winning the war and keeping their troops as safe as possible? We will never know the number, but one is one too many. Am I too cynical? Perhaps I'll be satisfied when those $6.6 to over $18 billion American dollars are recovered in Iraq, and the thieves tried and convicted. I am not holding my breath.

Chapter 13

SEX AND THE VIETNAM SOLDIER

When boot camp instructors call soldiers 'girls' or 'ladies' to insult them, it is impossible for the same soldiers and their officers to regard women as anything but inferior.
— Former Vietnam nurse Mary Reynolds Powell, from her book *A World of Hurt.*

Televised images of violence against blacks by law-enforcement officials in the South and reports of violence against civilians by U.S. soldiers in Vietnam called into question the real meaning of obscenity. What danger could erotic material pose compared to racism and war?
— David Allyn, from *Make Love, Not War: The Sexual Revolution, an Unfettered History.*

Actress Marilyn Monroe was found dead in her bed on August 5, 1962, wearing only her usual Chanel No. 5 and surrounded by pill bottles. At that moment, many of the guys who would be going to Vietnam in later years were deep in the throes of puberty, with photos of the greatest sex symbol of them all secreted somewhere in their bedroom. If you turned to this chapter first, expecting a cheap thrill, I must inform you right up front that there are no pictures, and certainly no fold-outs. However, I can assure you that military service, and especially the war in Vietnam, offered a variety of sexual opportunities and experiences to the Vietnam-era G.I. Young and virile, far away from home, and struggling to find his place in the "sexual revolution," the kid next door was challenged to accept his own mortality, even as he was tempted by all the forbidden delights that have surrounded military bases throughout history.

The late '50s, the '60s and the early 1970s were an inspiring and glorious time to experience puberty and adolescence in America! Whether via television or the movies, advertising images or the foldout photos of "men's" magazines, post-war America celebrated sex in unprecedented and uninhibited ways. Perhaps it was the media attention that made many beautiful young women sex objects, and maybe it was the permissiveness that seemed to follow the dark years of World War II just as the "roaring twenties" followed the first World War. Movies and magazines had always featured pretty women, and now television offered a dazzling new arena for viewing beautiful people.

In the early sixties America was ripe for a sexual revolution. The name of the show may have been *I Love Lucy*, but there was no hint of a sex life between Lucy and Desi, ever! Dick Van Dyke did not sleep in the same bed as his sexy wife Laura, played by Mary Tyler Moore. It was a time when married couples on TV always slept in separate beds. In similar fashion, music, even rock 'n roll, was very reluctant to suggest anything sexual in the late 1950s. In 1960, Brian Hyland scored a big #1 hit record with *Itsy Bitsy Teenie Weenie Yellow Polka-Dot Bikini*, about a young lady who was afraid to be seen in her sexy new swimsuit. Blushing was much more common in those days.

The television audience was shocked, and a little bit titillated, when it was announced that *Peyton Place,* a sex-drenched popular novel by Grace Metalious, would be made into a TV series. The first ever prime-time soap opera, *Peyton Place* aired from 1964 until 1969, at one point appearing three times per week. Johnny Carson joked that it was "the first TV series delivered in a plain brown wrapper." Compared to the sexual content of today's daytime soap operas, *Peyton Place* was actually quite tame. The show featured a lot of talk and innuendo about rampant adultery, philandering, and edgy topics such as teenage pregnancy, but no nudity or on-screen love-making. Still, it was revolutionary for its time simply because it acknowledged that sexual activity was happening in a typical middle-American community. Oh, my! Not everyone was happy to see that made public.

When I graduated from high school in 1965, a couple of classmates had dropped out because they had become pregnant. The proprietor of the town's one gas station was arrested for "selling drug paraphernalia" to underage children when it became known that teens were purchasing condoms from the machine in the men's room. Teenage guys handed around clandestine copies of *Playboy* and other men's magazines, while it was rumored that our fathers or neighbors sometimes got together to drink beer and watch Super 8 porno movies in someone's garage.

The first issue of *Playboy* appeared in December of 1953, and by the early sixties the magazine and its creator, Hugh Hefner, had become cultural institutions. Always classy, *Playboy* featured beautiful girls tastefully nude (not yet "full frontal" below the waist) and bold suggestions of uninhibited sex for pleasure, even without a wedding ring. Adolescent boys, and obviously a lot of their fathers, dreamed of becoming a *Playboy* photographer, or someday owning a Playboy Club key. Heaven would be an invitation to Hugh Hefner's Playboy mansion in Chicago. For most of us, the photos in *Playboy* and similar magazines were our first introduction to the mysteries of female anatomy, and while we realized that those images were carefully chosen and air-brushed, we looked upon them as high art.

To be fair, we often *did* read the articles. The magazine regularly included short stories by the greatest novelists of the time, from Ian Fleming to Valdimir Nabokov, Saul Bellow, P.G. Wodehouse, or Arthur C. Clarke. Unlike much of the literature we were assigned to read by our high school English teachers, the articles in *Playboy* were timely and relevant, and we felt sophisticated discussing them over the lunchroom table. The *Playboy Philosopher* was a monthly feature that discussed the magazine staff's outlook on many of the social controversies of the day. I would even dare to suggest that we learned a great deal about presenting ideas and arguments in a written format from our furtive investigations of *Playboy*, as it subtly showed us how to structure our essays, reports and term papers for school assignments even as it opened our eyes to the important debates that were shaking our society. *Playboy* showed us how to dress fashionably, and how to dazzle a young lady with our sophisticated knowledge of the finest wines, music, theater, literature, men's grooming, and virtually anything that mattered.

In the early sixties, America was still very up-tight and conservative regarding sexuality. Occasional glimpses at magazines like *Playboy* allowed teenage guys hints of a more exotic lifestyle that might be happening in big cities or far-off exotic locales like Paris or London, but sex was not discussed in polite company. Adolescent guys whispered and winked, exaggerated their exploits in locker room conversations, and desperately looked for any opportunity to add to their limited knowledge of the subject. Very few American communities had "art" theaters where European films were shown, but magazines like *Life*, *The Saturday Evening Post*, *Look*, and *Time* couldn't resist reporting on the latest daring movies and their fabulously sexy stars. We were fascinated by exotic continental beauties, especially the ones who dared to flaunt their sexuality on the screen. Brigitte Bardot was a legendary "sex kitten," while Sophia Loren (perhaps the most beautiful woman in the world even today) won an Oscar and a series of European awards for her acting. Gina Lollobrigida, Catherine Deneuve, Claudia Cardinale, and Anita Ekberg were all favorites as we were growing up.

Ann-Margret was born in Sweden but raised in the U.S., and always incredibly beautiful and sexy. I saw her with Bob Hope at Christmas, 1968 in Korat, Thailand, a show I will never forget. All-American favorites included the iconic Marilyn Monroe, and also Natalie Wood, Raquel Welch, Jane Fonda (whose outfit in the movie *Barbarella* was truly out of this world), Elizabeth Montgomery, Cybill Shepherd, Faye Dunaway (who dared to suggest oral sex in *Bonnie and Clyde*), Jayne Mansfield, America's first Bond girl Jill St. John, the ultimately sexy Ronnie Spector of the Ronettes all-girl singing group, teenage heartthrob Shelley Fabares of *The Donna Reed Show*, and Julie Newmar who played "Catwoman" on the campy TV show *Batman* before being replaced by the equally sensual Eartha Kitt. The British TV show *The Avengers* brought us Diana Rigg, often in tight leathers. In 1962 Sean Connery played British secret agent James Bond in the first Bond film, *Dr. No*, which featured perhaps the sexiest movie scene of all time as the amazing Ursula Andress emerged from the surf in that incredible white bikini. Meanwhile, popular music offered beautiful, sexy women such as Diana Ross and the Supremes, and the slinky, sexy Shangri-Las, who toured with the Beatles, the Rolling Stones, the Drifters, and James Brown.

As noted previously, the mini-skirt was introduced in London in the early 60s, just about the time that a number of English rock 'n roll bands came to America in a "British Invasion" that captivated pop culture. The ultimate in fashion at that moment was a colorful, playful look called "mod," short for modern, from the youth-oriented designers on Carnaby Street in London. Men wore flowered shirts and broad leather belts, and young women wore whatever felt comfortable and free to fit their lifestyle. It was a rocking, joyous time and the mini-skirt seemed to set leggy young women free. There were skeptics, of course, and adults who were shocked at the sight of a young lady's thigh.

By the early '70s the ladies were going natural, leaving their bras home, and some lingerie manufacturers actually built fake nipples into their bra cups so the wearer would appear to be braless. Designer Rudi Gernreich created a stir with a topless swimsuit, but for all the hoopla I doubt that any young lady ever wore one on an American beach. From garter belts and stockings, modern science created panty hose. Hippy girls and dedicated non-conformist women began to wear jeans in public, and still the planet spun on its axis. Guys wore flared or bell-bottom jeans, fashionably faded and scuffed, with "heavy" worn leather boots. Facial hair was a fashion statement, from mustaches and beards to elaborate bushy sideburns. There was only one purpose to dressing in style, and that was to be attractive to the opposite sex.

To an adolescent bulging with hormones, the sixties and early seventies provided all manner of provocative images and suggestions. A popular ad campaign featured beautiful women living exotic fantasies above the caption "I dreamed I was (the fantasy of the month) in my Maidenform bra!" Cosmetics manufacturer Coty offered body paints. "Nobody who loves mini, kicky, bare-as-you-dare fashions looks dressed without it." The lady could choose from green, blue, mauve, or one (or more?) of four flesh tones. The kit came with a miniaturized, very personal pan and paint roller all packaged in an industrial-looking bucket. Betsy Johnson offered a clear vinyl dress, with an optional five-dollar bag of stick-on "copper coin dots, silver stars, and metallic blue rays" to maintain one's modesty in more formal circumstances.

In 1962 airline stewardesses threatened to go on strike if they were not allowed to color their hair, while many young women ironed their tresses to make them straight. *In Fashion* magazine declared that the topless swimsuit and the mini-skirt were "intended to prove that women were in control of their destiny and would choose whom they wished to mate with…" A generation of adolescent males immediately raised their hands to volunteer.

As automobiles multiplied, we discovered the wonderful opportunities offered by the 4,000 drive-in movie theaters scattered across the U.S. These "passion pits" were dark, semi-private places where the more daring movies often played on warm summer evenings. In those days the majority of cars had full-bench front seats, not buckets, and shift mechanisms on the steering column, so a guy and his date could slide over a little and meet in the center of the car to cuddle or snuggle and watch the show together. Hormones being what they are, we occasionally missed portions of the movie! These adventures were commonly known as "making out," not to be confused with the infinitely more serious "going all the way."

The legal age for buying alcohol was 18 in New York, and I once had a most memorable evening when I took a six-pack and a full-blooded Native American girl to the drive-in to see *How the West Was Won*. The film was an "epic" featuring two dozen Hollywood stars including John Wayne, James Stewart, Gregory Peck, Henry Fonda, Spencer Tracy, Richard Widmark, Debbie Reynolds, Carroll Baker, and George Peppard, but

I did not learn any lasting American history lessons that evening. I like to think that I did my part to bridge the gap between two races that had known conflicts in the past. I was not a virgin when I was sent to Vietnam, but I was far from sophisticated.

Not entirely of my own free will, I avoided the draft by enlisting in the army in late 1966. I reported for the swearing-in ceremony in downtown Buffalo the morning of December 30th, and was amazed to find that we were turned loose in the city until we would meet our train to Fort Dix late in the evening. In the company of a raucous band of frightened strangers, I found myself in a burlesque theater watching middle-aged strippers bump and grind. It was cold, so I purchased a bottle of scotch before catching the train.

We arrived in New York City, transferred to buses, and at Fort Dix we were met by a contingent of snarling, loud, nasty drill sergeants. I include this anecdote because from the very start of our military experiences, we were called "ladies" or "girls," an insult to our masculinity. We soon found ourselves standing in a frigid warehouse stark naked, surrounded by a few hundred other guys who were equally undressed and uncomfortable. For the next eight weeks we were constantly called "pussy" or "miss," and most of us were in far closer contact with other men than we had ever been before. By the time we were eligible for a weekend pass at the end of week six, we were desperately eager to escape the testosterone-rich environment of the barracks and find some female company. I broke the rules and flew home for the weekend, but as we signed out from the military compound we were "encouraged" as only drill sergeants can do to take a few "raincoats" from the punchbowl of condoms situated alongside the sign-out book.

In the book *Beyond Combat* by Heather Marie Stur one veteran recalls a drill instructor who assured the young group in his charge, "the man who don't f**k, don't kill." From the very first day of basic training, the objective was to destroy every recruit's sense of self. In eight weeks, he would be expected to graduate as a new person, fully committed to obey without hesitation, and to lay down his life for his country or his comrades. He had become physically toughened by a strenuous program of exercise, and he was expected to be mentally tough after an intense period of "training" that resembled brainwashing. The object of this curriculum was, of course, not to destroy the man. There had to be some acknowledgement of his worth, some possibility of reward at the end of his ordeal. That reward was the promise of a better sex life, and it was damned near impossible not to dream the dream. At every opportunity, we were expected to visit the local prostitutes. "This is my rifle," the saying went, "and this is my gun" (Hand to

SEX AND THE VIETNAM SOLDIER

crotch, long before Michael Jackson made it fashionable.) "This one's for fightin', and this one's for fun." Make no mistake, we were an army of virile young men undergoing some harsh physical training far from home and contemplating the possibility we might be sent to a war zone soon, and very few if any of us were offended by the moral implications of this permissive new environment. (At this point, youthful readers are encouraged to become familiar with the masculine medical condition known as "epididymal hypertension" which can be readily accomplished by Googling *blue balls*. The condition is far more common than Google suggests.)

Throughout my army experience, there was a constant focus upon going downtown, buying sexual pleasure, and "wearing your raincoat," yet a surprising number of guys became infected with a wide variety of sexually transmitted diseases. From Fort Dix, we were directed toward New York City, and I seem to recall suggestions of 7th Avenue, but I may be thinking of Paul Simon's song "The Boxer." From Aberdeen Proving Grounds we were directed to "The Block" in Baltimore, a neighborhood of strip clubs, sex shops, burlesque houses, and "adult entertainment" businesses where a guy could find a place to "dip his wick" or "get his pipes cleaned." M.P.s (Military Police) patrolled these areas to prevent fighting or muggings, and to assist drunken soldiers, but they looked the other way at prostitution, assuming "boys will be boys."

American soldiers in Vietnam were plagued by loneliness and sexual desire, as are all men sent off to war. If there was a difference in Vietnam, it was that a large percentage were there against their will, and watching, or taking part in a surreal extravaganza of destruction and killing unprecedented in all the history of wars. The "only 19" factor loomed large, as they were at their sexual peak . Far from home, lonely and often morally troubled by the ravages of war around them, they were eager for a few moments of physical pleasure, especially if the young lady was skillful at seeming to understand. In an environment where the G.I.'s individuality was suppressed and even outlawed, where fear was always present and creature comforts were nonexistent, a few minutes of self-indulgent pleasure in the private company of a beautiful, talented woman allowed a young man a release of tensions, and a small measure of confidence-building self-indulgence. For those few minutes, the G.I.'s individual feelings and needs mattered. There wasn't much else to spend your money on in Vietnam, so an investment in self-indulgence was especially satisfying.

It was November, or maybe it was December, of 1967. I was stationed in Pleiku, in the central highlands, and there was North Vietnamese ac-

215

tivity in the area. We spent a lot of time supporting the outpost in distant Dak To, patching up the trucks that ran constant supply convoys up and down the primitive dirt "highway." Sometimes, when drivers were needed, we volunteered to get a change of scenery. In late November the 173rd Airborne began to run into large numbers of North Vietnamese regulars in the hills around Dak To, and then all hell broke loose and the result was the Battle of Hill 875, the biggest battle of the Vietnam War to that point. I volunteered to drive a truckload of ammo to Dak To one morning, and it was a terrifying, life-changing journey. I had hoped that I might experience real combat away from my friends. I wasn't at all confident that my actions might not put my buddies at extra risk, so this adventure seemed to offer an opportunity to test myself in a scenario that would keep them safe. I experienced terror beyond anything I had ever imagined, but that's another story.

Meanwhile, somewhere in the midst of all the turbulence and raw terror, word got around that the new issue of *Playboy* showed pubic hair for the first time! The PX had a limited number of copies, so the limit was one per man. Danger seemed to be closing in around us, the fighting near Dak To was hell on earth, it was the holiday season at home and we weren't in any position to do Christmas shopping, and now we had to plot a strategy to get to the PX and purchase the landmark "girly book"!

Under the auspices of the United States military, in close cooperation with the Army of the Republic of Vietnam (ARVN), the taxpayers of our fine country unwittingly provided a chain of supervised bordellos throughout South Vietnam for the entertainment and solace of American G.I.s. One noteworthy example was a twenty-five-acre compound near An Khe, a village about halfway between Pleiku and the important port city of Qui Nhon. An Khe was an important American helicopter base located along a major supply route. Truck convoys carried supplies west through the An Khe Pass, a frequent scene of ambushes, to the highlands, often stopping for the night so the drivers could visit "Sin City." American MPs guarded the compound, and supposedly, American military doctors checked the girls regularly.

In Pleiku, we enjoyed access to a similar but much smaller operation. I'm sure "government houses" operated in the vicinity of many American bases. Supposedly, Vietnamese government officials took care of all the business operations of these institutions, and many Vietnamese refugees and displaced women sought employment in the government-operated houses because they would be better protected against venereal diseases, and would be treated if they became infected. However, for every one "government house" there were probably fifty to a hundred independent businesses trying to attract horny G.I.s. Massage parlors and "boom-boom houses" surrounded every American base.

In Saigon, bar girls sidled up to a G.I. and asked him to buy "Saigon tea," a tiny dollop of colored water in a miniature goblet. Depending upon the bar and the young lady, the price of a Saigon tea could be anywhere from $5 American up to $50, a steep price that actually purchased a few minutes of the girl's time so that negotiations for a far more serious encounter might ensue. It was not unusual for these negotiations to require more than one Saigon tea. Every American had heard of this scam by 1968, but it was looked upon as a game or contest, and far less threatening than the contest taking place out in the bush.

In a "benny" or benefit similar to an annual vacation, G.I.s stationed in Vietnam were allowed a five-day R & R, or "rest and recreation" break once a year. The military coordinated the comings and goings at the designated R & R cities, which included such exotic locations as Sydney, Australia; Singapore; Tokyo; Manila in the Philippines; Taiwan; Bangkok; Kuala Lumpur; and the Malaysian island of Penang. It was expected that a G.I. on R & R would enjoy female companionship, and all were supplied with guidelines to the local money system and "usual" rates for a lady's company during the flight to the destination city. Disembarking from the R & R center, the G.I. was immediately accosted by a huge throng of "agents" or pimps waiting to introduce him to a bevy of ladies who were eager to welcome him and make his vacation memorable.

It must be noted that married men were allowed to meet their wives in Honolulu, and unmarried men were strictly forbidden from taking their R & R in Hawaii. While prostitution was taken for granted in the exotic Asian cities and even in Australia, it was a generally accepted fact that an American city like Honolulu would not and could not offer that type of entertainment. Heaven forbid that anyone suggest we have prostitutes in America! The hypocrisy of the Vietnam War extended in many directions.

The incidence of venereal diseases among G.I.s was rampant in Vietnam. The U.S. Army Medical Department Office of Medical History states: In World War I, venereal diseases "ranked second only to influenza as a cause of disability and absence from duty, being responsible for the loss of 6,804,818 days and the discharge of more than 10,000 men. During World War II, the incidence of VD varied widely among the theaters of operation. Between 1941 and 1945, worldwide incidence in the army averaged 42.9 per 1,000 strength per year. This figure doubled during the postwar period (1946 to 1950) to 82.3 per 1,000 strength per year. With the troop build-up in Korea, the case rate once again doubled to 184.0 per 1,000 average strength per year for the period 1951 to 1955. The incidence remained consistently high in the ensuing ten years, exceeded only by that of American troops in Thailand. Similar high rates of venereal disease appeared in Vietnam as American "advisors" arrived in 1963. The overall average incidence was 261.9 per 1,000 strength per year during the period of 1963 to 1970. In comparison with other common diseases, venereal disease was the number one diagnosis from 1965 to the conclusion of the war. During the same period G.I.s assigned to stateside bases became infected at a rate of only 31 per 1,000.

In Vietnam 90% of VD cases were gonorrhea and slightly over 1% were syphilis. According to widespread G.I. legends, the other 9%, or some portion of them, were made up of one or more virulent, often fatal, *incurable* strains affectionately called "the black syph." According to legend, the G.I. who became infected with "the black syph" or similar "Viet-nereal diseases" would soon see his male equipment "turn black, shrivel up and fall off!" Upon diagnosis, he was immediately hustled away to a lifetime of total quarantine at an infamous military hospital located on one of the least populated islands of Japan in a joyless American military institution known as "Camp Crotchrot."

Historians and experts have analyzed and investigated every aspect of the war in Vietnam including this one, and very few give the story much credence. In the forty-odd years since the American occupation of Vietnam, a number of drugs have been developed that have proven very effective in curing or controlling venereal diseases. I have been unable to find even the slightest evidence of any G.I. being cured and returning to his home and family from "Camp Crotchrot." There are a few veterans who insist that the camp did exist, but I have never seen the slightest bit of evidence. I suspect this legend is exactly that, and nothing more. But, who knows?

Another prominent G.I. myth involved prostitutes who were Viet Cong sympathizers who supposedly kept razor blades in their sex organs to injure horny G.I.s in the most devastating manner imaginable. While booby traps of every type and description were common in Vietnam, and with the caveat that I am no medical authority, I have doubts that the ladies could accomplish such a feat without incurring serious injury themselves. I'm also inclined to think that, while sexual techniques vary, more fingers might be injured by this practice than penises, especially after the rumor became so widely spread. I love the suggestions by John Laky, Director of the Connelly Library at LaSalle University. In a paper titled "White Cong and Black Clap: The Ambient Truth of Vietnam War Legendry," Laky writes,

> One might wager safely on the power of this particular threat to gain the wide-eyed attention of a post-pubescent male – talk about 'just say no!' More to the point, though, the moral implication of GI's being injured in this ghastly way during the precise carnal act usually reserved for joyous rites of passage, is obviously a very fertile cluster of images for interpretation.

Perhaps this legendary story was a Viet Cong or North Vietnamese attempt at psychological warfare?

Like the actual number of Americans assigned to Vietnam, the number of Vietnamese prostitutes working at any point during the war is subject to debate. Official estimates generally indicated 20,000 to 70,000 female prostitutes working throughout South Vietnam, but those estimates probably only included the ladies working at the government-operated bordellos. Other sources estimated as many as 600,000 women, and perhaps another 100,000 young men. Pulitzer Prize-winning journalist Peter Arnett estimated the number of women at 300,000 but there is no indication of how he arrived at that number. Senator William J. Fulbright described both the city of Saigon and the whole of South Vietnam as "a brothel" with "over 500,000 prostitutes, one for every American soldier" in-country. Another half-million entertained Americans assigned to support the war from bases in Thailand, and the sex industry catering to American troops in the Philippines was estimated to employ 300,000 to 600,000.

Several factors led to the high incidence of prostitution among Vietnamese women during the war. First, prostitution was widespread during the war against the French prior to the American involvement. Once American combat troops were introduced in 1965, the Americans' concept of a "war of attrition" included the systematic destruction of villages, homes, livestock, and crops. While the introduction of chemical defoliants such as Agent Orange was usually justified as a means of denying cover to the enemy, vast areas of rice paddies were sprayed from helicopters in order to destroy the crops and weaken the resolve and the physical strength of the Vietnamese people. To destroy the very meager possessions of a peasant family, as well as their crops and livestock, was to leave them with literal-

219

ly nothing. Many young women were widowed when their soldier husbands were killed. Uneducated and without any skills to offer a potential employer, many peasants were forced to resort to the most extreme means in an attempt to stay alive. Parents had to send their children, sons as well as daughters, to the cities and towns to try to earn a few Piastres to keep the family going. The Vietnamese soon realized that the Americans were horny and flush with cash, and so the old law of supply and demand ruled the marketplace. Americans had come expecting to find an Oriental society where beautiful women were taught to be submissive to men and adept at the most sensual and exotic techniques of lovemaking in the world.

Sadly, no discussion of sex and the Vietnam War can fail to address the subject of rape in the war zone. I was not a combat infantryman, and I don't want to generalize or paint anyone with a broad brush. I have come in contact with a lot of Vietnam veterans, and this is a subject that rarely comes up in conversation. In 1971, Vietnam Veterans Against the War (VVAW) held a public discussion of war crimes and atrocities they had participated in while in Vietnam. The Winter Soldier Investigation featured testimony from about 75 veterans and four civilians who had worked in Vietnam. That testimony, and many other confessions and observations over the years, make it clear that rape was common and widespread in Vietnam. Further, it seems obvious from the accounts that American and Korean troops resorted to rape most often. The Communists committed many atrocities, but rarely rape. Likewise, the South Vietnamese were rarely rapists. The history of the Vietnam War is often murky and distorted, but in this instance it is quite clear. To be realistic, there has probably never been a war without abundant raping. War is traditionally a male endeavor, and the bodies of women have always been among the spoils of war. It is natural to be uncomfortable with these facts. The solution to the problem, clearly, is to make wars obsolete. More wars will not eliminate the occurrence of rape.

One other sad aspect of sex and the Vietnam War was the large number of Amerasian children that resulted. Once again, the actual number will never be known but estimates range from 50,000 to 100,000 or perhaps far more. These children were ostracized and referred to as *bui doi* or "dirt of life," and never accepted into the Vietnamese community, so they were condemned to a life of bitter poverty and very limited opportunities. A small number of the Amerasian kids have been brought to the U.S., and a few charitable organizations have tried to assist them. When the Communists came to power they offered virtually no help to these children, and many of the children of American fathers grew up to become prostitutes.

The Communists claimed to have eradicated prostitution in Vietnam, but businessmen and tourists have reported that it is still very much available, especially in Ho Chi Minh City (formerly Saigon) and Hanoi.

There were certainly a lot of sex fantasies running rampant through the baby boomer generation, and especially the guys who were sent to Vietnam. To an American kid in Southeast Asia, the ultimate girl of our dreams would have round eyes. We wanted to go home and fall in love with an all-American girl. Like many others, I had a very serious romantic attachment to a wonderful, beautiful young Chinese woman I met while on R & R in Penang, Malaysia. Still, my ideal fantasy woman would have been Ursula Andress, Natalie Wood, Ann-Margret, or singer Ronnie Spector of the Ronettes.

There were round-eyed women in Vietnam! We caught glimpses of them from time to time. Most were nurses, and a few were "Donut Dollies," volunteers of the Red Cross Supplemental Recreational Activities Overseas (SRAO) program, who came by once a month or so to smile and play tape-recorded rock 'n roll music while they emceed contests even more ridiculous than daytime TV game shows. Exactly 899 ladies served as Red Cross "Donut Dollies," visiting the G.I.s in the field to distribute donuts and smiles, play silly games, and "support our troops" with smiles and incredible bravery. They were always cheerful, attractive, they wore skirts and lipstick, and their eyes were round. They faced enemy fire at times, incoming mortars or rockets, mined roads and snipers, choppers taking ground fire, but they were American women, chosen for their good looks and ready smiles, surrounded by half a million lonely, hurting American soldiers who were only too eager to be reminded of the pleasures that we would experience if we survived and returned home. Only later did we realize and appreciate what they did for us, and the courage they showed day after day.

Former "Donut Dolly" J. Holley Watts self-published *Who Knew! Reflections on Vietnam*, a collection of her poems and memories that is uniquely heart-wrenching, patriotic, and sincere. The following is taken from that book:

Who knew…
How completely naïve I was.
It wasn't until decades after her death
That I'd learn my mother's greatest fear of me going to Vietnam
Was my possible encounter with sex.
All that time I thought it was the war.

The reader will be surprised to learn that the experts are unable to tell us how many women went to Vietnam. In the 1996 book *Vietnam Shadows*, author Arnold Isaacs suggests that "the most exhaustive post-war study of the veterans' experience reported that 7,166 women served 'in or around Vietnam' during the war." Does that include Donut Dollies, or nurses who volunteered to work with wounded civilians, like Patricia Walsh, the author of *Forever Sad the Hearts?* It is a terrible disgrace that Donut Dollies and USAID volunteers are ineligible for any post-war medical benefits.

The war in Vietnam saw a new medical strategy, the Trauma Center. Helicopters made it possible to bring critically injured G.I.s to Evacuation hospitals, where the latest medical equipment and techniques saved a great many guys who would never have made it to a hospital in World War II. The medical personnel in Vietnam were fantastic, and none more so than the nurses. They were young, usually just out of nursing school, and they were all volunteers. They may not have realized all that they were going to see and experience, but they came to Vietnam to help their fellow Americans. They worked enormous hours under the most trying of conditions, and they were always able to smile, squeeze a hand, and whisper encouragement. They had round eyes, and huge hearts, and they were angels.

Not to be maudlin, but I must ask the reader to imagine a 19 year-old kid who has dreamed of being close to a round-eyed American girl again, finding himself in the hospital, critically wounded, blown apart, perhaps burned, his "it won't happen to me!" braggadocio lost along with his legs or intestines or face, blown away out in a rice paddy. She smiles and tells him he's going to be all right. She may not believe it herself, but in a land where lies run riot she tries to help him believe he's going to be alright. The patient knows what she is seeing. He is broken and bloody, but she smiles and cares for him, and he will try his damnedest to make it through the night so he can see her pretty round eyes again tomorrow. The doctors and nurses who deal with war's wounded are angels come to Earth, and they deserve every benefit, every accolade that can possibly be offered them. They were, and are, truly war heroes.

* * *

In his book *Hanoi Jane: War, Sex, and Fantasies of Betrayal*, author Jerry Lembcke notes that "the gains made by the American women's liberation movement during the 1960s and early 1970s were perceived by many men to have come at the expense of their own social and economic standing." Lembcke also suggests, "The status loss felt by many men was heightened by the one-two punch of war-front, home-front indignities, a combination that helped write a cultural narrative spelled "class." Steve Mason, in his epic poem "To Brooklyn With Love" from his 1988 book *Warrior For Peace* uses similar words to express the sexual angst many Vietnam vets were feeling:

All American men my age
suffered the bad luck and ill-timing
of drawing Vietnam and women's lib
in the same ten years!

Sort of like getting hit by a truck
the same day they told you
about the stomach cancer.

John Wheeler, a West Point grad and Vietnam Veteran, in his 1984 book *Touched With Fire: The Future of the Vietnam Generation,* observes,

Something more was happening. Men grew long hair. They started "sharing" an idea instead of 'telling' it. Some men looked like women, and vice versa, and Americans were doing a double take. The culture became a *bit* more feminine. But for a big country, a bit is a lot.

Writing about divisions of American society during the Vietnam War years, he notes,

First, the man who wore the uniform was separated from the man who did not. Then, woman was separated from man, as the "all bets are off" attitude of the 1960s freed the women's movement, and as the factor of a despised war fed a feminization of the culture and disaffirmation of a distinctly masculine ideal.

Wheeler, it must be noted, contributed greatly to the building of the Vietnam Memorial in Washington, but he found his masculine role models in the Reagan administration's support for the brutal Contras in Central America. The changing attitudes moved the great Gloria Emerson to write, in the prologue of her book *Some American Men,*

In a decade when so much has changed at last for American women, it has been odd, and even unsettling, to keep making discoveries about men during a time when they have been denounced as childlike, brutish, inchoate, unfeeling, bullies, and deficient in both decency and imagination.

Later, she writes of Vietnam veterans,

"…whose deepest hopes for themselves have also been lost."

While I am skeptical of claims that soldiers returning from Vietnam were spat upon in airports, or by anti-war protestors, it is an inescapable fact that Vietnam vets met with an invisible but very solid wall of anxiety or uneasiness as they tried to return to the lives they had left behind. Women, newly emancipated, were strident and confrontational, some looking for any excuse to deride all men as "chauvinist pigs."

Returning veterans, fresh from the land of unlimited prostitution-on-demand, were not prepared for the feminist attitudes that painted them as "chauvinist" predators and selfish, incorrigible boors. We came home seeking, even desperately needing, feminine company and nurturing, and we were ill-prepared to deal with the aggressive feminists. Most of us ultimately found someone to love, but American society and attitudes toward sex had changed drastically while we were away. Also, economic factors were making it necessary for more and more women to enter the workplace, so returning vets found fewer opportunities for employment. This was especially frustrating for many, because they had been drafted or pressured into the military soon after high school, and were only eligible for entry-level jobs. Their classmates who had attended college were graduating and finding professional career positions.

Eager to start a career and looking forward to supporting a family someday, the veterans were entering the workforce at a lower level than their peers, and to lose out on a potential job opportunity to a "housewife" whose husband was earning a good wage was disappointing. Among all the other readjustments we had to make upon returning home, the acceptance of new attitudes and gender roles provided obstacles few had anticipated.

As a veteran of the American war in Southeast Asia, I must admit that I participated rather enthusiastically and enjoyed a variety of exotic adventures with the ladies of Vietnam and Thailand. After the war I returned home and met the most wonderful woman in the world, got married and raised a family. Carolynn and I have been married for more than forty years, and like all marriages, we have had our ups and downs. I fully accept that I alone am responsible for my actions prior to being a husband, and since. Still, I suspect that some of my expectations, and some of my reactions when faced with hard times, might have been considerably different if I had never been taken into the military and assigned to Southeast Asia.

At eighteen and nineteen years old a young man is expected to "sow his wild oats," and I would be the last one to discourage that activity. But I must point out that, from the very first day of basic training, the military experience was designed to strip a young man of his civilian identity, and train him to be a soldier. That training included a strong element, if not an indoctrination, of sexism that was in sharp contrast to civilian attitudes we left behind when we became soldiers, and in even greater contrast to new feminist standards when we returned to civilian life. Life in an army barracks, and I assume the same was true in the other services, was made up of harsh realities today and vivid fantasies of tomorrow, with sex a central theme of the barracks banter and fantasies. In a war environment a soldier is exposed to sights, sounds, fears, and psychological realities that are extremely difficult to rationalize, especially for a young, inexperienced soldier far from home and in fear for his life. Our training and instruction clearly suggested that, in an attempt to escape from the horrors and terrors, if only for just a few minutes, a man can relieve his stress and refresh his masculinity by enjoying a sexual encounter with a woman.

Of course, very few of the guys in the barracks, then or now, would disagree with this strategy. But things were changing, rapidly and drastically, out in the civilian world, and we came home with deeply ingrained attitudes about sex that would have some very difficult repercussions later in life. I suppose, with the increased presence of women in today's military, the curriculum has had to change. But MST, or Military Sexual Trauma is a major problem in today's military, with one out of every three women raped by a co-worker in her first enlistment, and intense retaliation if she reports the assault. The spouse of a military veteran should anticipate a wide variety of problems related to sexual attitudes and habits.

One final thought. Years after I had returned from Vietnam, I enjoyed a leisurely afternoon lunch and conversation at a New York City sidewalk café with a few people who had read and approved of ... *and a hard rain fell*. One of those was a tall, elegant, blonde, and very attractive PhD, the former head of Human Resources for a Fortune 500 company. In the course of the conversation I was surprised to learn that this sophisticated lady had left the corporate rat-race and was presently Manhattan's premier dominatrix. "At least ninety percent of my clients are either Holocaust survivors or combat veterans," she said softly. "Why do you think that is?" I'm sure my answer sounded as fumbled and ridiculous as it felt, but the question has remained in the back of my mind ever since.

Today, the remaining veterans and survivors of World War II are reaching advanced age and soon the last will be gone. Before long there won't be any more Holocaust survivors. I don't know whether the dominatrix profession might be in any danger of disappearing. But, as war continues to curse our world, I kind of doubt that's the case. Erica Jong wrote that the point of power is the freedom to cultivate roses. Of course, the thorns mandate that the beautiful flower must be handled with care, but the bloom brings a smile to a lady's lips, and so the rose will always be symbolic. Vietnam veterans have experienced far greater divorce rates than our peers who were never in the military, stark evidence of the emotional and psychological baggage we brought home from the war.

Chapter 14

THE GREAT MYTH

The willingness with which our young people are likely to serve in any war, no matter how justified, shall be directly proportional to how they perceive veterans of earlier wars were treated and appreciated by our nation.

– George Washington.

I processed out of the army in Oakland, California and flew home from San Francisco. I remember seeing the most outrageous hippies at the airport, but they certainly didn't say or do anything negative or adversarial towards me. I was in uniform, although in those days we did not wear combat fatigues in public places. When I got on the plane a businessman assigned to the seat next to me asked to be moved. There was a stop in Dallas, and another in Detroit, and each time the same thing happened. There was no spitting, no real animosity. People just didn't want to be close to a guy in a military uniform, and I thought it was probably because they didn't know what to say. And frankly, I didn't really mind because I didn't know what to say either. When I got home I kind of expected the neighbors to come by and welcome me back, but that didn't happen. I was sitting in the back yard when the next-door neighbor came out to mow his lawn, and he offered a big wave and a smile, and that was fine.

Today, when I see soldiers in the airport I make it a point to smile and nod, and I've bought a few meals without getting too close. I expect them to have thoughts and memories that I should not access, and I certainly respect their privacy.

It is generally accepted as fact that Vietnam veterans were widely disrespected, spat upon, and called "baby killer" upon returning home, especially in airports. I'm pleased to tell you, none of those things ever happened to me. I'm sure they happened to some vets, but I am convinced the few genuine instances have been blown way out of proportion.

Following are a few of my personal experiences that I believe illustrate that the American people were actually supportive of the troops in Vietnam, and returning veterans. That concept, by the way, shouldn't really surprise anyone. We were, after all, loved ones, the kid next door, former members of the high school football, basketball, baseball, track and field, wrestling, or tennis teams. We had pumped gas, served up ice cream cones, delivered newspapers, won scouting merit badges, or played in school bands. To suggest that any significant number of the American people harbored personal resentments against Vietnam veterans is simply out of character and offensive.

It was a time of intense emotions, and sometimes those emotions overwhelmed good sense. If instances of that sort happened, they would certainly be contrary to the general nature of the American people, and I don't believe that abuse of returning Vietnam veterans was at all common or universal. A few friends and acquaintances from my age group have gone out of their way to assure me, in the most agitated tones, that someone they knew had been spat upon or called "baby killer," always exactly the same stories, and always in airports, but I believe they are being sincere. If you're a vet and something ugly actually happened to you when you returned from Vietnam, I'm very sorry. There are jerks everywhere, and it's a damned shame you ran into one... or more. I just cannot accept that a large part of the American public felt or acted that way.

Long before we met, my future wife Carolynn was a nursing student at Genesee Hospital School of Nursing in Rochester, NY. One evening a lady representing an organization called "Operation Morale" came into the dorm and asked the students to write letters and send packages to local guys serving in Vietnam. (Women were not excluded, but they were extremely rare in combat zones in those days.) Each of the students covered her eyes and ran a finger down the list, stopping at random names. Carolynn chose three names, including mine. She was reluctant to write to me because I was a mere Private First Class, or Pfc., but rules are rules. Her letters were wonderful! Her school was located close by the downtown Rochester Chevy dealership where I had worked, and she walked through that area often. She described the holiday decorations in store windows, snow storms, and the venues where local bands like Wilmer & the Dukes were playing. Familiar places, places I could see in my mind's eye, and I was so grateful to learn that they were still there, and life as usual was still going on. Her letters always contained a liberal portion of Avon "Somewhere" body powder, and I often went to sleep holding the envelope over my nose to escape the foul scent of war. She sent boxes filled with home-made cookies, hard candies, newspaper clippings, and precious reminders of home, but mostly it was the cheerful tone of those letters that endeared her to me. One of her three pen-pals was killed, and Carolynn took his letters and photos to his mother. Carolynn's grandparents lived near the race track at Watkins Glen, and you could hear the sound of the race cars clearly from the homestead. She won my heart in a variety of ways.

When I returned home I dated a little bit. I was eager to see and hear the latest bands, but by that time psychedelics had become popular, and the flashing light-shows and booming music reminded me of incoming rockets and mortars and made me uncomfortable. One evening I dug out Carolynn's home address, looked up the number in the phone book, took a deep breath and called her. Her mother was just going out bowling. We had a wonderful conversation, and were still on the call when her mom came home! We were married in September of 1970, barely a year after I had returned from Southeast Asia.

At one point we actually visited "Mama Kay" Robinson, the lady who had originated Operation Morale. Years later, Amie Alden, the Livingston County, NY Historian, became interested in Operation Morale. She compiled an enormous amount of data, artifacts, and photos of the organization, and presented her findings at a number of events across upstate New York in the early years of the 21st century. Clearly, Operation Morale had been a large endeavor, an outpouring of support for the troops from all of western New York. Ms. Alden soon found that her audiences were surprised to learn of the scope of the operation, and the serious commitment of a great number of people to helping their neighbors fighting in Vietnam. That history had been de-emphasized, distorted, revised, or ignored.

It doesn't take a lot of imagination to realize that there were programs like Operation Morale all across the United States while American kids were fighting in Vietnam. The American people were looking for opportunities to help their neighbors. I hope this small mention will find its way to every person who gave of their time, or donated goods, to one of those organizations. You will never know how much the letters and packages were appreciated. THANK YOU!

Meanwhile, back in Vietnam, as I was receiving letters from Carolynn, the sister of one of my high school friends sent my name and address via HAM radio to a friend in Cincinnati, Ohio. Somehow, that address was printed in a Sunday newspaper, and I began to receive incredible mail, both in amount and content. I had never been to Cincinnati in my life, and I have no idea what the article said, nor how many names were listed. I began to receive a lot of letters from women, total strangers, all completely supportive and endearing. (Other than my father, I don't believe I ever received a letter from a guy while I was in Vietnam.) I actually received so many that I gave some away. There was no time to answer them all, and I felt very self-conscious carrying bundles of letters away from the mail shack while some of my buddies were getting no mail at all. I shared a lot of letters, and I did write to a few favorites in Cincinnati throughout my time in Vietnam. I broke off exchanging letters with Carolynn when I went to Thailand, and I don't know if I continued with any of my Cincinnati correspondents. I doubt it. Sadly, I don't have any of their names or addresses today, but I retain many fond memories.

At any rate, their support for a soldier in Vietnam was a sincere and most appreciated outpouring. I also received boxes of cookies, candy, Kool-Aid, and other snack foods. I must also mention that a few of the letters contained Polaroid photos of the ladies in the nude or in very sexy lingerie, and vivid descriptions of how they intended to welcome me home if I would only visit Cincinnati after returning. Lack of support for soldiers in Vietnam indeed!

When ... *and a hard rain fell* came out in 1985 and attracted a lot of attention in the local newspaper, I received a very emotional call from a lady who wanted to meet with me. A highly respected ex-legislator from Maryland's House of Delegates, she came to our home and settled into a comfy chair in the living room and began to tell her story. During the Vietnam War, her husband was an Air Force officer assigned to Andrews Air Force Base near Washington, D.C. The ladies of the Officers' Wives Club were looking for a project, and someone mentioned that a lot of flights were bringing in wounded G.I.s from Vietnam. Some of the wounded were still in muddy combat fatigues, and many were able to get around a little. Most were headed to Walter Reed Army Hospital or Bethesda Naval Hospital. Wouldn't it be nice if the Club could learn about the flights in advance, and welcome the returning soldiers with homemade cookies, magazines, and cheerful greetings?

The plan was begun. When a plane was due, phone calls alerted all the participants. Some baked cookies. Others took bathrobes and necessary baskets for carrying laundry. Regardless of the hour, day or night, when the soldiers arrived they were met with a committee of welcoming women. There were snacks, hamburgers and hot dogs grilled over charcoal, home-made salads, ice cream, and warm, emotional greetings. Men in dirty clothes were given robes and slippers to wear while their laundry was whisked away to designated homes where it was washed and even pressed. The ladies held fundraisers and provided fresh underwear and socks, razors, toothbrushes, and magazines. The program was a huge success, and the G.I.s seemed to really appreciate it. Then, mysteriously, the notifications of incoming flights stopped.

A delegation of the wives went to the base commander to inquire. They had done nothing wrong, he assured them, but they would not be meeting any more planes. There was no explanation offered. Now, many years later, this tearful woman wanted me to know that they had tried to welcome the troops home, but the Air Force had put an end to it. "Please tell the Vietnam veterans that we tried!" She was very emotional, and sincere. Of course, I was never able to ask the base commander why the program had been stopped, but I believe it was because the military did not want Vietnam vets, especially wounded Vietnam vets or guys right out of the field, to talk with housewives as soon as they got off the plane. Who could predict what they might say? As I have pointed out at numerous other points throughout this book, morale was bad in Vietnam. The powers did not want a lot of negativity passed on to officers' wives on the fringes of Washington, D.C., of all places. The war was being waged cruelly, and not at all in the best interests of the Vietnamese people. It would not do to have that message reach the heartland, and especially not via the wives of Air Force officers stationed in the nation's capital.

In Vietnam, in combat, every moment counted. Every movement, every circumstance was life-or-death, every thought was confrontational with the deadly environment that surrounded us, and we had to learn to function despite the terror that was so intense and immediate that it eliminated all but life itself. Sometimes it took that, too.

We came home changed, and to a profoundly changed environment. While we had been serving our country's militarism and imperialism in Vietnam, but also in Korea, Germany, at bases or on ships all around the globe, our classmates had been getting an education and preparing for successful careers. Women were demanding an increased presence in the workplace, and two-income families were becoming more necessary. When we went looking for jobs the interviewer asked, "What have you been doing since high school?" Sadly, in far too many cases we found that the recruiters and the sergeants had lied, and our military specialties really hadn't prepared us to work in high-tech positions in the space-age work environment. We had to play catch-up, and it was damned hard sometimes, but the slow progress in career advancement was not really discrimination against veterans so much as it was the law of supply and demand.

Avon, New York is a small town. Located about thirty miles south of Rochester, it is a bedroom community surrounded by farms and agriculture. I was so relieved to come back! But I had forgotten one important fact during the two years I was away in Southeast Asia. Over there, a siren signaled an attack. Avon has a volunteer fire department, and they sound the siren to summon the firemen. I wasn't home for long, sound asleep in my bed, when the fire siren sounded. I rushed out of bed, banging and crashing in a terror-filled rush to find my pants and my gear, and promptly fell down the stairs!

How do you explain about times like that to your mother? How do you describe them to a next-door neighbor, or a co-worker, or a girlfriend? They can't imagine such intensity, and they certainly can't help you to shed it. It seems there will never be a good time to talk about it. They think you have changed, and they are probably right. Acknowledging the change, everybody walks on egg shells, wondering how many nights it will take until the poor vet settles down, relaxes, and remembers that his family should play an important role in his life? Why is it so hard to acknowledge the changes you feel inside to a parent, a sibling, or a lover? Why? I know a lady whose Vietnam veteran husband could only make love to her while he was holding the business end of a loaded pistol against her temple! One day he turned the pistol on himself. Should she be relieved? How should anyone deal with that anguish? And why should they have to? "Be all you can be" indeed.

Very few of us were welcomed home with open arms, except by family, and even that wasn't a given. We grew our hair, stretched our minds, learned some skills, and found a small circle of lovers and friends. We hid or denied our memories and worked to catch up, and to pay mortgages and car payments. We knew we were different, and it was often a point of stubborn pride. We could endure and overcome anything, and most of us proved our worth. In business, veterans are usually overachievers. For many of us, it was years later when we began to hear that some of our brothers had found a cruel reception when they got home. It was troubling to hear those stories, and a few vets set up "vet centers" and rap groups, and we talked about it all, and helped each other. Politicians beat their chests and promised to get to the bottom of it all, and they swore they had never disrespected Vietnam veterans. (We were of age to vote by that time, and they wanted our votes.)

Slowly, steadily, the PR experts convinced the American public that Vietnam veterans had gotten a raw deal... from the American people, *not* the government or the military! This myth became a convenient fact for those who needed someone to blame. Finally, one Vietnam vet investigated the claims. In his 1998 book *The Spitting Image*, veteran Jerry Lembcke describes the great lengths he went to investigating the myth, and he came up empty. There are zero published reports of returning Vietnam veterans being spat upon or harassed to be found in America's newspapers, TV news films, or police reports. While many veterans persist in their stories, and perhaps their recollections, Lembcke was unable to find a shred of proof that Vietnam veterans were confronted or abused by antiwar protestors upon arriving home. I suspect some vets felt that their Vietnam combat experiences were not valued, and those feelings led to exaggerated expressions and stories, but again, I feel strongly that the actions described would be terribly out of character for the great majority of Americans.

Vietnam veterans came home to a divided American populace, and it was quite natural that some would take the criticisms of the war to be personal attacks against them. There are uncouth, misspoken, boorish zealots and fools throughout our nation, in the military, on the street corners of America's home towns, and, perhaps especially, in bars and taverns. There is no doubt the peace movement, overall, welcomed us home from Vietnam, as evidenced by the major role that Vietnam Veterans Against the War were invited and encouraged to play in the national anti-war strategy.

By the time of Desert Storm and the American reaction to Saddam Hussein's invasion of Kuwait in 1991, we had seen a flurry of glitzy "Welcome Home" parades, ten years or more after we had actually returned from the war. The President and his fellow chicken-hawk neo-cons promised to make everything right on the evening news while they quietly hid behind the walls of the White House or the Capitol and chopped our benefits. American troops invaded Panama and Grenada, almost as if the militarists were checking to see if the anti-war crowds were still watching. The media were not invited, and there are no photographs of the bulldozers digging mass graves in the carpet-bombed barrio of El Chorrillo, where foreign journalists and civil rights groups witnessed thousands of dead and wounded.

Operation Desert Storm was just a little war, about 45 days long, and America was adorned with "support our troops" bumper stickers, signs, and magnetic yellow ribbons. President George H.W. Bush crowed that "Vietnam syndrome" had been cured. Then, in response to 9/11 his son invaded Afghanistan and 18 years later we are all eager to see how that works out. In 2003, "W" invaded Iraq again, after the "shock and awe" bombardment of downtown Baghdad. Eight Americans were captured by the Iraqi army, but we remember only Jessica Lynch, who was described as bullet-riddled before she heroically spoke out to set the story straight.

"W" masqueraded as a jet pilot and declared, "Mission Accomplished," adding one more lie to the "weapons of mass destruction" fallacy that hung over the war for so many years after. The Pentagon's marketing and merchandising people used their overflowing budgets to misinform the American people and lure recruits to the all-volunteer military by sowing a storm of misplaced guilt, and the myth became accepted as fact. They spread lies and misrepresentations about Vietnam veterans not being welcome when we returned home and created a myth that has lasted to the present day.

After the Middle Eastern wars, a substantial number of veterans of those wars reported a variety of illnesses including chronic fatigue, gastrointestinal disorders, and birth defects among their offspring. The Veterans Administration has been reluctant to investigate these claims or provide any real relief to affected veterans, and it is noteworthy that they refer to the range of maladies as "Gulf War Syndrome," once again implying that the conditions are more mental than physical. Perhaps the American people with those yellow ribbon stickers on their automobiles supported our troops more than the military or government? Again? Just sayin'.

The Vietnam War was a debacle for America's military, forced to swallow defeat for the first time in our history, and they were eager to move beyond the embarrassment and shame. Certainly, there was concern that memories of the Vietnam disaster would carry over and have a negative effect upon recruiting for the all-volunteer military. The "Be all you can be" TV commercials had worked pretty well for a number of years, but then there was Operation Desert Storm and the gloves were off, and it appeared we might need to attract a lot of cannon fodder soon.

Just prior to the second invasion in 2003, it was widely disseminated and believed by many that Saddam Hussein had a vast arsenal of chemical weapons. CBS TV's *60 Minutes* revealed that our brave young troops were being issued old, used, dilapidated gas masks patched up with duct tape. Newer masks had been ordered, but they would not be ready before the anticipated invasion. No one ever really explained what the urgency of that moment was all about. Shortly after the invasion, our troops complained that their Hum-Vees and other vehicles were not properly armored, and the infantry was not being issued Kevlar jackets. They had to write home to their parents and loved ones, who bought flak jackets in hometown army-navy surplus stores and shipped them to the Middle East. G.I.s were scrounging through scrap yards in Iraq, looking for discarded metal panels they could hang on the sides of their vehicles to act as makeshift armor. When one brave young G.I. was filmed by a TV news crew confronting visiting Secretary of Defense Donald Rumsfeld about this issue he was derided and labeled unpatriotic! No, he had discovered he was just cannon fodder, and he knew exactly who had put him in harm's way.

Once again, America was undergoing tumultuous times as our young people were drawn into a questionable war, made possible by the "events of 9/11." It seemed that the Pentagon policy makers were conspiring to lure a new generation of recruits, and even appease their anxious parents, by conducting a vast disinformation campaign to make the American public feel guilty for "mistreating" Vietnam veterans when they came home. It would not be the first time the government had misled its people about the history of the war in Vietnam.

The second half of the twentieth century saw great changes in American culture. While our military and space technology seemed to overcome all challengers, the quality and desirability of products for the home consumer deteriorated. Once completely dominant, the "Big Three" Detroit automakers produced an endless parade of obsolete, inefficient, and problem-plagued vehicles that were woefully incapable of competing with Japanese and European cars. For a time, it seemed that Detroit was putting more effort into lobbying against the imports in Washington than engineering and designing fuel-efficient and safe vehicles for sale to the American public. By 1980, American products had been eclipsed by Japanese and European products in a number of vital industries such as airplane and ship building, the production of medical instruments and equipment, and home electronics.

Much has been written about American businesses outsourcing their manufacturing overseas where factory workers are willing to accept lower wages and fewer benefits. Washington's increased emphasis upon war-making severely impacted the manufacturing sector, and consumers turned to imported goods to make their lives comfortable. The neglect of our "representative" government to create incentives and trade barriers to protect American jobs has been a shameful national tragedy. Over the last five decades, we have seen our manufacturing economy relentlessly moved overseas to maximize profit for corporate interests who care nothing about the welfare of the American worker. It has been led by the Republican Party, with Democrats mostly standing by and impotently wringing their hands while they go along to get along and keep the big campaign contributions coming.

In the mid-sixties, our newspapers were ablaze with revelations of waste and fraud by Pentagon purchasers. Six hundred-dollar toilet seats and three hundred-dollar claw hammers outraged the public, but no officials were ever held accountable. Of course, those outrageous transactions are still happening today. By the time of the Vietnam War, big business had realized that the road to big profits and happy stockholders led directly to the Pentagon. By the 1980s, it was reported that over 80% of all college engineering graduates were finding work in defense-related industries. The top 80%. The remaining 20% were hired by the "people products" industries and tasked with competing against such foreign powerhouses as Toyota, Honda, Volkswagen-Audi, Mercedes-Benz, Nissan, Michelin, Bridgestone, Seiko, Sony, Panasonic, JVC, Toshiba, Yamaha, Suzuki, Kawasaki, Samsung, and so many others. Emboldened foreign companies brought a vast array of new products to America.

America's textile industry self-destructed, and today the vast majority of the clothes we wear have been manufactured overseas. American furniture companies have failed, and today the majority of the furniture sold in the U.S. is made in China. Examples are evident everywhere. In 2006 I was working at a Honda dealer in Northwest New Jersey, and construction of our new service department was delayed for six weeks while a steel beam, not available in the American marketplace, was imported from Canada. The dealership was located about an hour's drive from Bethlehem, Pennsylvania, where the site of the old Bethlehem Steel plant is today a casino.

The sad fact is that today American manufacturing is mostly in the business of death and destruction. Our economy has been shifted from "people products" like wristwatches, TV sets, medical instruments, and smart phones to war machines, bombs and drones and spy satellites. Today corporations and businesses are allowed to spend unlimited amounts of money to influence politics at every level, and some of their campaigns have been frighteningly effective. We see corporate names on NASCAR and other series' race cars, and on the stadiums and facilities where our favorite sports are played.

Vietnam veterans returned home to find a changing industrial environment, and without college degrees many had a hard time finding a good job. Vietnam vets could go to college with financial assistance from the G.I. Bill, something today's returning veterans do not have. In the divisive political environment of the late sixties and early seventies, many aspects of American tradition and culture were questioned and attacked. Vets returned home from the Vietnam war only to find their family or community had disintegrated into armed camps of "hawks" and "doves," just as today's American social structure is divided by allegiances to "liberal" or "conservative" political viewpoints. Today's Middle East veterans are struggling to reintegrate back into the American mainstream, daily suicides are epidemic, and that is far more a result of the harsh economic environment than any antagonism or lack of appreciation on the part of the American public.

The effects of American industry's emphasis upon maximum profits (no matter the cost to the worker) and those lucrative Defense contracts have been disastrous for many American families. Remember the 8-hour day, or the five-day work week? Remember when companies paid a large part of your health care, and when you earned a retirement pension in return for your loyalty to an employer? Those things were standard just a few years ago. Not only veterans have been hurt by Washington's "pro-business" agenda.

Americans care about their veterans and try to honor them at every opportunity. Unfortunately, our country has overspent its budget. In eight years, Ronald Reagan took America from the world's greatest lending nation to the most indebted country on the planet, drastically cut veterans' benefits, and turned thousands of mentally ill people out into the street. For the record, George W. Bush cut veterans benefits more than any modern President. The American public's respect for veterans can be seen on Memorial Day, the 4th of July, and Veterans Day every year, in the cemeteries and ceremonies held in communities all across the nation. The government's flowery speeches aside, their lack of caring for veterans is disgraceful, and far too often constitutes a blatant breach of contract in violation of agreements forged and promises made by the military recruiters.

A large part of the Pentagon's budget is used to attract recruits to the all-volunteer military. An example is the Obama administration's multi-million-dollar 50th anniversary commemoration of the Vietnam War, which proved to be an excuse to get recruiting teams into high schools and social events. I love race cars, but I am opposed to watching top fuel dragsters, funny cars, and NASCAR stock cars on TV with millions of tax-dollars providing commercials that are clearly designed to attract young race fans to join the military, as if war is just a real-life video game, while at the same moment thousands of hurting veterans are forced to wait months and even years to get their claims approved by a VA system that is economically incapable of doing the job it has been assigned. Until our Defense budget is brought into line with all the other nations of the world and our education and health-care systems are repaired to be representative of the richest country in the world, the propaganda from the Pentagon is self-serving and offensive.

I'm afraid our government is actually trying to divide us as it systematically squanders our national wealth with no regard for the best interests of the American people. If the powers can stir our emotions by exaggerating claims that hippies spat on veterans half a century ago and distract us from the 22 American veterans that commit suicide every day, they can continue to award unnecessary "defense" contracts to the corporations that line their pockets with campaign contributions or other favors and continue to bankrupt our country both financially and morally.

The government fears nothing more than people in the streets. The huge Women's March on the day after President Trump's inauguration was an indication of the American mood that swept an unprecedented number of women into Congress in the mid-term elections of 2018. If there is any lesson to be learned from the Vietnam War, it is precisely that our government will conspire, sabotage our gatherings, and use all the latest state-of-the-art technology and techniques to keep the public in line. Our "representatives" are too often unapproachable, isolated from constituents but available to any corporate representative with a checkbook in his hand. In a number of election results, those 2018 mid-terms showed that the corporate-backed candidates can be defeated and sent back home if enough voters turn out. Democracy is threatened in America, but it still works despite the conditioning and hype.

Chapter 15

PEACENIKS, PATRIOTS, AND PROVOCATEURS

We're not really pacifists, we're just nonviolent soldiers.

– Joan Baez

Do not … regard the critics as questionable patriots. What were Washington and Jefferson and Adams but profound critics of the colonial status quo?

– Adlai Stevenson

O ver the years I have been privileged to speak to many classes and participate in interviews, written communications, and e-mail exchanges with high school, college or university students all around the world. As the war in Vietnam fades further and further into the mists of history, I find that the majority of students and younger people are convinced the protesters who demonstrated against the war were all "hippies." When asked to define hippies, students often refer to a vast group of young people with long hair, dressed in "funny," often dirty clothes, stoned on drugs and with questionable sexual morals. Occasionally the protesters are described as cowards, or Communist sympathizers, anarchists, or a scruffy band of rebellious hedonists opposed to capitalism, materialism, civic responsibility, and the American Dream. I often get the impression that the students are just repeating what they have been taught or picked up from parents, grandparents, teachers, or political authority figures; but there's a little curiosity lurking just below the surface. They are usually at the rebellious age themselves, and perhaps they secretly relate to a generation of youthful insubordinates who made history.

Speaking with today's students, I don't believe I've ever heard the word "patriotism" used to describe the people who protested the war in Vietnam, or even the suggestion that they may have acted out of a sincere love of country. I have gradually come to recognize that many of the teachers who are speaking to today's youth were not even born when the last American troops left Vietnam. Their knowledge of the war has been gathered during a period of intense militarism and propaganda in America that has strategically aimed to revise the true history of the war. In this age of the all-volunteer military, the last thing the Pentagon wants to see is a body of students and young people who question our nation's "exceptionalism" or militarism, or who might come to understand and associate with the peace movement.

In the very early days of America's involvement, as grade school students we had never heard of Vietnam. When we entered high school, at the very most we might have been aware that there were a few "advisors" in a poor little country somewhere in Southeast Asia. They were there to aid and assist the people, of course, alongside Doctor Tom Dooley, who wrote best-selling books about his work providing medical assistance to the Laotian and Vietnamese peasants. Much later we learned that he was a covert CIA agent, but when his books were popular we had no idea of that.

In those days, most Americans, if they *had* ever heard of Vietnam, probably couldn't find it on a map. As more "advisors" were sent, a few people became alarmed. At first, the critics were mostly religious types, missionaries, or pacifists, folks at the fringes of the diplomatic community. Congress was asked to appropriate money once in a while; but compared to the costs of the Cold War defending primitive Vietnam against creeping Communism was small potatoes. When things began to escalate, students picked up on it, and college students always made up a large percentage of people who vocally opposed the war. A few college students achieved notoriety for their anti-war activities, but they were not the only ones to recognize that America had no business getting involved in Vietnam.

In the November 21, 1960 issue of *Time* magazine, an editorial stated, "Diem has ruled with rigged elections, a muzzled press, and political re-education camps that now hold thirty thousand." We were beginning to realize that Cuba under Fidel Castro had brought Communism to within just ninety miles of Florida's coast, but very few Americans were concerned that the Communists might take over in a far-off land called Vietnam.

President Kennedy's bold efforts to craft a nuclear disarmament treaty with the Russians faced widespread opposition from cold warriors who very intently recalled the result of appeasement with Hitler prior to World War II. Years after Kennedy's death, the peace movement tried desperately to encourage legislators to support nuclear disarmament. Compared to the threat of nuclear annihilation, the conflict in Vietnam seemed insignificant, and proponents of the test-ban treaty did not want any other issue to draw attention from the ultimate goal of averting the possibility of nuclear war.

The people surrounding President Johnson were, as we have seen, both guiding the expansion of America's military involvement in Southeast Asia and contesting the American public's growing disenchantment with the military-industrial-intelligence community. The "peace" organizations working for non-military solutions to international tensions were driven by religious or moral intensity, but because they were unknown and unappreciated by the vast majority of Americans, a significant portion of their activity was devoted to competitive fund-raising and PR efforts. Competing anti-war groups often fought each other with as much passion and zeal as they opposed militarism and bellicose foreign policy. To a great extent, those economic struggles, as much as any philosophical differences, would ultimately inhibit the effectiveness of the peace movement throughout the Vietnam War era. They are still a formidable barrier to the movement's effectiveness today.

Many who became aware of the growing American involvement in far-off Southeast Asia viewed the war as a parallel concern to the civil rights movement here at home; youthful idealists were convinced that one could not address one injustice without challenging the other. Folk singers on the college circuit began to reflect the youthful social movement, and a few singers and songwriters began to address some very important issues.

As noted elsewhere, every authority figure, every parent and teacher and religious leader had lived through World War II and the Korean War, and civics or social studies classes emphasized the horrors of the holocaust and the dangers of creeping communism. Many young people grew up in households scarred by America's recent wars, and we were taught that America was a uniquely good place, the hope of the poor and downtrodden all around the world. But the times were a'-changin', and it was difficult to square the reports of racial segregation and violence in the South with platitudes about all men being equal in the USA, or news reports of H-bomb tests in Nevada with classroom lectures that war was obsolete and unthinkable in the nuclear age. Young people were becoming skeptical and critical of The Establishment. We had little faith that the world had learned from the great wars, and they could be avoided in the future.

241

Our optimism was challenged by Russia's Sputnik satellite, the communist takeover in Cuba, the Cuban missile crisis, the Berlin Wall, and especially by the assassination of President Kennedy. Resistance to the civil rights movement was violent, implacable, and threatened every aspect of America's basic freedoms. We had never heard of Vietnam, but we might be drafted and sent to a war there. The baby boomer generation, unprecedented in its numbers and its prosperity, came of age as the TV evening news brought a vast number of challenges into our living rooms.

Reformers came to the fore, only to be systematically vilified, ridiculed, or, if dangerous enough to the Cold Warriors' agenda, eliminated. The American public did not accept politically-inspired murder quietly, but who were the bad guys? By the time the National Guard opened fire on protesting students at Kent State University in 1970, many Americans had gained a cynical, even fearful respect for what America's government had become. Many thought the protesters were to blame, setting buildings and their draft cards on fire, marching and carrying signs, disrupting traffic, causing turmoil, and questioning the very foundations of our society.

Our parents had endured years of child-rearing with high hopes for their children's future, only to see them drafted and sent halfway around the planet. Thousands of flag-draped coffins were coming home, and for what? Then the government attempted to address the inequities of the draft system by initiating a lottery, and even more middle-class moms and dads saw their children snatched away and sent into the meat grinder. Taxes were raised to fund the war, politicians were found to be crooked, many of the questions being asked by the sign-carrying kids in the streets were quite valid. Middle-class moms and dads with established influence in Washington began to challenge the war head-on.

Yes, there were "hippies" protesting the war, but they weren't a splinter group of unwashed bohemians from the wrong side of the tracks; they were about 98% of all of us. Long hair and faded jeans were in fashion, along with flowered shirts, ankle-length skirts, and T-shirts printed with clever political or social commentaries. Colors were all the rage, for guys and gals. Sandals were popular, except in winter. Pop-culture "hippies" read *The Hobbit, Lord of the Rings, Jonathan Livingston Seagull, One Flew Over the Cuckoo's Nest,* poets like Ginsberg and Richard Brautigan, listened to Ravi Shankar playing his sitar or the Beatles or Rolling Stones, smoked a little "pot" when we could get it, and decorated our walls with psychedelic posters advertising rock concerts, mandalas or symbols from Hinduism and Buddhism, or prints of colorful paintings by Peter Max, Maxfield Parrish, Andy Warhol, or Leroy Neiman. We discovered "health foods" like yogurt and tofu and washed it down with quantities of beer or wine. We became concerned about pollution and the misuse of our planet, about rivers on fire and air you could see due to smog. Earth-friendly lifestyles were heavily influenced by *The Whole Earth Catalog* and the Foxfire books. To some extent, young people adopted the hippie look, but went on with their mainstream lives. After work or school, we read the news with a newfound cultural cynicism, and discussed concepts of social and government reform. We could no longer quietly accept "that's just the way it is."

As the sixties came of age, the radical "hippies" embraced the nonviolent ideas of the counterculture movement and, taking their cue from Timothy Leary, decided to "tune in, turn on, and drop out" to create experimental communities that were usually loosely governed by a makeshift system of no-pressure socialism mixed with "free love" sexuality and self-sustaining natural agriculture. With the assassinations of the Kennedy brothers, Martin Luther King, Jr., and Malcolm X, American politics had become too "intense" and corrupt for many to become directly involved.

The post-World War II economy had given rise to rabid consumerism and the pursuit of "status symbols." The hippies rejected materialism and capitalism, and they made a statement by resigning from the frenetic and intensely competitive economic and political landscapes. They questioned every aspect of society, choosing to live together in communes where families were often unstructured and everyone shared what they had to offer, and tried to love and accept each other regardless of what an individual might be able to contribute.

Of course, with severely limited incomes, many of the communes chose to conduct their experiments in moderate climates like California and the Southwest, but attempts to drop out of society and lead the new Socialistic lifestyle were scattered all across the country and throughout the free world. One particularly high-profile hippie enclave occurred in San Francisco, centered in the neighborhood around the intersection of Haight and Ashbury streets, but it was widely publicized and soon overrun with runaway kids, moochers, and capitalists who wore the colorful costumes but ripped off their neighbors. The Summer of Love in 1967 was the "high" point (pun intended) of the San Francisco experiment, but it gradually deteriorated and Haight-Ashbury became crime-ridden and unsafe. The inescapable economic reality is that drugs and food cost money.

At that moment in American history, the vast majority of young people and many of our parents were committed to social and political change.

We had long hair and love beads, but we were hard at work on careers as well as setting The Establishment straight. While the true radical hippies withdrew from mainstream society, most of the young people found avenues to get involved, stand up and defy the status quo. It was, after all, the Age of Aquarius, the dawning of a new time when peace and love would replace war and hate. Our enthusiasm and commitment scared hell out of The Establishment.

These were desperate times, and when the flag-draped coffins began to come home from Vietnam in quantity we knew that a high percentage of the guys in Vietnam were disadvantaged or black, but they were our brothers. Educators were hearing challenges from their students that could not be taken lightly. College courses must become more relevant, and basic civil rights extended to all. Education must not be theoretical. The real issues facing our country demanded immediate and effective action, and institutions of higher learning were expected to prepare their students to make a real difference. Longstanding curricula written by, for, and about The Establishment were considered irrelevant and rejected. If the college was reluctant, an army of students occupied the administrative offices until a compromise could be reached.

Overseas, even in countries we had helped to rebuild after World War II, America's military adventuring in Vietnam was being debated. Europe was acutely aware of the French defeat in Vietnam, and there was anxiety when the world's great super power, the only country to have dropped atomic bombs in wartime (upon Asians), chose to show no restraint in bombing, torturing, assassinating, immolating or poisoning Asian peasants in a mad, headlong, and vicious effort to confront Communism. The American Way of Waging War had become so bold and brutal that even our allies began to question and protest the senseless slaughter.

A wide variety of Americans spoke out or marched in the streets in opposition to the war. There was no interactive "Social Media" in the sixties, but we had the telephone and the good old U.S. Postal Service and no worries about being hacked. Affluent college communities spread the word through letters and phone calls, along with underground newspapers and a growing underground network that was remarkable in its resourcefulness and effectiveness. Hundreds of thousands of American citizens showed up to protest the war and exercise their first amendment rights. It was an awesome effort, and it was, in the end, surprisingly effective!

Bertrand Russell was a highly-respected mathematician and philosopher, outspoken historian, writer, social critic and political activist who had been awarded the Nobel Prize in Literature in 1950. Russell was a devout social-ist and pacifist, and in March of 1963 he attracted a great deal of attention by writing a letter to the editor of the *New York Times* decrying the paper's reluctance to print "articles which exposed the lies and distortions of the American Government" regarding the political opposition and potential al-ternatives to the American-backed Diem regime in South Vietnam. Russell pointed out that the *Times* had indeed printed an article by correspondent Homer Bigart on July 25, 1962 in which Mr. Bigart described the indiscrim-inate killing of Viet Cong prisoners, and the "charred bodies of women and children in villages destroyed by napalm bombs." Russell also acknowledged that the Times had reported the use of chemical weapons in Vietnam on New Year's Day of 1962, and had described a "crop-killing programme" of chemical warfare taking place in South Vietnam on January 26 of that year.

A lively exchange ensued, including an April 8, 1962 editorial in which the *Times* stated, "We have been deeply concerned, as most thinking Amer-icans have, about the increasing military commitment in South Vietnam, and we have not shared Washington's excessive optimism about American successes." The paper accused Russell of "arrant nonsense" when he accused the U.S. of "prevention of far-reaching social reforms" by backing the repres-sive Diem government. "There are many questions to be raised about the extent and the wisdom of the American commitment in South Vietnam," the *Times* editorial admitted, "and about the need for reform of the govern-ment that the United States is supporting there; but to call the United States the aggressor and to say nothing about the Communist push for domina-tion against the will of the inhabitants in Vietnam is to make a travesty of justice and a mockery of history."

Russell responded that "U.S. support of Diem is driving more and more of the inhabitants of South Vietnam into the arms of the Commu-nists – a result to be deplored.... The war is an atrocity," he wrote. "It is an atrocity because such things as napalm bombs are being used – bombs which do not simply kill, but which burn and torture, and that chemi-cal warfare is employed to destroy crops and livestock and so starve the people of South Vietnam." Bertrand Russell continued to be an outspo-ken critic of U.S. policy in Vietnam until his death in 1970. He was not particularly effective in America, but his opinions were highly regarded throughout Europe and the United Kingdom, and he was widely quoted by anti-war protestors in the U.S.

David Dellinger graduated Phi Beta Kappa from Yale in 1937 with a degree in economics. He was awarded a fellowship to study at New College, Oxford, England, and upon returning home he enrolled at Union Theological Seminary in New York. In 1940 he became a conscientious objector and refused to register for the draft. He spent a year in federal prison; then in 1943 he once again refused to report for an induction physical and was imprisoned for two more years. Dellinger undertook a hunger strike in prison to protest the racial segregation of prisoners during meals, and was force-fed. Upon his release, he began a life-long career of pacifism and Ghandi-inspired nonviolence. Dave Dellinger envisioned a world of peace and social justice, and he was an important link between Rev. Martin Luther King, Jr. and the black civil rights movement and the white anti-war community.

In April of 1963 Dellinger took part in an Easter Peace Walk in New York City in support of a nuclear test-ban treaty between the U.S. and the Soviet Union. A number of marchers carried signs opposing the burgeoning U.S. presence in Vietnam, and the organizers of the march ordered them removed. Dellinger insisted the signs be allowed, and he expressed opposition to the American involvement in Vietnam during his remarks. As a result, SANE, one of the groups organizing the march, warned him that he would never again be allowed to speak at one of their rallies.

Dave Dellinger became a highly respected, outspoken and effective opponent of the war in Vietnam, and this most peaceful man was one of the "Chicago 8," accused and convicted of conspiring to create violent rebellion at the 1968 Democratic National Convention in Chicago. The convictions were later overturned, but the persecution of David Dellinger stands as a prime example of The Establishment's efforts to discourage the peace movement during those passionate times.

The Chicago 8 were a disparate and colorful assemblage of personalities. They were Dellinger, Abbie Hoffman, Jerry Rubin, Bobby Seale, Tom Hayden, Rennie Davis, Lee Weiner, and John Froines. Black Panther activist Bobby Seale continually spoke out and disrupted court proceedings until he was bound and gagged in the courtroom, and his case was separated from the others, leaving the Chicago 7. Perhaps the most outrageous conduct at the trial was exhibited by Judge Julius Hoffman (no relation to Abbie), a prickly and disrespectful personality who made no attempt at judicial impartiality. The trial became a nationally televised circus, and an example of all that was wrong with America's Establishment system of justice.

Doctor Benjamin Spock's 1946 book *Baby and Child Care* had become one of the best-selling books of all time, and a staple reference for parents, especially young mothers, as they faced the many challenges of raising the baby boomer generation. The book's messages were "you know more than you think you do" which encouraged its readers to trust their instincts, and to feel free to express love and affection for their children.

Prior to Dr. Spock and the arrival of the baby boomers, parents had been taught to maintain strict discipline and avoid touching their children too much, not to respond to a child's tears, and to withhold hugs, kisses, and other shows of affection. Spock encouraged parents to listen to their child's feelings. Instead of spanking them when they wouldn't eat their spinach, allow them to watch *Popeye* cartoons on television and be lured into liking spinach. So pervasive was Dr. Spock's philosophy, it became a strong influence on TV shows like *The Mickey Mouse Club, Captain Kangaroo, Howdy Doody, Leave It to Beaver*, and *Father Knows Best*.

Critics claimed the Doctor's teachings promoted self-indulgence and lack of respect for authority, and it has been widely suggested that the generation reared according to Dr. Spock were outspoken, defiant, self-important and "soft," which contributed to America's first defeat in war. Certainly, the times they were a-changin' for the parents who raised children in the post- World War II era just as certainly as for their offspring. Housewives demonstrated against the war, as did every facet of authority in the baby boomers' lives. Doctor Spock was very outspoken, and was actually arrested for his anti-war activities.

Many religious leaders opposed the war, along with teachers, professors, attorneys, writers, civic leaders, senators and congressmen, and Presidential candidates. Reverend Martin Luther King, Jr. defied his advisors, spoke out against the war, and was silenced soon after. William Sloane Coffin was a noted cleric who spoke out against the war, and religious groups such as Sisters of Notre Dame de Namur and Clergy and Laymen Concerned About Vietnam objected to the war on moral grounds and encouraged prayer for peace. The brothers and anti-war priests Philip and Daniel Berrigan each individually defied authority and committed acts of civil disobedience to actively challenge the war in Vietnam.

As mentioned previously, boxer Cassius Clay refused to be drafted on religious grounds and was stripped of his Heavyweight Champion of the World title.

Senator Vance Hartke (D., Indiana) spoke out and authored a book, *The American Crisis in Vietnam*, that was extremely critical of American policy and the war, and Senator J. William Fulbright (D., Arkansas), the Chairman of the Senate Foreign Relations Committee, authored two books, *The Arrogance of Power* and *The Pentagon Propaganda Machine*, to express his frustrations over the war and fears about the arrogance and hubris of America's top political and military leaders. Highly respected writers such as Norman Mailer and Gore Vidal wrote inflammatory, passionate books about the war and the upheavals in American society at home. As noted elsewhere, comedians Tom and Dick Smothers invited guests to their TV variety show to speak out, were ultimately censored and the show taken off the air over their opposition to the war. Army doctor Howard Levy refused to teach Green Berets, whom he described as "murderers of women and children" and "killers of peasants." He was court-martialed and sentenced to three years in prison, but his conviction was later overturned by The U.S. Court of Appeals. William Colby was Chief of the CIA's Saigon station and the agency's Far East Division, and also head of the CIA's Civil Operations and Rural Development effort, as well as overseeing the Phoenix Program. While he was away, his wife Barbara regularly took part in Washington protest marches opposing the war.

Dean Rusk's son was a former Marine who became an anti-war activist and a member of Vietnam Veterans Against the War while his father was a leading proponent of the war and Secretary of State to Presidents Kennedy and Johnson. Poets Allen Ginsberg and Robert Bly opposed the war, along with writers such as Grace Paley and Andrea Dworkin. Many entertainers and actors opposed the war, notably Jane Fonda and Donald Sutherland, and of course the vast majority of influential rock 'n roll and folk musicians.

As the war dragged on, many labor unions gradually came to oppose the war, especially after the Tet Offensive and the election of Richard Nixon as President in 1968. The Teamsters, United Auto Workers, the American Federation of State, City, and Municipal Employees, and the Amalgamated Clothing Workers represented thousands of blue-collar workers across the country, and their voices were very influential in Washington.

The Presidents of many of America's colleges and universities spoke out, and after the Kent State shootings President Nixon invited a group of them to discuss the outlook. Harvard President Nathan Pusey declared, "no longer are we dealing with a small group of radicals, but rather a broad base of students and faculty who are upset." Henry Kissinger, who sat in, had previously told President Nixon "the university presidents are a disgrace."

After the bloody confrontations at the Democratic National Convention in 1968, factions within the anti-war movement wanted to meet violence with violence. Women were particularly turned off by this development, and they split off from the movement and created or joined their own groups such as Women Strike for Peace, Another Mother for Peace, and Women's International League for Peace and Freedom.

On April 7, 1967 at an anti-Vietnam War protest march in New York City, a number of Vietnam veterans showed up and were placed prominently near the front of the parade along with their wives, girlfriends, and children. Someone in the organizing committee noticed them and hurriedly produced a banner that read "Vietnam veterans against the war." One of the vets was 23-year-old Jan Barry Crumb. Crumb was born in Ithaca, New York, the home of Cornell University, and grew up in the tiny hamlet of Interlaken in the Finger Lakes. He left college to join the army and see the world, and in1963 found himself in Vietnam. Although the U.S. "officially" had no combat troops in Vietnam, Crumb saw enough to turn him against the war, even in those early stages. Upon returning from Vietnam, he was appointed to the U.S. Military Academy at West Point, but he did not attend for long before resigning, unable to accept the academy's stiff doctrine or the military's institutional contempt for the peasants he had witnessed in Vietnam.

Within a couple of months, Jan Barry Crumb, who had adopted the professional name of Jan Barry, had created an organization with its name taken from the slogan on the parade banner, Vietnam Veterans Against the War. Never before in American history had America's military veterans spoken out against a war that was currently being waged. From that humble beginning, VVAW became a solid, if sometimes unconventional, organization that was hated and feared by President Nixon, and subjected to a wide variety of infiltrations, government surveillances, and an assortment of "dirty tricks" by every facet of the FBI, COINTELPRO, and local police.

By about 1967, the government began a subtle campaign to keep returning Vietnam veterans away from civilians. Discontent and organized opposition to authority had become so widespread in the military that the government could no longer allow soldiers to mingle with civilians for fear they would speak out against the conduct of the war or the government's policies behind it. Soldiers in the war zone were often photographed wearing peace signs or flashing the "peace sign," and anti-war slogans were everywhere on American bases in Vietnam. A disturbing number of vets returning from Vietnam dared to speak out against the racism of the war being waged against the Vietnamese, and within the

American military itself. Seventy percent of all Americans killed in Vietnam were black, and the draft was clearly aimed at America's disadvantaged communities. As the flag-draped coffins came home, far too many families and friends mourned the loss of loved ones or friends who had paid the ultimate price without ever understanding why they had been sent to Vietnam. Letters home had made it clear that they didn't believe in the war, and they didn't want to be involved in the massacre of thousands of Vietnamese peasants "in order to help them."

The simple truth is that a large cross-section of the American populace opposed the Vietnam War, and that group grew and evolved as the war dragged on. In the early days, opposition to the war was centered mostly in colleges and a few pacifist religious groups such as the Quakers. When Norman Morrison, a Quaker, and then Roger LaPorte, a Catholic, doused themselves with gasoline and struck matches in late 1965, they were decrying the violence of war in general, and as practiced by their country, the United States of America, in particular. Morrison was responding to a news account of a Catholic church in Vietnam that had been destroyed by American bombs. The French priest had buried seven of his parishioners, all "blown to bits." LaPorte lived long enough to say, "I'm a Catholic Worker. I'm against war, all wars. I did this as a religious action." In Detroit, eighty-two years old and a refugee from Hitler's Germany, Alice Herz had also set herself ablaze. She told firemen, "I did it to protest the arms race all over the world." She left a note for her daughter in which she wrote, "I do this not out of despair but out of hope. I choose the illuminating death of a Buddhist to protest against a great country trying to wipe out a small country for no reason." During the years 1965-1970, eight Americans protested the war by immolating themselves.

No discussion of the anti-war movement would be complete without addressing Jane Fonda. The daughter of beloved movie star Henry Fonda, at the age of 23 she received the first of two Tony Award nominations for the 1960 play *There Was a Little Girl*. She went on to several very successful movie roles such as *Period of Adjustment* in 1962, *Sunday in New York* (1963), *Cat Ballou* (1965), *Barefoot in the Park* (1967) and *Barbarella* in 1968, in which her space-age costume made her a full-fledged sex symbol. She was nominated for an Academy Award for 1969's *They Shoot Horses, Don't They* and won the Best Actress Oscar in 1971 for *Klute*, and again in 1978 for portraying the wife of a PTSD-troubled Vietnam veteran in *Coming Home*. Fonda was also nominated for Oscars for her roles in *Julia* (1977), *The China Syndrome* (1979), *On Golden Pond* (1981), and *The*

Morning After (1986). She has also won an Emmy and four Golden Globe Awards.

However, Jane Fonda is also famous for her anti-war activism, especially for her 1972 trip to Hanoi and the photographs of her sitting, grinning, on an anti-aircraft gun that's sole purpose was to fire at American bombers. Earlier, she had met with a group of POWs and delivered letters from their families, and when she asked them about their treatment in captivity, she was perhaps a little too accepting of their assurances that they had been well treated. The meeting was filmed for use as North Vietnamese propaganda, and one of the prisoners later claimed that he had blinked his eyes to spell out "torture" in Morse code. In her 2005 autobiography *My Life So Far,* Jane Fonda describes the situation at the anti-aircraft gun, and the deep regret that she has lived with all these years.

Jane Fonda had not been politically active until the Tet offensive in early 1968 shocked her into action. Suddenly she became an outspoken advocate for American Indians' rights; she also supported Angela Davis, the University of California professor who was being pressured because she would not abandon her Communist and Black Panther associations. Fonda helped raise funds for the Black Panther Party's program to provide breakfasts for inner-city school kids.

In an attempt to end the war in Vietnam, she wrote letters to the North Vietnamese delegation to the peace talks in Paris, and the CIA illegally opened those letters and began to monitor her activities, along with the FBI. She met a former Green Beret, now a VVAW member and activist working to encourage war resistance within the military, and soon she bankrolled and participated, along with actor Donald Sutherland, in a country-wide tour of shows known as the "FTA Tour." A play on the army's recruiting slogan "Fun, Travel, and Adventure," the antiwar tour's title supposedly was meant to say "Free the Army," but every G.I. recognized the initials, which had been ubiquitous even when I was in the service in early 1967, as an acronym for "F*#% the Army." The troupe toured to the proximity of military bases across the country, providing entertainment and anti-war discussions to huge audiences of active-duty G.I.s who were always enthusiastic.

When Jane Fonda went to Hanoi, over 300 American peace activists had preceded her. The purpose of her trip was to photograph the damage that American bombing was doing to the dikes, locks, and dams that controlled the Red River north of Hanoi. European diplomats in Hanoi had reported the bombings, and the great threat of flooding and destruction of the irrigation systems that fed the rice paddies. When the North Vietnamese invited Ms. Fonda to visit Hanoi, she accepted on the condition that she would be given the opportunity to see and photograph the evidence of bombing to the dikes. Readers are encouraged to read her autobiography, especially the chapter "Hanoi," to understand all that she experienced while visiting the enemy. Her experiences during the bombing, visiting hospitals, a display of the various anti-personnel bombs dropped by American planes, and seeing the extensive damage done to civilian areas is jarring testimony that parallels the descriptions from many others who visited North Vietnam during the war, and especially during Nixon's all-inclusive "carpet" bombing after 1971. Former LBJ administration Attorney General Ramsey Clark visited North Vietnam with a group of current and former international dignitaries just a few weeks before the Fonda trip, and reported on the bombing damages and the obvious targeting of civilian residential areas, schools, churches, hospitals, and also the damage done to the critical dikes.

Jane Fonda was too trusting during her visit to North Vietnam and allowed herself to be photographed in a most compromising position and exploited by the Hanoi regime. In many other activities before and after, she supported American soldiers in Vietnam and Vietnam veterans, and donated her time and money to aid them and address their needs.

To the author, it is ironic that many veterans vilify Jane Fonda and call her a traitor. It should be noted that this activity really took root in the 1980's as President Reagan was urging the country to reject "Vietnam syndrome" and aid the Contra "freedom fighters" in Nicaragua. Reagan doubled the Defense Department's budget and sent $90 million to aid the cruel dictatorship in El Salvador. While adding manpower to America's armed forces and pushing for huge increases in allocations to fund the purchase of new ships, planes, high-tech equipment, and expand militarism into outer space, Reagan quietly authorized his budget director, David Stockman, to cut $900 million dollars from the VA's funding, and eliminate 20,000 VA medical and health care employees, plus another 3,200 from the VA's Department of Veterans' Benefits. Stockman, who had enjoyed a college deferment during the war, sought to cut VA programs to aid disabled vets, a program that provided vocational rehabilitation for the disabled, the Incarcerated Veterans Project, legal services assistance, kidney dialysis for veterans, the VA's medical research programs, and unemployment compensation for vets who declined to reenlist. He cut funding to CETA, the Comprehensive Employment and Training Act which included a network of veterans' self-help groups, and the Center for Veterans' Rights. The Reagan-Stockman team sought to close the national chain of storefront Vet Centers, and impounded funds that had already been allocated for veterans' health care. So blatant and offensive was their assault upon veterans that Senators Alan Cranston and Chiles introduced a resolution that condemned Stockman for usurping authority from congress. Cranston actually sued Stockman in Federal District Court to force him to release the VA's funding, and was successful. All of these cuts, of course, were part of the "Conservative" president's campaign to "cut the fat" in government. In reality, during his eight years in office, Ronald Reagan transformed America from the world's greatest lender nation to the world's greatest debtor nation.

In the same era, the ultra-conservative, liberal-bashing Rush Limbaugh's radio talk show began to be broadcast nationally in 1988. The nation wanted to forget the agonies of the Vietnam years, and underwent a knee-jerk backlash political transformation that gave newly resurrected "neo-conservatives" the opportunity to denounce and deride all things liberal, leftist, anti-war, or pro-peace. It was a time when Vietnam veterans were struggling to find their place in mainstream American society; when the storefront Vet Centers gave them a much-needed opportunity to get together with other vets in "rap groups" and discuss their feelings and frustrations.

The Reagan administration cut funding for 91 Vet Centers, then dismissed Vietnam veteran and multiple amputee Max Cleland from his position at the head of the Veterans Administration. Reagan recommended another Vietnam vet, James Webb, for the job but Webb declined, citing the administration's lack of "good signals" and the threat of more budget cuts looming over every aspect of Washington except the defense budget. Two other Vietnam vets were nominated for the position but rejected by congress. Finally, Robert Nimmo, a World War II veteran, was approved and installed. He promptly "cut the fat" by spending $54,000 redecorating his office and sending the old furnishings to his daughter. Nimmo was repeatedly caught living the good life at taxpayer expense. He felt the nation should stop "coddling Vietnam vets" and derailed a congressionally mandated study of the medical effects of Agent Orange.

Like many Vietnam-era veterans, I came away from my military experience with the feeling that once your usefulness was used up, you were discarded by the system and left to fend for yourself. The promises made when you enlisted, never committed to print, were meaningless. And the damage done to your mental or physical health, or the health of your off-spring, were simply additional aspects of your "obligation" to the United States. Reagan's cuts to veterans' benefits were just one more indignity from a government that demanded obedience while it reneged on every promise.

Ronald Reagan and his "conservative" cohorts not only sought to deny veterans their hard-earned benefits and take away their assistance and health care. By the end of his term, it should be remembered, an unprecedented 138 members of his administration had been convicted, indicted, or were the subject of investigation for official misconduct and/or criminal violations. Setting the stage for the neo-conservatives to come, Reagan believed regulations were actually needless limitations on both government overreach and the almighty corporate interests, and the fat he urged his administration to cut ended up in many of his associates' pockets. In the years since Reagan, other conservatives have attempted to eliminate or pare down veterans' benefits, but none have been so cold-hearted or effective as Ronald Reagan.

The Reagan years were a critical period for Vietnam veterans, as they attempted to re-enter the American mainstream. Ten or fifteen years after coming home, many vets were beginning to feel the full effects of PTSD. As we have seen, the environment in Reagan's Washington was not especially favorable to veterans. After a long, hard political fight, Congress allocated an area on the National Mall for the construction of a (privately funded) Vietnam Veterans Memorial. Almost immediately, a spirited debate erupted among vets over the design of the memorial. The winner of the design contest was the awesome V-shaped black stone wall we see today, designed by college student and artist Maya Lin.

A number of veterans objected, calling the design a "black gash of shame" and openly complaining that the designer was an Asian woman. Veterans took sides all across America, and Maya Lin's wall was ultimately approved… with the addition of a more traditional statue to be erected nearby. In the midst of these various controversies and setbacks, a contingent of vets became angrier, and they seized upon Jane Fonda as the icon of all that was wrong about the way America had dealt with their war over the years. Ms. Fonda has repeatedly apologized for her visit to that anti-aircraft gun in Hanoi, and she has continued to support a variety of Vietnam veterans' programs.

Often overlooked, the film *Coming Home* starred Jane Fonda, Jon Voight as an angry, troubled paraplegic Vietnam vet, and Bruce Dern. Released in 1978, the film was nominated for eight Academy Awards including Best Picture, and won for Best Actor (John Voight), Best Actress (Jane Fonda), and Best Original Screenplay. Conceived and brought to the screen by Jane Fonda, *Coming Home* was made with a cast and crew who had been opposed to the war, but were entirely cognizant of the problems facing Vietnam veterans and supportive of veterans in every respect. In the opinion of this Vietnam veteran, Jane Fonda has given of her time, finances, creative abilities, and of her heart to oppose the war that was chewing up young Americans like a meat grinder, and to bring the plight of vets to the attention of the American public after the war.

The bitter guys who call her "traitor" should read the history of the war and focus their anger upon people like Lyndon Johnson, Robert Mc-Namara, William Westmoreland, General Julian Ewell, Henry Kissinger, Richard Nixon, Allen Dulles, McGeorge Bundy, Ronald Reagan, David Stockman, and many more. Their treachery and greed killed millions and they truly betrayed Vietnam veterans in their time of need. Just sayin'…

* * *

The Vietnam War was a huge, tragic event that damaged America, but it was made up of many individual events that did serious harm to businesses, communities, families and individuals throughout our country. No one was immune. Many of those who protested it or refused to take part went to prison, where they were often mistreated. Others chose to flee. Canada offered refuge in those days, as did Sweden, Costa Rica, and other countries. The throngs who chose exile did so in full expectation that they could never return to visit families or friends.

One of my wife's high school classmates and his wife were college students in the mid-west when the National Guard opened fire on non-violent protesters at Kent State University in Ohio, killing four. Appalled, the young couple left America for good, and they have contributed much to their new homeland community in Canada. They rarely visit the U.S.

We knew a vet, a Marine who had survived the siege of Khe Sanh only to be reassigned to a stateside base where he was constantly harassed with taunts like "Come on, Mister Vietnam vet, you're a tough guy, show us how it's done." After months of this hounding he left a note on his locker door, "Gone fishing," and escaped to Canada.

Veterans were ignored, ostracized, or scapegoated, perhaps more within the military than in civilian life. Upon leaving the military, however, veterans were often not hired when they mentioned they had gone to Vietnam after high school, not college. The wounded and maimed had an especially terrible time. Ron Kovic was on his second tour in Vietnam, a gung-ho Marine, when a bullet smashed his spine. In his classic book, *Born On the 4th of July* which became a movie starring Tom Cruise, Kovic tells of life in a VA hospital on Long Island where his mother brought him bread which he tossed to the rats at night in hopes they would not gnaw on his lifeless toes. When he spoke out against the war, Kovic was dumped out of his wheel chair and beaten and kicked.

No one escaped the passions, the bitterness and raw emotion that ripped America apart, wounds that still afflict us. Corporations prospered, soldiers won medals and promotions, politicians got elected by promising to win or end the war, and a whole lot of people got hurt or killed. That was acceptable to some, and they upheld the war, sometimes violently. It was unacceptable to many others, and some of them became so frustrated that they also turned to violence. Mothers and fathers, students and veterans, teachers and congressmen, even some hippies, all kinds of people protested the war. All kinds of people became soldiers, and all kinds of people died or were torn apart. It was a terrible time in America's history.

In 1959, Students for a Democratic Society (SDS) was formed. In June of 1962 a number of members of SDS met at a United Auto Workers facility in Port Huron, Michigan and hammered out a document they hoped would be the blueprint for a new America. Written by Al Haber and Tom Hayden, the "Port Huron Statement" declared that the movement:

> maintain(s) a vision of a democratic society where at all levels the people have control of the decisions which affect them and the resources upon which they are dependent. ... it feels the urgency to put forth a radical, democratic program counter-posed to authoritarian movements both of communism and the domestic right, [and saw the new movement as] civil libertarian in its treatment of those with whom it disagrees, but clear in its opposition to any totalitarian principle as a basis for government or social organization.

Predictably, over time and under great pressure, the young architects and members of the movement had disagreements. Passions ran deep, groups splintered off and soon we had the "Weathermen" robbing a bank and shooting it out with police in Nyack, New York – all to promote non-violence and peace! When a Greenwich Village townhouse exploded in March of 1970, investigators discovered that the Weathermen had been preparing a dynamite bomb in the basement. Three members of the group were killed. Tom Hayden later wrote,

> So, when the New Left suddenly emerged it was a group of very intelligent people, but suddenly we were asked to do things that adults would normally do, like lead an overdue civil rights revolution, stop a war, end poverty... and the average leader of this movement was about twenty years old.

To be fair, in the early sixties, most Americans were in favor of any action that would slow the advance of dreaded Communism. Throughout most of the war years, a majority backed the government's policy. Eventually, many middle-class Americans were sick of the whole thing, but they also strenuously disapproved of the actions of many anti-war protesters. After President Nixon began withdrawing troops from Vietnam, the numbers of protesters in the streets diminished noticeably. The American people were tired of the war overseas, and just as tired of the social strife and emotional struggles at home.

It is difficult to understand how peace advocates could find it necessary to turn to bombs and shoot-outs with police. But it was also frightening to learn that the federal government could so easily oppose the public's 1st Amendment right of freedom of speech, and resort to infiltrating the peace movement with informants, secret agents, and *agents provocateur* who actually instigated many outlandish actions in hopes of arresting some of the leaders of the movement. Telephones were illegally wire-tapped, burglaries conducted, offices broken into, files rifled or stolen, misinformation distributed, and "enemies lists" from the Nixon White House sent to the IRS with an order to harass the President's opponents, even if they were members of Congress from the opposing party. Americans who tried to stop the madness were hounded, slandered, and if they were too powerful, even murdered to silence them! We can immediately point to JFK and RFK, the Reverend Martin Luther King, the four students at Kent State, two more at Jackson State, and there were many others whose names are forgotten.

General William Westmoreland is gone, as are Richard Nixon, LBJ, Robert McNamara, Allen Dulles, and all the other architects of death and destruction save Henry Kissinger (still spouting foolish observations about the war that he helped prolong and never understood). Vietnam showed what America had become, both in the rice paddies of Southeast Asia and here at home. And America has never been the same since.

Today, it seems America's most relevant and honest news coverage is found on *Comedy Central* or *The Late Show With Stephen Colbert*. The state of our nation is dire. Under Donald Trump, the current White House sinks to astonishing depths of blatant lies, racism, nepotism and financial corruption, anarchist "conservatives" dismantle health care, national parks, education and anything decent or kind about our country in their mad lust for power and profits. Immigrant children die in cages, Canada is considered a security threat, America is divided almost as severely as during the Vietnam War, and our president snubs old allies while he indulges the world's cruelest despots and dictators. Fifty years from now, what will the historians write about America since Vietnam?

* * *

My father died in 1986 after a long fight against prostate cancer that spread to his bones and then his lungs. His last days were sad and pathetic as he suffered. I flew to South Carolina for his funeral, then home to Maryland where I grabbed some fresh laundry and jetted off to Las Vegas for the gala introduction of Toyota's new models. I was surrounded by my staff, a great group of guys, and they kept my mind off my loss. On the last morning, before we caught our flights home, we were enjoying breakfast in the casino-hotel's coffee shop. Never much of a gambler, I was amused to see a small train powered by a lawn tractor making its way through the slot machines. Buckets upon buckets of coins were loaded onto the carts, freeing the slots to accept the day's fresh harvest as soon as the sun rose a little higher.

Someone had a *USA Today*, and my attention was seized by a color photo and headline on the front page. In Washington, D.C. four veterans were beginning a water-only fast to protest the Reagan administration's activities in Central America. The article said that an acquaintance, Brian Willson, along with World War II vet Duncan Murphy and two other vets I didn't know would fast until their action made America aware of the actions of our government in Central America. George Mizo was a Vietnam vet, as was Charles Liteky. A photo showed Liteky placing his Congressional Medal of Honor at the base of the Vietnam Memorial along with a letter to President Reagan asking him to stop what Liteky saw as "another Vietnam" in El Salvador and Nicaragua. He had heard about the problems in Central America and gone there to see for himself. Reagan did not acknowledge the protest. Today, Liteky's medal and the letter are on display at the Smithsonian Institute's Museum of American History.

The article said that another vet, Art James, had also returned his medals for the same reason. I knew Art James! Something clicked in my head.

My dad had suffered terribly in his last days, getting nourishment through tubes, and now these guys were threatening to starve themselves to death on the steps of the U.S. Capitol! I went often, after work, just to be with the fasters, to support them. I had read enough to know that America was on the wrong side in another conflict, and a lot of innocent civilians were being killed again for all the wrong reasons.

I soon learned that Charlie Liteky had been a Catholic Chaplain in Vietnam. In December of 1967 he accompanied an infantry patrol "to see what it was like," and they were ambushed. Liteky crawled out under intense fire, and saved more than twenty wounded G.I.s by dragging them back to be air-lifted out. He suffered a number of wounds himself but carried on until all of the injured were evacuated. Charlie Liteky was the first recipient of the Congressional Medal of Honor to return it.

The fasters said they would continue until they saw "a significant sign" that the American people were aware of what our government was doing in Central America. Long story short, in an attempt to prevent them from starving themselves to death on the steps of the Capitol I put together an action that I hoped would be "a significant sign." I got the authors of about 40 books about Vietnam to send copies of their books, along with statements opposing American activities in Central America. After the display of books on the Capitol steps, I had agreed to put the books and statements at the base of The Wall where they would be collected and kept as a part of history. A date was set, and a number of authors agreed to stand with me on the Capitol steps and deliver the message that "the truth is available at your public library. Please learn what our government is capable of doing, and join us in opposing the U.S. policies in Central America."

The night before my event the fast was ended. The fasters were too weak to go on, doctors ruled, so they acknowledged the crowds that had supported them and were taken to the hospital. My event was authorized under the permission granted to a peace group whose name I can't remember. With the fasters gone, they wanted to call off the book display. "We can use you better somewhere else," they said, and I assured them that I was a Vietnam veteran and I had been "used" before. Finally, they agreed to go ahead with the event, and it drew a considerable amount of attention.

A few years later I was invited to speak in West Virginia, and I learned that Charlie Liteky was also invited. I called him and offered to give him a ride, which he graciously accepted. I was privileged to spend a few hours with Charlie traveling to and from our speaking engagement, and I grew to admire the man more than ever. The talk was at a small college in West Virginia, and I apologize for not remembering the name. We have moved three times since then and I assume my souvenirs are in a box somewhere in the garage.

We each made a short statement, and then there was a time for questions and answers. Vietnam veteran Art James was very strident in exhorting the students to read about Mahatma Ghandi and Reverend Martin Luther King, and then dedicate themselves to a life of non-violent resistance. The audience showed no inspiration to do that. At breakfast the next morning, Art was frustrated and a lively discussion ensued. Charlie Liteky and I talked about the peace movement all the way back to Washington. He is gone now, but I consider him a true American hero.

The sad truth is, in America every organization needs funds to do its work, from Cub Scouts or Little League to neighborhood associations and peace groups. When I was told "we will use you" by the group in Washington, they were only one of hundreds of peace and social justice groups struggling to gain attention and attract funding so they could pay the rent, buy a meal, and survive to wage the good fight. The peace movement, the civil rights movement, Occupy Wall Street and all the other "progressive" groups have dared to suggest changes to the American way, and often to defy predatory capitalism, so they are opposed by the big money guys like the Koch Brothers and Donald Trump.

As we drove back from West Virginia, Charlie Liteky and I agreed that the peace movement needs to market and merchandise its message in a manner that invites newcomers to stick a toe in the water before jumping in over their heads. War is the most abhorrent condition on planet Earth. Very few people, regardless of country, political persuasion, or religious background want war. But the fact is, there's a lot of money to be made from wars, and a lot of power and authority to be grabbed. Smedley Butler famously called it a racket.

Until the peace movement, or for that matter the environmentalists, civil rights movement, LGBT or women's rights groups or the Occupy folks trying to challenge Wall Street find a way to package and distribute their messages in a way that will attract moneyed backers, the bad guys with the big wallets will continue their crusade to control everything and everybody.

Most of our media have been bought up by a few far-right leaning tycoons. Does the name Rupert Murdoch ring a bell? Google him and get scared. Then look up the Koch Brothers, or Sheldon Adelson. Since the

Supreme Court declared that corporations should have the same rights as real people (Citizens United vs. the Federal Election Commission, decided in January of 2010), many of America's political leaders and the seats of power have been for sale to the highest bidder.

A surprising number of high schools and colleges continue to offer courses on the Vietnam War. There is no standard curriculum or focus for these courses, but as I pointed out at the beginning of this chapter, the ones with which I've become familiar tend to teach the students that only a bunch of "hippies" protested the war in Vietnam. I hope this meager chapter has instilled a little doubt about that idea, and perhaps even shed some light on the issues that brought thousands of Americans into the streets. And, while the war didn't end immediately upon the occasion of the first protest, it is obvious that the anti-war protests were eventually effective in limiting the extent of the Vietnam War, and refreshing many Americans' views of the promise of American democracy, in spite of our government's authoritarian madness!

Today's young people sense that the Vietnam War caused great and passionate rifts in American society, but there are scant resources available to the student who seeks to understand the emotions or divisions of the time. Far too many facts concerning the war have been mislaid, forgotten, or at times, even purposefully overlooked or revised. It is vital to America's survival that its people have access to all the facts. It is especially vital that students have access to realistic views of history. The history of America's war in Vietnam has been systematically revised or obscured over the years.

To those of us who lived through the era, it was such a colorful, meaningful, and insightful time in our nation's history it remains vivid in our memories. It is troubling to recognize how little today's young people are learning about that time, and how pasteurized and revised is the material they are being taught. Still, some bold educators offer realistic classes or courses about the Vietnam War for high school or college students. I wrote this chapter to honor their contributions, aid their efforts, and offer food for thought to a few of their students.

Chapter 16

PTSD, Suicide, and Damage from War

To kill on military orders and be a criminal, or to refuse to kill and be a criminal is the moral agony of America's Vietnam War generation.
— Jan Barry, Founder of Vietnam Veterans Against the War

War is eternity jammed into frantic minutes that will fill a lifetime with dreams and nightmares.
— John Cory

Every soldier thinks something of the moral aspects of what he is doing. But all war is immoral and if you let that bother you, you're not a good soldier.
— General Curtis LeMay, Chief of Staff of the Air Force and George Wallace's American Independent Party vice presidential running mate in 1968.

On any average day, the Veterans Administration estimates that about 20 American veterans commit suicide. The Vietnam Memorial in Washington, D.C. displays the names of 58,315 Americans who died in the war. It is one of the most-visited and effective memorials in the city, but few of its visitors are aware that an estimated 200,000 or more Vietnam veterans have committed suicide since returning home from the war. Veterans make up less than 9 percent of the U.S. population, but they contribute 18 percent of all suicides.

The truth is, no one knows the real number. There are no reliable statistics about suicides overall, and even less about veteran suicides. Most states and localities do not have any established procedure or office to submit suicide reports to the VA, to determine if the deceased had served in the military, and in many cases the local examiners are not sure if the death was indeed self-inflicted. Many self-induced deaths are recorded as accidental because the actual cause of death cannot be determined, or out of respect for the victim's family.

Far more than veterans of other wars, Vietnam vets have been reluctant to go to the VA for help, or to join the various veterans' organizations. A sizable community of Vietnam vets, called "trip wire" vets, are reclusive, living in hand-crafted cabins in remote areas where they are out of touch with everyone, including family. As a result, while we are confronted with overwhelming and heart-wrenching evidence indicating that suicide has become far more prevalent among veterans since the Vietnam War, the statistics that might clearly define the scope of the problem simply don't exist.

That the professionals who deal with the problem day-to-day estimate such staggering numbers is a sobering and thought-provoking indication that something is, or was, wrong in the state of our nation's military. Realistic numbers will never become available, from the government or military, because of the negative impact they might have on the costs of VA health care, or on the recruiting efforts so vital to the all-volunteer military. Suicide is the ultimate expression of PTSD, and it must be noted that there are approximately ten survivors of suicide attempts for every death that occurs.

It is important to realize that suicides among active-duty troops are a very different statistic, and also at record levels, regularly killing more of our soldiers than enemy actions in recent years. In 2014, U.S. forces sustained 55 combat deaths and 269 suicides. The Pentagon has reported that suicides among active-duty soldiers have started to decline, but they have increased among the elite Special Operations forces. A December 18, 2018 article in the *New York Times* said the suicide rate among veterans is rising. Among veterans age 18 to 34, the rate is now 45 deaths per year for every 100,000 people, more than three times the national average. The actual numbers are very rarely disclosed, but it is widely acknowledged that the rate is significantly higher among both veterans and the active-duty military than in the general population.

In the twentieth century, wars killed as many as 200 million human beings, the majority of whom were non-combatants. Since World War II, America's military academies, corporations, laboratories, think-tanks and war colleges have developed the science of brutality, killing, destruction, and terror to unprecedented levels of sophistication. General Westmoreland saw the war in Vietnam as an "opportunity to test our latest weapons and tactics," and in that respect, and *only* in that respect, the war was an overwhelming success. Somewhere between three and five million Vietnamese, Cambodian, and Laotian peasants died, along with those 58,315 Americans. Thousands more were maimed, mutilated, torn, burned, punctured, tortured, poisoned, or simply disappeared. Our state-of-the-art weaponry and tactics were "field-tested" beyond question. We dropped more tons of explosives on Vietnam, an impoverished agricultural country the size of New Mexico, than were used in all of World War II. Napalm was widely used to destroy villages and their inhabitants in huge balls of flaming gasoline. Agent Orange and other defoliant chemicals poisoned thousands of acres of fertile farmland, even as they caused birth defects and cancers among the Vietnamese peasants and the Americans who handled it. Similar destruction of Laos and Cambodia provided America's military-industrial complex with enormous quantities of "test results" even as it devastated those countries.

Officially, PTSD is an acronym for Post-Traumatic Stress Disorder. I prefer to define PTSD as Post-Traumatic Stress *Damage*, because I do not view the revulsion, trauma, mania, depression, nightmares, and other common symptoms that so many soldiers and veterans experience after participating in modern warfare to be a "disorder." Post-Traumatic Stress Damage is a normal and predictable reaction by the human heart and soul to experiencing the horrors of war, the unthinkable destruction of brick and mortar and life and limb.

I believe modern war, and especially the American Way of Waging War, with all its high-tech weapons and "war of attrition" tactics, presents scenes and attitudes so cruel and repulsive that the average kid-next-door American soldier is often emotionally scarred by them. The casual, matter-of-fact ways that young recruits are trained, or brainwashed, to accept and to inflict unprecedented degrees of man's inhumanity to his fellow man has become morally troubling, even objectionable to many. To witness modern combat often exposes the young soldier to the gruesome, heart-rending effectiveness of modern weapons, many of them "developed" to levels of mechanized barbarity far beyond anything we saw in Vietnam.

I believe PTSD is a normal reaction to such scenes, and the person who can view the blood, gore, and destruction of modern warfare *without* feeling his or her humanity and morality challenged is the one with the dangerous disorder. Too often, our vets come home knowing that they have been emotionally damaged, but there are few if any resources available to help them cope. "Keep it in the family," they are told. "Just deal with it." "Don't be a pussy." Often the effects of PTSD are not acknowledged until months or even years after the vet returns from war.

I am a Vietnam veteran, and I cannot escape my memories of the barbarity, cruelty, and destruction I witnessed. I have been diagnosed with "severe" PTSD. America's war in Vietnam and Southeast Asia, like the present ones, was born of lies, propaganda, and misrepresentations, and prolonged for years while the military garnered its ribbons and promotions, and the "defense" contractors wallowed in obscene profits.

Like all post-war baby boomers, I grew up at a time when the accomplishments of our country's military in World War II were universally applauded. As a boy I played soldier with the neighborhood guys, wearing a helmet, web belt and canteen from the army-navy surplus store. I remember Memorial Day parades with phalanxes of veterans all marching in step, accompanied by colorful flags and bands playing stirring patriotic music.

As a high school student, I worked after school and weekends with a distinguished older gentleman, George Studley, who was at that time the only person in the world authorized to make half-size miniatures of American military medals. Mr. Studley had a magnificent personal collection of medals, decorations and military commendations from around the world. He enjoyed a very lucrative business, and had a barn full of military equipment and surplus accumulated over the years as he purchased whole collections in order to gain access to a prized medal or decoration he needed.

George Studley taught me many lessons, and my association with him brought me into contact with a fascinating array of American veterans and heroes. My hands-on experience with those medals and ribbons and reading the letters from veterans who were not at all reluctant to describe how they had earned their awards gave me a deep-seated respect for those who had gone before me. Although I felt no attraction to the military whatsoever, when the draft made it inevitable that I must become a soldier I approached my military "obligation" reluctantly, but with a sincere appreciation for valor and military traditions.

I mention that I was at least somewhat familiar with veterans and wartime experiences because, until years after my return from Southeast Asia, I had never heard the term PTSD, nor any veteran described with the words, "You know, he's changed. He just hasn't been the same since he came home from the war." Sure, I was vaguely aware of "shell shock" and "battle fatigue," but I had also heard of bubonic plague and elephantiasis, and I'd never known anyone who was suffering from those maladies either.

We did not sit around in Vietnam and spend our idle time discussing how the war might affect our thinking or emotions when we got back home. Perhaps we should have. It was widely acknowledged that the war we were witnessing turned our stomachs. Some revolted at the time, but most of us just kept our mouths shut and our heads down and waited for our short-timer calendars to expire. Then we caught the "freedom bird" and returned to the neighborhood expecting to leave all the bad memories behind. Most of us addressed our anxieties by "sucking up" and acquiring college degrees, careers, car payments, wives and families, mortgages, credit cards, and all the other trappings of modern-day life. But in far too many cases, it didn't work.

Clearly, the Pentagon will not shine its patriotic spotlight on the veterans suffering from PTSD forty and fifty years after returning from Southeast Asia, or the thousands who have taken their own lives. "*Those who cannot learn from history are doomed to repeat it,*" wrote George Santayana, and as the Pentagon seeks to commemorate the war in Vietnam with a rehashed menu of the same old lies, distortions and misrepresentations, and as our current conflicts in the Middle East drag out endlessly and unsuccessfully, we must look at what's being done to our brave young soldiers and strive to be realistic in every respect. One can only hope that a national conscience will emerge one day and rein in America's rampant militarism.

For 14 years I kept my war memories "in a box on the shelf" while I focused on career and family. In 1982 my box fell off the shelf and spilled across the floor. For years, I could not describe or explain the changes I felt, the anger and bitterness. The lasting effects of my military experiences have had a severe impact upon my life, and the lives of my family. I resent the fact that so many lives have been damaged in far worse ways than mine, by participation in a war that was completely unnecessary and blatantly misrepresented. I guess that's my bitterness coming through.

I am amazed and saddened to see that the American people, especially parents and loved ones, have become conditioned to steadfastly support their children when they enlist and accept with sad resignation that they are likely to come home "changed" and suffering from PTSD. While the young recruits are of age to make their own decisions, the parents and loved ones quietly accept the emotional damage that will likely result as if it is some sort of modern-day taxation – a necessary cost of "patriotism." Today, kids stifle their fears and stoically accept service in the military as an honorable American tradition, proudly citing their ancestors' participation in our country's wars of old, blissfully unaware that times have changed. Few question why so many private charities have popped up in recent years, many of them blatantly corrupt, to take up collections because the military does not take care of its wounded veterans.

The author is not a mental health professional, but I believe I have learned a lot about PTSD as both a participant and a spectator, and by a fair amount by reading. I know the experts say PTSD can be the result of other devastating events – a plane crash, an automobile accident, an assault, virtually any traumatic experience – I don't mean to downplay the importance of those other causes, but I believe the trauma caused by modern war is of a different variety. Earlier armies throughout history have suffered from "nostalgia," "cowardice," "battle fatigue," "soldier's heart," or "battle-related neurosis."

Perhaps there is no more moving description of early efforts to deal with "shell shock" than those found in the landmark book, *Long Time Passing: Vietnam & the Haunted Generation*, by Myra MacPherson, with accounts of techniques used by the British in World War I to deal with "malingerers." To the Brits, maintaining "a stiff upper lip" in the face of extreme challenge was a proud national trait, and the inability to cope with the fear and horror of trench warfare was viewed as a failure or defect in personal character, calling for "disciplinary" action. Remedies included injecting the traumatized warrior with ether, "not dangerous but extremely painful," applying electric shocks "strong enough to be extremely painful," pressing the lighted ends of cigarettes into the tongue, and applying red hot metal irons to the tongue or roof of the mouth.

One can only suppose that some sufferers were motivated by these tortures to return to the front, where they would supposedly fight on to defend the mother country from the vile brutality practiced by, in that case, the beastly Germans. I hope God saved a special place in heaven for them, Similar threads of senseless barbarity run through all the recorded history of warfare.

Some soldiers are affected by PTSD and others aren't, and the military has long sought to portray the afflicted veterans as somehow pre-disposed, weak or susceptible. Contrary to the military establishment's self-serving declarations, virtually all mental health professionals agree that the com-

267

bat veteran's mental state, inherited family genes, social status, education level, astrological sign, or any other naturally-occurring traits are rarely if ever related to his or her PTSD problems. The simple fact remains that a great many American soldiers are understandably troubled by what they have seen in modern war zones, and the emotional and moral dilemmas they feel are the mental roots that flower into PTSD.

Calling the variety of conditions known as PTSD a "disorder" or a "syndrome" trivializes the damage and gives the impression that the victim is sick or infected in some way; that he or she brought along some pre-existing debilitating condition when they joined the military; that their exposure to the rigors of combat simply brought their innate weaknesses into the light. The military loves to suggest the seeds of the illness were there all along, just waiting to manifest themselves – like mental measles or chicken pox.

Veterans struggling with PTSD know that what they have learned of man's inhumanity to his fellow man has resulted in their emotional reaction to experiencing war, to seeing human bodies mutilated, burned, torn, shredded, dismembered, disemboweled, poisoned, or penetrated by modern weapons which is not at all similar to catching a cold. PTSD is a form of overload more of the heart and soul than a strictly mental condition. It is an outpouring of the soldier's intrinsic humanity, of his or her respect for other human beings and their life's worth and accomplishments, and the revulsion of seeing these things defiled. Call it conscience or morality, many veterans are simply unable to cope with scenes of such horror and destruction, which upsets the soldier's heart and head so profoundly that he cannot accept his experience or fit it into the framework of normal thought processes. If he survived there and made it home, he must readjust to a far different environment at work, in the home, and in stressful situations like traffic.

The United States has been fortunate in that we have not experienced war upon our soil since the Civil War, but as a result the folks at home have little real appreciation for what an American soldier has seen or experienced. They are especially vulnerable to the Pentagon's slick marketing and merchandising campaigns.

If war is the most extreme condition in all of human existence, it is only logical that it will present the most searing and difficult challenges to the individual's conscience. The wanton, widespread destruction and blind hatred, the overwhelming emotions that surge when a buddy or an innocent is horribly disfigured or killed, are not stored quietly away in a convenient brain-locker; they are indelible and will emerge, often at the most inopportune moments.

We honor our warriors with medals and feel-good stories in the media, but it is too much to ask them to just accept and forget all that they have seen and done. The veteran must live with it forever. Those who would help him cope with his PTSD can only urge him to deal intellectually with the desperate conflict occurring in his head and his gut while caught between the proverbial rock and that very hard place.

Today, as death by suicide takes an ever-increasing toll, we see the mental health community beginning to recognize and accept the true nature of PTSD, referred to as "moral injury" or "moral damage from war." One of the first institutions to use these terms in their work with veterans is the Soul Repair Center at Texas Christian University's Brite Divinity School. Founding co-director Reverend Rita Brock recognizes those realities. She points to the weeks and months of training and indoctrination that a recruit experiences upon joining the military, and contrasts it with the negligible reconstructive counseling that's done before the combat veteran is discharged back into civilian society. "The rest of us just think, well, they'll just get over it and go on with their lives and be the same. And they're never the same."

A number of noteworthy books on the subject have emerged, including two influential and critically acclaimed books by Dr. Edward Tick, a clinical psychotherapist. Dr. Tick's *War and the Soul* was originally published in 2005, and his follow-up, *Warrior's Return*, in 2014. In conversation, Dr. Tick explained that PTSD is a phenomenon that occurs among the soldiers of aggressive nations who are invading foreign lands and waging wars primarily in the civilian communities there. "The Vietnamese don't exhibit PTSD," Tick told me over dinner. "They have grief, immense grief, but not PTSD. They defended their homeland against the invaders and lost three million family members and friends, comrades. They were finally able to beat off the invaders and create an independent Vietnam after years of colonial rule. That makes all the difference."

Doctor Jonathan Shay is a staff psychiatrist with the Department of Veterans Affairs Outpatient Clinic in Boston, and the author of two highly regarded books about PTSD and Moral Damage, *Achilles in Vietnam: Combat Trauma and the Undoing of Character*, and *Odysseus in America: Combat Trauma and the Trials of Homecoming*. His patients are predominantly Vietnam veterans:"It's titanic pain that these men live with," he has written. "They don't feel that they can get that across, in part because they feel they deserve it, and in part because they don't feel people will understand it." The concept of Moral Damage from War is being widely discussed and accepted in academic and mental health circles. All of this is positive and reassuring and long past due, but Vietnam veterans have lived with that damage, whatever name we assign to it, for almost half a century... except the many who haven't.

The Pentagon and the VA will not seriously address PTSD or suicide, or any of the other social problems resulting from war, because they cannot admit that war is a bad thing. It is the business they are in, and business has been very, very good. Not surprisingly, both the Pentagon and VA have refused to acknowledge the concept of Moral Damage from War. Faced with the daunting suicide problem, the services have revised some of their training to address readjustment problems such as "inner conflict." The consensus among the military brass appears to be that if anyone utters the word "moral" in a discussion of the role of today's military, the word "immoral" might be brought into the conversation. Oh heavens, we wouldn't want that! Scholarly institutions that receive huge grants from the military are obviously loath to admit that war is always a gruesome, emotionally shattering experience.

As they try to paint war as noble cause, the true believers, profiteers, and warmongers must use a broad brush, unrealistic colors, and many thick coats. Still, from time to time the truth bleeds through, almost like graffiti scrawled upon the wall in a Pentagon restroom. The primary modes of treatment are always pharmaceutical, developing medications, psychic vaccines that might eliminate PTSD from future armies, never daring to think, or publicly admit, that war itself is the problem.

PTSD and military service-related suicides are occurring at disturbing levels among post 9/11 veterans and active-duty troops. Surely, today's soldiers are not more sensitive or less thick-skinned than their predecessors. As PTSD and Moral Damage have become widely recognized, the old "Be All You Can Be" recruiting slogan has been retired, replaced by the telling motto "An Army of One." To be perceived as weak or vulnerable does not fit well with the military's macho "kill, kill, kill!" environment. Far too often, if today's active-duty soldiers report feelings of PTSD or troubled conscience they are isolated and subjected to intense retaliation and humiliation, giving them a new and troubling connotation to that "Army of One" advertising slogan.

Should a soldier in today's military admit to feelings of regret or attacks of conscience; if they confess to feeling compassion for the people of Iraq or Afghanistan, or if they dare to question the basic morality of the military's mission in those countries, they are likely to bring down a firestorm of harassment and discrimination upon themselves. Since a soldier's personal medical and mental health records are not subject to the confidentiality we take for granted in civilian life, any comments or expressed feelings that might "jeopardize the soldier's ability to perform the mission" are immediately passed on to the G.I.'s superiors. It is not uncommon for these issues to be dealt with in a very public arena, subjecting the afflicted G.I. to scorn and harassment from his or her peers and leaving them to feel ostracized, truly a lonely "army of one."

One young woman I know, an Iraq War veteran, was sexually assaulted by a superior officer in Iraq. When she reported him, she was verbally abused and humiliated in front of her unit, then treated as a mental case and sent home to a psychiatric facility where she was given drugs to the point where she was incoherent. Her horrified parents helped her to escape and hide until the effects of the drugs wore off.

There was, predictably, a long and nasty legal proceeding in which she was considered guilty until she proved the facts in her case. Her commanding officer was found guilty and demoted, but allowed to continue his military career. She was discharged from the army, and today she is a housewife with two small children. Her memories haunt her and PTSD affects every aspect of her life. She was, throughout the ordeal that lasted years, truly "An Army of One." In today's military, one in three female recruits will be raped, most often by a person who outranks them, within the first two years of her service. The ensuing trauma they experience is known as MST, or Military Sexual Trauma.

Most traumatized G.I.s simply "man up" or "grin and bear it," saying nothing in the hopes that their problems will go away when they get stateside or out of the military.

What does "support our troops" mean if not listening to them when they try to tell us what they have experienced? Why does the military persecute them if they ask for help? I suggest it is because the military leaders know that their methods and weapons are so excessively inhumane and destructive that they cannot be morally defended. Their only available strategy is strict censorship, or secrecy. During Wikileaks whistleblower Chelsea Manning's trial, she was charged with giving information to the enemy. The Iraqi and Afghan peoples already knew all too well the harsh truths that Manning made public. Chelsea Manning was only guilty of exposing those truths to the non-military American public and embarrassing the warmongers. Sentenced to 35 years in Leavenworth prison, her sentence was commuted by President Obama shortly before leaving office. One can only deduce that, in the eyes of our military establishment, the American people are the real enemy.

The Department of Veterans Affairs is a cabinet-level government entity that operates the nation's largest integrated health care system with more than 1700 hospitals, clinics, community living centers, domiciles, readjustment counseling centers, and other facilities. The VA also administers a variety of benefits and services to provide financial and other forms of assistance to service members, veterans, their dependents, and survivors, and it operates 131 national cemeteries in the U.S. and Puerto Rico. With a 2019 budget over $200 billion, the VA is one of the federal government's largest operations functioning at the grassroots level. The revelations of 2014 revealed that many within the VA were profiting and living the good life while our veterans were committing and attempting suicide at a rate never seen before, or waiting for months to get an appointment at the local VA facility.

The current Secretary of Veterans Affairs, Robert Wilkie, was sworn in by President Trump on July 30, 2018, the fourth person confirmed by the Senate to hold this position since 2014, although there have also been 3 additional interim Secretaries during that period. In addition to Wilkie, President Trump is also guided by three mysterious members of his Mar-a-Lago club in Florida who are completely unqualified to give any advice on medical care or administration of the largest entity of our federal government without any accountability, transparency, or oversight. They do, however, have plenty of authority, making many demands of VA officials with no regard for government rules or protocol. VA officials who oppose the Mar-a-Lago triumvirate soon disappear.

Republican legislators have been pressured by the Koch brothers to privatize the VA, which would eliminate a shining example of government-run health care and steer even more money to the greedy medical Establishment, probably impairing the medical benefits available to veterans in the process. The majority of veterans and veterans' organizations are opposed to privatization, with the exception of Concerned Veterans for America (CVA), a group funded by the Koch brothers.

A 2014 study by RAND compared the VA's mental and behavioral health programs to those in the private sector. The study was focused upon common veterans' problems, specifically PTSD and MDD (major depressive disorder), and found that only 30 percent of the private sector clinicians used state-of-the-art evidence-based therapies, compared with VA clinicians at 75 percent. The evidence-based therapies have proven in a variety of scientific studies to be among the most effective techniques available for dealing with PTSD in a clinical environment.

The Pentagon now spends $2 billion a year on mental health care for the active-duty military alone. The Veterans Administration's budget has skyrocketed to more than $200 billion in 2019. Despite all that spending, veterans take it for granted that VA doctors will attempt to treat any malady by prescribing vast quantities of pills, and mental health concerns are no different. Since 2003, the VA's rate of prescriptions for psychiatric drugs has soared. These drugs are not intended or expected to cure anything. They mask the symptoms, generally calming or sedating the patients in hopes of avoiding violence or acts of self-destruction. But many of these psychotropic drugs exhibit side effects such as aggressiveness, thoughts of suicide, and the threat of addiction. Overall the hope seems to be that the risks of side effects will be offset by the immediate short-term benefits which allow the veteran to walk out of the VA office and presumably resume a normal life. The suicide rate seems to indicate that that hope is ill-founded at best.

Perhaps someday a "real cure" pill for PTSD may be discovered. Sadly, until that unlikely day, our brave young soldiers must accept the fact that the only official response to their misery will be the fashionable but hollow slogan "Thank you for your service." Ultimately, the answer to PTSD and suicides caused by exposure to war is to abandon war and militarism as the foundations of our foreign and economic policies, but until that day we have to deal with our current problems in a realistic manner.

Over the years, the media has reported that veterans are poorly treated, most notably at Walter Reed Army Hospital a few years ago, and more recently at a few VA hospitals and medical centers across the country. Late in 2014 it was discovered that a VA hospital in Arizona was manipulating computer records to make it look like they had reduced the wait times for appointments. Their computer games resulted in the death of a number of veterans while they were waiting for appointments that would never be. The heads of that hospital were rewarded with sizable bonuses until their scam was discovered. In an effort to earn bigger bonuses, personnel at a few VA hospitals cheated and reported wait times for appointments that were as bogus as those body counts the military used to feed to reporters at the "five o'clock follies" in Saigon. Over the past few years, many of the scheduling problems have been solved or improved. I am not aware of any VA officials going to jail.

It must be noted, however, that most VA hospitals give exceptionally good care. In fact, studies show that care in a VA hospital is far better than in most for-profit hospitals. Decisions regarding care in VA hospitals are always governed by what's best for the veteran, never by what's profitable for the hospital administration. Under President Trump, the pressure for privatizing the VA has increased. Virtually all of the nation's veterans' groups oppose privatizing the VA. What's really needed are far more VA facilities, more staff, and, anticipating the problems of all the veterans returning from the Middle East, even more budget. As this is written, the VA medical system reports it has 49,000 vacancies.

Back in 2013, over a million veterans of the wars in Iraq and Afghanistan had been treated at VA hospitals and clinics, and they were continuing to see about 10,000 new patients per month. Articles in the October 31, 2013 *International Business Times* and *Forbes* reported that the Department of Veterans Affairs has quietly stopped releasing the number of non-fatal casualties of the Middle East wars. How many of those injured young people might have escaped harm (and injuries that have to rely upon non-government charities for medical attention!) if officials in the Pentagon were attending to business instead of stealing trillions? (See Chapter 21.) Again, the VA will no longer report the actual numbers of suicides and casualties they are treating. They say this is for "security" reasons. I suggest it is for recruiting reasons!

American military leaders thrive in an environment where the United States officially refers to torture as "enhanced interrogation" and civilian deaths as "collateral damage" even as our government pumps millions of taxpayer dollars annually to recruiting and propaganda. Death and destruction due to the American Way of Waging War are being word-managed to obscure the truth from the public. A carefully camouflaged provision of the 2012 defense budget authorization bill erased *all* domestic laws limiting propaganda. In effect, there are no longer any limits to what the Pentagon or the State Department might tell the public or foreign audiences. "Official" information from the United States government can now be accurate, completely false, or anything in between. Clearly, President Trump has enjoyed this troubling development. And, if your kid is approaching the age when he might be eligible for the all-volunteer military, you can bet today's recruiters are very aware of that fact.

Unfortunately, since the Vietnam debacle our nation has embraced war as the answer to our capitalistic business needs, and given our military a virtual blank check to grow its influence in every direction. Morality has been all but abandoned in the halls of the military-industrial-government power complex Eisenhower warned us about, to the obvious benefit of Wall Street where the only loyalty is to maximization of profit no matter the cost to our common interests, and damn the consequences. When we read that the U.S. spends more on militarism than the next 10 nations combined, it is important to keep in mind that a very large percentage of those dollars go directly to the defense contractors. Ultimately, a significant portion flows to the employees of those companies, and their employees. It will not be a small task to steer America toward a national agenda of peace. Sadly, the only real cure for our soldiers coming home "changed" by PTSD, MST, MDD, or other emotional problems is to change our country's course and de-emphasize militarism and war. I believe it would help our country in many ways if we could go back to a Department of Defense that was really focused on defense, and not offensive activities. And yes, I mean offensive in every meaning of the word.

Many of our veterans, proven strong individuals, cannot live with themselves when they realize what they have taken part in, and what it says about America as a country. Many more struggle to consolidate what they have seen with the image of our country as a benevolent force for justice and freedom around the world. Disillusioned, our vets came home and got involved in jobs and families, but the troubling thoughts, the memories and nightmares just wouldn't go away. Our children or grandchildren are growing up in this toxic environment of a warlike society. I don't want to see my grandchildren sent away to be "changed."

As the Pentagon folks commemorate the "noble" aspects of the war in Vietnam, I hope the American public will seize upon the occasion to step back and look at what America has become since the assassination of John F. Kennedy and the phony Gulf of Tonkin incident. What do we tell our young students about the dark experiences that have resulted in so many unnecessary deaths and traumatized so many veterans? About the Iraqi "weapons of mass destruction" that turned out to be weapons of mass deception? Do our high schools prepare their students, our children, to be productive members of a civilized society, or to be soldiers? Do we raise our children for fifteen or twenty years only to see them in ROTC training, or basic training, being brainwashed, de-sensitized and prepared to follow orders without question? Careful, don't answer too quickly.

Today, America's military permeates every aspect of our society, and we must acknowledge that our children or grandchildren are targeted to become tomorrow's soldiers. American grade school kids are learning foreign languages – valuable knowledge that never becomes obsolete – but the programs are funded by the Pentagon's National Security Education Program with the stated purpose of providing "a cadre of highly qualified candidates for employment in the national security community." Is that program involved in your kid's schooling?

We the people must insist that our government pursue peace as the primary goal, not military domination or empire-building. With rigorous civilian oversight, the tactics and strategies employed by our military must be realistically reviewed and then modified in such a way that someday we can promise young Americans who volunteer for military service that they will emerge from that service feeling proud that they have done the right things, for the right reasons, and will have made their country and the world a better place. Should they be injured or harmed, we must assure them that they will receive the very best of care. The questions are not about the recruit's inherent morals or mental state. The fundamental questions America faces are about the moral integrity of our government, military, intelligence, and corporations, the paths they choose, and the profits they reap. Can we overcome today's ethical ambiguity and regain civilian control and oversight over the Pentagon, the CIA, NSA, 15 other intelligence organizations, the "defense" industries, "contractor" mercenary firms, and all the other rogue entities profiting from the destruction and death that we export in unthinkable quantities?

Fifty years later, Americans are still being "wasted." Today's American Way of Waging War demands that we, as a people who profess to hold dear the unalienable rights of all men to life, liberty, and the pursuit of happiness, must confront the military-industrial-political juggernaut and all the other interrelated offices of government, and demand that America deliver on its claim to be a moral and ethical model to the world. If we settle for anything less, I'm afraid our country is doomed to experience a devastating pandemic of Moral Damage from War.

Chapter 17

VIETNAM: WHAT WAS
ALL THE FUSS ABOUT?

*We flattened cities in Germany and Japan in World War II. I don't
know what's so sacred about Hanoi. Let world opinion go fly a kite.*
                                        – Senator Mendel Rivers

*The price we pay for corrupting the soldier is our own corruption. The
political greatness of a nation is ill founded upon the demoralization of
a class. If only for the nation's sake, it is time to abolish the soldier; if
only for the soldier's sake, it is time to abolish war.*
– Walter Walsh, *The Moral Damage of War* (published 1906, Ginn
                                        & Company, Boston)

In October of 2017, PBS TV presented a massive documentary series titled *The Vietnam War*. The series was ten episodes and eighteen
hours long, a very in-depth look at the history of the war crafted by
America's preeminent documentarian, Ken Burns and his faithful director
and long-time associate Lynn Novick. In publicity prior to the airing of
the first episode, Burns predicted the series would "inspire our country
to begin to talk and think about the Vietnam War in an entirely new way."
The anticipation was great as we settled around the television for the airing of the first installment on a Monday evening. In the credits preceding
the film, we saw that it had been funded by David Koch, one of the far-
right activist Koch brothers, and the Bank of America. In 1971, a Bank of
America branch in Santa Barbara, California was burned down to protest
the bank's deep involvement in the war. When the documentary began,
the audience was immediately informed that America's involvement in

the war "was begun in good faith by decent people out of fateful misunderstandings, American overconfidence, and Cold War misunderstandings."

I did not find Ken Burns' "new way" to be "inspiring." History does not show America's "good intentions." The people who instigated and initiated American involvement in the conflict in Vietnam were, arguably, far from decent people. When France tried to reinstate its colonial dominance over Vietnam after World War II, at the point of a gun, America paid 85% of the costs of the ensuing war. American fliers and planes were secretly assigned to take part, without disclosure to Congress or the American people. When the French were finally defeated, the U.S. rushed to take up the fight. Covert intelligence agents masquerading as "advisors" recognized the vast flow of resources heading to Southeast Asia, and by moonlight they set up elaborate operations to personally profit. The "Golden Triangle" had never known so much gold, and it was low-hanging fruit.

After decades of French dominance, the Vietnamese people saw America's attention as another invasion by an imperialist power. In Hanoi, Ho Chi Minh had long ago seen American involvement as betrayal of the Viet Minh's efforts in World War II, not a "Cold War misunderstanding." When the promised elections were canceled and the Americans created and propped up the corrupt and brutal Diem regime , the majority vigorously opposed the American presence. Recognizing the ever-increasing opportunities for profit, powerful organizations descended upon Southeast Asia disguised behind a variety of flags, and they did business with great skill and determination. A large part of that business was in opium and heroin from the Golden Triangle. When threatened, they were utterly ruthless. The Ken Burns series failed to describe those activities, it failed to reveal that the Gulf of Tonkin incident was a lie, and by giving credence to those landmark misrepresentations the series failed miserably to "inspire new thinking."

While the architects of America's involvement spoke of protecting the people of Vietnam from Communist brutality, their "good faith" was belied by the greedy, cruel efforts of the profiteers and power-hungry to demolish Vietnam under the most intense bombardments in the history of warfare. American bombers dropped more than 700 pounds of explosives and anti-personnel bombs for every man, woman, and child in South Vietnam. We now know that hospitals and schools were intentionally blown to smithereens, that thousands of acres of crop lands were poisoned with defoliants or consumed in flaming infernos of napalm. As the crops of heroin and opium flowed through Vietnam and Laos, the blood of assassinations began to flow freely and governments were toppled. Nothing was allowed to get in the way of business. Soon, the profits to be gained from military struggle eclipsed even the drug business, and the international situation became uncontrollable. Most of the carnage was rained upon Southeast Asia's civilian peasants. The poor peasants being blown "back to the stone age" did not misunderstand. Millions of American kids who witnessed the death and destruction did not misunderstand, and the journalists tasked with describing the devastation were often unable, in good conscience, to portray its motivation as "good faith by decent people."

The Vietnamese were not grateful to the Americans. In fact, they felt the Americans should thank them and be grateful for the use of their land as a place to fight their war against Communism, against the Soviet Union and Communist China and the terrifying theories of Karl Marx, who dared to challenge Capitalism. On the surface, the war in Vietnam was the inevitable coming-to-blows between the two dominant ideologies. But it was more, far more, because the innocent, nearly helpless Vietnamese peasants were caught between the jaws of the great military powers.

The politicians guiding the military forces, and the generals, by instructing their minions as they did, gave poignant definition to what the various countries and their systems represented. The Soviet Union and Communist China sent supplies, weapons and ammunition, but also fuel and food to sustain the fighters. The North Vietnamese worked the populace to the bone carrying supplies southward along the Ho Chi Minh Trail. When trucks weren't available, they transported the weapons of war balanced upon the seats of bicycles or carried upon their backs. The North Vietnamese enlisted their people to fix the infrastructure after the bombings, to aid the injured and rebuild time and again, and they continued to ask more and more, promising nothing until the fight was won. The people answered the call, suffered terribly, and never lost hope that one day their country would be reunited.

The United States flung its bulging wallet at the foe and misled its own people, obscuring the facts as it heaped more and more wealth and power upon those who were already wealthy and powerful. When the common people objected, when they pointed out that the United States had abandoned morality and good sense, the powers turned their authority and weapons upon their own citizenry both at home and abroad. The voice of the people was choked with tear gas in the shadows of the monuments to our founding fathers, and the flag-draped coffins came home by the thousands for no good reason.

We the people were an adversary, a force that questioned, and to those who had much to hide public scrutiny was an act of war. The White House, the Capitol, and the Pentagon became fortresses where the powers retreated to avoid not only the questions, but also the sounds of truth, reason, sorrow or fear. They sent out their armies to quell the disturbance; the National Guard, the FBI, CIA, local police departments, COINTEL-PRO, infiltrators and agitators, the IRS, and even the White House Plumbers. It got so bad, so important, that the veterans came home and marched against the government by the thousands, and threw their hard-won medals back at the Capitol.

In the end, Richard Nixon did not publicly acknowledge the emotions of the great throng gathered outside to call for an end to the suffering. He considered them "enemies" and conducted covert and illegal activities to undermine and sabotage them. Nixon sacrificed everything America represents to ensure he would be re-elected, and damned thousands more of his countrymen to be killed or wounded needlessly on the far side of the planet. Together with Henry Kissinger, President Nixon made a secret deal with the North Vietnamese to continue the war for a "decent interval" until he had been re-elected. Nixon sold out the American people, and he sold out the South Vietnamese, but he won the election of 1972. Within two years Vice-President Spiro Agnew was forced to resign because he was found to be corrupt. Then the President himself was caught in his own web of high crimes and misdemeanors, and he resigned to avoid official impeachment (knowing that Gerald Ford had his back.).

For years, the daily news brought revelations of corruption, torture, atrocities, mistakes, conspiracies and cover-ups, a seemingly endless parade of the worst the human race can inflict upon its fellows. When it was finally over we breathed a great sigh of relief and went on with our lives, foolishly hoping that it would never happen again. No one was held accountable, the important questions were rarely asked and never answered, some of the dead were remembered on stone memorials, and the history was told and retold countless ways to confuse the public and continue the profiteering.

We have grandchildren now, young innocents who will inherit the America we leave for them. The Vietnam War was a great human tragedy, and it exposed a myriad of defects in our American systems and practices of government, business, and culture. The Ken Burns series did not "inspire our country to begin to talk and think about the Vietnam War in an entirely new way." We can only hope that that inspiration happens. "Vietnam," and the truths it exposed, are enormously important to the America our kids will inherit.

The Vietnam War created a social upheaval in the United States unlike anything the nation had experienced since the Civil War. Most young people are aware that something of significance happened, although they are largely unaware of the root causes or the scope of the unrest.

Because many of the questions raised serious doubts about the roles and practices of American big business, our government, and our military as they affect our nation's involvement in the world community, broad expanses of history have been de-emphasized, ignored, or misrepresented. Passionate as the debates over Vietnam were, perhaps the efforts to downplay them reflect the government and big business's desires to sweep the sordid dirt of their real history under the rug. As a result, it is difficult for today's students to find information and resources that might contribute to a realistic understanding of the effects of the war upon day-to-day life here in America. Following are some questions that might help the reader to realize the importance of Vietnam, to investigate further and, hopefully, find ways to end America's policies of war for profit.

1. The Vietnam War was not an actual war. America never declared war on North Vietnam as required by U.S. Constitution. Was it, therefore, illegal and unconstitutional?

2. Because the Gulf of Tonkin incident was found to be a fabrication, should someone have been held accountable?

3. The United States was a party to the Geneva Agreements when the French were defeated and driven out of Vietnam in 1954. Those agreements called for a general election to be held in 1956 in South Vietnam to determine who would lead. Fully realizing that Ho Chi Minh and his Communist party would win by a sizable majority, the U.S. ignored and violated the agreement and backed the very unpopular President Diem and his regime . Did this make the war illegal according to international law? Again, should someone have been held accountable? (The decision appears to have been made by President Eisenhower, acting upon the advice of his advisors.)

4. Does might make right? Even if it kills millions of people? The U.S. played a major role in orchestrating the coup that overthrew President Diem. What are, or should be, the limits to U.S. intervention into the affairs of another country? Is the United States enti-

tled to send covert teams to overwhelm the leadership of another country? To conspire with its generals or any other group to plan a coup? To influence that country's politics, or re-write its policies or laws? To take any part in the assassination of another country's leaders? What can be done to stop these practices?

5. While the military consider themselves professional experts in conducting warfare, according to the U.S. Constitution they are always subject to oversight by Congress and the Commander in Chief. What should be the parameters of the military's authority in conducting operations without previously consulting the government? The question is, does the military answer to our government? Or should the government turn the military loose to wage war as they deem necessary, without limits?

6. If Congress is reluctant to oversee or restrict the activities of the military, what can be done?

7. There is a perception that "the government" or "Congress" did not allow the military to win in Vietnam. Critics suggest we should have invaded North Vietnam, or perhaps used nuclear weapons on Hanoi and, if necessary, Peking and Moscow. Some vets suggest we should have landed a force at the southern tip of Vietnam and marched north, killing anything that moved until they reached the border with Communist China. Keep in mind, instead of that strategy, the U.S. subjected Vietnam, and especially South Vietnam, plus Laos and Cambodia, to the most intense and deadly bombing in history. History tells us the U.S. government was very concerned about igniting a nuclear war with Russia or China that could eliminate all life on the planet. Did the President or the Congress prevent America's military from achieving victory in Vietnam?

8. Did we really send American troops to Vietnam for the benefit of the Vietnamese people? How would success be recognized?

9. Is a policy of attrition, and specifically, of bombing or destroying civilian homes and neighborhoods in an enemy area, ethical or acceptable behavior in war?

10. When the military conducts covert operations, or classifies information as "top secret" for purposes of misleading or keeping the truth from its own people as opposed to an enemy, what should be the ramifications? Should anyone be held accountable when the truth is learned? What punishment might be appropriate?

11. Because supplies and troops were flowing from North Vietnam down the Ho Chi Minh Trail through Laos and Cambodia to South

Vietnam, was President Nixon justified to expand the war by sending American troops into Laos and Cambodia? Was he justified to order carpet bombing of those countries?

12. The CIA is a non-elected organization, its only powers and authority assigned by the Executive branch of government. When it is found to be involved in overseas coups, torture, shipments of arms and military equipment to foreign countries or groups, assassinations, gun-running, or fund-raising to enable operations without the knowledge or permission of Congress, is that illegal activity? Who is responsible? Who can be held accountable? When a military field commander oversteps his bounds resulting in unnecessary death and destruction in a foreign country, should he be held accountable? Does it make a difference if those unnecessary losses are to a friendly or enemy population?

13. Are business concerns such as access to natural resources valid reasons for America to send armies to foreign lands, to wage war, or to overthrow popularly-elected governments to help American business interests improve their profit pictures?

14. Does the government of a free society have the right to seize its citizens and force them to take up arms and be subjected to great risk when the conflict is not seen by the individual as worthy of such sacrifice? If no war has been declared? If a draft is instituted, what should be the criteria for avoiding military service, either temporarily, or in total?

15. Should every American citizen be obligated to a period of national service?

16. At what age is a person "ready" for military service?

17. Should women be drafted? (Women are now assigned to combat roles)

18. Does the President, or any other elected official, have the right to compile an "enemies list" and wage a campaign of harassment or retribution against American citizens without going through the conventional legal system?

19. When a war is unpopular, how should the American public treat the veterans who come home from participating in that war? Should lower-ranking personnel be treated differently from NCOs or commissioned officers?

20. Precisely what are the obligations of the government (as representing the American people) to a combat veteran?

21. Can the expression of opposition to a war or military conflict be construed as criminal when in fact no criminal acts of violence or destruction have occurred? Is the mere expression of opposing thoughts a criminal act? Is dissent a crime, or a sacred right?

22. Is an individual soldier empowered to refuse to participate in activities that would, in the soldier's opinion, violate the standards declared at the Nuremburg trials at the end of World War II, or any other international standards governing the conduct of war, and/or standards defining war crimes? Is a clear and readily achievable path available for that soldier to opt out of participating in activities he, or she, finds morally unacceptable without recrimation or punishment?

23. When a soldier hears his military superiors, including the Commander in Chief, lying to the American people about military policies or events that are, or would be, opposed by public opinion or international law, what opportunities exist for that soldier to opt out of participation in that operation, and to make the truth known to the American public?

24. Should President Gerald Ford have pardoned Richard Nixon for criminal acts related to the Watergate break-in? Should other members of the Nixon administration have been pardoned?

25. At the conclusion of the Vietnam War in 1975, should President Ford have pardoned deserters from the U.S. military? Draft dodgers? Should veterans who had received less-than-honorable discharges, often for conduct that would have been considered "free speech" in a civilian court, have had their records cleared so they would be eligible for veterans benefits?

26. The Vietnam Memorial in Washington, D.C. is unlike any other memorial. It has no statues (although two separate statues related to the war have been installed nearby), but simply lists the names of all American soldiers killed in the war. Do you approve of the unique design of "The Wall"?

27. Can the government of the United States still be influenced by peaceful demonstrations of the will of its people? What means are available to the citizenry to effectively voice opinions, oppose illegal or immoral actions, and affect our country's policies and activities?

This is just a partial list of the endless issues we still live with from that Great Schism called the Vietnam War, but the author hopes it might serve as a thought-starter.

Clearly, many of these questions and answers which have been evolving over the past 50 years are enormously significant as the United States attempts to chart its political and social path into the future. Resolution of many of these issues will determine how the U.S. government interacts with the other governments and peoples of the world, as well as how our government will rule over our children and grandchildren. Many of the precedents established by the way the Vietnam War was run have shown up again and again in more modern times, especially in the Middle East.

Chapter 18

TELLING MOMENTS

Whether you can say it or not, keep trying to say it.
— Beatle George Harrison on censorship, *The Smothers Brothers Comedy Hour*, Nov. 17, 1968.

Why should we hear about body bags and death ... I mean, it's not relevant. So why should I waste my beautiful mind on something like that?
— Former First Lady Barbara Bush, on ABC TV's *Good Morning America*, March 18, 2003

... and a hard rain fell was originally published in May of 1985. Over the past thirty-odd years I have had a variety of amazing and heart-rending experiences, but back when the book was about to appear I was scared to death. I was just a mechanic, body and fender repairman and welder when I served in Vietnam. How would combat-infantry vets react to my story? Well, most of the response has been overwhelmingly positive, and I need to tell the reader about a few of the people I've met and the experiences I have enjoyed as a result of the book.

Shortly after *... and a hard rain fell* was published, I was invited to attend a conference on Vietnam at Gettysburg College. In the afternoon, a grizzled old Sergeant Major from the nearby Army War College pointed to author Bill "W.D." Ehrhart and myself and told the audience "These whining, complaining veterans will die off. The history of the Vietnam War your grandchildren will read has been written, and it will not reflect much of what has been said here today." He did not characterize his version as truth. If it would aid enlistment in the future that was enough for him. I have struggled to keep *... and a hard rain fell* available on America's bookstore shelves just to frustrate the bold and blatant warmongers like that crusty old Sarge.

I had never written more than a high school term paper when I began to record my impressions of my Vietnam experiences. I set out to write a few pages, a letter to my wife that my daughters could read when they were older, and hopefully understand why their daddy acted a little odd at times. A chain of incredible coincidences that seemed "meant to be" brought my story to the shelves of bookstores across America and around the world. Now, more than 30 years later it is still on the shelf in many bookstores.

Over the years, the book has evolved. The original Macmillan hardcover featured a thought-provoking high school yearbook-inspired cover designed by Vietnam vet John Beam, a celebrity of sorts for the poignant sign he carried at the dedication of The Wall in Washington, D.C. There were lyrics to a number of important songs from the era. After two printings in that form, the book went paperback via Simon & Schuster Pocketbooks. They insisted upon changing the cover to feature a painting of a tired, woebegone soldier, but the first draft referred to me as "mind shattered" and stressed the book's sex, drugs, and rock 'n roll. The word "understanding," so prevalent in the book's many reviews and endorsements, was nowhere to be seen. Pocketbooks refused to change it, my literary agent told me I was crazy, and I contacted a friend of my mother-in-law who just happened to be a legal counsel for Vietnam Veterans of America. He was upset at the wording and its depiction of Vietnam veterans, and presumably so was someone in the hierarchy of VVA; we were less than two hours from filing a class-action lawsuit pitting Vietnam Veterans of America vs. Simon & Schuster to stop production of the book when the publisher relented and agreed to change the words but not the cover painting. In that form the book stayed alive for many years and multiple printings.

One of the proudest moments of my life came the day my Simon & Schuster editor suggested I begin to describe my book as a best-seller. "We are going to another printing on your book," he told me, "while we are renting warehouse space to hold all the unsold copies of Ronald Reagan's memoir." Soon after Pocketbooks decided to end production, an article in the *Washington* (New Jersey) *Observer* brought my attention to an area literary agent working for a new agency. I contacted her, and she created my hugely successful relationship with Sourcebooks. The lyrics to those iconic songs are long gone, however.

A number of wonderful moments have happened over the years. I will never forget my first talk to a high school class, shortly before the book was first published. My nerves were trembling but everything went well until a young lady asked the question she hadn't been able to ask previously. "I have two sisters," she said softly, "and both have serious birth defects. I know my father blames his service in Vietnam and something called Agent Orange, but when anyone mentions Vietnam he goes into his room and closes the door, and sometimes he won't come out for days. My question is, what is Agent Orange?" I had a hard time answering over the huge lump in my throat. We lost our son at the age of fourteen days, to birth defects I believe were related to Agent Orange and my time in Vietnam. Moments like that one come less often now, but I take huge satisfaction from my meetings with students. I only hope my thoughts encourage them to investigate further, and to think.

Back in the 1980s, I often found I was speaking to young people who were living in a home where the damage, emotions, or loss of Vietnam were a traumatic everyday presence, but the parents couldn't or wouldn't talk about the war. The students were a whole new generation of post-war "baby boomers," and more than once their questions brought tears to my eyes. I hope my words were a comfort to some of them. The pressure I felt was enormous.

Gradually, my audiences became more removed from the emotions, but always curious. Over the years I have always found that high school and college students are very interested in Vietnam, both the war and the era. They seem to sense that the history of that time is critical to understanding today's America, and the current wars in the Middle East. Many of them still cry and tell me about their fathers or uncles who were damaged by their service in Vietnam, or about their parents who opposed the war. Far too many describe funeral services for veterans of Iraq or Afghanistan, former classmates or relatives. Sometimes, the veteran took his own life, leaving the student bewildered. It is all past history now, but the emotional legacies from the Vietnam years are still affecting many American families. I thought I had said everything I needed to say about Vietnam in *… and a hard rain fell,* but the questions are endless. When I retired I knew I had to put together the book you are holding in your hands.

I was invited to speak to a 1988 Veterans Day assembly at Roxbury High School in Succasunna, New Jersey. I traveled by train from Maryland to New York to do a talk at Columbia University, and then by bus, \d ultimately I found myself knee-deep in an early snowstorm in rural

New Jersey. No one expected over a foot of snow in early November, but it was a blizzard! The assembly was under way when I finally arrived at the school; I spoke briefly, warning the students that they should stay aware of current events because America's militarism was threatening to start other wars and they could be sucked into horrific experiences like my own.

Before long, school officials interrupted with the announcement that, due to the storm, they were closing the school and summoning the school buses to take the students home. The assembly immediately disintegrated into chaos as the students scattered to retrieve their coats and head for the buses. Backstage, I was approached by a man my age accompanied by a child. He said he had come especially to meet me, and to introduce me to his son who was a victim of Agent Orange. Most of all, he wanted to thank me for my book. We spoke briefly, I was very moved, but the school was closing and we were being encouraged to exit the auditorium. I have long regretted that I didn't get his name or address. I wonder how his son is doing today.

I had no idea how I might get from the high school to my train back to Maryland. Originally, one of the faculty was going to drive me to Newark, but the storm made that impossible. There was lively discussion in the lobby outside the auditorium, when a limousine pulled up outside. Because the buses would be coming, the position of the limo attracted a lot of attention, and then a gentleman exited the vehicle and came into the school. He was arriving late due to the storm, but he was a recognized New Jersey personality and candidate for the U.S. Senate, and school officials fussed over him with appropriate concern, explaining that the ceremony had been interrupted and the students were being sent home due to the storm.

Pete Dawkins had been Captain of Cadets at West Point, captain of the undefeated football team and winner of the Heisman Trophy; a Rhodes Scholar at Oxford, a heavily decorated Vietnam veteran, and the youngest brigadier general in the history of the army. I was amazed to hear that he expressed no disappointment over the cancellation of his talk to the students. I only heard him say "To hell with the kids, is the press here?"

I was not able to hear what he told the press, as arrangements had been made to get me out of the high school and headed toward home. I was driven to a local train station where I could catch a train to Newark, although I would arrive at a station some way from the terminal, where I would have to catch the train back to Maryland. I emerged in Newark to find myself still in the midst of the blizzard. I was directed to wait for a bus and stood in the snow for a long while. No buses came, so finally I went across the street into a convenience store to inquire about a bus or even a taxi that might take me to the train station. Luckily, a customer saw my VVAW button and drove me to my train. He was a fellow Vietnam vet, and he delivered me safely to my destination. "You've got to be careful around strangers in Newark," he grinned.

The train was delayed by deep snowdrifts, and I arrived at the Baltimore airport train station long after dark. My car was buried. I dug it out and headed home, plowing through the after effects of the storm. When I arrived home, Carolynn informed me that Nicaraguan President Daniel Ortega was in Washington and wanted to meet with a group of supportive Vietnam veterans at the Vietnam Memorial the next day, and we were invited. I arranged another day off by blaming the snow storm, and we managed to drive to the nearest Metro station and make it to the Memorial, where a group of vets were eagerly awaiting the arrival of President Ortega. Alas, we waited in vain, until the cold and disappointment chilled us, and we went home. The next day's *Washington Post* had pictures of President Ortega buying fashionable new glasses.

Another time I was invited to speak at SUNY (State University of New York) in Albany, by Fred Wilcox, the author of the landmark book *Waiting for an Army to Die* about Agent Orange and its effects upon Vietnam vets. Fred was teaching a class, which I think was on Vietnam, but it was a long time ago and my memories are completely dominated by the freezing weather. We had to walk a long, long way from Fred's designated parking spot to the building where the class was held and, of course, back again afterwards. It was a few degrees below zero and the wind was fierce. Fred's hospitality was excellent, I believe my talk went well, but what I remember most is the bitter cold.

On another cold January day, I was asked to speak at Archbishop Spalding High School, very near to our Maryland home at that time. Every year, the staff at Archbishop Spalding set aside one day to expose the Senior class to a variety of "peace and social justice" organizations and opportunities they might pursue after graduation. I was a regular guest on those occasions, reading a short passage from my book, warning the students that the military recruiters might not be telling them the whole truth, and acquainting them with some of the peace groups in the area. The school was located less than ten miles from Fort Meade army base and the headquarters of the National Security Agency (NSA), so many of the students had been brought up in a home atmosphere that didn't always make them aware of such groups.

On this particular day I was a little apprehensive as a local gentleman had contacted the school and asked to also speak to the students to offer an alternative point of view to my comments. He was a former infantry officer in Vietnam, and he felt that my book gave an unrealistically negative view of army officers in general, and their performance in Vietnam in particular. The school called and asked if I would mind an opposing view, and of course I said no, but I had no idea just what I was facing as I entered the school that morning. I met the gentleman and he was very cordial, and we talked briefly before our segment of the program was scheduled to begin about ten o'clock. We agreed that he would go first, but he gave me no idea what he was going to say.

He was very professional, dressed in a nice suit, and he had a relaxed, comfortable manner of speaking. He started off explaining his background, and that he asked to be here today because he had felt that my depictions of army officers in ... and a hard rain fell were overly harsh. He wanted to tell my audience that not all officers in Vietnam were as unfeeling or unprofessional as the ones with whom I had come in contact.

There was a pause, and then he held the microphone close and spoke softly, and proceeded to tell the students that he had looked at my book a few nights ago as he was preparing his comments for today's talk, and after reviewing a few passages he suddenly realized that, in all his actions in Vietnam, he had focused on surviving, and performing in a manner that might help him earn a successful career in the military. After the war he had worked in an office in the Pentagon for a time, and he was very proud of his accomplishments, but he had left the army after a while to pursue a business career. He paused again, obviously struggling with his emotions, and then he told the audience that he had suddenly realized that in all his years as an army officer, and especially leading an infantry team in heavy combat, he had never felt any responsibility or real caring for the men under his command. His voice broke a bit as he gestured in my direction and urged the Senior class to listen to what I had to say because I would be telling the truth.

At that very moment someone burst into the room and hollered that the space shuttle Challenger had just exploded moments after lift-off, killing everyone aboard! There was a TV set up in the gym, and everyone was encouraged to go there immediately to see the news reports of the tragedy. The students rushed off – and the precious moment was lost. It was January 28th, 1986, and the space shuttle Challenger had exploded moments after lift-off killing everyone aboard.

I have cardboard boxes of letters from readers, and some of them tell me that their son or brother came home from the war "changed" and unable to relate to his family. For long years he had resisted any contact, but the writer had read my book and found understanding in its pages, sent it on to the vet, and the book had led to renewed communication. Some vets finally came home for Thanksgiving or Christmas, and their families wrote to thank me. My daughters are older now, and I have saved those letters in hopes that someday they will be proud that I found a way to turn the negative experience of Vietnam into a positive. In fact, when Source-books agreed to publish *... and a hard rain fell*, because it had originally been published years before, there was no computer text of the book. My youngest daughter spent her Christmas vacation typing the book onto floppy discs, the first time she had read it through. I paid her (handsome-ly), and a series of touching and meaningful discussions resulted.

I was invited to Chicago's Vietnam homecoming parade back in about 1989, supposedly to speak out in contrast to the parade's Grand Marshal, General Westmoreland. I was with Chris Noel, the beautiful Armed Forc-es disc jockey from Vietnam, when a helicopter whisked the General away "for his own safety." At one point I walked within a couple feet of "Westy," and I controlled myself. I used to hold out hope that those responsible for the Vietnam war would be held accountable for their crimes, but it is obvious that will never happen. Over the years, I've observed that regardless of the scope of the disasters they have created, people in government or positions of authority, celebrities, and religious zealots in today's United States are rarely held accountable for their actions.

I attended a Vietnam Veterans Against the War party that weekend in Chi-cago, and met many of the names I had read in newsletters. From the start, VVAW spoke for me more than any of the other veterans' organizations.

In the Spring of 1990, I was invited to speak to a class at the Naval Academy at Annapolis, Maryland. As I do at most of my meetings with students, I started the class by circulating a piece of shrapnel from Viet-nam. We were rocketed one night and spent most of the evening in our sand-bagged bunkers watching the perimeter in case the rockets were followed up by a ground attack. The next morning some of us were sent back to clean up and refresh the bunkers, and I was chosen for this chore. When I reached my assigned position, I noticed that one of the sand bags in the top row where I had leaned with my rifle was nearly empty and most of the sand lay in a small pile on the outside edge of the bunker. I took a closer look and found that the bag had been punctured by a piece of shrapnel just four to six inches below my face and neck! I wrapped it up and sent it home to my parents. I've found that most students have heard the word "shrapnel," but they have no idea what it looks like.

As a point of trivia, the concept of making the casing of an artillery round in such a manner that it will explode and spread many small, jagged pieces of ragged metal, making the round an anti-personnel weapon, was invented by a lieutenant in the British Royal Artillery in 1784. Henry Shrapnel was rewarded for his idea, and ultimately promoted to Major General. Shrapnel died in 1842, but his deadly invention lives on.

The piece I retrieved from the sand bag is jagged and lethal-looking. As it was passing hand-to-hand among the Midshipmen, one of the Middies stood up and interrupted my narrative. "What are you doing?" he asked, holding my souvenir over his head. "We are going to be professional military officers, and you are trying to scare us!" I agreed, and said I thought professional military officers should be familiar, not just with the word "shrapnel," but what the real object could do to them. I was never invited back to speak at the Naval Academy.

It has not been easy for my wife to be married to an author and Vietnam vet. One reader, a divorced and underemployed Native American writer, brought his teenage children to our house as he slowly and painstakingly rebuilt his life. "Roy" needed furniture, and we donated an old rocking chair. He needed friendship and understanding. We tried. He bought his daughter a sweater, and I helped him buy a Christmas tree to put it under. One night he sat in our old chair and got drunk. That night he didn't call me; he put a gun to his head and ended his journey.

Another vet, a Marine who had been at Khe Sanh, was reassigned to a base in the States where he was subjected to a load of abuse ("Show us how it's done, Mister Vietnam Vet."). "Tom" put a note on his locker door to tell the Marines he was "going fishing," and he deserted and went to Canada. He was able to return to the states under Jimmy Carter's amnesty, but his wife had divorced him and would not allow him any contact with, or information about his young daughter. He called one Friday night to say goodbye. He couldn't do it anymore. I shamed him into coming to the house, saying he owed me better than just a phone call, and Carolynn and I talked with him night and day until late Sunday afternoon when he announced that he would give it another try.

Throughout that weekend Carolynn looked after our two toddlers, trying desperately to entertain them and explain why Daddy wasn't available today. I was willing to help a friend in trouble, but in retrospect I think it is a shame that my wife has had to be haunted by these events. My daughter tells me she and her sister hated the family trips to the Vietnam Memorial in Washington where I would meet old friends and leave them alone with Mom, completely ignoring them.

I have been very fortunate. I never intended to write a book. Today I have a huge collection of letters, "fan mail" from readers who were touched by ... *and a hard rain fell*. People all over the globe have written to tell me my story has helped them to understand, and has brought comfort and compassion to their families. Sometimes, a reader will reach out to me, and our telephone has rung at all hours of the day or night. It is obvious that the hurt caused by the Vietnam War has continued to resonate throughout America in many poignant situations. It is shameful that there is so little relief or help available. I try to make myself available.

I have had the good fortune to travel all over America and meet veterans and their families, kind people who have shared some very poignant moments with me, and often with Carolynn. Thanks to the book, my wife and I have had the opportunity to meet victims, survivors, heroes, housewives, activists, many published authors, writers and thinkers, "true believers," and a few celebrities. Sometimes it has been heart-rending to meet veterans from America's more recent wars, Gold Star Mothers who lost their sons, the parents of a high school buddy who didn't make it home from Vietnam, survivors of U.S. sponsored violence in El Salvador and the Middle East, Vietnamese doctors working with Agent Orange victims, and Americans who fled the Vietnam War and have built successful lives in Canada. We have met countless Americans who remain active in what is loosely referred to as "the peace movement," and have been inspired by them.

Contemplating the history and effects of the war has had a severe impact upon every aspect of my life, creating a jumbled jigsaw puzzle that I have tried to solve in part by organizing and researching this book. It is intimidating to go through hours of testing and be diagnosed as having "severe PTSD." I am reminded of the Paul Simon tune "Maybe I Think Too Much."

On the weekend when so many VVAW members gathered in Washington to help IVAW pull off Winter Soldier II, Carolynn and I were in rural Sussex, New Jersey. A lady from Washington, Susan Austin-Roth, has written a play titled *Missing Pages* that contrasts a World War II intelligence officer with Alzheimer's to his son, a Vietnam vet with PTSD. We saw the play presented as a reading at the Kennedy Center for the Performing Arts, and on that Saturday evening it was presented again at a small town theater in rural New Jersey. At the end of the play the entire audience was in tears, including me. The playwright has openly stated that the character of Andy, the Vietnam vet, was taken from my book. I am honored beyond words.

Carolynn discovered that one of her community college students was an Iraq War veteran who had been sexually assaulted by her commanding officer. When she reported the incident, the young lady was remanded to a psychiatric ward and quieted with an assortment of medicines. The story of her escape, and the agonies and frustration of rebuilding her life were heart-breaking, but today she is married and a mommy, and embittered but bravely moving on with her life. The army investigated approximately 15,150 reports of sexual assault within its ranks in 2009. Only 8% were prosecuted, and only 2% resulted in a conviction. The Pentagon has stubbornly resisted any efforts to address Military Sexual Trauma, while they encourage that the hypothetical draft be expanded to include women.

Another of Carolynn's acquaintances, after learning of my book, confided that her son-in-law had gone to Iraq on his second deployment with eight other guys from our small rural community. A year and a half after returning, four of the nine had committed suicide, and she feared her daughter's husband would become the fifth. His legs had been severely wounded by an IED, but the VA refused to give him knee replacements because he was "too young." The local newspaper did not make its readers aware that the loss of those young men might have been related to their common military service. These are the situations that are quietly happening in home towns all over America, to too many veterans of too many wars.

I find it difficult to sit quietly by. There is much work to be done. Today America's militarism and imperialism threaten to bankrupt our country. At the very least, expenditures for war-making will have a terribly negative impact upon the quality of life to be inherited by our children and grand-children. When the government of the United States finds it necessary to cut the budgets for education and repairs to our infrastructure in favor of funding new weapons systems that the Pentagon doesn't even need or want, and perpetual unwinnable wars while VA benefits are cut or misappropriated and propaganda supplants truth in our children's educations, I have to protest. We need to down-size the military and install a system of low-cost universal health care in America. We need to stop meddling in other countries, stop overthrowing their duly-elected leaders, stop assassinating their officials, and stop promising to install "democracy" there when we can't even make it work here in America.

We need to, somehow, overturn the Supreme Court's "Citizens United" decision that treats corporations as "people" with individual rights but no individual responsibility. And we need to recognize that self-labeled "conservatives" have without exception increased government deficits beyond any previous level, wasted trillions of dollars and done more damage to the American standard of living than any other political movement throughout our history. We need to amend our constitution to eliminate the dollar influence of special interests and return to the concept of a representative democracy that reflects the will of all the people. We need to dismantle a large portion of our military and intelligence communities in order to afford these changes, and stop trying to dominate the world.

Prior to the war in Vietnam, the United States of America was the greatest, most prosperous, and the most promising country in the world. Since Vietnam, America's status and the quality of life of its inhabitants have steadily deteriorated even as its arsenals have increased beyond all imagination. Depending upon which comparison you read, we outspend the next 10, or 12, 15, or 17 of the world's most militarized nations combined, on death and destruction – but we are far from the top of the list in such categories as the costs of medical care or the survival rate of newborn infants.

Yes, the Vietnam experience shed light upon many dark, secretive aspects of our current government system and its corrupt, self-serving methods. Realistically, an American life is no more precious than a human life anywhere else on Earth, and we need to adjust our policies and prejudices to acknowledge that basic fact. Doing so will yield a "homeland security" our country has not enjoyed since Pearl Harbor, and loosen up the funds to improve all Americans' quality of life to standards that used to be described as "the American Dream."

These are the themes I have talked about to many high school and college students, and I look forward to sharing these thoughts with many more. When I started, my children were toddlers and now I am advocating for my grandchildren. I can't say that I've changed the situation much, but I've tried.

> You may say I'm a dreamer
> But I'm not the only one
> I hope someday you'll join us
> And the world will live as one.
> From "Imagine" by John Lennon

Chapter 19

FAQs

1. **What is Agent Orange?** Agent Orange is one of a family of chemical defoliants that were widely used in Vietnam to kill the vegetation. Much of Vietnam is jungle or thick vegetation which gave the enemy cover. The U.S. used Agent Orange to cause the green leaves to shrivel, turn brown and fall off, taking away the enemy's hiding places. In addition, rice paddies and other crops were sprayed to deny the enemy food, but of course this also caused great hardship to all the Vietnamese peasants. At the time, we thought defoliation was a good thing, but Agent Orange was heavily laced with Dioxin, one of the most toxic chemicals known to man. In the years after the war, a wide range of serious health problems began to afflict veterans, and also the Vietnamese population.

Research linked these problems, which included tumors, birth defects, cancers, and skin ailments to Agent Orange, but for a long while the U.S. government and the manufacturers of the chemicals refused to acknowledge those links. The government found Dioxin in American communities of Times Beach, Missouri and Love Canal in New York, and immediately condemned the areas and forcibly evacuated all residents, but they steadfastly refused to help Vietnam veterans.

Over time, we learned that more than 19 million gallons of Agent Orange and similar chemicals were sprayed over 4.5 million acres of South Vietnam between 1961 and 1972. Of course, Vietnam was primarily an agricultural society and this spraying had a devastating effect upon both the food supply and the country's economics.

For years, the Vietnamese have borne large numbers of children with grotesque and debilitating birth defects. U.S. acknowledgement and assistance to the Vietnamese victims of this chemical warfare has been paltry at best. The government has reluctantly offered some medical assistance to Vietnam veterans who were exposed to Agent Orange. Today, it is common for young men to leave a specimen at a sperm bank before entering military service.

2. **Did you kill people?** No, I'm grateful that I never had to do that. I had a Viet Cong sapper in my sights one night, but he retreated and saved us both from harm.

3. **How could you, low-ranking soldiers far from the management of the war, determine that the war was unwinnable seven years before it ended?** There were many clear signs. First, we couldn't help but be aware that the vast majority of the Vietnamese people opposed their government and our support for that corrupt rule. Second, although most of the G.I.s in Vietnam were relatively uneducated, we were neither blind nor stupid. We could see that there was no overall strategy to win the war. The "war of attrition" was entirely focused on inflicting quantities of death and destruction upon the Vietnamese people that were so devastating they would give up the fight and quietly buckle under to the Saigon regime.

Clearly, if the U.S. ultimately won, the Saigon regime would rule over a desolated landscape and the ragged, hopeless remains of its population. Had the ARVN army, the representative embodiment of the Saigon government we saw every day, been inspired or dedicated, we might have been motivated by them, but they weren't, and so it was obvious they would not win the war. And of course, we could not win the "hearts and minds" of the Vietnamese people without them.

4. **Do you believe American POW/MIAs are still being held against their will in Vietnam?** No. Absolutely not. I do suspect that some former POWs might have opted to remain in Vietnam instead of returning home, only because a number of American veterans have chosen to return to Vietnam permanently.

5. **Would you do it all again?** No. However, I will qualify that answer by adding, given the circumstances at the time, I would probably make the same decisions I made in 1966. Given what I know today, I would refuse induction. Whether I would go to prison or just escape from the United States is a question I cannot answer. I spend too many nights still considering the question.

6. **What do you think about the Vietnamese "boat people" who escaped after the communists took over and came to the U.S. as refugees?** At the risk of stirring up old controversies, I will only say that most of the Vietnamese I saw lived in abject poverty. I suspect that anyone who could afford to pay to board those boats had probably gotten rich at the expense of his fellow countrymen. That's just an observation, but I think the best Vietnamese were left behind.

7. Do you see parallels between the Vietnam War and the 21st century American wars in Iraq and Afghanistan? Yes, completely. Once again, the American effort has no clear strategy to win the wars, conquer the enemy, and leave the people of those countries better off than they were before we came. The current American Way of Waging War relies upon our firepower to "shock and awe" the enemy forces. The destruction of both countries has been devastating, creating widespread resentment and despair, and millions of desperate refugees.

The people of Iraq and Afghanistan have learned that the Americans bring nothing constructive to their countries or communities, so the young people fight the invaders to save their homeland while the elderly and weak just see everything they have accomplished in life being systematically destroyed, and they can only feel bitterness and hate.

8. Many people feel that the government interfered with the military in Vietnam, and kept them from winning the war. Is that true? I don't agree with that opinion, and here's why. The military in Vietnam, and also Cambodia and Laos, inflicted more bombing, more artillery fire, and more sophisticated anti-personnel weapons than had ever been used in any previous war in history. We used chemicals like Agent Orange to destroy their crops and poison their water supplies. Overall, it was the cruelest and most destructive war ever waged. The government ordered the bombers to avoid areas too close to the border, which kept the Chinese from entering the war as they had done in Korea.

Although nuclear weapons were moved to the area, they were never used. A nuclear war with the forces of worldwide Communism was averted. Thank God for that!

The Vietnam War was lost because of two significant factors. First, the American public learned a lot about the lies and corruption that were so rampant in America's prosecution of the war, and the ineffectiveness of the American strategy overall. As the war dragged on for years, these factors took on more and more importance, and the public's support of the war disintegrated. The second factor was that the common soldiers in-country witnessed the same factors, and also the enormous devastation and cruelty of the American Way of Waging War, and they revolted. By 1971, the American military was so affected by desertions, AWOL, mutiny, fragging, drug abuse, and sabotage that it could no longer function.

9. When the Communists took over Vietnam, were they good for the people? Did they punish former ARVN soldiers, or

people who had worked with the Americans? When the North Vietnamese took over the South, they were quite brutal to their former enemies. Tens of thousands who had worked with the Americans were killed, and many others were imprisoned. South Vietnamese who had been ARVN soldiers, politicians, or who had worked with the Americans were generally sent to re-education camps to be punished and brainwashed. Some were held in the camps for five or six years or even longer until they were considered reformed and able to re-enter the general population. Many South Vietnamese sought to escape when the Communists took over, often resorting to rickety boats in hopes of finding refuge in Thailand or Malaysia. Those countries became overcrowded with refugees and began to turn them away. Also, the reunited Vietnam fought a bitter war against Pol Pot's brutal Khmer Rouge regime in Cambodia in late 1978, pushing the murderous Khmer Rouge out of the capital city of Phnom Penh and ending their rule in early January. In response, China attacked North Vietnam, but the Vietnamese overcame the Chinese troops and restored the border. The history of wars between China and Vietnam goes back over 2,000 years. In 1978, Vietnam was supplied mostly by the Soviet Union, and China's conflict with Vietnam was thought to be a provocation of the Soviets. Vietnamese troops remained in Phnom Penh until the Soviet Union fell apart in 1989. With the Soviets no longer a threat in Southeast Asia, the border between Vietnam and China was formally established at that time. Two years later, the United States began taking steps to reestablish ties with Vietnam. In 1994, President Bill Clinton ended the post-war trade embargo, and formal relations were normalized in 1995.

Although the government of Vietnam is strictly authoritarian, it has allowed capitalism into the marketplace and today Vietnam is a thriving business hub with products exported to markets all around the world. Sadly, however, corruption and rampant profiteering have left the working poor of Vietnam in a powerless and poverty-ridden state. While the Vietnamese endured the heaviest bombardments in history and defeated the most powerful and best-equipped army in the world, it appears from afar that many of the intentions and goals of Ho Chi Minh have been betrayed.

10. **Did the U.S. help Vietnam to rebuild after the war?**
The simple answer to this is, of course, no. When America withdrew from Vietnam in 1975, they left behind a devastated wasteland. The bombing from American planes was the most concentrated in the history of warfare, and far more destruction was rained

upon our ally nation, South Vietnam, than North Vietnam. Roads, railroads, bridges, and canals were all devastated by the bombing, and unexploded artillery shells, bombs, and land mines littered the country. Again, Vietnam was an agricultural country approximately the size of New Mexico, and the unexploded ordnance hiding in the soil or under water in the rice paddies made agriculture extremely risky or impossible in many areas. Almost twelve and a half million acres of forest and farm land had been killed or rendered unusable by chemical defoliants such as Agent Orange. The new government in Saigon estimated that two-thirds of all the villages in the South had been completely wiped off the map by American bombing and ground actions. The Americans had left behind 10 million refugees, approximately 880,000 orphans, about 360,000 amputees and invalids, and over a million war widows. Three million people in South Vietnam were unemployed and completely dependent upon the government for their day-to-day survival. Inflation was at approximately 900%, making the money basically worthless. At the peace talks in Paris, the U.S. had agreed to pay $3.5 billion in reparations, but never paid anything at all. In fact, the U.S. insisted the new Communist government repay millions of dollars borrowed by the old Saigon regime, and Hanoi did actually pay off that debt. The U.S. imposed a trade embargo upon Vietnam, and urged many of the world's nations to also refuse to trade with the devastated nation. Having bombed Vietnam "back to the stone age," the U.S. pressured agencies such as the International Monetary Fund, UNESCO, and the World Bank to deny aid to the struggling country. Years later, America acknowledged that Agent Orange had caused a variety of serious illnesses and birth defects, and offered some compensation to veterans, but nothing to more than two million Vietnamese victims. Only in 2015 did the U.S. send a paltry sum, under $2 million, to aid the Vietnamese victims of Agent Orange.

11. What is your opinion of the movies about Vietnam? I find most of the movies about the war in Vietnam to be shallow and unrealistic. I admit that I haven't seen all of them, but they always show the Vietnamese scenery as neat and orderly, and it was never either of those. I found *Apocalypse Now* to be too artsy and unrealistic. Many of my students are shown *We Were Soldiers*, the 2002 film starring Mel Gibson, in class. This film shows the Mel Gibson character walking upright in a fire-fight, which is absurd. I tell students Mel Gibson read the script and knows he won't be killed, but in a real battle there is no script, and everyone is terrified. My favorite Vietnam movie is *The Deer Hunter*. It is artsy, but the theme of Russian roulette is very effective in showing that the soldier has absolutely no control over whether he lives or dies, and the madness brought on by the corruption of war.

12. **Many of your ideas seem to contradict many of the more common opinions of the majority of Vietnam veterans. Do you feel confident that a sizable number of Vietnam vets will agree with the ideas suggested in this book?** Yes, although the ones who disagree may be louder. Over the 30+ years that *... and a hard rain fell* has been on the market, I have received countless letters, phone calls, e-mails, and personal assurances from fellow veterans that they agree with most, if not all of my points of view. The majority have opted to quietly work and raise their families. The reader should keep in mind that for a number of years I "put my memories of Vietnam in a box on the shelf." My box fell and spilled. Each of us has had to deal with his personal demons in his own way. I feel confident, based upon the love I have received from Vietnam veterans and their families, that *... and a hard rain fell* allowed me to turn a very negative experience into a positive, and I am grateful to everyone who took the time to contact me. I have, by the way, personally answered every "fan" contact regarding the book I have ever received.

Chapter 20

THE WALL

The Wall reminds us to be honest in our telling of history. There is nothing to be gained by glossing over the darker portions of a war, the Vietnam War, that bitterly divided America. We must openly acknowledge past mistakes, because that is how we avoid repeating mistakes.
– Secretary of Defense Chuck Hagel, Veterans Day, 2014.

When I look back at all the crap I learned in high school
It's a wonder I can think at all
But my lack of education hasn't hurt me none
I can read the writing on the wall
– Paul Simon, "Kodachrome"

The following information has been widely circulated on the Internet. There is no indication of the source in any version I have seen. It seems to have been composed about 2010, so a few of the numbers may have been updated since then. When this information was originally circulated, it said there were 58,267 names on The Wall. That number is now 58,315 so the additions may have increased some of the other numbers. The author sincerely hopes no one will be offended if I make this information available to a wider, interested audience. It is extremely important to the overall story of the Vietnam War.

Interesting Statistics on the Vietnam Memorial wall:

There are 58,315 names listed on that polished black wall, current as of a December, 2017 mailing from the Vietnam Veterans Memorial Fund.

The names are arranged in the order in which they were taken from us by date and within each date the names are alphabetized.

• The first known casualty was Richard B. Fitzgibbon, of North Weymouth, Mass. Listed by the U.S. Department of Defense as having been killed on June 8, 1956. His name is listed on the Wall along with that of his son, Marine Corps Lance Cpl. Richard B. Fitzgibbon III, who was killed on Sept. 7, 1965.

• There are three sets of fathers and sons on the Wall.

• 39,996 were just 22 or younger when they died.

• 8,283 were just 19 years old.

• The largest age group, 33,103 were 18 years old.

• 12 soldiers on the Wall were 17 years old.

• 5 soldiers on the Wall were 16 years old.

• One soldier, PFC Dan Bullock was 15 years old.

• 997 soldiers were killed on their first day in Vietnam.

• 1,448 soldiers were killed on their last day in Vietnam.

• 31 sets of brothers are on the Wall.

• 31 sets of parents lost two of their sons.

• 54 soldiers attended Thomas Edison High School in Philadelphia.

• 8 women are on the Wall. They died nursing the wounded.

• 260 soldiers were awarded the Medal of Honor for actions that occurred during the Vietnam War; 153 of them are on the Wall.

• The most deaths for a single day, 245, occurred on January 31, 1968. That date marked the beginning of the Tet offensive.

• The most deaths for a single month, 2,415, occurred in May 1968.

• Beallsville, Ohio, population, 475 lost 6 of her sons.

• There are 711 West Virginians on the Wall.

• West Virginia had the highest casualty rate per capita of any state in the nation.

• The May/June 2017 issue of *The VVA Veteran*, newsletter of Vietnam Veterans of America, in an article titled "The Veterans Initiative: Trip 25 regarding the continuing search for the remains of Americans in Southeast Asia" states that, as of February 23, 2017 there were still 1,616 Americans missing and unaccounted for in Vietnam and areas of Cambodia and Laos that were controlled by the Vietnamese during the war.

Most Americans who read this will only see the numbers that the Vietnam War created. To those of us who survived the war, and to the families of those who did not, we see the faces, we feel the pain that these numbers created. We are, until we too pass away, haunted with these numbers, because they were our friends, fathers, husbands, wives, brothers, sons and daughters. The Wall screams out its terrible truth to all who venture into its dark divide. Nothing was won, but so much was lost.

Chapter 21

THE HIGH COST OF
AMERICA'S MILITARISM

Of all the enemies to public liberty war is, perhaps, the most to be dreaded because it comprises and develops the germ of every other. War is the parent of armies; from these proceed debts and taxes ... known instruments for bringing the many under the domination of the few.... No nation could preserve its freedom in the midst of continual warfare.
　　　　　　　– James Madison, *Political Observations*, 1795

A nation that continues year after year to spend more money on military defense than on programs of social uplift is approaching spiritual death.
　　　　　　　– Rev. Martin Luther King, Jr.

As of early January, 2019 America's national debt is $21.8 trillion.

On Veterans Day 2017, the Costs of War Project at Brown University's Watson Center announced that they estimated the U.S. had spent over $5.6 trillion on war-making since the 9/11 attack on the World Trade Center. That amount, much of it borrowed, is equal to approximately $23,386 for every American taxpayer. The report includes the immediate costs of the wars, plus "war-related spending by the State Department, the Department of Veterans affairs, and Homeland Security," relevant to the wars in Iraq, Afghanistan, Syria and Pakistan. It does not include actions in Libya, Yemen, Somalia, or South Sudan. It does not include state or local expenses related to veterans' care, nor the costs of military equipment "gifts" and awards to the nations named above. "In sum," the report states, "although this report's accounting is comprehensive, there are still billions of dollars not included in its estimate."

In fiscal 2018, the U.S. plans to spend approximately $892 billion on military activities. That amount includes a base budget of $616.9 billion for the Department of Defense (DOD), along with another $69 billion in overseas contingency operations (OCO) for the DOD to fight the War on Terror. An additional $181.3 billion is allotted to the Department of Veterans Affairs, the State Department, Homeland Security, the FBI, the Department of Justice for cybersecurity, and the National Nuclear Security Agency of the Department of Energy, which oversees our nuclear weapons arsenal. An additional $18.7 billion goes to the State Department and Homeland Security to fund their activities in the War on Terror.

A few important facts lend perspective to those figures:

1. Experts expect total military spending during this period to exceed $1 trillion.

2. This budget, and the accompanying spending, is more than the military spending of the next ten countries combined.

3. America maintains more than 800 military bases around the world. This is far more than all the other countries of the world combined.

4. The United States has not participated in a declared war since World War II ended in 1945.

5. America has 19 aircraft carriers, including 10 massive ones, while the rest of the world's navies have a total of 12, and none in the "massive" category.

6. At an estimated cost of $400 billion over ten years and up to a trillion dollars over the next thirty years. The budget above includes provisions specified by Congress to safeguard our military bases from climate change. Facilities in the 100-year floodplain must be designed to remain functional with ocean levels rising two feet, despite the Trump administration's insistence that climate change is "just a hoax."

7. Over the next few years, the Navy is upgrading our submarine fleet from the Ohio-class to Columbia-class at a cost of more than $100 billion, and Northrop-Grumman will build a new long-range bomber, the B-21, to replace the B-52 and B-1 fleet at a cost in excess of $55 billion.

8. America currently spends approximately $2,000 per person on "defense" per year, according to the International Institute for Strategic Studies. China, with a population of 1.35 billion people, spends just $83 per person. Russia spends $475, Saudi Arabia about $2,100, the U.K $900, France $797, Japan under $400 per person, and Germany about $540.

9. All of the military spending in the world was estimated at just over $2.0 trillion dollars in 2017. The United States spent $610 billion, or 35.0% of that total. China was second at $228 B, or 13.0%, Saudi Arabia was third at $69.4 B, or 4.0%, Russia was fourth at $66.3 B and 3.8%, India came fifth at $63.9B and 3.7%, France was sixth at $57B and 3.3%, the U.K. seventh at $47.2B and 2.7%, Japan was eighth at $45.4B and 2.6%, Germany ninth at $44.3B and 2.5% of the total, South Korea was tenth at $39.2B and 2.3%, Brazil was eleventh at $29.3B and 1.7%, Italy nearly tied for eleventh with $29.2B and 1.7%, Australia came in thirteenth at $27.5B and 1.6%, Canada was fourteenth at $20.6B and 1.2%, and Turkey was fifteenth at $18.2B and 1.0%. Please note that North Korea and Iran don't even make the list of the top fifteen. (www.SIPRI.org)

10. In Chapter 12 we noted that in 2004, somewhere between $6.6 and over $18 billion in $100 bills were loaded onto pallets, flown to Iraq aboard 21 C-130 cargo planes, and promptly disappeared. Congress, ignoring its constitutional role of overseeing the Pentagon, has never investigated. One can only presume that this is considered just "a cost of doing business."

Looking closely at item #9 above, we can see that the money spent by the United States on military equipment and activities, $610 billion, is greater than the spending of the next 11 countries combined ($605.5 billion). Using 2018 data, we see that we spend another $269 billion on military topics that SIPRI doesn't even count. While the politicians in Washington contemplate cutting or abolishing expenditures to address climate change, health care, education, Medicaid, Medicare, Social Security, and our country's infrastructure, it is time for the American people to look at this ridiculous imbalance and complain. If we cut our basic military spending in half (to $305 billion using SIPRI's 2017 numbers), we would still spend more than China and Russia combined.

The total interest due on our national debt in 2019 will be $67,018,850,756.40. That's more than $67 billion, or more than Russia will spend on military matters.

Commenting on the national debt of more than $21 trillion on Truth-dig.com in November of 2018, comedian Lee Camp attempted to describe just how much money $21 trillion dollars might be. He notes that the GDP of the United States is $18.6 trillion, and the total amount of money invested in the stock market is $30 trillion. The calculator I use to track the family bills doesn't have that kind of capacity, but Camp's tells him if $1000 bills were stacked on top of each other, *twenty-one* trillion dollars would create a stack 1323 miles high! Camp also suggests that a worker earning $40,000 a year would require 25 million years to accumulate *one* trillion dollars, or 525 million years to earn $21 trillion. I envy Lee Camp his calculator, and his patience.

Perhaps it is time to look at what we are getting for our money.

Incredible as it seems, the Pentagon's spending has never been audited. In 2009 Congress passed a formal law that required the Defense Department to be prepared for a full audit by 2017. In 2011, Obama's Secretary of Defense Leon Panetta ordered that key areas of the department's books be available for audit by 2014. It didn't happen. However, also in 2011, the DFAS office in Columbus, Ohio made errors totaling $1.6 trillion, (that's trillion with a TR), in Air Force financial records, an amount that far exceeded the Air Force's total annual budget for the year! DFAS is the Defense Finance and Accounting Service, an agency of the Department of Defense established in 1991. It is an internal accounting department tasked with monitoring the financial management within the DOD.

Ahhh, but $1.6 trillion is chump change. Hidden somewhere in the dark corners of the Pentagon, in dusty shoe boxes, desk drawers, under couch cushions, or maybe even in a few generals' or admirals' Swiss bank accounts, there is a pile of missing money 1323 miles high. In 2016 (when Obama was still President), Mark Skidmore, a Professor of Economics at Michigan State University learned that a Department of Defense Office of Inspector General report had found $6.5 trillion in unaccounted-for Pentagon spending in the year 2015 alone! Skidmore was incredulous, as that amount is more than the gross domestic product of the entire United Kingdom. A bean-counter at the highest professional level, Skidmore did some investigating, examining a variety of government websites dating back to 1968. With the assistance of Catherine Austin Fitts, a former assistant secretary in the Department of Housing and Urban Development, Skidmore assembled a collection of official government documents revealing that "unsupported adjustments" totaling $21 trillion had been reported to the DOD and HUD through the years 1998 to 2015! This enormous story was published by *Forbes* magazine on December 8, 2017, and backed up by a very detailed article in *The Nation* on January 7, 2019.

On November 15, 2018 it was announced that the Pentagon had failed its first-ever audit. A small army of auditors, headed up it seems by the prestigious firm Ernst & Young, announced that they had reached a point where they could go no further. The DOD's records, they said, were "riddled with so many bookkeeping deficiencies, irregularities, and errors that a reliable audit was simply impossible."

Is this an ironic coincidence or what? The national debt is $21.8 trillion, and the Pentagon can't tell us where $21 trillion of its funds have gone.

Skidmore found that in 2015 the army was allocated $122 billion as an annual budget, but the Treasury Department made a cash deposit of $794.8 billion to the army's account. That amount was larger than the Pentagon's entire military appropriation for the year, and at the same time the army records alone showed accounts payable, or bills due, of $929.3 billion. What in the world were they buying? And from whom? The most questionable items were a large number of "unsupported adjustments," or sums of taxpayer money that disappeared by "adjusting" entries to reports and journals. Skidmore says he found unorthodox bookkeeping practices "so obtuse" that it was simply impossible to discover exactly where that $21 trillion was pilfered from, or where it went. Thousands of records had simply disappeared. It is possible some of the money was used for legitimate purposes, but it is also possible that some or all of it disappeared illegitimately.

This is nothing new. *The Nation's* article points out that Donald Rumsfeld, secretary of Defense under George W. Bush, and his notable extremely hawkish Vice President Dick Cheney, told a press conference on September 10, 2001 that "according to some estimates we cannot track $2.3 trillion in transactions" by the DOD, which had a total budget of $313 billion that year. America's adversary, Rumsfeld said, was not China or Russia. "It's closer to home: It's the Pentagon bureaucracy," he warned. Rumsfeld's statement might have attracted far more attention in the press had not the U.S. come under attack the next day, commonly known as 9-11. There has never been any official explanation of where the missing money went.

To quote the article in *The Nation*: "For decades, the DOD's leaders and accountants have been perpetuating a gigantic, unconstitutional accounting fraud, deliberately cooking the books to mislead the Congress and drive the DOD's budgets ever higher... DOD has literally been making up numbers in its annual financial reports to Congress – representing trillions of dollars' worth of seemingly nonexistent transactions... according to government records and interviews with current and former DOD officials, congressional sources, and independent experts."

The *Forbes* article points out that after Mark Skidmore began looking into these matters, "the Pentagon response was stonewalling and concealment." Detailed reports, replete with errors and dead-end adjustments, have been removed from the DOD inspector general's website. The unsupported and unexplained adjustments were 54 times the level of total spending authorized by Congress. Remarkably, Congress has ignored this incredible discrepancy.

The Pentagon says it is "unable" to keep track of its finances, hardware, weapons, ammunition, wages, or any other expenses. The Department of Defense, headquartered in that iconic five-sided building, is the only area of the entire federal government that has never complied with the law that requires all federal departments to submit annual audits of their budgeted operations. A July 2016 report by the Department of Defense's own inspector general found that the Pentagon's Finance and Accounting Service (DFAS) based in Indianapolis could not account for $6.5 trillion in 2015 year-end expenses to the Army General Fund!

While there are no solid indications of theft or embezzlement in those reports, it is obvious that the military routinely avoids providing financial tracking, journals, purchase orders, itemized bills, transaction dates, or any documentation whatsoever that might provide trillion-dollar tracks in the DOD budget snows. More than 16,500 documents and records disappeared from the Defense Departmental Reporting System in the third quarter of 2015 alone, with no explanation of why they were removed or where they went.

In an extensive 2013 report called "Unaccountable," investigative reporter Scot Paltrow of Reuters documented an environment of bold and blatant fraud and abuse. Paltrow summed up his findings writing: "For two decades, the U.S. military has been unable to submit to an audit, flouting federal law and concealing waste and fraud totaling billions of dollars." All of this kinda makes me wonder what they're teaching at the military academies. A few years ago, West Point announced it was discontinuing its ethics classes.

The 2016 OIG (Office of the Inspector General) report concludes that the unexplained and missing trillions of dollars are the result of the Department of Defense's "failure to correct system deficiencies." Next time the family checkbook doesn't balance, try using that excuse with your mortgage company.

The Government Accounting Office (GAO), the watchdog of federal government spending, says the major obstacle to controlling government spending is "serious financial management problems at the Department of Defense that made its financial statements unauditable." The Defense Department claims "it is not feasible to deploy a vast number of accountants to manually reconcile our books." When Al Capone used a similar excuse, he ended up in jail. In December of 2012, when the federal government was at the precipice of the "fiscal cliff," the Department of Defense declined to explain to the House of Representatives Appropriations Committee, which controls federal spending, how and where it planned to cut to meet "fiscal cliff" requirements. The arrogant Generals do not feel that the American people have any right to know how much they spend or where they spend it, and there is little pressure from Congress to evaluate or rein in military spending.

The author contacted his Virginia Senator, Tim Kaine, concerning these reports. In a return letter dated December 17, 2018 Senator Kaine reassured me that "Congress is concerned about the impact that budgetary pressures and continued combat have had on the readiness and combat effectiveness of the Armed Forces.... The Fiscal Year 2019 National Defense Authorization Act (NDAA) authorizes critical funding for the Department of Defense (DOD) to rebuild a ready and capable force by increasing the strength of our naval forces necessary for power projection, procuring combat aircraft and munitions, and reducing the shortfall in end strength... Throughout my time in the Senate, I have worked to remove non-strategic sequester cuts and budget uncertainty, which has hurt Virginia, our national security, and the economy.... This year's defense authorization identifies efficiencies to make the best use of taxpayer dollars and authorizes approximately $175 million for 12 critical military construction projects throughout the Commonwealth at Fort Belvoir, Fort A.P. Hill, Dam Neck, Joint Base Langley-Eustis, and other locations... It is important we make smart budgeting decisions consistent with a sound defense strategy."

There is no shortage of funding for America's military. When it comes to acquiring hardware, it seems we strive to outdistance our own shadow in terms of military preparedness. The Pentagon and the Joint Chiefs of Staff have said they don't need or want the F-35 fighter, additional upgrades to the M1 Abrams tank that will cost us $3.5 billion, the global Hawk drone, the C-27J Spartan transport aircraft, or plans for an East Coast missile defense system with a $3.6 billion price tag that General Martin Dempsey, at the time the Chairman of the Joint Chiefs of Staff, described as "unnecessary." The Pentagon has recommended cost cutting that would save at least $487 billion over 10 years, but the same Congressmen who call for cuts to food stamps, education, Medicare, and Social Security make darn sure their pork barrels and earmarks are included in the budget, and all those projects mentioned above are on track to be built.

It has long been the position of Congress and the Senate, Democrats and Republicans alike, that we "must" increase defense spending every year, supposedly because we are in jeopardy of "falling behind." We may be falling behind on the interest payments on our national debt, but that's certainly not going to be helped by shoveling more billions of dollars toward the Pentagon.

Every president and political and military leader praises America's military as "the finest fighting force in the history of the world," as President Barack Obama did in his 2016 State of the Union address. Obama also described our armed forces as "the best-led, best-trained, best-equipped military in human history." Certainly, it is the best-funded. We can only suppose that a large portion of those missing trillions have actually gone toward equipping our armed forces. Clearly, they have too much hardware, allowing them to donate large amounts of equipment to police departments across the country, even as our troops are at war in the Middle East.

As American citizens, we appreciate the kid next door who volunteers for service in the armed forces. His, or her, bravery and sacrifice are commendable. We must, however, never forget that taxpayers are footing the bill for all this armed prowess. It's a very different subject, especially if embezzlement or theft are being committed. With over $21 trillion in national debt in 2019, many anxious Americans, especially outside of the Washington beltway, are casting worried glances the Pentagon's way. If our military is compared to the family car in the driveway, we have purchased a top-of-the-line Rolls-Royce with all the accessories, but ol' Betsy is performing like a dilapidated, worn-out used car. For all the money we have spent, and are intending to spend, we cannot seem to get to the corner store.

While the Pentagon spends more than half of all our country's discretionary budget and maintains more than 800 bases and facilities around the world, they are completely incapable of explaining how our troops are provided with toilet paper. They spend enormous amounts of our taxpayer dollars indiscriminately. In today's America, the ultimate status symbol is not a Rolex watch or a Rolls-Royce, it is a Defense contract, a license to make money. The good ol' boy deals in the millions are filled with legendary overspending like sixteen hundred-dollar toilet seats and seven hundred-dollar claw hammers. The Center for Public Integrity reports that a partly-plastic roller wheel with a market value of seven dollars at Lowe's or The Home Depot is billed to the Defense Department at $1,678! In Afghanistan, the Pentagon found that defense contractor companies had ordered $138 million worth of spare parts, despite the fact that ample stores of those parts were stacked in warehouses in-country. Another unit, the Combined Security Transition Command – Afghanistan ordered $370 million worth of spare parts for vehicles we had supplied to the Afghan National Army, but it was unable to account for $230 million of them when audited. The simple fact is, we the people can no longer afford to watch as our government borrows trillions only to have them disappear into the nooks and crannies of the Pentagon.

Pentagon generals have hired vast numbers of contract firms to do much of the support work for our wars in Iraq and Afghanistan. Conveniently, the Pentagon does not have to report the number of contracted employees as part of its war zone troop counts. Companies like Blackwater, (which, after well-deserved exposure of its crimes and abuses, has changed its corporate name to Academi, and has been sold), has provided "security services" for the CIA for $250 million a year, (I can see no reason why the CIA would be insecure!), and for the State Department for another $92 million. The founder and former head of the company, Eric Prince, has pressured his friend President Trump to turn over every aspect of the wars in Iraq and Afghanistan to his company, which would allow our armies to come home.

Meanwhile, the brother of Secretary of Education Betsy DeVos, contributor to the Trump campaign, and a frequent guest on far-right Breitbart radio, Prince has announced that he will be training Chinese troops at two Blackwater-style camps. There is a possibility that these activities will violate sanctions against providing military services or equipment to China. Many of our contractor personnel know no loyalties but to adrenalin and money.

The Pentagon cannot tell us how many private contractor companies it employs, but the number is thought to be in excess of 600,000! The 2006 film *Iraq for Sale: The War Profiteers* by Brave New Films reveals the scale of corruption and profiteering, and the poor performance of four major defense contractor companies – Blackwater, K.B.R.-Halliburton, CACI, and Titan who were hired to support the American forces in Iraq. These companies contracted to do "virtually everything except the actual killing," including food services, laundry, housing, security, intelligence-gathering, garbage pick-up, and interrogations. The film reveals their high-cost but inferior performance, shoddy materials and workmanship, and negligence that often jeopardized American fighting forces or denied them the few comforts the Pentagon sought to supply to our troops in the war zone. Former Vice President Dick Cheney is no longer head of Halliburton, but he gets an annual check from the company. It must be a big one.

A Pentagon review in 2011 found that service contractor companies had become "increasingly unaffordable." Why do we have 600,000 "unaffordable" contractor companies working for the Pentagon? No one seems to be questioning these costly transactions, and no one is really sure how many defense contractors are currently on the Pentagon payroll, but if we cut defense spending to half its present amount, I predict the howling from those defense contractors would tell us exactly how many there might be.

The 2016 book *The Burn Pits* by Joseph Hickman reveals the very troubling history of severe respiratory illnesses, cancers, and deaths among our forces deployed to Iraq and Afghanistan. It seems the military have to keep their garbage incineration pits within their compounds, and any and all manner of trash are burned, from toxic waste, oil, rubber, asphalt shingles, tires, pesticides, asbestos, chemically treated uniforms, plastics, medical waste, even body parts. They smolder constantly, emitting thick clouds of dark black smoke that has had a disastrous effect upon our soldiers. It is thought likely that the burn pits were responsible for the brain cancer that killed Major Joseph R. "Beau" Biden, the son of Vice President Joe Biden in 2015. Many soldiers have suffered from various illnesses that seem to be caused by breathing the smoke from the burn pits, but the DOD denies there are any health-related issues related to the burn pits, and the VA has denied all veterans' disability claims. However, technically the burn pits have been outlawed since 1978 when a DOD report stated that open air incineration of trash on overseas bases would be allowed only on a temporary basis until high-temp mechanical incinerators can be installed. Of course, our military has been in Afghanistan for 17 years and Iraq for 15. The definition of "temporary" is being contested on many fronts.

The burn pits have been and are operated by the infamous Halliburton Corporation and its spin-off, KBR. When the U.S. invaded Afghanistan, those two companies were awarded a no-bid contract to provide services for $50 million, and that was just for starters. When Vice President Dick Cheney left Halliburton to join the George W. Bush ticket, he received a corporate severance package worth $36 million, plus another $20 million in stock options. In the first ten years of the war in Iraq, KBR was awarded nearly $40 billion in contracts. When President Obama's troop withdrawal began, KBR continued to bill the government for personnel who weren't there, phantom charges of between $193 million and $300 million. Defective showers constructed by KBR electrocuted at least ten American soldiers in Iraq, and KBR's records show that hundreds were shocked due to defective electrical wiring installed by the company.

When one Pennsylvania family attempted to sue for negligent homicide, "patriotic" KBR claimed the case should be tried under Iraqi law because the incident happened in Iraq. It was estimated that there were 90,000 showers to be inspected in Iraq. It's good to know that our invading army enjoys the opportunity to be fresh and clean during their activities in that hot desert environment.

The author would be remiss not to mention a long and contentious debate over the Incinerator at Radford Army Ammunition Plant in southwest Virginia. Operated by defense contractor BAE, Radford is acknowledged to be the single greatest polluter in the state of Virginia. Plans to construct a closed incinerator are discussed and batted back and forth endlessly, while the plant continues to burn refuse chemicals from its ammunition manufacturing in outdoor "burn pans." Of course, the smoke from those pans is uncontrolled. The DOD regulations for outside burning of refuse listed in *The Burn Pits* have never been enforced in Virginia, let alone on overseas bases.

While this chapter has been focused upon the Pentagon and military spending, it is also necessary to consider a few other significant expense items. Our federal government currently includes 17 separate intelligence agencies. Can you name them?

For the record, they are the Central Intelligence Agency (CIA); the National Security Agency (NSA); the Defense Intelligence Agency; the Federal Bureau of Investigation (FBI); the Department of Homeland Security Office of Intelligence Analysis; the State Department Bureau of Intelligence and Research; the Treasury Department Office of Intelligence and Analysis; the Drug Enforcement Administration Office of National Security Intelligence; the Department of Energy Office of Intelligence and Counterintelligence; the National Reconnaissance Office; the National Geospatial Intelligence Agency; Air Force Intelligence, Surveillance, and Intelligence; the Office of Naval Intelligence; Army Military Intelligence; Marine Corps Intelligence; Coast Guard Intelligence; and, to coordinate all of these disparate operations, the Office of the Director of National Intelligence (ODNI).

Do we really need 17? What does the National Reconnaissance Office do that the CIA and NSA don't? How exactly have the 17 organizations benefitted us over the past fifty or sixty years? Do they cooperate, work together, and freely exchange information? The total budget(s) for these operations are estimated to be about $70 billion a year in addition to what is covered in the Defense budget. What are we getting for our tax dollars?

Isn't it about time we recognize that many of our worst enemies are lurking in Washington, D.C.? When we've heard it from Donald Rumsfeld, we have to believe it's true! Unless they are profiting from this corruption, no American taxpayer approves of this type of highway robbery. It's not a partisan problem, but one can't help wondering why the "conservatives" who favor tax cuts and smaller government don't call attention to this atrocious waste of our tax dollars from corruption and profiteering?

There is no single political party to blame for our exorbitant national debt, but there is also no political party willing to take on the power brokers and solve the real problems. With a national debt over 20 trillion dollars, you would think someone would interrupt this grand larceny before the country goes bankrupt. Sooner or later, the American people have to ask, "Who are these guys?" running the Pentagon and our wars and "conflicts." Our military is fat, bloated, and corrupt … and with the exception of "Operation Desert Storm" which was a virtually uncontested skirmish, it hasn't won a war since World War II, more than 70 years ago!

Throughout history, great empires have claimed that they are forces for good, and of course the United States justifies its "exceptional" worldwide military activity as being moral and beneficial when the actual results of most of its actions since World War II have been military failures with devastating results to the countries we are supposedly helping. The war in Vietnam was supposed to stop the spread of Communism and install a democratic form of government. In the end, Vietnam was united under a Communist flag, and so were Laos and Cambodia. Millions died or were horribly wounded, and vast areas of all three countries were destroyed or left unworkable due to chemical poisoning or unexploded ordnance.

In Iraq, American intervention has totally disrupted a society that was working; our firepower has destroyed homes and businesses, schools and medical facilities, and most of the worthwhile achievements of the Iraqi population. Sadly, America's military adventures have replaced all that the citizens of Iraq had accomplished before we invaded them with piles of rubble, anxiety and fear. The exodus of millions of refugees from Iraq, Afghanistan, Syria, and Libya has overwhelmed Europe. Those refugees are the direct result of America's misguided and incompetent military adventures and their effects upon those countries, and the Trump administration has chosen to deny immigration of the refugees, supposedly to "keep America safe." I suggest it is also to keep America uninformed. The Generals, with all their "surges" and firepower, and all their attempts to create a benchmark democracy in the Middle East, have given rise to the incredibly brutal Islamic State, or Isis, and a worldwide assortment of other spin-off terror groups.

The lessons of Vietnam? It looks to me like the American people learned nothing, and the profiteers, bureaucrats, and crooks learned how to perfect their scams and increase their dirty profits while generation after generation of soldiers and civilians bleed and die. Like Vietnam, once again we don't know why our young people are at war, and we don't know where trillions of dollars are disappearing to. Isn't it time we insist upon real audits, controls, and cutbacks? Where, and why, are we spending at a rate that is out of proportion with all the other countries on the planet? And, how can we bring that spending into line? Today's high school and college students will have to deal with those questions and bring the United States back to fiscal responsibility, or our country will perish. Perhaps there is an opportunity for some aggressive young entrepreneur to invent and market a hand-held calculator with the capacity to work with numbers in the trillions. Realistically, that might be far easier than trying to change the culture in the U.S. Capital and the Pentagon. It appears that the costs of militarism might be a greater threat to America than the Viet Cong, Al Quaeda, or Isis.

America spends more dollars on military equipment and adventuring than any nation in history, but those efforts have done little to further the goal of peace on earth. Why do the lessons of Vietnam matter? Because while all the activities and travesties listed in this chapter are still going on, teachers across America have to go to discount stores and buy pencils for their students out of their own pockets. When will it ever end?

318

Recommended Reading:

SIPRI, the Stockholm International Peace Research Institute. (www.SIPRI.org)

www.InternationalComparisons.org is a research site that compares the quality of life in a number of countries. Their data offers a thought-provoking look at what we, the people are getting for our tax dollars, along with those trillions of borrowed dollars.

Chapter 22

SUMMING UP: MY MESSAGE

Patriotism is your conviction that this country is superior to all other countries because you were born in it.

– George Bernard Shaw

We need to decide that we will not go to war, whatever reason is conjured up by the politicians or the media, because war in our time is always indiscriminate, a war against innocents, a war against children. War is terrorism, magnified a hundred times.

– Howard Zinn

As I said at the start of this book, I am the stereotypical angry and bitter Vietnam veteran. Prior to this chapter, I have tried to present history in the form of historical facts and personal experience. Before I end this book, I need to speak from the heart about the lessons I have drawn from my two years in Southeast Asia and a life of curiosity, of investigations and conversations, and reading extensively about the history of Vietnam, the Cold War, the assassinations of the 1960s, and the later events that have shaped American and world history throughout our lifetime. I am a curmudgeonly old man with my mind made up. I encourage the reader to explore your own world, turn over a few rocks, read some books and form your own conclusions.

I have learned that when a person has witnessed the madness of war, their memories are usually corrosive to the soul and a ponderous burden to carry around throughout the rest of one's life. Shouldn't this be obvious? Clearly, to humanity's great shame, it is only rarely acknowledged, if at all. I acknowledge that war and war-making are good business.

I've learned that people are basically the same around the world. There is good and evil in every community and every country. The majority of the world's people are good, kind, caring souls who strive to provide themselves and their families with shelter, security, adequate food, and a brighter future. Still, we can never forget that there are evildoers, misguided folks, tyrants and zealots. The great technological advancements since the Second World War have given the bad guys frightening abilities to do harm on a grand scale. As baby boomers, we were fortunate to grow up in an environment devoid of terrorism. Today, those seem like the proverbial good old days.

I carried a Ford Motor Company business card for a time, and proudly! I had no idea that Henry Ford, one of America's great industrialists and business leaders, despised democracy and the concept of one man, one vote, or that he wanted to bring Fascism to America. I did not know that many of America's most prominent businessmen agreed with Ford, and conspired to install a dictator and align America with Fascism and the Nazis prior to World War II. Why wasn't that taught in high school?

We have named one of America's great airports after John Foster Dulles who, along with his brother Allen, gained wealth and power by laundering vast quantities of the Nazis' stolen loot, acts recognized and described as "treason" but never prosecuted. They prevented many of the architects of the Holocaust from being tried for their inhuman crimes, and even brought some of those notorious mass murderers to America and installed them in government and defense operations. Many historians believe Allen Dulles was deeply implicated in the assassination of JFK, to prevent him from waging peace. I have been distraught since I discovered the obscure history of that coup attempt during the time of FDR, or realized that the threatening and pernicious sentiments that drove that pro-Fascist movement are alive and well in the hearts of many American businessmen and politicians today.

I am dismayed to learn that some of the same secret opponents of democracy created the Cold War and tried their damnedest to initiate nuclear wars against Cuba, the Soviet Union, Communist China, and even Vietnam ... while hundreds of thousands of Americans were there! I am amazed to discover that these traitorous warmongers had unmistakable links to the assassinations of President Kennedy, Martin Luther King, Robert Kennedy, and the overthrow and murders of many duly-elected heads of state around the world. They fabricated the war in Vietnam to enhance their careers, and profited handsomely by introducing air transport to benefit another group of corrupt "businessmen" setting up worldwide distribution avenues for heroin, opium, and other drugs from the fertile fields of Southeast Asia to the world's drug markets. Then, they kept the war going long after it was obvious it couldn't be won so they could continue to wallow in illicit profits of enormous proportions.

In far-flung corners of the world like Chile, the Congo, Guatemala, El Salvador, Iran, and Nicaragua, they have spread their tyrannical political philosophies at the point of a gun, maximizing profits for Defense contractor corporations, gun runners, and always, it seems, drug traffickers. The ghosts of more than three million Southeast Asian peasants are a stark testimony to this dark side of "big business."

Today we are engaged in an even longer, costlier, and more corrupt war in another of the planet's most fertile drug-growing regions. Coincidence? We must accept the fact that America is in the business of death and destruction, that dollars make anything palatable, and then we must return to the basic principles of allowing all the citizens of the world to seek life, liberty, and the pursuit of happiness... and we must oppose, not aid, anyone who would infringe upon those rights regardless of the dollars at stake.

In Washington, today's political parties are primarily acting as carnival barkers for big business interests, while American democracy has been rendered almost obsolete and legislated nearly to death. The Supreme Court's 2010 decision, Citizens United vs. Federal Election Commission, has allowed corporations the "same rights and privileges as people," allowing business interests to spend enormous sums of money influencing politicians. As long as political power in America is for sale to the highest bidder, any suggestion of democracy is terribly unrealistic and misleading. We continue to teach our children that we live in a Democracy. We can only hope they believe it, and that they will take back power from the corporations. Once in a while we still see voters stirred up to the point where an election actually brings about change. Democracy is like muscle. It can be fed and exercised to become incredibly strong, or it can be neglected and allowed to become weak and ineffective. We have to hope our young people can keep American Democracy going.

It is a testament to the true American spirit that a vast literature of the war in Vietnam has poured forth from witnesses as diverse as Marilyn Young, Ron Kovic, Gloria Emerson, Daniel Ellsberg, Morley Safer, Frances Fitzgerald, Robert Mason, Philip Caputo, David Halberstam, C.D.B. Bryan, Bernard Fall, Patricia Walsh, Neil Sheehan, Myra MacPherson,

Wallace Terry, Colonel David Hackworth, Steve Mason, Arnold Isaacs, Archimedes Patti, Seymour Hersh, Lynda Van Devanter, Larry Heinemann, Oliver Stone, Jerry Lembcke, W.D. Ehrhart, Stanley Karnow, Christian Appy, David Harris, Arnold Isaacs, Tim O'Brien, and Nick Turse, to name only a few.

All were astounded by the truths of Vietnam, but they knew those truths must be told. What they (we) have seen and experienced in Vietnam, or in the halls of power in Washington, D.C., has illuminated the darkest corners of reality that hide under the thick, dark blankets of "patriotism" and "defense." Their stories speak of heroism and bravery, but they also reek of disillusion, corruption, treachery, foolishness, betrayal, suffering and waste. They do not find fault with the young, lower-ranking men who went to Vietnam. Most have recorded painful passages to describe the suffering and destruction they witnessed. All are hopeful that the accumulated weight of their individual observations and testimonies might turn the tide of public opinion and bring about changes that would ensure that nothing like America's war in Vietnam will ever happen again.

I believe the series of Apollo spaceflights to the moon and back were a high point of American history, and the Vietnam War was the beginning of the decline and fall of the United States and its experiment in representative government. I believe the assassination of John F. Kennedy was essentially a coup d'etat, a takeover of the United States by the military-industrial-intelligence complex, aided by a massive cover-up in our mainstream media. Certainly, since that terrible day the U.S. government has rarely proven beneficial to the people of the United States, or to the world at large.

As I read history, we admire constructive acts and individuals. From the ancient cave man who discovered fire to the Egyptians who built the pyramids, then on to the ancient Greeks and Romans with their architecture, their arts, language, and literature, to the Renaissance, and on to the age of mechanics and technology, the human race celebrates those who contribute to mankind's overall good. We admire the great artists and thinkers, Socrates and Plato, Leonardo Da Vinci, Thomas Edison, Marconi, Madame Curie, Karl Benz, Mozart, the Wright brothers, Beethoven, Mark Twain, Bach, Lennon and McCartney, Hemingway, Thomas Jefferson, George Lucas, Abraham Lincoln, Walt Disney, Steven Spielberg, Albert Einstein and many, many more.

This country went from horse-drawn carts to steam boats, cross-country railroads, automobiles and interstate highways, to biplanes and supersonic aircraft, and ultimately the lunar lander and a satellite sending back close-up photos of Pluto. We have gone from quill pens to the telegraph, to television, Microsoft Windows and I-Pads, and cellular telephones that can control the home thermostat and feed the family dog from the other side of the continent. We have progressed from candle light and torches to the light bulb, glowing neon, and LEDs; from fireplaces to central air conditioning, from witch doctors and "bleeding" procedures to heart transplants and incredible microscopic surgeries.

But there is another side to the human psyche, and we do not admire the men who were destructive. Adolf Hitler, of course, and Charles Manson, John Wilkes Booth, Jesse James, Idi Amin, Machine Gun Kelly, Pol Pot, Joseph Stalin, Osama Bin Laden, the mad scientists who developed the atomic bomb or chemical warfare, or the twisted ideologues who created Auschwitz or Bergen-Belsen.

We have seen great evil in our time. Richard Nixon's "enemies list," the string of burglaries by his "Plumbers," and attempts to assassinate the character of his political opponents while he destroyed the Constitution are examples, but Nixon was allowed to resign and go away to write books and live comfortably. The most blatant and evil American personalities have rarely been held accountable. As this is written, President Donald Trump and his cabinet of anarchists seem to be destroying much of the American framework in a mad orgy of contempt. History will record the degree of their success.

I am troubled by the huge amount of human toil, wealth, attention, resources, hard work, energy, and curiosity committed to discovering and perfecting better methods of killing or wounding our fellow man and destroying all he has built. What if that energy and all those resources were re-directed toward curing diseases, educating the illiterate, feeding the hungry, nurturing the children, or rebuilding our nation's infrastructure?

"Ahh!" You say, "But those things don't pay!" What might happen if we abandoned our rampant militarism, cut 50% or more of our funding from the destructive, and reallocated it to the constructive? We could make building bridges, healing the sick, reducing homelessness or teaching children more lucrative than selling weapons to the Pentagon... or to the terrorists overseas. We could rebuild our manufacturing base and put Americans back to work. We could afford universal health care like all the other major countries of the world, and I'll bet we could find the cures for cancer, heart disease, Lou Gehrig's Disease, AIDS and many other afflictions a lot sooner. We could bring smiles, alleviate suffering, heal wounds, and possibly even restore the planet's environment. We could welcome immigrants and help them to become established as contributing American citizens. We could… we can (!) return to a constructive national agenda

When I was an adolescent, before Vietnam, my country stood for hope. It offered a sanctuary where humanity and kindness were available to all, where the constructive pursuits could flourish. After the assassinations of John and Robert Kennedy, of Martin Luther King, Malcolm X and John Lennon, after Hiroshima, Nagasaki, and Vietnam, our country has changed drastically. I am not "just" a Vietnam veteran who was too poor or stupid to find a draft deferment and escape the war. I have read extensively about Vietnam, about Panama, Bosnia, Somalia, Iran, Iraq, Afghanistan, Syria, Yemen, corruption in Washington, and all the American history that has happened during my lifetime. I have talked with the veterans returned from Iraq and Afghanistan, good men and women who have told me about today's American Way of Waging War.

We have seen the President of the United States supporting "freedom fighters" in Central America whose agenda was precisely the same as that of the Taliban in Afghanistan: kill all the teachers and doctors, destroy the schools and hospitals, eradicate literature, history, music, and enslave the peasants. I have seen our government leaders condoning torture! I have children and grandchildren. I fear for them, and their futures. I have become an opponent of militarism and war. I must try.

We don't begin to know the real scope of the intelligence community's "covert" actions. The heads of the CIA and NSA are not elected, but they are empowered to make policy and even intervene in the affairs of other nations. Today we have more than 70,000 covert "Special Forces" guerrilla warriors at work around the world. Today the CIA and NSA, along with some unknown combination of those other 15 intelligence operations, have become a rogue 4th branch of government, unelected, and defiantly resistant to any oversight, let alone checks and balances. When American forces arrived in Afghanistan in 2001, the farming of heroin poppies had been all but eradicated. Today it is thriving, at levels never seen before. Perhaps it's just coincidence…

As I read history, societies that have been destructive, particularly those that have tried to conquer the world militarily, like Greece under Alexander the Great, Rome under the Caesars, or Germany under Hitler's Nazis, have *all* ultimately failed miserably and seen their influence disappear. Other great evildoers such as Stalin, Vlad the Impaler, Mussolini, Pol Pot, or Idi Amin destroyed their countries with their brutality. History is clear: violence and hate do not make a society successful. In fact, countries under totalitarian control rarely last long. Since the Vietnam War, there is a clear international perception that America's moral influence is deteriorating despite our increased militarism. It appears that we have abandoned our national standards of morality and attempted to bully the world with our guns, bombs, spooks and nukes.

I experienced war up close and this entire book is intended to tell you that there is nothing honorable or noble about war. I define war as the complete breakdown of all things civilized, and the utter failure of human beings to respect each other. I did what my country asked. I went, against my will, and one day long ago I saw a young woman, a civilian, explode, and the death spray from her body splashed hard across my face. No matter how many times I've washed my face over 50-odd years, I cannot wash those stains away. I pray that as we come to understand the history of lies, misrepresentations, and fabricated pretexts that our political leaders have fed us to rationalize far too many wars and military adventures in our lifetimes, one day soon the American people will rise up and say "No more!" "Not in our name!" I have faith it can happen. President Eisenhower, a 5-star General who had commanded all of the Allied forces in Europe in World War II, said: "*Indeed, I think that people want peace so much that one of these days governments had better get out of the way and let them have it.*"

My parents brought me up to recognize right and wrong. I was also influenced by the insights of John Lennon, Bob Dylan, Barry McGuire, Joan Baez, Paul Simon, John Fogerty, Bruce Springsteen, and Country Joe McDonald, and I'm darned proud to say so. I believe our wars in Vietnam, Iraq and Afghanistan have all been immoral, illegal, ill-conceived... and *unaffordable*. I love to imagine an America with universal health care, pothole-free super highways, the best educational system in the world, a thriving economy that rewards everyone proportionate to what they produce, but that takes care of our disadvantaged and affords them the very finest quality of life.

I have looked back at my military experiences, the things I saw in Vietnam, and I don't want my children or grandchildren to ever have to see anything so horrible... or so wrong! I pray for the time when Veterans Day will become unnecessary because there won't be any more veterans, and Armistice Day will return to being a celebration of *peace* in America, as it was originally intended. Like John Lennon, I oppose destruction as political or social activity, and I too *Imagine* all the people of the world living life in peace. I choose to work toward that end, and to stay separate from the folks who propose or support wars as if they might bring some benefit.

War is the surrender to hopelessness. The victims of war have cried out for justice since time began, and have been largely ignored. The purveyors of war have profited, and even more obscenely in recent years. Today, neocon candidates run for office on a platform of 100 years of permanent war as if that idea held some promise. PTSD, suicide, and desertion are at epidemic levels in today's militaristic environment. The lessons of Vietnam? They are so obvious, but largely ignored.

As I wrote in ... *and a hard rain fell*, one loves the sick child but curses the disease. I am not anti-American. Not at all. I believe America's militarism is a disease that is killing our country like a cancer. I believe that Capitalism must be regulated or it becomes a voracious wild animal preying upon us all. Our American for-profit health care system is a terrible example. Those who make money hurting other people, denying help to the oppressed, or putting a price on human kindness are the essence of evil.

If World War II was a "good war" and necessary to stop Hitler & Company's atrocities, the history sketched out in this book should be extremely troubling to the American public. Yes, Vietnam matters! If you think you can take American freedoms and democracy for granted, you are terribly mistaken. If you have read to this point, I hope you will be a little more skeptical and aware the next time you read a newspaper, watch the evening news on TV, or enter a voting booth. Please don't just take my word for any of this. I have included a huge bibliography of recommended books where you can learn much more and form your own opinions. Contrary to Donald Trump and Betsy DeVos, education is the most precious commodity of all, and education allows opinions to be based upon facts.

My baby boomer generation has seen so much history, both good and bad. I doubt that any other generation in human history has witnessed the technical progress, or the human history that we have experienced. Today, Vietnam Veterans Against the War (VVAW) are graying old men with a lot less hair than back in the day. Veterans For Peace has struggled to become an effective international voice against war. Iraq Veterans Against the War (IVAW) are speaking to a new generation, and telling a frightful new collection of truths.

America's war in Southeast Asia was a travesty and a tragedy. The history of the Vietnam War lies at our feet, fallen to the ground and broken into myriad pieces with a loud and dissonant clunk while all the king's horses and all the king's men have gone off to wage wars in other countries. Yes, those scattered pieces can be arranged to form a telling mosaic. Sadly, in far too many situations, we did not celebrate the true heroes of the Vietnam era. We did not incarcerate the corrupt. We had too little compassion for those that suffered. We watched the whole sordid business like it was a TV drama, and it was. We did not insist that the politicians, the businessmen, or the generals learn from their mistakes. We watched *Laugh In* and *The Smothers Brothers Comedy Hour* while napalm and white phosphorous bombs were falling upon Vietnamese schools, hospitals, and villages, killing millions of people. We listened to the Beatles and the Doors, but not to our veterans. We squandered our country's fortune, its wealth, its morality, and its humanity. We abandoned the American dream.

Make no mistake … it is not the veterans who have lied, who have misrepresented, or who have sold out. Our veterans are what they have always been … just common, everyday Americans caught up in something far bigger and more sinister than they ever imagined. Time and again they have gone to war, usually for all the right and honorable reasons, although some have been forced by economic situations beyond their influence or control. Far away from home, in an alien and terrifying environment, they have tried to make the best of a bad situation. Often betrayed, our veterans have generally tried to do the right thing, the honorable thing, even while surrounded by horror and suffering beyond imagination. And then they, or we, have come home from the wars, and tried to go on with the rest of our lives.

Far too many of us have come home changed, often unable to talk about what we've seen, or what it means. Yes, some of us are proud of what we've done. Many of us are proud of our individual acts, our integrity and humanity in the face of institutional brutality, but we are troubled by what we have seen. And, far too many have seen sights so awful, so unthinkable, that they cannot live with the knowledge. I have tried to resolve all this, and this book is the result. Today I choose to describe myself as an opponent of militarism and war. I hope that I honor my fellow veterans, and serve my country by doing so. And I also hope you will investigate, read and comprehend, discuss these issues, and consider what kind of country you want the United States of America to be in forty years when our grandchildren have inherited what we build for them today.

Chapter 23

AFTERWORD
"THANK YOU FOR YOUR SERVICE"

This piece was originally published as a letter to the editor of the Roanoke (Virginia) Times on Veterans Day, 2014. It has been widely reprinted since.

Please don't thank me for my service. I was taken against my will, yanked away from all the hopes and plans I had for my life, and made to see and experience things that contradicted anything and everything I had ever been taught about right and wrong. I heard the screams of someone dying, far away from home, a fragile human being blown apart, for no good reason. I saw burnt, bloodied, maimed children. And men, and women. I smelled the scent of open wounds, of flowing blood and burnt flesh. I felt the splatter of someone's loss of life as it exploded across my face, and no matter how many times I have washed my face over the past 47 years I cannot wash away that horrible stain. And you would thank me for that? I abandoned my morality. I lost my equilibrium.

I cannot tell you much of what I learned, but it wasn't worth a damned thing in the civilian workplace, in my baby's nursery, or at the checkout of the grocery store. It is only a spectre, a dense dark monster that pursues me in the night; that colors my view every day in ways no one else can see. Too many nights, almost half a century later, the horror twists my stomach into knots.

Oh, I know, you thank me because you don't know anything else to say. You still hope that it was all about freedom and democracy and good things like that, and not just about profits and power, authority and career advancement and some ancient goddamned illicit definition of the word masculine. It was about corporate profits and garish stripes sewn onto a sleeve, about genocide and the screwed-up notion that you can make a total stranger's existence better by killing or maiming him. I was playing in a rock 'n roll band when they came for me, reciting songs about understanding and brotherhood and love. They took me against my will, stripped me naked and beat me bloody, and they sent me to the other side of the world where death fell out of the sky and exploded, and its shards tore up anything and anybody they hit. I learned to lie as flat as possible on the mud, to will my body to become a puddle and sink down into the ooze. I learned to overcome the terror, the violent tremors, and I learned that none of those things matter when your number is up. I learned it happens to the very best guys, in the very worst ways, and there's nothing right or righteous about it; they were just wasted. Please, oh please don't thank me. If you want to express something, promise me you will get involved in the struggle to abolish wars. Nothing else will say that you understand.

Then, I will thank *you*.

John Ketwig

Chapter 24

RECOMMENDED READING: BIBLIOGRAPHY

"If the legacy of the Vietnam War is to offer any guidance, we need to complete the moral and political reckoning it awakened. … Only an honest accounting of our history will allow us to chart a new path in the world. The past is always speaking to us, if only we listen."
Christian G. Appy, from *American Reckoning: The Vietnam War and Our National Identity*

O ne of the primary inspirations for constructing this book was to provide information for students assigned to study or research the war in Vietnam and its various legacies and impacts upon America and Americans. At the same time, the author has endeavored not to mire the reader in a visual obstacle course of footnotes and specific references. I have found most of the information in this study by reading books, and I hope some readers, especially students, might be encouraged to search some of the following recommended books to look further for additional details or information. This bibliography contains an alphabetical listing of the books, and a few recordings, movies, and additional related media offerings from which I have sourced information, and the chapters to which they are relevant. I have not included page numbers, paragraphs, or computer sites, as I feel those details would only make this book more difficult to access, enjoy, understand, or appreciate. I believe the information throughout this book to be completely factual, and I have endeavored to present it in a manner that is historically relevant. Doing so, I am fully aware that many volumes concerning the history of the Vietnam War have seen things from different perspectives, or have presented their chosen facts for different purposes. That is, I believe, why libraries and book stores offer shelves of books about any given subject. In the end, I have been there, done that, and have studied extensively in an attempt to make sense of what I saw in Southeast Asia, and what I have learned since. So many of the books by Vietnam veterans attempt to answer the basic question: "Why?" I hope the information gathered here might prove helpful to a wide variety of readers.

Also, hoping to encourage the reader to read and explore, a number of these books are recommended, or even highly recommended, by the author. This collection will offer a wide variety of information on the Vietnam War, the times, and war in general. It should be noted that war is a horrible situation, and many of these books include adult language and themes. They are listed in alphabetical order, with indications of the chapters within this book where information from the book has been utilized. These books are all important. (For the author, it is wonderful to be retired and have time to read the many books that have been "waiting" for much too long.)

Bibliography:

A Bright Shining Lie: John Paul Vann and America in Vietnam, Random House, 1988, by Neil Sheehan. Chapter 11

A Farewell To Justice, Potomac Books, 2005, by Joamn Mellen. Chapter 4

A Reporter's Life, Knopf, 1996, by Walter Cronkite. Chapter 11

A World of Hurt, Greenleaf Enterprises, 2000, by Mary Reynolds Powell. Chapter 13

Achilles In Vietnam: Combat Trauma and the Undoing of Character, 1994, Touchstone / Simon & Schuster, by Jonathan Shay, M.D., Ph.D. Chapter 16

After Sorrow: An American Among the Vietnamese, Penguin Books, 1995, by Lady Borton. Chapter 17

Alice's Restaurant Massacree, recorded song from the album *Alice's Restaurant,* Warner Brothers records, 1967, by Arlo Guthrie. Chapter 10

Alice's Restaurant, American comedy film co-written and directed by Arthur Penn, 1969, based upon the song by Arlo Guthrie. Chapter 10

American Reckoning: The Vietnam War and Our National Identity, (**Recommended**), Viking, 2015, by Christian G. Appy. Chapter 15

America's Deadliest Export: Democracy, Zed Books Ltd., 2013, by William Blum. Chapter 16

America's Vietnam War, Clarion Books, 1992, by Elizabeth Becker. Chapter 11

A Piece of My Heart: The Stories of Twenty-Six American Women Who Served in Vietnam, Presidio Press, 1985, by Keith Walker. Chapter 16

A World of Hurt, Greenleaf Enterprises, 2000, by Mary Reynolds Powell. Chapter 13

Backfire: A History of How American Culture Led Us Into Vietnam and Made Us Fight the Way We Did, **(Recommended)** Doubleday & Co., 1985, by Loren Barritz. Chapter 3

Behind the Lines – Hanoi December 23, 1966 – January 7, 1967, Harper & Row, 1967, by Harrison E. Salisbury. Chapter 11

Best Evidence: Disguise and Deception in the Assassination of John F. Kennedy, **(Recommended)** Macmillan, 1980, by David S. Lifton. Chapter 4

Beyond Combat: Women and Gender in the Vietnam Era, 2011, Cambridge University Press, by Heather Marie Stur. Chapter 13

Bloods: An Oral History of the Vietnam War by Black Veterans, Random House, 1984, by Wallace Terry. Chapter 16

Boomer Nation: The Largest and Richest Generation Ever and How it Changed America, Free Press, a division of Simon & Schuster, 2004, by Steve Gillon. Chapter 6

Born On The Fourth of July, McGraw-Hill, 1976, by Ron Kovic. Chapter 15

Brilliant Disaster: JFK, Castro, and America's Doomed Invasion of Cuba's Bay of Pigs, Scribner, a Division of Simon & Schuster, 2011, by Jim Rasenberger. Chapter 4

Brothers: The Hidden History of the Kennedy Years, Free Press, A Division of Simon & Schuster, 2007, by David Talbot. Chapter 4

Charley Company: What Vietnam Did to Us, William Morrow and Company, 1983, by Peter Goldman and Tony Fuller, with Richard Manning, Stryker McGuire, Wally McNamee, and Vern E. Smith. Chapter 16

Chickenhawk, Viking Press, 1983, by Robert Mason. Chapter 7, 16

Coming Apart: An Informed History of America in the 1960s, Times Books, 1971, by William L. O'Neil. Chapter 15

Cover Up: The Army's Secret Investigation of the Massacre at My Lai 4, Random House, 1972, by Seymour M. Hersh. Chapter 11

Crossfire: The Plot That Killed Kennedy, Carroll & Graf Publishers, 1989, by Jim Marrs. Chapter 4

Dangerously Funny: The Uncensored Story of the Smothers Brothers Comedy Hour, Touchstone, a division of Simon & Schuster, 2009, by David Bianculli. Chapter 7

Dispatches, Alfred A. Knopf, 1968, by Michael Herr. Chapter 11

Don't Cry, It's Only Thunder, Doubleday & Company, 1984, by Paul G. Hensler with Jeanne Wakatsuki Houston. Chapter 17

Embers of War: The Fall of an Empire and the Making of America's Vietnam, Random House, 2012, by Fredrik Logevall. Chapter 3

Farewell America, Frontiers Publishing (Lichtenstein), 1968, by James Hepburn. Chapter 4

Fatal Politics: The Nixon Tapes, The Vietnam War, And the Casualties of Reelection, University of Virginia Press, 2015, by Ken Hughes. Chapter 8, 12

Fire In The Lake, Random House, 1972, by Frances Fitzgerald. Chapter 7, 11

Flashbacks: On Returning to Vietnam, Random House, 1990, by Morley Safer. Chapter 11

Forever Sad the Hearts, Avon Books, 1982, by Patricia L. Walsh. Chapter 13

Going to Jail: The Political Prisoner, Grove Press, by Howard Levy, M.D. and David Miller. Chapter 15

Hanoi Jane: War, Sex, & Fantasies of Betrayal, University of Massachusetts Press, 2010, by Jerry Lembcke. Chapter 15, 13

Hardhats, Hippies, and Hawks: The Vietnam Anti-war Movement as Myth and Memory, Cornell University Press, 2013, by Penny Lewis. Chapter 15

Home Before Morning: The Story of an Army Nurse in Vietnam, Beaufort Books, 1983, by Linda Van Devanter. Chapter 13

Homecoming: When the Soldiers Returned From Vietnam, Ballantine Books, 1989, by Bob Greene. Chapter 14, 16

Home From the War: Vietnam Veterans, Neither Victims nor Executioners, Simon & Schuster, 1973, by Robert Jay Lifton. Chapter 14, 16

Home To War: A History of the Vietnam Veterans' Movement, Crown Publishers, 2001, by Gerald Nicosia. Chapter 10, 14, 15

Inside the Pentagon Papers, University Press of Kansas, 2004, Edited by John Prados & Margaret Pratt Porter. Chapter 15

I Refuse: Memories of a Vietnam War Objector, The Broken Rifle Press, 1992, by Donald L. Simons. Chapter 15

Jane Fonda: My Life So Far, Random House, 2005, by Jane Fonda. Chapter 15

JFK: An American Coup D'Etat, **(Highly Recommended)** John Blake Publishing, (London, England), 2013, by Colonel John Hughes-Wilson Chapter 4

JFK and the Unspeakable, **(Very Highly Recommended)** Touchstone, a Division of Simon & Schuster, Inc., 2008, by James W. Douglass. Chapter 4

JFK: The CIA, Vietnam, and the Plot to Assassinate John F. Kennedy, Carol Publishing Group, 1996, by L. Fletcher Prouty. Chapter 4

JFK – 9/11: 50 Years of Deep State, Progressive Press, 2014, by Laurent Guyenot. Chapter 4

Kerry: Agent Orange and An American Family, Dell Publishing, 1982, by Clifford Linedecker with Michael and Maureen Ryan. Chapter 17, 18

Kill Anything That Moves: The Real American War in Vietnam, (**Very Highly Recommended**) Metropolitan Books, 2013, by Nick Turse. Chapter 3, 4, 5, 6, 16

Life After the Bombs, National Geographic Magazine, August 2015, by T.D. Allman. Chapter 17

Long Time Passing: Vietnam & The Haunted Generation, (**Highly Recommended**) Doubleday, 1984, by Myra MacPherson. Chapter 14, 16

Mafia Kingfish: Carlos Marcello and the Assassination of John F. Kennedy, McGraw-Hill, 1989, by John H. Davis. Chapter 4

Make Love, Not War: The Sexual Revolution, an Unfettered History, Little, Brown and Company, 2000, by David Allyn. Chapter 13

Mary's Mosaic: The CIA Conspiracy to Murder John F. Kennedy, Mary Pinchot Meyer, and Their Vision for World Peace, (**Recommended**) *Skyhorse Publishing,* 2013, by Peter Janney

McNamara's Folly: The Use of Low-IQ Troops in the Vietnam War, Infiniti Publishing, 2015, by Hamilton Gregory. Chapter 10

Moral Dilemmas of Modern War: Torture, Assassination, and Blackmail in an Age of Asymmetric Conflict, Cambridge University Press, 2010, by Michael L. Gross. Chapter 16

My Lai 4: A Report on the Massacre and Its Aftermath, Random House, 1970, by Seymour M. Hersh. Chapter 11

My Life So Far, Random House, 2003, by Jane Fonda. Chapter 15

Nam: The Vietnam War in the Words of the Men and Women Who Fought There, Morrow, 1981, by Mark Baker. Chapter 17

Nixon's Secrets, Skyhorse Publishing, 2014, by Roger Stone with Mike Colapietro. Chapter 12

No Peace, No Honor: Nixon, Kissinger, and Betrayal in Vietnam, Touchstone / Simon & Schuster, 2001, by Larry Berman. Chapter 7

Nuremberg and Vietnam: An American Tragedy, Bantam Books, 1971, by Telford Taylor. Chapter 17

Our War: What We Did in Vietnam, and What it Did To Us, (**Recommended**) Random House, 1996, by David Harris. Chapter 15, 16

Patriots: The Vietnam War Remembered From All Sides, Viking, 2003, by Christian G. Appy. Chapter 16, 17

Payback: Five Marines After Vietnam, Alfred A. Knopf, 1984, by Joe Klein. Chapter 14, 16

Perfectly Clear: Nixon From Whittier to Watergate, Quadrangle, The New York Times Book Company, 1973, by Frank Mankiewicz. Chapter 12

Plausible Denial: Was the CIA Involved in the Assassination of JFK?, Thunder's Mouth Press, 1991, by Mark Lane. Chapter 4

Recovering From The War: A Woman's Guide to Helping Your Vietnam Vet, Your Family, and Yourself, (**Very Highly Recommended for Vietnam Vets**) 1990, Penguin Books, by Patience H.C. Mason. Chapter 16

Reflections On The Wall, Stackpole Books, 1987, by Edward Clinton Ezell. Chapter 21

Secrets: A Memoir of Vietnam and the Pentagon Papers, Penguin Group, 2002, by Daniel Ellsberg. Chapter 15

Sensing the Enemy: An American Woman Among the Boat People of Vietnam, The Dial Press, 1984, by Lady Borton. Chapter 17

Sherman's March and Vietnam, Macmillan, 1984, by James Reston, Jr. Chapter 17

Shrapnel in the Heart: Letters and Remembrances from the Vietnam Veterans Memorial, Random House, 1987, by Laura Palmer. Chapter 20

Some American Men, Simon & Schuster, 1985, by Gloria Emerson. Chapter 13

Stealing From America: A History of Corruption From Jamestown to Reagan, Paragon House, 1976, by Nathan Miller. Chapter 12

Tet, Doubleday & Company, 1971, by Don Oberdorfer. Chapter 11

The Arrogance of Power, Random House, 1966, by Senator J. William Fulbright. Chapter 7, 17

The Billboard Book of Top 40 Hits, Billboard Books, 4th Edition, 1989, by Joel Whitburn. Chapter 2

The Devil's Chessboard: Allen Dulles, the CIA, and the Rise of America's Secret Government, (**Highly Recommended**) Harper Collins, 2015, by David Talbot. Chapter 3, 4

The Draft and the Vietnam War, Walker and Company, 1966, by Jacquin Sanders. Chapter 10

The Electric Kool-Aid Acid Test, Farrar, Straus, & Giroux, 1968, by Tom Wolfe. Chapter 6

The Greedy War, also sometimes available under the British title of *A Very Personal War,* (**Very Highly Recommended, see below**) David McKay Company, 1971, by James Hamilton-Paterson. Chapter 12

The Haight-Ashbury: A History, Rolling Stone Press / Random House, 1984, by Charles Perry . Chapter 6, 7

The Hidden History of the JFK Assassination, Counterpoint Books, 2013, by Lamar Waldron, Chapter 4

The Hidden History of the Vietnam War, 1995, by John Prados. Chapter 4

The Invisible Wounds of War: Coming Home From Iraq and Afghanistan, Prometheus Books, 2012, by Marguerite Guzman Bouvard. Chapter 16

The Khaki Mafia, Crown Publishers, Inc., 1971, by Robin Moore and June Collins. Chapter 12

The Making of a Quagmire, Random House, 1964, by David Halberstam. Chapter 3

The Military Draft, The H. W. Wilson Company, 1981, edited by Jason Berger. Chapter 10

The New American Militarism, (**Recommended**) Oxford University Press, 2005, by Andrew J. Bacevich. Chapter 16

The Pentagon Propaganda Machine, Liveright Publishing, by Senator J. William Fulbright. Chapter 7, 17

The Plot to Seize the White House: The Shocking True Story of the Conspiracy to Overthrow F.D.R., (**Recommended**) Skyhorse Publishing, 2015, by Jules Archer. Chapter 3

The Politics of Heroin: CIA Complicity in the Global Drug Trade, (**Recommended**) Lawrence Hill Books (an imprint of Chicago Review Press), 1972, second revision 2003, by Alfred W. McCoy. Chapter 3

The Real War: The Classic Reporting On the Vietnam War, Pantheon Books, 1988, by Jonathan Schell. Chapter 11

The Rolling Stone Encyclopedia of Rock & Roll, Fireside / Simon & Schuster, 3rd Edition 2005, edited by Holly George-Warren and Patricia Romanowski. Chapter 2

The Secret Team: The CIA and its Allies in Control of the United States and the World, 2011, Skyhorse Publishing, by Fletcher Prouty. Chapter 3, 4

The Spitting Image: Myth, Memory, and the Legacy of Vietnam, New York University Press, 1998, by Jerry Lembcke. Chapter 14

The Ten Thousand Day War, (**Highly Recommended**) Eyre Methuen Ltd., 1981, by Michael Maclear. Chapter 3, 4, 5, 6, 7, 8

The Vietnam War: An Almanac, Bison Books Corporation, 1985, General Editor John S. Bowman. Chapter 3, 4, 5, 6, 7, 8,

The Vietnam Wars 1945 – 1990, **(Recommended)** Harper Collins Publishers, 1991, by Marilyn B. Young. Chapter 3, 4, 5, 6, 7, 8,

The Village of Ben-Suc, Alfred A. Knopf, 1967, by Jonathan Schell. Chapter 4

The Wall: Images and Offerings from the Vietnam Veterans Memorial, Collins Publishers, 1987, by Sal Lopes. Chapter 20

The War and the Protest: Vietnam, Doubleday & Company, 1971, by James Haskins. Chapter 15

The War Behind Me: Vietnam Veterans Confront the Truth About U.S. War Crimes, Basic Books, 2008, by Deborah Nelson. Chapter 16

The Winter Soldier Investigation: An Inquiry Into American War Crimes, Beacon Press, 1972, by Vietnam Veterans Against the War. Chapter 16

The Wounded Generation: America After Vietnam, Prentice-Hall, 1981, Edited by A.D. Horne. Chapter 15

They Killed Our President: 63 Reasons to Believe There Was a Conspiracy to Assassinate JFK, Skyhorse Publishing, 2013, by Jesse Ventura with Dick Russell and David Wayne. Chapter 4

They Were Soldiers: How the Wounded Return From America's Wars… The Untold Story, **(Highly Recommended)** Haymarket Books, 2013, by Ann Jones. Chapter 16

To Heal a Nation, Harper & Row, 1985, by Jan Scruggs and Joel L. Swerdlow. Chapter 20

To Move the World: JFK's Quest For Peace, Random House, 2013, by Jeffery D. Sachs. Chapter 4

Touched With Fire: The Future of the Vietnam Generation, Franklin Watts, Inc., 1984, by John Wheeler. Chapter 13

Trading With the Enemy: An Expose' of the Nazi-American Money Plot 1933-1949, Delacorte Press, 1983, by Charles Higham. Chapter 3

Vietnam: A History, **(Recommended)** Viking Press, 1983, by Stanley Karnow. Chapter 3, 4, 5, 6, 7, 8

Vietnam Revisited: Covert Action to Invasion to Reconstruction, South End Press, 1986, by David Dellinger. Chapter 17, 15

Vietnam Shadows: The War, Its Ghosts, and Its Legacy, **(Recommended)** The Johns Hopkins University Press, 1997, by Arnold Isaacs. Chapter 11, 13, 15

Vietnam: The History of an Unwinnable War 1945 – 1975, **(Recommended)** University Press of Kansas, 2009, by John Prados. Chapter 3, 4, 5, 6, 7, 8, 15

Vietnam: The War at Home, Grossman, 1973, by Thomas Powers. Chapter 10, 15

Vietnam Witness 1953-66, Frederick A. Praeger Publishers, 1966, by Bernard B. Fall. Chapter 11

Waiting For An Army To Die: The Tragedy of Agent Orange, Vintage Books / Random House, 1983, by Fred A. Wilcox. Chapter 17

War and The Soul: Healing Our Nation's Veterans From Post-Traumatic Stress Disorder, Quest Books, 2005, by Edward Tick, Ph.D. Chapter 16

War Is: Soldiers, Survivors, and Storytellers talk About War, Candlewick Press, 2009, Edited by Marc Aronson and Patty Campbell. Chapter 16

War Is The Force That Gives Us Meaning, (**Recommended**) Public Affairs Publishing, 2002, by Chris Hedges. Chapter 11

Warrior For Peace, (**Highly Recommended**) Touchstone/ Simon & Schuster, 1988, by Steve Mason. Chapter 13, 16, Dedication

We Gotta Get Out of This Place: The Soundtrack of the Vietnam War, University of Massachusetts Press, 2015, by Doug Bradley and Craig Werner. Chapter 2

Westmoreland: The General Who Lost Vietnam, Houghton Mifflin Harcourt, 2011, by Lewis Sorley. Chapter 5

What Do Women Want?, Harper Collins Publishers, 1998, by Erica Jong. Chapter 13

When Heaven and Earth Changed Places: A Vietnamese Woman's Journey From War to Peace, Doubleday, 1989, by Le Ly Hayslip with Jay Wurts. Chapter 17

White House Call Girl, Feral House, 2013, by Phil Stanford. Chapter 12

Who Knew?: Reflections on Vietnam, 2004, by (former Vietnam "donut dolly") J. Holley Watts. Chapter 13

Who Really Killed Kennedy?, WND Books, 2013, by Jerome R. Corsi, PhD. Chapter 4

Who Spoke Up?: American Protest Against the War in Vietnam, 1963 – 1975, Holt, Rinehart and Winston, 1984, by Nancy Zaroulis and Gerald Sullivan. Chapter 15

Why the CIA Killed JFK and Malcolm X: The Secret Drug Trade in Laos, Chronos Books (UK), 2014, by John Koerner. Chapter 4

Why Vietnam?: Prelude to America's Albatross, University of California Press, 1980, by Archimedes L.A. Patti (Patti was the American who negotiated with Ho Chi Minh at the end of World War II). Chapter 3

Winners & Losers: Battles, Retreats, Gains, Losses, and Ruins From a Long War, (**Recommended**) Random House, 1972, by Gloria Emerson. Chapter 11, 14

Winter Soldier Iraq and Afghanistan: Eyewitness Accounts of the Occupations, Haymarket Books, 2008, by Iraq Veterans Against the War and Aaron Glantz. Chapter 16

Without Honor: Defeat in Vietnam and Cambodia, **(Recommended)** The Johns Hopkins University Press, 1983, by Arnold R. Isaacs. Chapter 11, 17

Witness to War, Bantam Books, **(Recommended)** 1984, by Charles Clements, M.D. Chapter 7

Working-Class War: American Combat Soldiers & Vietnam, **(Recommended)** The University of North Carolina Press, 1993, by Christian G. Appy. Chapter 16

Writings For A Democratic Society, City Lights Books, 2008, by Tom Hayden. Chapter 15

12,20 & 5: A Doctor's Year in Vietnam, E.P. Dutton & Co., 1972, by John A. Parrish, M.D. Chapter 16

1968 in America: Music, Politics, Chaos, Counterculture, and the Shaping of a Generation, Weidenfeld & Nicolson, 1988, by Charles Kaiser. Chapter 6

The most important, highly recommended book about Vietnam I've ever found!

The Greedy War British title: *A Very Personal War* by James Hamilton-Paterson. David McKay Company, 1971. (The author considers this to be the ultimate book describing the real essence of the wars in Southeast Asia, and the folly of America's involvement. It is a relatively small book, but it offers great insight into modern war, and a sincere warning about the financial costs of war. According to many used book stores, many copies of this book were bought up and disappeared by mysterious buyers back in the 1970s. The term most commonly used was, this book was "suppressed by the government." Originally, prior to the Internet, it took me years to find a copy. Today, a few used copies can be found on-line at Amazon.com, or at ABEbooks.com.) This book is the true story of Mr. Cornelius Hawkridge, who I consider to be the ultimate hero of the Vietnam War.

Poetry by Vietnam veterans

Johnny's Song: Poetry of a Vietnam Veteran, Bantam Books, 1986, by Steve Mason

Warrior For Peace, Touchstone / Simon & Schuster, 1988, by Steve Mason

The Human Being: A Warrior's Journey Toward Peace and Mutual Healing, Touchstone / Simon & Schuster, 1990, by Steve Mason

Winning Hearts & Minds: War Poems by Vietnam Veterans, 1st Casualty Press / McGraw-Hill, 1972, edited by Larry Rottman, Jan Barry, & Basil T. Paquet

Index

JOHN KETWIG

John Ketwig is retired from a career in automotive service and parts, which included factory management positions with Toyota, Rolls-Royce / Bentley, Ford, Hyundai, and Prevost high-line buses and motor homes. He is a lifetime member of Vietnam Veterans Against the War, and a member of Vietnam Veterans of America and Veterans for Peace. John is the author of the critically acclaimed memoir *... and a hard rain fell: A G.I.'s True Story of the War in Vietnam* (Macmillan, 1985) and has written for numerous magazines and publications. John is a jazz/rock drummer, and he and his wife Carolynn enjoy exploring the back country roads of Virginia's Blue Ridge Mountains in their Miata sports car.